Public Personnel Management

Current Concerns, Future Challenges

Fourth Edition

Edited by

Norma M. Riccucci

Rutgers University Newark

Longman

New York San Francisco Boston
London Toronto Sydney Tokyo Singapore Madrid
Mexico City Munich Paris Cape Town Hong Kong Montreal

Executive Editor: Eric Stano
Senior Marketing Manager: Elizabeth Fogarty
Production Manager: Stacey Kulig
Project Coordination, Text Design, and Electronic Page Makeup: Pre-Press Company, Inc.
Cover Designer/Manager: Wendy Ann Fredericks
Cover Illustration/Photo: ©Jeremy Woodhouse/Getty Images, Inc.—Photodisc
Manufacturing Buyer: Roy Pickering
Printer and Binder: R.R. Donnelly and Sons
Cover Printer: Phoenix Color Corporation

Library of Congress Cataloging-in-Publication Data

Public personnel management / edited by Norma M. Riccucci.-- 4th ed.
    p. cm.
 Includes bibliographical references and index.
 ISBN 0-321-36468-6
 1. Civil service--United States--Personnel management. 2. Civil service--Personnel management.
I. Riccucci, Norma.

 JK765.P947 2006
 352.6'0973--dc22
                              2005019412

Please visit http://www.ablongman.com

1 2 3 4 5 6 7 8 9 10—DOC—08 07 06 05

ISBN 0-321-36468-6

To my dear friend Carolyn Ban, whose support, guidance, and friendship throughout my career have been invaluable.

Contents

Contributors

David Arellano Gault is a Professor in the Public Administration Division at the Center for Research and Teaching in Economics (CIDE) in Mexico City. He has recently published two books "Reformando al Gobierno" (Reforming Government) 2000; and "Más allá de la reinvención del gobierno" (Beyond Reinventing Government) 2004; some of his most recent articles are "Public Management policy and accountability in Latin America: performance-oriented budgeting in Colombia, Mexico and Venezuela (1994–2000)," *International Public Management Journal* 7 (1): 49–71, and "Maturation of Public Administration in a Multicultural Environment: Lessons from the Anglo-Saxon, Latin and Scandinavian Political Traditions," *International Journal of Public Administration* 27 (7): 519–528. He is also editor of the academic journal *Gestión y Política Pública* (Public Management and Policy). He received his Ph.D. from the University of Colorado.

Margo Bailey is Director of Planning & Evaluation at Melwood Training Center, Upper Marlboro, Maryland. Her most recent work "Cultural Competency and the Practice of Public Administration," examines the relationships between equal employment opportunity (EEO), affirmative action, managing diversity and cultural competency, and the importance of each for public managers. Dr. Baile, has served as Assistant Professor in the Department of Public Administration at American University, policy analyst for NASA, and evaluation consultant to various nonprofit organizations.

Carolyn Ban is Dean of the Graduate School of Public and International Affairs (GSPIA). She has written broadly on human resources and administrative reform, both in the U.S. and in Russia. She received her Ph.D. in Political Science from Stanford University, and her career has spanned the public and private sectors as well as academia. Her current research focuses on reforms of the civil service system in the federal government and on nonprofit leadership.

Evan M. Berman is professor of public administration at Louisiana State University. He is active in the American Society for Public Administration and is past Chair of the Section of Personnel and Labor Relations. He has numerous publications in human resource management, productivity, ethics, and local government. His recent books include *The Professional Edge* (M.E. Sharpe, 2004, with West, Bowman, and Van Wart), and *Essential Statistics for Public Managers and Policy Analysts*

(Congressional Quarterly Press, 2002). He is the Managing Editor of *Public Performance & Management Review*.

Dennis M. Daley is a Professor of Political Science and Public Administration at North Carolina State University. He is the author of *Performance Appraisal in the Public Sector: Techniques and Applications* (1992) and *Strategic Human Resource Management* (2002). He currently serves as Chair of the Faculty (2003–2005). He teaches classes in human resources, public personnel management, and labor relations. He holds a BA from Montana State University, an MA from the University of Montana, and earned his Ph.D. at Washington State University. He has published over fifty articles and book chapters. He has also held faculty positions at Minnesota State University (Mankato), Iowa State University, and the University of Mississippi.

Sergio Fernandez recently joined the faculty at the School of Public and Environmental Affairs, Indiana University, where he teaches courses in public management and public organization theory. His research focuses on a variety of issues relating to privatization and contracting for services, organizational change, and public sector leadership. His publications have appeared in the *Journal of Public Administration Research and Theory*, *Public Performance and Management Review*, and several edited books. He earned his Ph.D. in public administration from the University of Georgia in 2004.

Heather Getha-Taylor is a Ph.D. Candidate at the Maxwell School of Citizenship and Public Affairs at Syracuse University. Her research focuses on human resource management and government performance.

Charles W. Gossett is professor and Chair of the Department of Political Science at California State Polytechnic University, Pomona. He is the author of several articles in the area of civil service reform and gay and lesbian politics at the local and state government levels.

Patricia W. Ingraham is Distinguished Professor of Public Administration at Syracuse University's Maxwell School. She was the Founding Director of the Alan K Campbell Public Affairs Institute and is a Fellow of the National Academy of Public Administration. Ingraham is the recipient of the Dwight Waldo Award, Donald Stone, and Paul Van Riper Awards for Distinguished Research Career and Distinguished Service from the American Society of Public Administration and the John Gaus Award for Distinguished Career Contributions from the American Political Science Association. Her major research interests are the performance of public organizations and leading and managing the people of those organizations.

J. Edward Kellough is Associate Professor in the Department of Public Administration and Policy at the University of Georgia where he teaches and directs the MPA and Ph.D. programs. His major area of academic interest is public personnel administration/human resources management. His research has addressed such topics as equal employment opportunity and affirmative action, representative bureaucracy, reinventing government, and civil service reform. He is the author of a book of federal equal employment opportunity, numerous articles in academic journals, and several book chapters. Professor Kellough is also co-editor, with Lloyd Nigro, of a forthcoming book on civil service reform in the states.

Donald E. Klingner is a Professor in the Graduate School of Public Affairs at the University of Colorado; co-author of *Public Personnel Management* (5th edition 2003), also published in Spanish and Chinese; consultant to the UN, World Bank, and IADB on public management capacity-building; visiting professor at the National Autonomous University of Mexico (UNAM); Fulbright Scholar in Central America; International Coordinator and former chair, ASPA's SPALR and SICA; and co-editor, *Comparative Technology Transfer and Society*. He has also been a faculty member at Indiana University–Indianapolis and Florida International University. He worked for the US government's central personnel agency (1968–1973) prior to earning a Ph.D. in Public Administration from the University of Southern California (1974).

Carol E. Lowman is a procurement analyst with the United States Army. She is a doctoral candidate in Public Administration at the University of Georgia's School of Public and International Affairs.

Lloyd G. Nigro is Professor of Public Administration and Urban Studies at Georgia State University in Atlanta, Georgia. He is currently the department chair. He received his Ph.D. in Public Administration from the University of Southern California in 1972. Before joining the GSU faculty, he held tenured faculty positions at Syracuse University and the University of Southern California. He is the co-author with Felix A. Nigro of multiple editions of two widely read texts, *Modern Public Administration and The New Public Personnel Administration*. He has also published numerous book chapters and articles in the areas of public personnel policy, civil service reform, administrative ethics, and public administration and American political thought.

Joan E. Pynes is Director and Professor of Public Administration at the University of South Florida. She is the author of *Human Resources Management for Public and Nonprofit Organizations* (2nd edition, 2004), published by Jossey-Bass, Inc. Her major areas of research include public and nonprofit human resources management, labor relations, and public and nonprofit management.

Hal G. Rainey is Alumni Foundation Distinguished Professor in the Department of Public Administration and Policy in the School of Public and International Affairs at the University of Georgia. His research concentrates on organizations and management in government, with emphasis on performance, change, leadership, incentives, privatization, and comparisons of governmental management to management in the business and nonprofit sectors. The third edition of his book, *Understanding and Managing Public Organizations*, was published in 2003. He was recently elected as a Fellow of the National Academy of Public Administration.

T. Zane Reeves is Regent's Professor of Public Administration at the University of New Mexico, where he has been since 1981. His books include: *Case Studies in*

Human Resource Management, Managing Human Resources, Personnel Management in the Public Sector, Collective Bargaining in the Public Sector, and *The Politics of Peace Corps and VISTA.* He has also published numerous articles and consulted with organizations in areas of employee performance appraisal, discipline, grievance handling and alternative dispute resolution. He has served as a Personnel Hearing Officer for the cities of Albuquerque, Lake Havasu City, Rio Rancho and the Maricopa County Merit Commission (AZ), and is on the labor arbitration panels of the American Arbitration Association, Federal Mediation and Conciliation Service, Tinker AFB/ American Federation of Government Employees, US Postal Service/American Postal Workers Union and National Association of Letter Carriers, and the Rio Grande Credit Union.

Norma M. Riccucci is Professor of Public Administration at Rutgers University, Newark Campus. Her research and teaching interests lie in the broad area of public management. Most recently she published *How Management Matters: Street-Level Bureaucrats and Welfare Reform* (Georgetown University Press), and *Managing Diversity in Public Sector Workforces* (Westview Press). She is the recipient of the Distinguished Research Award from the American Society for Public Administration and the National Association of Schools of Public Affairs and Administration, and the Rita Mae Kelly Award for Research Excellence from SWPA, the American Society of Public Administration

David H. Rosenbloom is Distinguished Professor of Public Administration in the School of Public Affairs at American University in Washington, DC. He is the 2001 recipient of the American Political Science Association's John Gaus Award for Exemplary Scholarship in the Joint Tradition of Political Science and Public Administration. Rosenbloom holds a BA degree from Marietta College and MA and Ph.D. degrees in political science from the University of Chicago. He is a member of the National Academy of Public Administration and served on the 1992 Clinton-Gore Presidential Transition Team for the Office of Personnel Management.

James D. Slack is a Professor in the Department of Government at the University of Alabama at Birmingham (UAB). He serves as a senior scientist in the UAB Medical School's Center for AIDS Research, and he holds senior scholar positions in two centers in the UAB School of Public Health: the John J. Sparkman Center for International Public Health Education and the Lister Hill Center for Health Policy. His research, which focuses on anti-discrimination workplace policies, has been published in a variety of social science journals and in five books. He is currently researching "theocentric values, political community, and the public service."

Jonathan P. West is Professor and Director of the Graduate Public Administration program in the School of Business Administration at the University of Miami. His research interests include human resource management, productivity, local government, and ethics. Professor West has published over 70 articles and book chapters. His books include *The Professional Edge* (M.E. Sharpe, 2004, co-authors), as well as *The Ethics Edge* (1998) published by the International City/County Management Association. He is the Managing Editor of *Public Integrity*.

Introduction

Much has changed since the first edition of this book appeared in 1991. First, Carolyn Ban regrets that her administrative responsibilities as dean and her participation on a major research project made it impossible for her to participate as co-editor on this fourth edition, although she is very happy to still be a participant as an author.

In terms of substance, the changes that have appeared in each new edition of this book certainly signify the dynamic aspects of the field of public personnel management. The last fifteen years have been marked by rapid change in government as a whole as well as in the broader society. This fourth edition reflects the most current issues and challenges in public personnel management. The book is designed to provide readers with a broad understanding of the key policy and management issues facing the field today. As with previous editions, the book is not a "how-to" manual, with detailed instructions on the nuts-and-bolts of developing and implementing personnel procedures (e.g., an affirmative action plan).

In the opening chapter, Lloyd Nigro sets the stage for the issues that have shaped the field of public personnel management over the past several centuries. In particular, he focuses on the evolving role of public personnel in the governance of American society. As he suggests, assuring responsiveness and accountability in our personnel management systems is key, given the democratic framework within which our society operates.

New and challenging developments in all areas of public personnel management are subsequently addressed. For example, Patricia Ingraham and Heather Getha-Taylor point to the historic shift currently underway in the federal civil service in the United States, as nearly 45 percent of the federal civilian workforce is now covered by legislative provisions that were created for the Department of Homeland Security and the Department of Defense. These provisions place emphasis on performance and flexibility and, in effect, curtail the traditional protections provided to public employees under civil service law. The provisions also limit the role of federal employee unions in federal personnel processes.

In addition, revolutions across the globe have created changes in the public personnel systems and practices of many governments. Donald Klingner and

David Arellano Gault provide an overview of the evolution of public personnel systems in developing countries, and then look more closely at Mexico's federal professional career service. Their chapter shows the twists and turns that civil service reform in Mexico has taken, and the challenges that continue to exist as Mexico transforms into a more accountable and legitimate democracy.

Additional issues and ongoing challenges to the field are also addressed in this book. Topics such as affirmative action, diversity, HIV/AIDS, public sector labor unions, employees' legal responsibilities, and privatization are but a few that receive in-depth coverage. Also covered are the unique issues surrounding nonprofit organizations' personnel systems (see Pynes, Chapter 15); the issues pertaining to lesbians and gay men in public sector work forces (see Gossett, Chapter 6); the importance of strategic human resources practices to employee and organizational productivity (see Daley, Chapter 11); and the need for government organizations to develop systematic strategies of ethics management, including a commitment to continued ethics training (see Berman and West, Chapter 13). These are the critical issues that will shape and define the field of public personnel management in the years to come.

Chapter 1

Public Personnel Management and the Challenges of Democratic Governance

Lloyd G. Nigro

In this chapter, I will trace in very general terms the history of our thinking about the purposes of public personnel management in the United States. My focus here will be on the evolving role of public personnel management in American governance. As students of public personnel management have regularly observed, on one level it is and has always been about power, about controlling and allocating scarce resources—especially jobs and the powers associated with them. More broadly, it embodies a complex and dynamic set of explicit and implicit public policies or beliefs concerning the role public personnel management should play in the governance of our society (Ingraham, 1995).

THE POLITICAL ROOTS OF PUBLIC PERSONNEL MANAGEMENT IN THE UNITED STATES

Over the first century of its existence (1790–1890), the mechanisms associated with recruiting, selecting, and managing the performance of the public service on all levels of government in the United States were overtly and, some might say, proudly partisan. Technical competence at some level might have been necessary, but it was far from sufficient as a standard for assessing system as well as individual performance. The minimum qualification for employment was a demonstrated record of support for and loyalty to an executive policy agenda or program, elected officials (executive and legislative), and the political party in power. Most public workers were expected to actively work for, and to financially support, political parties and their candidates for elective office on all levels of government. In contemporary terms, there was no separation between partisan politics and public administration and that was considered to be a normal and indeed desirable state of affairs.

1

The widely accepted point of view was that truly democratic governance, as opposed to rule by elites, required a civil service that was motivated from top to bottom to be fully responsive to public opinion as articulated by elected officials. In the United States, the system of public personnel management seen as best suited to this purpose was a patronage or spoils system—hiring and firing based on or at least significantly influenced by partisan associations and loyalties. In theory, hiring and firing on the basis of loyalty and active support for political parties and their candidates allowed personnel management systems, however rudimentary by modern standards, to build highly responsive civil services (Fish, 1904; Van Riper, 1958).

GOVERNANCE BY GENTLEMEN

The policy of the first six presidents of the United States (1789–1829) was to make appointments to federal offices on the basis of "fitness." Fitness meant that the person was of good character, was able to do the work involved, *and* agreed with the political views and goals of the chief executive and his associates. Normally, *all three standards* had to be satisfied. For all practical purposes, the Federalists wanted their personnel management systems to establish and perpetuate a national civil service that legitimized the new central government and extended its capabilities (Caldwell, 1944; White, 1948, 1951). Democratic participation in government and responsiveness to the opinions of "common people" were secondary concerns at best. The national government's workforce was drawn almost exclusively from the American upper class. For the most part, these personnel systems performed well. As Paul Van Riper (1958) put it, "The government of our early days was a government led by the well-educated, the well-born, the prosperous, and their adherents" (pp. 17–18). At least on the national level, public personnel management was working as intended by the Federalists. This situation was not to last very long.

A DEMOCRATIC PUBLIC SERVICE

By 1829, the United States was undergoing a profound social, political, and economic transformation. The governing order established during the colonial period was being pushed aside by an energetic industrial and market system based in rapidly growing cities. The values driving the new system included rugged individualism, egalitarianism, and a belief that wealth, power, and status should be and could be *achieved* by the common person through a combination of opportunity, hard work, ambition, intelligence, and a willingness to take risks (Miller, 1972). In short order, ideologically as well as in practice, public personnel systems came to embody these values.

President Andrew Jackson emphatically rejected the elitist views of his Federalist predecessors and urged a much more democratized vision of public service, an approach that allowed members of the Democratic party that had elected him to displace the losing Federalists and their allies (White, 1954). Jackson argued that the doors to federal jobs should be opened to all segments of society and that there was no need for permanence since most federal jobs were simple and did not require experience (Van Riper, 1958). Jackson's election is often described as the beginning of spoils-based personnel management on the federal level, but this does not mean that the system had not been fundamentally partisan in its organizing logic and goals under the Federalists.

In light of what happened during the second half of the nineteenth century on all levels of government in the United States, Jackson could hardly be called a high priest of raw spoils (Mosher, 1968, p. 62). Nonetheless, his egalitarian rhetoric did much to open the gates for spoils on the national level, and those who followed were far more inclined to sweep out incumbents and to replace them with party loyalists. The goal was a practical one: to win elections by strengthening the party machinery from the grassroots up. By 1861, when Abraham Lincoln assumed the presidency, the spoils system had developed to the point that it "had an adhesive grip upon the political machinery of the United States" (Van Riper, 1958, p. 42). The same could be said of personnel management in the states and cities, especially the large cities where the "machines" prospered and the "bosses" ruled (Freedman, 1994). New York City's Tammany Machine of the 1880s is an example. Its explicit goals were, "To nominate candidates for public office, get out the vote, and win elections" (Riordon, 1963, p. xii).

George Washington Plunkitt, a Tammany district leader or ward boss, defended the spoils system in a series of classic interviews with William Riordon of the *New York Evening Post*. What outcomes should be expected of the public personnel systems of the times? Plunkitt expressed his point of view emphatically:

> What is representative government anyhow? Is it all a fake that this is a government of the people, by the people and for the people? If it isn't a fake, then why isn't the people's voice obeyed and Tammany men put in all the offices? . . . We stood as we have always stood, for rewardin' the men that won the victory. . . . First, this great and glorious country was built up by political parties; second, parties can't hold together if their workers don't get the offices when they win; third, if the parties go to pieces, the government they built up must go to pieces. . . . (Riordon, 1963, pp. 12–13).

Plunkitt placed spoils-driven public personnel management at the center of his version of democratic governance, and he was far from alone in these sentiments. Nonetheless, concepts of governance and the core values of public personnel administration were beginning to change by the end of the nineteenth century.

GOOD GOVERNMENT AND THE RISE OF MERIT SYSTEMS

Plunkitt and his Tammany associates were afraid that the civil service reform movement of the times was undermining democracy as they understood it. The very foundation of their political power was indeed under attack. Civil service reform was a key element of the larger progressive political movement of the late nineteenth and early twentieth centuries. The Progressives advanced a very different vision of democratic governance and they advocated many administrative ("good government") reforms. One of them was the destruction of the party machines that ran the nation's major cities. In their eyes, these machines were corrupt, inefficient and wasteful, technically incompetent, and intent on ignoring the interests of electoral minorities while taxing them heavily. The reform movement included the banking and commercial sectors, middle and upper income groups, and many university-trained professionals who were excluded from public employment by the machines (Schiesl, 1977, pp. 149–170). They wanted a stable infrastructure for their commercial activities and to "take the reins of power away from the lower classes and the Irish bosses" (Freedman, 1994, p. 17).

The implications of this reform agenda for governance in the United States were profound. By advancing "neutral competence" as the main goal of public personnel management, the civil service reformers sought a set of interrelated political outcomes: 1) to eliminate patronage as the machine's base of electoral power, 2) to create conditions under which overtly partisan considerations could be applied to only a few government jobs at the very top of the administrative hierarchy, and (3) to establish civil service commissions and personnel offices as powerful regulators charged with protecting and enforcing the "merit principle" in all phases of personnel management. The merit principle was to be the normative core of the personnel management enterprise.

In application, the merit principle requires that appointments, promotions, and all other personnel actions should be made exclusively on the basis of relative ability and job performance. Political beliefs and party affiliations should not be factors. This means competitive examinations and other job-related objective tests must be used if the merit principle is to be satisfied. For other personnel actions such as pay raises and dismissals, employees' "merit" should be determined through fair and objective performance appraisals, not some kind of partisan political test. In O. Glenn Stahl's words: "In its broadest sense a merit system in modern government means *a personnel system in which comparative merit or achievement governs each individual's selection and progress in the service and in which the conditions and rewards of performance contribute to competency and continuity of the service*" (Stahl, 1962, p. 28).

Later, Justice Lewis F. Powell's dissenting opinion in *Elrod v. Burns* (1976) underscored a long-standing debate over the contributions public personnel management should be asked to make to successful democratic governance in the United States. One point of view, that of the civil service reformers, was that democracy is best served by a civil service that is highly qualified in a technical sense and entirely neutral in a partisan sense—neutral competence allows the efficient and effective implementation of public policy set by elected officials. Another school of thought argued that administrative partisanship is in certain cases essential to democratic government (Daniel, 1992).

In *Elrod v. Burns*, a majority of the Supreme Court ruled that removals of "non-policymaking" employees solely for reasons of their affiliation with a political party violated their First Amendment rights. Powell disagreed, saying that it was naive to think that political activities were motivated by "some academic interest in 'democracy' or other public service impulse." He stated, "For the most part, as every politician knows, the hope of some reward generates a major portion of the local political activity supporting parties." Powell argued, "History and long prevailing practice across the country support the view that patronage hiring practices make a sufficiently substantial contribution to the practical functioning of our democratic system to support their relatively modest intrusion on First Amendment rights." This was the first of several Court decisions (*Branti v. Finkle*, 1980; *Rutan v. Republican Party of Illinois*, 1990) that limited constitutionally acceptable patronage to situations where the hiring authority could "demonstrate that party affiliation is an appropriate requirement for the effective performance of the public office involved" (*Elrod v. Burns*, 1976).

MERIT SYSTEMS AS REGULATORY ENTERPRISES

A primary thrust of the civil service reform movement was the effort to take control over personnel matters away from public managers and elected executives and to turn them over to disinterested experts who had the authority and resources needed to impose the merit principle. On the federal level, the U.S. Congress enacted the foundation for a merit system in 1883. The Pendleton Act was passed over a year after President Garfield was shot and killed by a "disappointed" office seeker. (In this instance, the personnel system clearly failed both the office seeker and the president.) A less sentimental reason was the incumbent Republicans' fear that the next president would be a Democrat who would remove many Republican officeholders and replace them with loyal Democrats. Initially, the Act covered only about 10 percent of the jobs in the executive branch. By 1952, well over 90 percent were covered and President Dwight Eisenhower, a Republican, was complaining about his inability to establish policy control over an "unresponsive" (Democrat dominated) bureaucracy covered by merit system protections.

The administrative machinery set up to carry out the Pendleton Act was a bipartisan Civil Service Commission (CSC) rather than an executive agency. As state and local governments adopted merit systems, they tended to follow the federal example and also created independent commissions or boards to administer them. As the machines and reform parties struggled for political control of the nation's cities and counties, it was not unusual for merit systems to come and go, depending on the outcomes of elections (Aronson, 1973, p. 38; Freedman, 1994, p. 39).

Although the number of civil service systems at least nominally based on the merit principle continued to expand between 1900 and 1930, the scope of their activities remained quite limited. At best, "merit" was making sure that public employees were appointed through entrance examinations, prohibited from blatantly engaging in partisan politics, and compensated on the basis of something resembling "equal-pay-for-equal-work." Those running merit systems concentrated on their regulatory functions, on "keeping the rascals out" by severely constraining or eliminating line managers' influence over personnel actions of all kinds. Little if any attention was paid to these systems' contributions to the efficiency and effectiveness of government operations and programs. Even less was paid to their effects on bureaucratic responsiveness to executive leadership and more generally on governance throughout American society.

THE BEGINNINGS OF HUMAN RESOURCE MANAGEMENT (HRM)

The first important deviation from the regulatory approach was an incremental effort to connect personnel policies and practices to organizational performance. The explosive growth of the federal government during the Great Depression of the 1930s and World War II quickly outpaced the Civil Service Commission's capacity to handle day-to-day personnel operations centrally. As Roosevelt's policies dramatically expanded the size of the classified civil service to encompass the New Deal agencies, it became clear that much of the Commission's work (not regulatory authority) would have to be decentralized to the agency level. It had become a serious bottleneck in the day-to-day personnel management of the federal government. This practical necessity led to FDR's 1938 Executive Order 7916 requiring the various departments to set up professionally staffed personnel offices.

Historically, Roosevelt's order signaled the arrival of "modern" personnel administration (U.S. Library of Congress, 1976, pp. 258–260). In this case, "modern" meant expanding departmental-level personnel units and improving the efficiency of services they provided, such as position classification, applicant testing, and record-keeping. It also meant that the CSC's responsibilities would gradually shift to policy formulation, research and development, and program evaluation and audits.

The concept of personnel administration as an arm of management (HRM) began to take hold, not only in the federal government but also in some states and localities. World War II greatly increased the pressure on departmental personnel shops to be responsive and supportive, and by the end of the war, the idea of personnel management as a regulatory function had been abandoned by leading practitioners and students of public administration. Simon, Smithburg, and Thompson (1950) were prepared to state in their influential textbook that personnel specialists deal with matters "that are of the greatest long range importance to the organization" (p. 312). They may have overstated the movement toward HRM somewhat. On the ground, the day-to-day practice of personnel management on all levels of government was still largely designed to sharply curtail management's role and to "police" the process.

Increasingly professional and formalized personnel operations, while successful in their own terms, were exercises in sub-optimization and goal-displacement in public managers' eyes. For personnel specialists, assuring that the managers followed the rules took precedence over actively supporting managerial and organizational performance. In fact, personnel offices typically were judged according to the degree to which the rules were followed and enforced in an efficient manner. All of this greatly frustrated line managers and executives who were focused on accomplishing organizational goals and implementing the policy objectives of elected officials. Personnel offices typically earned reputations with line managers as centers of legalistic bureaucratization where technical expertise in rules and procedures were all-important. Personnel specialists, in turn, were deeply suspicious of management's efforts to expand its authority and discretion in personnel matters. They saw their role as protecting the merit principle from the attacks of those who would return to the norms and practices of spoils under cover of arguments that more discretion was needed in order to meet demands for higher efficiency and effectiveness.

Despite determined resistance from defenders of merit systems and the ideal of neutral competence, pressures for "management-oriented" personnel policies and systems steadily increased. By the 1960s, a "perfect storm" of political, economic, and social forces had begun to form over the heads of those responsible for public personnel policy and management. These forces would do much to transform our understanding of public personnel management's role in the governing institutions and processes of American society.

UNIONIZATION AND COLLECTIVE BARGAINING

The "state of the art" described in public personnel management texts of the late 1950s would be obliterated by the changes that took place during the next twenty years. The first of these to hit the traditional systems with punishing force was the rapid spread of collective bargaining in the public sector. Prior to 1960, most merit system administrators thought of collective bargaining as something having no legitimate place in government. They assumed factory workers and craftsmen joined unions, not white collar government workers. By experience, personnel specialists had little or no familiarity with collective bargaining or appreciation of its institutional significance as a system of workplace governance in the private sector. To most it was a real menace to the merit principle and they believed that the unstated goal of most union leaders was to wipe out merit systems and to replace them with governing contracts negotiated under the threat of strikes and other disruptions of public services. For most professional personnel administrators in government, public employee unionization and collective bargaining were in the same category as spoils: something to be vigorously resisted on the legal, legislative, and organizational levels.

By 1968, however, the federal courts had firmly established that the First Amendment protected the right of public employees to form and join unions, and they identified no constitutional reason why public employers could not bargain collectively. State legislatures could enact laws requiring the state government and localities to engage in collective bargaining. In many states, organized employees were politically effective (and unions warmly received by workers who saw their pay and benefits falling behind those of the private sector), and collective bargaining was to dramatically change the landscape of personnel management.

By 1985, 40 states and the District of Columbia had statutes or executive orders setting up frameworks for collective bargaining with some or all of their employees. In the federal government, a limited form of collective bargaining began in 1962. Currently, about half of all state and local government full-time workers are members of employee organizations of one kind or another. The percentage of organized employees is even higher in such functions as education, highways, public welfare, hospitals, police, fire, and sanitation services. Many public employees now work in places where personnel rules and management are bilaterally determined (negotiated) and administered according to the terms of labor agreements or contracts. Since the late 1960s, offices of labor relations staffed by collective bargaining specialists have been common in the public sector.

INCLUSIVE PUBLIC PERSONNEL MANAGEMENT

In theory, merit systems do not discriminate in any aspect of employment for reasons of race, sex, religion, national or ethnic origin, or physical handicap. Stahl's definition of merit certainly leaves no room for hiring and other personnel actions based on anything other than objective measures of individuals' qualifications and job performance. Nonetheless, merit systems on all levels of government were in practice discriminating against minorities and women in 1962 when Stahl's book appeared. The merit principle often applied only to white males. Patronage systems predictably *excluded* minority groups that did not belong to their electoral coalitions.

The failure of public personnel systems of all kinds to assure equal employment opportunity (EEO) went virtually unchallenged until the Civil Rights Movement of the 1960s. A passive approach to the administration of even the strongest of merit systems also reinforced the pattern. Those running these merit systems argued that the very low representation of minority groups in public service did not mean that merit systems were not enforcing the merit principle. In other words, if there was no *overt* discrimination to be found, the absence of minorities was unfortunate but no fault of the merit system (U.S. Commission on Civil Rights, 1969).

By the mid-1960s, the Civil Rights Movement was transforming public personnel policy as well as American politics and society. The federal judiciary was increasingly inclined to void personnel practices that had adverse impact on minorities and to require affirmative action programs if public employers resisted voluntary remedies (*Griggs v. Duke Power Company*, 1971). The Civil Rights Act of 1964 was amended in 1972 to cover the public sector. While merit systems traditionally had concentrated on "keeping the rascals out," the 1960s and 1970s were marked by efforts to markedly increase the *inclusiveness* of public personnel policies and practices.

These efforts often took the form of affirmative action programs with goals and timetables for hiring minorities and women (*Regents of the University of California v. Bakke*, 1978). Presidents Johnson, Nixon, and Carter launched affirmative action programs, and federal rules and regulations requiring EEO and affirmative action plans of private contractors and governments receiving federal funds were set forth during this period (*United Steel Workers of America v. Weber*, 1979).

In addition to racial and ethnic groups, the federal courts interpreted the prohibitions in the Civil Rights Act of 1964 to include sex discrimination in employment. Intentional as well as "socially traditional" forms of discrimination against women, including sexual harassment, were ruled illegal, and the Equal Employment Opportunity Commission (EEOC) was empowered to investigate complaints by women as well as protected minorities against their employers. EEO protections were also extended to discrimination based on age and disability. The pressures on public personnel management systems were substantially increased. They were pressured to uphold the merit principle (neutral competence) in ways that were legal, constitutional, and without disparate or adverse impact on minorities and women.

Over time, the standards and performance criteria applied by courts, legislatures, and other stakeholders have shifted and conflicted, and judicial support for broad-gauged affirmative action programs has declined (Riccucci, 1997). Nonetheless, political and social pressures to maintain an inclusive orientation and to build and effectively manage a diverse workforce have persisted (*Patterson v. McLean Credit Union*, 1989; *Ward's Cove Packing Co. v. Atonio*, 1989; *Price Waterhouse v. Hopkins*, 1989; *Martin v. Wilks*, 1989; *Adarand Constructors v. Pena*, 1995; *State of Texas v. Hopwood*, 1996; Naff and Kellough, 2003).

CONSTITUTIONAL RIGHTS FOR PUBLIC EMPLOYEES

Public employers are now expected to understand and to protect the constitutional rights of their workers. The federal courts significantly strengthened the individual's constitutional position in the employment relationship, thereby weakening the powers of patronage as well as merit-based personnel management systems during the middle years of the twentieth century.

Historically, the courts had ruled that employees did not have *any* rights on the job that were based on the U.S. Constitution. Thus, in fixing the terms of employment, the public employer could deny workers civil and political rights universally enjoyed by those in the private sector. For example, the due process clauses of the Fifth and Fourteenth Amendments were held not to apply to public employees because, as the Supreme Court reasoned in *Bailey v. Richardson* (1951), government employment could not be considered property, life, or liberty. "Due process of law is not applicable unless one is being deprived of something to which he has a right." Accordingly, public employees were not entitled to substantive or procedural due process; they could be barred from political activity (substantive) and denied the right to a hearing in loyalty cases (procedural). In a famous 1892 ruling, Justice Holmes had stated for the majority that "The petitioner may have a constitutional right to talk politics, but he has no constitutional right to be a policeman" (*McAuliffe v. Mayor of New Bedford*, 1892). This interpretation was controlling over the following 60 years, and the scope of judicial review of personnel actions was very limited. In essence, public personnel systems were free to do as they pleased in structuring the employment relationship and the rules of the workplace.

Beginning in the 1950s, however, the federal judiciary progressively demolished its earlier "doctrine of privilege" (Dotson, 1955). This was replaced with the following standard: "Whenever there is a substantial interest, other than employment by the state, involved in the discharge of a public employee, he can be removed neither on arbitrary grounds nor without a procedure calculated to determine whether legitimate grounds exist" (Rosenbloom, 1971, p. 421). One of the most important changes was brought about by a series of Supreme Court decisions in the 1970s establishing that public employees may have property and liberty interests in their jobs that warrant protection under the due process clause of the Fifth and Fourteenth Amendments to the Constitution. Property interests include whatever affects the livelihood of an individual (e.g., welfare benefits, eligibility for occupational licenses). Liberty interests may come into play in situations where a personnel action affects the person's reputation, career prospects, or ability to find employment elsewhere (*Board of Regents v. Roth*, 1972; *Perry v. Sinderman*, 1972; *Arnett v. Kennedy*, 1974; *Bishop v. Wood*, 1976).

In general terms, the Supreme Court has meaningfully limited public employers' authority and discretion in several areas of the employment relationship. Public employees, for example, may not be required to take vague and overly broad loyalty oaths, and their freedom of political association cannot arbitrarily be limited by blanket prohibitions against membership in the Communist Party, or any other organization. Likewise, unless the public employer can show a rational connection between personal behavior and job performance, dismissals and other serious adverse actions stand a good chance of being reversed (Rosenbloom and Carroll, 1990; O'Brian, 1997). In short, today's public personnel management systems are expected to recognize and to embody contemporary definitions of the constitutional duties and obligations of government agencies with regard to their employees.

POLITICAL PARTICIPATION BY PUBLIC EMPLOYEES

Neutral competence, the hallmark norm of the merit system, called for a public service insulated from most political activities, especially partisan electoral politics. Much of the regulatory activity of merit systems was focused on preventing politics in any form from intruding into any aspect of personnel management. It was, accordingly, a long-standing practice in the U.S. to severely restrict political activities of public employees. In theory, these limitations were supposed to prevent partisan coercion of public employees, to assure the political neutrality of the civil service, and to protect the merit principle. Despite challenges to their constitutionality, the federal courts ruled that restraints on the political behavior of *public employees* were matters best left to legislative bodies (*United Public Workers v.*

Mitchell and *Oklahoma v. United States Civil Service Commission, 1947; United States Civil Service Commission v. National Association of Letter Carriers, AFL-CIO, 1973).* While restraints on partisan political activity are still common, blanket restrictions on political participation by civil servants have been largely abandoned.

The most widely recognized federal laws dealing with political activities by public workers are the Hatch Acts of 1939 and 1940. They placed severe limitations on many activities available to all other American citizens. The first was passed in large part because of Congressional fears that President Roosevelt was building an overwhelming power base in the federal bureaucracy by hiring large numbers of political allies non-competitively into the unclassified service and then later extending merit system coverage to their positions and agencies as allowed by the Pendleton Act. The 1939 Hatch Act applied to most workers in the federal executive branch. The Act's coverage was extended in 1940 to state or local employees "whose principal employment is in connection with any activity which is financed in whole or in part by loans or grants made by the United States."

By the 1960s, concerns that so severely restricting the political participation of about 15 percent of the labor force (much of it highly educated and socially involved) threatened the quality of American governance, which led to important policy changes in this area. In a 1974 amendment to the Federal Campaign Act, state and local workers covered by the 1940 Act were permitted to engage in certain partisan political activities (e.g., solicit votes in partisan elections and be delegates to party conventions) if state laws did not prohibit them from doing so. In 1993, for similar reasons, President Bill Clinton signed the *Hatch Act Reform Amendments of 1993*. These amendments authorized OPM to issue regulations on political activities intended to implement Congress' intent that that federal "[E]mployees should be encouraged to exercise fully, freely, and without fear of penalty or reprisal, and the extent not expressly prohibited by law, their right to participate or refrain from participating in the political processes of the Nation" (U.S. Office of Personnel Management, 1998). For most federal workers, they allow participation in political campaigns and running for election to *nonpartisan offices*, such as school boards. They prohibit candidacy for *partisan political office* and "soliciting, accepting, or receiving political contributions." Federal employees also are not allowed to receive political contributions or volunteer services from subordinates or to participate in political activities while on duty, while "wearing a uniform, badge, or insignia that identifies the employing agency," or if "he or she is in any room or building occupied in the discharge of official duties by an individual employed or holding office in the Government of the United States. . . ." (U.S. Office of Personnel Management, 1998, p. 4559).

Most state and local governments still restrict their employees' political activities to some extent. A few have laws more restrictive than the Hatch Act as amended; for example, they may prohibit voluntary contributions and not allow workers to express their partisan opinions publicly. The pattern on the state level is for most to permit general campaign activities while off-duty. About two-thirds allow their employees to be candidates in partisan elections, but there is no uniformity across the states (Thurber, 1993, pp. 45–46). The same variability may be found on the local level. Overall, however, public personnel systems are now expected to establish and administer a delicate balance between two sets of values—those related to neutral competence and those involving citizens' rights to participate in the political processes of a democratic society.

HRM AND RESPONSIVENESS TO EXECUTIVE LEADERSHIP

By the time Jimmy Carter assumed the presidency in 1976, pressure was building for yet another round of civil service reform. The first civil service reform movement sought to replace spoils with merit systems and to limit line management's control over many aspects of personnel administration. This was not what civil service reform meant in 1976. It referred instead to better aligning personnel policies and practices with the day-to-day needs of public managers, to improving the productivity of public employees, and to making bureaucracy more responsive to executive leadership. In other words, public personnel administration should become human resource management in its outlook and priorities.

Increasingly emphasis was placed on expanding the control chief executives and public managers had over the personnel function. Proponents of reform argued that the traditional merit systems imposed unnecessary barriers to managerial effectiveness. They directly challenged the belief that elected chief executives and line managers should be kept at arm's length because they could not be relied upon to protect the merit principle. There was, this second generation of reformers argued, no necessary contradiction between the merit *principle* and a management-oriented personnel system. The divide between executive management and the personnel function created by the first round of civil service reform had to be eliminated if government was to perform and to be responsive to public needs.

In part, this divide was to be closed through structural changes. The U.S. Civil Service Reform Act of 1978 (CSRA) abolished the Civil Service Commission and replaced it with the Office of Personnel Management whose director reports directly to the president, and the Merit Systems Protection Board (MSPB), which is responsible for the "watchdog" function historically assigned to the personnel offices. A growing number of states and localities followed the federal lead by abolishing their commissions or limiting them to advisory, appellate, and investigation functions. In most states, the personnel director's position or its equivalent now reports directly to the governor.

Deregulation and simplification were important elements of reform. Central personnel agencies and personnel offices in line departments were asked to eliminate the numerous "unnecessary" rules and regulations they traditionally used to closely control managers' discretion in personnel matters. If personnel management systems were to be partners with management in building effective and responsive public agencies, procedures had to be streamlined and oriented toward *enabling* or *serving* as opposed to *regulating* in areas such as recruitment, selection, and performance management (Campbell, 1978).

President Carter, of course, had little or no opportunity to implement the CSRA along lines he and Campbell intended. The Reagan Administration and its Director of OPM reverted to a regulatory posture in matters of personnel management (Ban, 1984, pp. 54–55). On the federal level, and in many of the states and localities struggling to deal with new political and fiscal realities, civil service reform (and even the idea of civil service as an important and valuable part of American government) lost much of its momentum.

By the mid-1980s, reform along lines advocated by the authors of the CSRA had stalled, at least on the federal level. By the end of the decade, serious concerns about the capacity of the civil service to function in an effective and responsive manner on all levels of government were developing. In its 1989 report, the National Commission on the Public Service observed that the United States' need for a highly competent and trustworthy public service was steadily growing, not diminishing. Its recommendations for changes in federal personnel policies and practices were intended to address what some called the "quiet crisis" of the civil service. By the end of the 1980s, evidence of declining competence, existing or impending shortages of needed human resources, and slumping morale in many areas of the nation's public service was accumulating at a rate that could no longer be ignored. The Commission's central message was clearly stated: the U.S. needed to build a national consensus on the importance of a truly excellent public service and to take steps needed to make it a reality (National Commission on the Public Service, 1989, p. 1).

The Commission urged the George H. W. Bush Administration to pursue some fifteen goals related to personnel policies and human resources management. While each addressed specific issues, the Commission's general purpose was to focus attention on three basic problem areas: building and sustaining a high-quality senior civil service, improving recruitment and retention in order to achieve a civil service staffed by the "best and the brightest," and increasing productivity by establishing a "culture of performance."

Demanding high levels of performance was not enough. The personnel system had to be supportive. The Commission's report stated:

> The commitment to performance cannot long survive, however, unless the government provides adequate pay, recognition for jobs done well, accessible training, and decent working conditions. Quality service must be recognized, rewarded, and constantly reinforced. It is not enough to exhort the work force to do better—government must provide tangible signals that performance matters (National Commission on the Public Service, 1989, p. 34).

The Volcker Commission's report set the stage for renewed reform efforts across a broad front of organizational and personnel-related functions. On the federal level, this process began in earnest with the Clinton-Gore "reinvention" and "re-engineering" initiatives, which continued to emphasize decentralization, deregulation, simplification, cooperative labor relations, *and* downsizing the federal workforce. These reforms reflected a broader shift away from support for traditional bureaucratic forms of organization in both the public and private sectors (U.S. General Accounting Office, 1995a, p. 3). This shift included a growing emphasis on:

1. Integrating personnel functions with organizational planning and policy-making activities.
2. Treating employee development and training as an investment in the human capital required to maintain and build organizational capacities.
3. Valuing people as assets to be developed and encouraged, as opposed to costs that should be minimized (U.S. General Accounting Office, 1995b, pp. 5–6).

In 1993, the National Commission on the State and Local Public Service issued an influential report (The Winter Report) that identified important reform needs on the state and local levels. The Report of the National Performance Review (Gore, 1993) issued by Vice President Al Gore and the Winter Report shared the general orientation described earlier, and both recommended extensive decentralization of the personnel function, delegation of hiring and other authorities to the agency level, and streamlining of personnel processes such as recruitment, hiring, position classification, and appeals (Thompson, 1994). Both reports also recommended changes that should increase the authority of chief executives over personnel policy through control over top-level appointments and organizational structures.

By the 1990s, the key elements of the civil service reform agenda were as follows (Kellough and Nigro, 2005; Walters, 2002):

- Structural decentralization and delegations of many human resource functions to line organizations
- Broad grants of discretion to agencies and departments in such areas as recruitment, selection, hiring, and promotions
- Streamlined and simplified job classification and pay systems
- Streamlined reduction-in-force, grievance, and appeals processes
- Performance management systems using a variety of merit-pay systems intended to reward individuals
- Lowering labor costs and achieving other efficiencies through contracting-out or privatization
- Moving toward "at will" employment relationships under which public employees do not enjoy the job-tenure protections afforded those holding classified positions in traditional merit systems

CLOSING THE CIRCLE

By the early twenty-first century, public personnel management systems were being asked to engage many problems and challenges that were simply unimaginable during the early years of the Republic. Many of the "deregulating and decentralizing" civil service reforms implemented on all levels of government over the previous decade were still in place, but as one observer noted, concerns about accountability and responsiveness were surfacing as politicians found that they had "far fewer levers available to . . . control the civil service" and deregulation and decentralization reduced their "capacity as leaders to exert as much control over policy implementation as they might have had in the past" (Peters, 2001, p. 138).

The core mandate had not changed in its fundamentals: today's personnel management systems are still asked to promote and sustain a civil service that is reliably responsive to public policies and executive leadership. Elected officials—executives and legislators alike—are held accountable in a variety of ways for the performance of public personnel management systems. As the overview presented here suggests, assuring accountability and responsiveness in a system of democratic governance is and always has been at the heart of the enterprise (Kettl, et al., 1996). The ongoing challenge has been and continues to be the "invention" of public personnel management systems that promote responsiveness in its broadest sense, foster the accountability to electorates and other segments of society required of a strong democracy, *and* offer the human resources management needed to achieve desired performance outcomes. Most importantly, in a democracy, these systems should enjoy broad public support and confidence (Hays, 1996).

REFERENCES

Adarand Constructors v. Pena, U.S. Secretary of Transportation. 1995. WL347345.

Arnett v. Kennedy. 1974. 416 U.S. 134.

Aronson, Albert H. 1973. "Personnel Administration: The State and Local Picture." *Civil Service Journal* 13:3: 37–42.

Bailey v. Richardson. 1951. 341 U.S. 918.

Ban, Carolyn. 1984. "Implementing Civil Service Reform: Structure and Strategy." in Patricia W. Ingraham and Carolyn Ban, eds., *Legislating Bureaucratic Change: The Civil Service Reform Act of 1978.* Albany, NY: State University of New York Press, pp. 42–62.

Bishop v. Wood. 1976. 426 U.S. 341.

Board of Regents v. Roth. 1972. 408 U.S. 564, 92 S. Ct. 2701, 33 L. Ed. 548.

Branti v. Finkel. 1980. 445 U.S. 507.

Caldwell, Lynton K. 1944. *The Administrative Theories of Hamilton and Jefferson.* Chicago, IL: University of Chicago Press.

Campbell, Alan K. 1978. "Testimony on Civil Service Reform and Organization." *Civil Service Reform, Hearings of the U.S. House Committee on Post Office and Civil Service.* Washington, DC: U.S. Government Printing Office.

Daniel, Christopher. 1992. "Constitutionalizing Merit? Practical Implications of Elrod, Branti, and Rutan." *Review of Public Personnel Administration* 12:2: 26–34.

Dotson, Arch. 1955. "The Emerging Doctrine of Privilege in Public Employment." *Public Administration Review* 15:2: 77–88.

Elrod v. Burns. 1976. 427 U.S. 96 S. Ct., 2673.

Fish, Carl R. 1904. *The Civil Service and the Patronage.* Cambridge, MA: Harvard University Press.

Freedman, Anne. 1994. *Patronage: An American Tradition.* Chicago, IL: Nelson-Hall Publishers.

Gore, Al. 1993. *Reinventing Human Resource Management: Accompanying Report of the National Performance Review.* Washington, DC.

Griggs v. Duke Power Company. 1971. 401 U.S. 424.

Hays, Steven. 1996. "The 'State of the Discipline' in Public Personnel Administration." *Public Administration Quarterly* 20:3: 285–304.

Ingraham, Patricia W. 1995. *The Foundation of Merit: Public Service in the American Democracy.* Baltimore, MD: The Johns Hopkins University Press.

Kellough, J. Edward and Nigro, Lloyd G. 2005. "Radical Civil Service Reform: Ideology, Politics, and Policy." In Stephen E. Condrey, ed. *Handbook of Human Resource Management in Government*, 2nd ed. San Francisco, CA: Jossey-Bass Publishers, pp. 58–75.

Kettl, Donald F., et al. 1996. *Civil Service Reform: Building a Government that Works.* Washington, DC: Brookings Institution Press.

Martin v. Wilks. 1989. 109 S. Ct. 2180.

McAuliffe v. Mayor of New Bedford. 1892. 155 Mass. 216, 29 N. E. 517.

Miller, Douglas T., ed. 1972. *The Nature of Jacksonian Democracy.* New York, NY: John Wiley & Sons.

Mosher, Frederick C. 1968. *Democracy and the Public Service.* New York, NY: Oxford University Press.

Naff, Katherine C. and Kellough, J. Edward. 2003. "Ensuring Employment Equity: Are Federal Diversity Programs Making a Difference?" *International Journal of Public Administration* 26:12.

National Commission on the Public Service. 1989. *Leadership for America: Rebuilding the Public Service.* Washington, DC: National Commission on the Public Service.

O'Brian, David M. 1997. "The First Amendment and the Public Sector." In Phillip J. Cooper and Chester A. Newland, eds., *Handbook of Public Law and Administration.* San Francisco, CA: Jossey-Bass Publishers, pp. 259–273.

Oklahoma v. United States Civil Service Commission. 1947. 330 U.S. 127.

Patterson v. McLean Credit Union. 1989. 109 S. Ct. 2363.

Perry v. Sinderman. 1972. 408 U.S. 593, S. Ct. 2694, 33 L. Ed. 2d 570.

Peters, B. Guy. 2001. *The Future of Governing*, 2nd ed, revised. Lawrence, KS: University Press of Kansas.

Price Waterhouse v. Hopkins. 1989. 109 S. Ct. 1775.

Regents of the University of California v. Bakke. 1978. 98 S. Ct. 2733.

Riccucci, Norma M. 1997. "Will Affirmative Action Survive into the Twenty-First Century." In Carolyn Ban and Norma Riccucci, eds., *Public Personnel Management: Current Concerns, Future Challenges.* New York, NY: Longman, pp. 57–72.

Riordon, William L. 1963. *Plunkitt of Tammany Hall.* New York, NY: E. P. Dutton.

Rosenbloom, David H. 1971. "Some Political Implications of the Drift Toward a Liberation of Federal Employees." *Public Administration Review* 31:4: 420–426.

———. and Carroll, James D. 1990. *Toward Constitutional Competence: A Casebook for Public Administrators.* Englewood Cliffs, NJ: Prentice Hall.

Rutan v. Republican Party of Illinois. 1990. 110 S. Ct., 2734.

Schiesl, Martin J. 1977. *The Politics of Efficiency*. Berkeley, CA: University of California Press.

Simon, Herbert A., Smithburg, Donald W., and Thompson, Victor A. 1950. *Public Administration*. New York, NY: Alfred A. Knopf.

Stahl, O. Glenn. 1962. *Public Personnel Administration*, 5th ed. New York, NY: Harper and Row.

State of Texas v. Hopwood. 1996. WL 227009.

Thompson, Frank J., ed. 1994. "The Winter Commission Report: Is Deregulation the Answer for Public Personnel Management?" *Review of Public Personnel Administration* 14:2: 5–76.

Thurber, Karl T., Jr. 1993. "Big, Little, Littler: Synthesizing Hatch Act-Based Political Activity Legislation Research." *Review of Public Personnel Administration* 13:1: 38–51.

United Public Workers v. Mitchell. 1947. 330 U.S. 75, 67 S. Ct. 556, 91 L. Ed. 754.

United States Civil Service Commission v. National Association of Letter Carriers, AFL-CIO. 1973. 98 S. Ct. 2880, 27 L. Ed. 2d 796.

United Steel Workers of America v. Weber. 1979. 443 U.S. 193.

U.S. Commission on Civil Rights. 1969. *For All the People . . . By All the People: A Report on Equal Opportunity in State and Local Government Employment*. Washington, DC: U.S. Government Printing Office.

U.S. General Accounting Office. 1995a. *Transforming the Civil Service: Building the Workforce of the Future*. Washington, DC: GAO/GGD-96-35, December.

———. 1995b. *Federal Personnel Management: Views on Selected NPR Human Resource Recommendations*. Washington, DC: GAO/GGD-95-221BR, September.

U.S. Office of Personnel Management. 1998. "Political Activity: Federal Employees Residing in Designated Localities." *Federal Register* 63:20: 4555–4560.

U.S. Library of Congress. 1976. *History of Civil Service Merit Systems of the United States and Selected Foreign Countries*. Washington, DC: U.S. Government Printing Office, December 31.

Van Riper, Paul P. 1958. *History of the United States Civil Service*. New York, NY: Harper and Row.

Walters, Jonathan. 2002. *Life After Civil Service Reform: The Texas, Georgia, and Florida Experiences*. White Plains, NY: IBM.

Wards Cove Packing Co. v. Atonio. 1989. 109 S. Ct. 2115.

White, Leonard D. 1948. *The Federalists*. New York, NY: McMillan.

———. 1951. *The Jeffersonians*. New York, NY: McMillan.

———. 1954. *The Jacksonians*. New York, NY: McMillan.

Chapter 2

Great Expectations but Hazards Ahead: Applying Lessons Learned from Past Demonstration Projects to Emergent Federal HRM Systems

Patricia W. Ingraham and Heather Getha-Taylor

INTRODUCTION

The story of the federal civil service in the United States is one of cycles and shifts, of moves from one set of values to another, and of nearly constant frustration with efforts to balance the practices and policies of stable bureaucratic organizations with demands of electoral and practical politics (Van Riper, 1958; Ingraham, 1995). As the civil service grew in the last century, it moved from patronage to coverage by the Pendleton Act, away from the Pendleton Act to more policy-based appointments, notably in the pre-World War II years, and back again to increased civil service coverage. We are experiencing another of these historic shifts, as nearly 45 percent of the federal civilian workforce will move into coverage by new legislative provisions created for the Department of Homeland Security and the Department of Defense. These provisions move away from some protections and provisions traditionally associated with civil service and toward a much greater emphasis on performance and flexibility. They also seek to dramatically decrease the roles played by federal employee unions in personnel processes.

These moves followed the much less sweeping changes of the previous twenty-five years: The Civil Service Reform Act of 1978 provided for greater managerial and agency discretion in testing, for other flexibilities under the conditions of demonstration projects, and created the Senior Executive Service, but did little to fundamentally alter the statutory provisions of USC Title V, the major statutory basis for civil service law. Special legislation exempted the entire

18

Federal Aviation Administration from most provisions of Title V in 1996. Reorganization legislation for the IRS in 1998 provided that agency with new personnel flexibilities and exemptions (Thompson and Rainey, 2003). The use of CSRA demonstration authorities continued to increase, notably in the Department of Defense, challenging Title V classification procedures by adopting such practices as *broad banding*. As hiring became more difficult for some agencies and occupations, an ever larger percentage of the federal workforce operated under hiring and pay authorities that excepted them from Title V's provisions (Ingraham, Selden, and Moynihan, 2000). Finally, entire organizations—the Foreign Service, the Postal Service, and Government Accountability Office, for example—operated with pay and personnel systems that were completely separate from Title V.

There were tensions in these creeping alterations, however, and some created serious obstacles to more fundamental changes. When the Patent and Trademark Office became a Performance Based Organization, for example, legislative provisions contained no mention of new personnel flexibilities. This was due largely to intense lobbying by the organization's largest union (Jacobson, 2003). The "reformed" organization, therefore, was to act more like a private sector company, but was to do so within the continuing confines of federal personnel rules. Other organizations struggled with balancing emphasis on traditionally defined principles of merit—fairness was frequently described as sameness—with more flexible and discretionary management practices. Virtually all faced recruiting challenges, even when armed with new flexibilities.

WHY CHANGE NOW?

Three events—two evolutionary, one unprecedented in the United States—caused changes to be more sweeping. The first change, the aging and graying of the federal workforce, was the result of demographic changes across government agencies, of downsizing and hiring freezes in the 1990s, and of a general inability to nimbly compete in the market for younger and more specialized talent. The cumulative impact left a large proportion of the federal workforce eligible for retirement over the next three to five years and some critical agencies such as NASA with enormous skill gaps (Partnership for Public Service, 2003).

The second change centered on defense, but was profoundly important to the federal workforce overall. DoD's 746,000 employees constitute a very large percentage of the total federal civilian workforce and DoD agencies have traditionally been bellweathers of personnel innovation (Barr, 2003). Since the end of the Cold War, the mission and the work of both military and civilian employees of the Defense Department have changed substantially—from waging and supporting large ground war operations to intense but smaller, shorter-term, and more strategic engagements. In this new context, Secretary of Defense Donald Rumsfield estimated that over 300,000 military personnel performed jobs that could be civilian, thereby increasing stress on military personnel (Rumsfeld Testimony, 2003). Military personnel continued to be placed in these positions, however, because they possessed relocation and other flexibilities that civil service law prohibited for civilians. Further, Pentagon planners argued, continued outsourcing of DoD jobs rendered many civilian jobs obsolete or less in demand, and substantial workforce restructuring was necessary. Civil service laws and union demands constrained such restructuring, even in the face of national emergency.

The third event leading to the rather dramatic swing in civil service reform was September 11, 2001. In the aftermath of that day, it became evident that traditional civil service laws did not support the integrated and swift responses the new world arena demanded. Civil service reform, therefore, became closely intertwined with national security (Moynihan, forthcoming).

Some of the proposed changes had been considered and discussed for years. Moynihan argues that the change could occur so rapidly in 2002 because public management was not the dominant policy issue in the debate, but was fully subsumed by national security. He notes, for example, that the Homeland Security Act represents a ". . . concern with flexibility that was already pursued under Clinton, and as far back as the Carter administration . . . [and that] the Bush administration had already developed a managerial agenda for reform before 9/11, which became the basis for the flexibility provisions in the HSA, albeit in a much more simplified and expanded version" (Moynihan, forthcoming).

The U.S. Merit Systems Protection Board (2004), clearly a protector of merit and the values it embodies, praised the direction of the changes—as well as their timing. The Board decried the complexity of current flexibilities: "Instead of strategically changing the way we do business, many of the new flexibilities have incrementally added processes onto the already complex structure of HR rules and regulations, making the system even more difficult to understand and navigate than ever before" (p. 11). Current personnel reforms have the potential to change the way public sector managers conduct their business—and the Merit Systems Protection Board applauded:

> If the new systems deliver what is promised, the human capital rules and regulations will be more flexible, managers will be more involved in and accountable for decisions, and HR staffs will receive the resources and support they need. If the new systems don't deliver, we may miss an opportune time for change (p. 11).

Employee union representatives, however, were not so sure. While unions were included in the planning of the DHS reforms, representatives argued that their concerns were not carefully considered or factored into the new human resource management system. Unions were included, but not so fully, in the DoD changes. In response, unions resorted to the courts. John Gage, national president of the American Federation of Government Employees, was vocal on this point: "We, the unions, had earnestly sought to design a new, efficient personnel system in collaboration with DHS managers . . . with our efforts rebuffed and our gravest concerns ignored, we now, unfortunately, have no choice but to pursue a remedy through the federal courts" (FedSmith, 2005a).

Given the swift and heated response to the DHS and DoD reforms, the hazards ahead can hardly be described as hidden. But union collaboration is not the only difficulty the new reforms will encounter. The changes are clearly taking place in a highly charged political environment—driven in part, at least, by a presidential management agenda that focuses on performance. The role and the politics of unions profoundly complicate this situation. Second, although there was serious dissatisfaction about the old system in many quarters—some referred to it as a "house of cards"—there was not complete agreement about the components of a new one.

Congressional debate about the reforms centered largely on the national security implications; only when new rules were published (after a year-long planning process) did members of Congress begin to focus on other implications. Senator Joseph Lieberman, D-Conn., was quoted: "Congress decided the Homeland Security Department needed extraordinary flexibility to waive civil service protections because of its unique security mission. Now that DHS is undertaking a grand experiment in revamping the civil service system, we should see how it works before we consider whether it would be appropriate for agencies without critical national security responsibilities" (Daily Briefing, 2005a).

Despite such concerns, government wide reforms—closely modeled on the DHS and DoD efforts—is on the agenda for the Bush administration. MAXHR, the adapted human resource management system based on the DHS and DoD reforms, is designed for application to 110,000 additional federal employees. The system is intended to "create an environment that enhances recruitment, retention, and development of superior talent. MAXHR will recognize and reward employee contributions, and achieve the highest levels of individual performance and accountability" (FedSmith, 2005a). Planning for such efforts continues despite union assertions that such changes are "gutting the civil service" (Daily Briefing, 2005b).

HOW WAS THE CHANGE PROCESS DESIGNED?

The DHS and DoD processes were not revolutionary. Indeed, they closely followed the recommendations set forth by the General Accounting Office (GAO) to guide major transformation:

- Ensure that top leadership drives the transformation
- Establish a coherent mission and integrated strategic goals to guide the transformation
- Focus on a key set of principles and priorities at the outset of the transformation
- Set implementation goals and a timeline to build momentum and show progress
- Dedicate an implementation team to manage the transformation

- Establish a communication strategy to create shared expectations and report related progress
- Involve employees to obtain their ideas and gain their ownership

The actual design of the system proceeded under the auspices of a joint task force convened by DHS Secretary Tom Ridge and OPM Director Kay Coles James. The task force presented a set of 52 options for consideration in November, 2003. The actual choices among the options were determined in January, 2004, more than a year after passage of the legislation in November, 2002. In DHS, there was full union participation in the planning process; as noted, in DoD, collaboration was more limited. Neither model of inclusion was satisfactory from the unions' perspective, however. In January 2005, four unions (American Federation of Government Employees, National Association of Agriculture Employees, National Federation of Federal Employees, and National Treasury Employees Union) filed suit against DHS in response to the announcement that the new personnel system would be implemented against union wishes. The unions want the implementation blocked on the grounds that the new system limits collective bargaining and the employee disciplinary appeal process. The unions see both as violations of Congress' original intent to design a flexible system to accompany the provisions of the 2002 Homeland Security Act.

While the role of the unions in the "politics" of reform cannot be denied, it is also important to examine the role played by the Office of Personnel Management in the reform process. Key OPM staff was involved in the DHS deliberations from the beginning. Secretary Rumsfeld initially declared, however, that OPM management of civilian employees at Defense was one of the major problems remedied by NSPS. DoD's original proposal was fundamentally for free rein of the Office of the Secretary of Defense in civilian personnel matters.

The DHS reform design team identified the following fundamental elements and guiding principles to focus their joint effort. Overall, the process contained four critical elements: 1) a joint OPM-DHS design team, 2) extensive consultation, 3) union participation, and 4) external review. These were elaborated to include specific elements, which are described in Table 2.1.

WHAT ARE THE CHANGES?

Three things are immediately clear. First, the reforms are mission-based. This is in obvious opposition to the classic "standardized across government" model that identified the civil service for many years. Second, the reforms are based on individual and organizational performance. They define merit as performance based; they do not emphasize standardized equity. Third, the changes are designed to be agile; flexibility and performance, not protection are their underlying values.

It is anticipated that full rollout of DHS provisions will occur over a five-year period; DoD anticipates a two- to five-year roll-out for the National Security Personnel System (but this timetable is subject to substantial revision). In many ways, DHS faces the more complex implementation challenge: combining the personnel

TABLE 2.1 Fundamental Elements and Guiding Principles for DHS Design Team

Fundamental Elements	The new system must be responsive to the mission of the agency
	The new system must be performance-based
	The new system must be agile enough to respond to twenty-first century threats
	The new system must be credible and fair
Guiding Principles	The new system must be mission-centered
	The new system must be performance-focused, contemporary, and excellent
	The new system must generate respect and trust
	The new system must be based on the principles of merit and fairness embodied in the statutory merit system principles
	The new system must comply with all other applicable provisions of law
	The process for developing the new system must be collaborative, reflecting the input of managerial and non-managerial employees at all levels in DHS and of employee unions

SOURCE: Federal Register (2004)

of 22 separate agencies into one, while also transforming the framework under which they operate (see Table 2.2).

But the sets of changes in DHS and DoD do have common characteristics. They move away from the strong role that collective bargaining has played in workplace conditions toward performance rewards and more stringent disciplinary systems. Both simplify and streamline disciplinary processes and keep them internal to the agency to a much greater extent. Both systems place strong emphasis on performance management and performance reward and will assess top management on their ability to make the new systems work. Both systems emphasize simplified hiring and promotion systems and eliminate automatic annual pay increases. Both systems emphasize—to a much greater degree than before—workforce planning with an eye toward workforce restructuring and potential downsizing (and additional contracting out). Both increase managerial discretion in these matters very substantially. Both obviously move away from standardization toward agency-specific tailoring and away from predictability toward agility and responsiveness.

Major components of the legislative changes emerged from quite disparate sources. To be sure, the private sector and its emphasis on performance are well represented (Ingraham, 1993). There are also elements of much broader management reforms such as New Public Management (Moynihan, forthcoming; Ingraham, 1997). To a large extent, however, much of the content of the new reforms emerges from earlier federal demonstration projects authorized by the Civil Service Reform Act of 1978. Examining the lessons of these demonstrations, particularly

TABLE 2.2   Positions Transferred to Department of Homeland Security

Originating Department	Originating Agency	Positions Transferred[1]
Agriculture	Import and Entry Inspection[2]	2,655
Commerce	Critical Infrastructure Assurance Office	50
Defense	National Communications System	105
Department of Energy		101
Federal Emergency Management Agency		8,542
General Services Administration		1,713
Health and Human Services		91
Justice	Immigration and Naturalization Service	36,769
Justice	Other	385
Transportation	United States Coast Guard[3]	60,403
Transportation	Transportation Security Administration	68,859
Transportation	Other	40
Treasury	United States Custom Service	22,028
Treasury	United States Secret Service	6,251
Treasury	Federal Law Enforcement Training Center	922
Treasury	Other	191
Total		209,105

[1] This column reflects positions—full-time, part-time, and vacant—and does not represent FTE employment or the total number of employees on board.
[2] This represents a specific function from APHIS that was transferred to DHS.
[3] This represents both civilian and military U.S. Coast Guard positions.
SOURCE: GAO (2003)

with an eye toward what their experience might forecast for DHS and DoD, is the subject of the next section.

LESSONS FROM THE DEMONSTRATION PROJECTS

Management flexibility reforms in the federal government have shown some strong similarities in the past twenty-five years. They range from the classification and pay reforms initially tested at the China Lake Naval Research Laboratory demonstration project, through recruiting and hiring simplification reforms, to recruitment and retention bonuses. These reforms were designed to combat what were perceived to be problems endemic in the civil service system: difficulties in recruiting top-notch candidates, extremely slow hiring processes, difficulties in rewarding good performance and punishing bad, and frustrations caused by too complex and rigid internal systems. None required major changes in base Title V law; all were deemed to be compatible with core Title V provisions.

To determine the efficacy of these projects, in 2002, the General Accounting Office examined existing flexibilities and asked federal managers which they found most useful. As an overview of experience, GAO reported that work-life programs, recruitment and retention incentives, incentive awards, and special hiring authorities were most favored by the federal mangers interviewed (GAO, 03 2, 2002). Thompson (1999) observed that in the Clinton administration's experiments with reinvention, simplification activities, especially as they related to classification and hiring, were also favored.

In 2004, the Office of Personnel Management identified 14 lessons that emerged from the implementation of CSRA demonstration projects. These lessons are divided into four broad categories: 1) primary lessons learned, 2) lessons on planning, 3) lessons on culture, and 4) lessons on resources. Lessons learned have applications to past demonstration projects, but also illuminate the challenges inherent to the current DHS and DoD reforms. A research team from the Maxwell School's Campbell Institute tested these findings with a group of federal managers; both OPM "Lessons" and Maxwell's findings are presented in Table 2.3.

FINDINGS: LESSONS LEARNED, BUT HAZARDS AHEAD

The interviews with senior managers yielded important information, including new lessons that directly apply to the Department of Homeland Security and Department of Defense flexibility initiatives. Using the Office of Personnel Management's lessons-learned framework as a guide, we gained new insights on alternative personnel systems as well as the inherent tensions in the DHS and DoD change processes.

While both sets of reforms reflect lessons learned, it is important to note that the current initiatives are occurring in a much more politicized environment than did any of the demonstration efforts. OPM was present early on in the DHS reforms, but was involved later, and at congressional urging, in the DoD reforms. Unions illustrated the intensely politicized environment by describing the DHS system as "a huge power grab from the Legislative Branch to the Executive Branch" (FedSmith, 2005b). In other words, union representatives believe that the reforms are taking on a new form and application that is not consistent with the authority granted by the Homeland Security Act.

Lesson Learned: An Executive Champion Is a Key to Success.   Based on our interviews, the first lesson learned from the demonstration projects, "Flexibilities Are Effective," is very widely accepted. All of our interviewees agreed that flexibilities *can be* effective HR management tools. But implementation of flexibilities must be clearly and strongly led. The managers strongly emphasized the need for consistent change managers and leaders. "You need disciplined planning in a serious way," said one manager. Another emphasized support throughout the change process. "Even the best designs can go astray without good leadership." Inspiring commitment to the cause requires frequent reminders, said one manager. We need to remind supervisors "of their objectives and why the demo was designed in the first place." Further, to be successful, demos require individuals who are intrinsically motivated. "We needed people who just took the initiative without having to be told."

TABLE 2.3   Office of Personnel Management—Lessons Learned from the Demo Projects (edited)

	Lessons Learned by Office of Personnel Management	Testing the Lessons: Questions Posed to Demonstration Project Managers
Primary Lessons Learned	*Flexibilities are Effective*: These are effective HR management tools that can have an impact on organizational effectiveness. However, large-scale organizational change does take time.	Can demonstration projects have an impact on organizational effectiveness? To what extent? How long would it be before you could tell? Can you provide an example?
	Potential for Wider Impact: There should be a method of converting successfully tested flexibilities to permanent programs and for making them available to other agencies—short of separate legislation.	Should successful demonstration projects be made permanent? Should successful demonstration systems be available to other agencies? Why or why not? What prevents this from happening now?
Lessons on Planning	*A Business Case for Change*: The flexibilities should support the agency's mission and should address the agency's human capital challenges. There must be clear objectives and performance criteria.	How can you measure alignment between agency mission and the flexibility project? Can you tell us about some of your objectives and criteria? Were they appropriate for the system and your agency?
	Diverse Pay Systems Can Create Inter-Agency and Intra-Agency Challenges: Consistency and equity are key concerns as are competition and increased costs.	Did you experience inter-agency or intra-agency challenges revolving around such issues as consistency or equity? How did you resolve these problems? (Or, why wasn't it a problem?)
	An Executive Champion Is a Key to Success: An individual at the agency level is needed to promote, defend, and support the initiative.	Can you tell us about executive champions within your agency for this demo project? Why did he/she step forth as a leader? Did he/she possess any special qualities that may have predisposed him/her for such a job? If none presented themselves, why?
Lessons on Culture	*A Supportive Culture Is Essential*: The existing culture often determines what will or will not work—systems change alone will not cure an unhealthy culture.	Please describe your organizational culture. Did you witness any cultural change within your organization after the demo project was implemented (specifics please)? Why or why not?

(continued on the following page)

TABLE 2.3 *(continued from the previous page)*

Lessons Learned by Office of Personnel Management	Testing the Lessons: Questions Posed to Demonstration Project Managers
One Size Does Not Fit All: If implemented governmentwide, there should be sufficient flexibility to allow for customization that will meet unique management expectations and organizational needs.	Do you think that your particular demo project would be appropriate for other agencies? Why or why not? Under what circumstances? Can you describe a potential demo project that would be applicable to all agencies? Or that wouldn't work at any?
Communication and Training Must Be Priorities: Employees must understand how the change impacts them on an individual basis and there should be ongoing training for managers, employees, and HR specialists.	What methods did you use to communicate with employees about the demo projects? What kinds of training did you provide for employees, HR specialists, and managers? What kind of feedback did you receive?
Employees and Employee Organizations Must Have "Buy-In": Employees and their representatives should be involved from the beginning. However, involvement and consultation do not guarantee buy-in.	What does "buy-in" mean in your organization—in regard to this demo project? Did you achieve "buy-in"? Why or why not?
Successful Tests Focus on Performance, Not Entitlement: Flexibilities support a performance culture, but may meet resistance from some employees who may focus on potential adverse impacts.	Did you encounter resistance to a culture change that embraces performance over entitlement? Can you give any specific examples?
Keep It Simple: Flexibilities should be simple—easy to understand, easy to implement, and easy to administer.	Was the demo project easy to understand (by employees, managers, HR specialists)? Easy to implement? Easy to administer? Why or why not?

(continued on the following page)

TABLE 2.3   *(continued from the previous page)*

	Lessons Learned by Office of Personnel Management	Testing the Lessons: Questions Posed to Demonstration Project Managers
Lessons on Resources	*Costs Can Be Controlled:* Although pay-based flexibilities are not cost neutral, there are tools to limit increases. However, there are additional costs associated with changing administrative, HR, and IT support systems that should be considered.	Did you experience problems with cost control in implementing the demo project? In what areas did you experience the most problems: salary increases, administrative costs, evaluation costs, or something else? What advice could you give to other agencies to control costs? Should cost control be a concern at all?
	Flexibilities Must Be Integrated into the Agency's HR System: Flexibilities should complement and strengthen the entire HR system—they do not work alone.	Did the demo project complement and strengthen your HR system? How so? Can you comment on the impact of the demo project on IT and HR support services?
	Ongoing Evaluation Is Important: Evaluation can help determine the effectiveness of the system as well as address adverse impacts and provide a basis for expansion to other agencies.	When and by what method (surveys, interviews, etc.) did you evaluate the demo project's effectiveness? Did you find surprising results? What was the evaluation report used for? What should it be used for?

Hazard Ahead: The Changes Occur in a Political Environment; Some Necessary Leaders Are Political Appointees with Short Tenure.   The experience of both public and private organizations suggests that change leaders must understand and communicate the purpose of the change clearly and consistently (Thompson and Rainey, 2003; Ingraham, Joyce, and Donahue, 2003). Thompson and Rainey credit much of the early success of the change at the Internal Revenue Service, for example, to the leadership of Charles Rossotti and his team, who were, in effect, "change champions." At DHS and DoD, top leadership is dealing with the daily crises of national security and war, as well as managing the change processes necessary for effective reform. Further, many of the political appointees who led and participated in the design of the reforms resigned at the beginning of the second Bush term; that is, at the beginning of implementation. This clearly suggests some lack of continuity and may well contribute to mixed signals about the importance of the reform effort.

Lesson Learned: Keep It Simple.   This suggests a move away from the burdensome process and procedure of the old system. Many of the demonstration projects did, in fact, stress simplicity in classification and in performance systems.

Hazard Ahead: Change Is not a Simple Process.   The managers we interviewed found this lesson to be laughable. "I don't think of any of this as simple. Good HR has some technicality and detail." Another respondent agreed. "Simple is relative. Simple doesn't mean it will work better—just that it will be understood." According to another respondent, these changes always require more than what is expected. "The change will require a lot of time, effort, and money—and it often takes 5–7 years to take root." What seems to be more important than simplicity is *clarity*. "This is not a simple process, but the intent and expectations should be clear."

Beyond clarity, timing and phasing were emphasized as critical in our interviews. One of the primary lessons that emerged from the interviews was that large-scale changes such as those proposed by DHS and DoD will take much longer than expected. One individual recommended that managers "expect a transition phase. It's a devil of a chore—there will not be a lot of happy campers." In order to facilitate such change, implementation must be phased. "You can't do it all at once," this manager continued. Another agreed: "bureaucracies are difficult to change; it is a matter of time." Recognizing that these changes will take time and will require implementation in phases will help ease the transition as well as temper expectations with regard to the evaluation of the flexibilities. Again, the significance of the politicized environment and turnover of key political appointees is important.

Lesson Learned: A Supportive Culture Is Essential.   Part of the problem with transferring flexibilities to other agencies is that cultural differences may influence the impact of such reforms, depending on the organization. The lesson learned from the demonstration projects supports this. It is critical that demonstration projects match the mission and culture of the organization. If a culture has to change to match the reform, managers must keep in mind that such change requires time and flexibility. A mismatched culture could be the death-blow of many well-intentioned flexibility initiatives. The new reforms are allowing for cultural diversity, however, by remaining a *framework*, rather than a set of specific procedures. The design team argued that this did indeed permit tailoring to specific mission and culture.

Hazard Ahead: Merging Diverse Cultures Is One of the Most Challenging Parts of Organizational Change.   "Some people don't understand why flexibilities don't work . . . but they have a completely foreign culture [that won't support the flexibility]," said one manager. In fact, culture is one of the primary reasons that not all flexibilities fit all agencies. According to one respondent, changing the organization's culture requires a strong sense of ownership and accountability among managers, both of which, said the respondent, seem to be in short supply.

The merger of 22 different agencies, with profoundly different missions and cultures, different leadership styles, and different constituencies is one of the most difficult tasks ever undertaken in the federal government. Only the creation of the Department of Defense compares in size and scope. The dimensions of change here are massive and very long term. At the same time, evidence of a "cultural merger" needs to be produced in the relatively near future.

The role of unions in both organizations also makes culture change a more complicated undertaking. The individual, performance-based focus of many components of the new reforms stands in stark contrast to the standardized definitions of "fairness" historically adopted by union leadership. Further, the unions have maintained an essentially confrontational stance, which suggests little real willingness to adapt. The lessons learned from the demonstration projects offer insight into this dynamic, because part of the resistance from union representatives is based on their concern that DHS reforms will be extended across federal agencies. The federal managers we interviewed shared this concern to some extent, and did not consider "potential for wider impact" to be a guiding principle across the board. According to this group of senior managers, flexibilities should be tailored explicitly for the agency and should not be made available to other agencies outright. However, the interviewees did voice strong support for learning through partnership with other agencies that are also utilizing flexibilities. However, that partnership doesn't mean simply taking flexibilities that work under one set of conditions and applying them to another environment. According to one manager, when you simply "copy and borrow from already established data" you risk creating solutions that are mismatched to the agency-specific problems.

Lesson Learned: Diverse Pay Systems Can Create Inter-Agency and Intra-Agency Challenges.   This is, in fact, one of the primary concerns of union representatives involved in the DHS reforms. Union representatives are concerned that, if applied broadly, the DHS personnel system and its accompanying emphasis on managerial evaluations of individual performance and market conditions will depress federal pay and "let everyone suffer equally" (Daily Briefing, 2005a). When we asked federal managers about this, one camp held to the following position: Government should not compete with itself. However, the other camp basically said: What's wrong with competition? "We should welcome some challenges," said one manager. "There may also be virtue in competition . . . who said uniformity is a virtue?"

Hazards Ahead: Pay Differences Can Be Perceived as Unfair.   Union representatives are currently very concerned that their worries about pay, collective bargaining rights, and employee appeal protections are going unnoticed. Another lesson, "Communication and Training Must Be Priorities," could speak to this, but effective communication necessitates fundamental conditions of trust and understanding. One of our interview subjects stressed that both communication and training must be "early and recurring." To offer sound communication, however, implementers must first fully understand the demo project themselves. Once there is shared understanding, managers must focus on employee morale. "You have to defend what you aren't doing and explain what you are," said one manager. "Good people need affirmation and recognition," said another.

When problems occur in the lines of communication between managers and employees, the managers reported, it may simply be a case of misunderstanding. "It's important that everyone understand the big picture," said one manager. To clarify these miscommunications, managers have to invest more effort into reaching employees. "It [communication] is needed in extreme doses." It is important to keep in mind that without constant communication and ongoing training, employees are likely to revert to old habits. "People will revert to old practices without training," said one interviewee. "You have to move your culture toward performance." However, human resource managers must remember that training is a large, but worthwhile, investment for the success of the demo project. Almost all of our respondents indicated that communication and training are problem issues in managing change and the DHS reforms are no exception.

Lesson Learned: Employees and Employee Organizations Must Have Buy-In.   The federal managers we interviewed indicated that unions in particular are of great importance during the design and implementation of flexibilities. "When unions are not involved, it can be a problem . . . [they] cannot be ignored." While important, unions can complicate the process. "Legal authorities for employees to unionize and bargain are new—they create problems in management." Even if unions make the process messy, mere symbolic interaction with unions will not satisfy employees.

A lesson learned from a less-than-successful collaboration with unions occurred when union representatives were invited to contribute to the design of the alternative personnel system, but none of the union's suggestions were taken into consideration. While it seems intuitive to include unions in the design and implementation process, it is even more obvious that employees should be directly involved as well. One way to include employees, said one interviewee, is through focus groups. "Lots of involvement is good for design and does not water down results." Including employees in the design and implementation can avert potential rifts in the form of "an 'us' versus 'them' attitude," which seems to have taken over in the DHS negotiations.

An equally important lesson here relates again to the importance of consistent leadership. Buy-in and the development of trust cannot occur in a setting in which priorities and loyalties are in constant flux. Leadership provides a consistent vision, a level of communication that facilitates understanding, and to an important extent, some protection from the exigencies of the unknown.

Hazard Ahead: Changes, No Matter How Well Planned, Threaten Many Employees. These reforms continue to be seen by some as threats to traditional civil service protections. Yet, nearly all of our interview subjects said that the goal of flexibilities should be performance. "Any performance management system needs to result in performance. It can't be an arbitrary system—there need to be distinctions in performance." Managers have to make tough distinctions in performance measurement and must reinforce those distinctions in promotion decisions. "Performance is the only way to advance," said one interviewee. "Send the message that the system is performance-based and raises are not automatic." Perhaps the most critical aspect of establishing such measurements is equal measures across the board. Managers need to "closely look at performance plans . . . since they will have to meet to ensure consistency." Last, the respondents emphasized the need to stress competency building. "Critical competencies should be stressed." Managers must help employees find ways to improve. "Let them know the areas they need to develop."

Lesson Learned: There Must Be Clear Measures of Accountability. In the new systems, accountability is clearly focused on improved performance—of the individual employees, of managers, and of the organization as a whole. The difficulties with performance-based pay are well known, but if the system is carefully designed and well managed, there is greater clarity in accountability. The Demonstration Projects clearly showed that one of the best ways to introduce accountability into the system is to introduce ownership. Regular and careful individual evaluations are also key. However, with added accountability, one respondent hinted at a growing tension between "good" and "average" employees as well as between supervisors and employees. "Supervisors like the concept," of performance and accompanying accountability for such performance. While good performers may prefer the new system as a way to be recognized for their contributions, one respondent noted that "average employees are frustrated."

Hazard Ahead: In a Mission-Based System, Full Accountability May Look Different From Organization to Organization. Even the most successful demo project in one particular organization can fail under different conditions. It will be necessary to allow for, and be tolerant of, "different routes for every site, given differences in mission and culture." According to one respondent, lessons learned from other agencies and programs "cannot guarantee better organizational results and better products; future evaluation needs to better capture the impact of workforce quality on the [organizational] mission."

Lesson Learned: Flexibilities Must Be Integrated into the Agency's HR System. Interviewees agreed with OPM that flexibilities "should complement and strengthen the entire HR system" if they are to support better performance and improved accountability. According to one respondent, reforms must integrate change management with human resource management in order to gain the intended results: "Changes that focus on only one or the other won't work." Further, several respondents sounded an alarm with regard to employee protections. "Safeguards need to be in place to protect employee rights." There should be "periodic human capital reviews to make sure that women and minorities are not receiving less than average ratings without a reason." And finally, flexibilities should retain avenues for appeal: "If agencies decide to provide an alternative appeals system, it won't be effective . . . unless it is an independent body. And it should be noted that there will be some decisions that go against agency management."

Hazard Ahead: But Don't Cast the New System in Stone.   We learned a new lesson from our interviews that applies directly to the DHS and DoD reforms: Personnel management reforms should evolve as necessary. This lesson emerged based on similar input from nearly every person we interviewed. "What is proposed is not perfect," said one respondent. "It may not work." The interviewees caution DHS and DoD implementers to be prepared in that respect. "Certain formulations just aren't right" for all organizations uniformly. Demos can and should be "changed when necessary," said one manager. The bottom line for these managers is that personnel systems should be flexible. "Nothing should be in stone." According to one respondent, the words "permanent" and "flexibilities" should not be used in the same sentence together. "You have to build in the ability to be flexible . . . with room to move." Specifically in the case of the DHS and DoD changes, one manager said that the regulations should "serve as an outline," but should allow "for different routes at every site given differences in mission and culture." A mechanism that would allow such flexibility should be built into the regulations, many of the managers said.

Lesson Learned: Costs Can Be Controlled.   According to one manager, implementing organizational reforms is not often cost-neutral, "but can make up for costs in productivity . . . you invest up front for return on improved performance, effectiveness, and efficiency." According to one respondent, this lesson should be rephrased: "Costs can be managed because costs are needed for training, IT, salary—and how you allocate costs all depends on what works best." And what works best for successful reform in most cases is a general reprogramming of the organization's culture. "If a large alternative system can gain effectiveness, it is usually because money was spent on reprogramming to apply to a large population."

Hazard Ahead: Market-Based Compensation Must Be Well Informed and Carefully Managed to Succeed.   According to the managers we interviewed, many government agencies have simply forgotten about market forces. Just as the managers said that agencies need to identify someone to manage the change process, they also need someone to think about "market issues." According to one manager, "This information is totally absent—we have to look to the private sector for direction." Market-based pay "can be done," said one manager, "but it needs to be done well." The idea of adapting the system to the environment and responding to markets, said one respondent, "is expensive." And perhaps in a line of thought that would inspire debates on the purpose and values of government agencies, one respondent indicated that government agencies need to be "less concerned with consistency and mission, and more with hiring and recruiting people in a competitive market."

We learned an additional lesson from our interviews that indicates wide support for DHS's emphasis on market forces in the evaluation process. However, if the force of competition is to successfully enter the federal workforce, changes must be made. "The Title V system is broken; it doesn't work to keep them [employees] competitive."

CONCLUSION

Certainly, we can learn from the experiences of senior-level managers in terms of evaluating lessons from the past—both successes and failures. But how does this knowledge assist us in our understanding of the current DHS and DoD initiatives? For one thing, history tells us that what is most important is not what went wrong in prior flexibility attempts, but what we can apply to the future. "DHS and DoD reforms are the picture of the future," one manager noted. "People are watching." While some criticize DHS and DoD for not accounting for the varied cultures and missions of the organizations within them, others say that the reforms are absolutely necessary—regardless of cultural differences. The challenge will be to obtain buy-in to support such sweeping personnel reforms. "People will think that the projects do not belong to them, but rather have been imposed by someone else." Both DHS and DoD will need the support of a variety of stakeholders ranging from managers to employees to union representatives to members of the public. According to one senior manager we interviewed, "Future reforms have to have public support for the public service. The public service needs to have a positive connotation."

The Office of Management and Budget agrees. Federal employees, it says, should be thought of as public servants and not as bureaucrats. And in order to facilitate that transition, OMB says the key is providing federal employees with the "tools they need to live up to their full potential" (Daily Briefing, 2005b). While the DHS and DoD reforms are seen by designers and implementers as those very tools, convincing other stakeholders of this will take some time. And perhaps this is the greatest challenge of all. The old "house of cards" has fallen and the bones of a new system have emerged. The political, leadership, and management demands are enormous. These are historic changes, with the potential to rewrite the practice of merit in the public service.

NOTE

1. Based on a reputational sample, we interviewed 20 senior managers in the Department of Defense and in civilian agencies, who were involved in the planning and/or implementation of alternative personnel systems and/or demonstration projects. We first asked these managers to comment on the lessons-learned framework as established by the Office of Personnel Management. We also asked these managers to include any additional lessons learned that were not included in the framework that are important in the context of current human resource management reforms. We inquired about the extent to which they thought the DoD and DHS reforms addressed the most significant problems the organizations were confronting. Finally, we asked them to describe a personnel system that would be capable of meeting the challenges of the next five years (limiting this to internal management changes, not external funding decisions). It should be noted that this is an ongoing research project and the following results are preliminary. This is not a representative sample of senior federal managers and the results must be considered in that light.

REFERENCES

Barr, S. 2003. "Massive changes at DoD." *The Washington Post* Dec. 26, 2003.

Daily Briefing. 2005a. Bush administration plan to reform civil service draws union ire. January 27. govexec.com/dailyfed/0105/012705sz1.htm.

Daily Briefing. 2005b. OMB to seek governmentwide personnel reform. January 26. govexec.com/dailyfed/0105/012605k1.htm.

Federal Register. 2004. Department of Homeland Security, Office of Personnel Management. 5 CFR Chapter XCVII and Part 9701. February 20.

FedSmith. 2005a. New Human Resource System for DHS Released (and Unions Announce Intent to Sue). January 27. www.fedsmith.com/articles/articles.showarticle.db.php.

FedSmith. 2005b. Plans to Expand New Personnel Rules Across Government Anger Union. January 31. fedsmith.com/articles/articles.showarticle.db.php.

Ingraham, P. W. 1993. "Of Pigs in Pokes and Policy Diffusion." *Public Administration Review* 53:4: 348–356.

Ingraham, P. W. 1995. *The Foundation of Merit: Public Service in American Democracy.* Baltimore, MD: The Johns Hopkins University Press.

Ingraham, P. W. 1997. "A Laggard's Tale: Civil Service Reform in the United States." In Hans Bekke, Theo Toonen, and James Perry, eds. *Comparative Civil Service Reform.* Bloomington, IN: Indiana University Press.

Ingraham, P. W., Selden, S.C., and Moynihan, D. 2000. "Report From Wye River: The Public Service of the Future." *Public Administration Review* 60:1: 54–60.

Ingraham, P. W., Joyce, P. G., and Donahue, A. K. 2003. *Government Performance: Why Management Matters.* Baltimore, MD: Johns Hopkins Press.

Jacobson, W. 2003. *Individual Motivation and Organizational Change in Two Organizations.* Syracuse, NY: The Maxwell School, Unpublished PhD Dissertation.

Moynihan, D. P. 2005. "Homeland Security and the U.S. Public Management Policy Agenda." *Governance.* 18:2: 171–196.

Partnership for Public Service. 2003. *Partnership Pipeline.* November.

Rumsfield, D. 2003. Testimony before the U.S. Senate Committee on the Defense Department Transformation Act. October.

Thompson, J. 2000. "Reinvention as Reform: Assessing the National Performance Review." *Public Administration Review.* 60:6: 508–521.

Thompson, J. and Rainey, H. G. 2003. *Transformation and Change in the Internal Revenue Service.* Washington, DC: Pricewaterhousecoopers Endowment for the Business of Government.

Thompson, James R. 1999 "Devising Administrative Reform that Works." *Public Administrative Review.* 59: 4: 283–292.

United States General Accounting Office. 2002. Human Capital: Effective Use of Flexibilities Can Assist Agencies in Managing their Workforces. GAO-03-2. Washington, DC: Author.

United States General Accounting Office. 2003. Human Capital: DHS Personnel System Design Effort Provides for Collaboration and Employee Participation. GAO-03-1099. Washington, DC: Author.

United States Merit Systems Protection Board. 2004. *Issues of Merit.* 9:3: 1–11.

Van Riper, P. P. 1958. *History of the United States Civil Service.* Evanston, ILL.: Row, Peterson and Co.

Chapter 3

Mexico's Federal Professional Career Service: Linked Changes in Public Personnel Management and Political Culture

Donald E. Klingner and David Arellano Gault

THE EVOLUTION OF PUBLIC PERSONNEL SYSTEMS IN DEVELOPING COUNTRIES

The evolution of public management in developing countries appears relatively uniform because pressures for modernization and democratization tend to parallel, though lag behind, those in the Western world. While many of these administrative innovations are diffused by Western consultants or adopted due to exposure to the West (Adamolekun, 1990; Sabet and Klingner, 1993), Western lenders have also often mandated administrative reforms as a condition of continued credit (Klingner, 1996; Salgado, 1997).

In the first stage, *elite leaders* of successful independence movements establish new nations. The transition to a second stage (*patronage*) follows as these emergent nations strive to strengthen the conditions in civil society that underlie effective government (such as education, political participation, economic growth, and social justice) by refining their constitutions, developing political parties, and creating public agencies. This transition is often difficult, particularly if the culture supports political leadership based on personalities rather than parties.

The third stage, if it occurs, is a transition from patronage to *merit systems* (civil service) marked by passage of a civil service law, creation of a civil service agency, and development of personnel policies and procedures. This stage results from internal pressures for efficiency (modernization) and human rights (democratization). International lenders and donor governments often add external pressures that emphasize government capacity, transparency, and citizen participation.

TABLE 3.1 Evolution of Public Personnel Systems and Values in Developing Countries

Stage of Evolution	Dominant Value(s)	Dominant System(s)	Pressures for Change
One	Responsiveness	"Government by elites"	Political parties + Patronage
Two	Responsiveness	Patronage	Modernization + Democratization
Three	Efficiency + Individual rights	Civil service + Patronage	Responsiveness + Effective government
Four	Responsiveness + Efficiency + Limited government	Patronage + Civil service + Collective bargaining + Privatization	Dynamic equilibrium among pro- and anti-governmental values and systems

Again, this transition may be difficult. Governments may be large or inefficient due to socialist traditions favoring public control of agencies (such as railroads, airlines, mining and petroleum, banking, health and hospitals, and insurance) that in developed countries are usually part of the private sector. Pressures for transparent, honest, and efficient government may be thwarted by corruption, use of the public sector as the employer of last resort, or a "brain drain" to the private sector because of a politically vulnerable, underpaid, and poorly qualified civil service.

If and when the transition to civil service occurs, developing countries then seek to balance conflicting values and personnel systems to achieve the contradictory objectives that characterize the fourth stage of public personnel management. They must establish an optimum level of public employment, maintain administrative efficiency and protect public employee rights, and achieve both uniformity and flexibility of personnel policies and procedures. As the economy develops, there is less pressure on the government to be the employer of last resort, and more support for government because professional public management is more effective at public service delivery of desired services to the public. However, the opposite may occur just as easily: Economic stagnation may generate political pressure to increase public employment. Colonial traditions and centralization tend to produce a uniformity that outweighs administrative flexibility and diversity. "Neo-liberal" economic policies (imposed by international lenders to promote economic development) do reduce external debt by cutting public employment and expenditures. But they may also increase unemployment, social injustice, and popular discontent with elected leaders or the entire political system.

Emergent systems do not supplant their predecessors, but instead conflict and combine with them. Thus, the evolutionary process results described in Table 3.1 results in increasingly complex combinations of patronage, merit, market-based contracting and privatization, and other public personnel systems.

At the same time, there is no guarantee that this evolutionary process will occur. A variety of political, social, and economic factors serve as benchmarks for

TABLE 3.2   Political Culture and Public Personnel Management Development

1. From Independence to Patronage

Indicator	–	+
Political freedom (speech and media)	low	high
Economic growth and development	export-based	balanced
Racial and ethnic discrimination	high	high
Basis of political leadership	charismatic	issues, parties
Electoral process	inadequate	functional

2. From Patronage to Civil Service

Indicator	–	+
Effective and transparent government	no	yes
Administrative formalism	high	low
Patronage influences	high	low
A civil service law has been passed	no	yes
A central public personnel agency exists	no	yes
Merit system procedures are in place	no	yes
Unemployment or underemployment	high	low
Public employee salaries and benefits	inadequate	adequate
Non-merit discrimination	high	low
Role of the military	intrusive	minimal
Source of pressure for reform	international	domestic

3. From Civil Service to Maturity

Indicator	–	+
Balanced uniformity–flexibility	no	yes
Balanced centralization–decentralization	no	yes
Balanced public–private employment	no	yes
Balanced employee–management rights	no	yes

the progression from one stage of public human resource management to another (see Table 3.2). This conceptual model was originally presented in Klingner (1996), and has been explicated elsewhere (Klingner, 2000; Klingner and Nalbandian, 2001; Klingner and Nalbandian, 2003; Klingner and Pallavicini Campos, 2002).

MEXICO'S PUBLIC PERSONNEL SYSTEM IN HISTORICAL CONTEXT

Although Mexico is nominally a federal republic, political power by tradition and Constitutional provisions is centralized in the executive branch of the national government. Since the 1920s, Mexico's government has traditionally been a one-party democracy dominated by the Institutional Revolutionary Party (PRI, for its Spanish acronym). In 1996, the PRI lost control of the national legislature for the first time. Following widespread allegations of electoral fraud in 1988, Mexico developed a professional civil service system for its newly created Federal Electoral Institute (IFE) (Estatuto, 1999; Méndez Martínez, 2000). This organization—designed to increase the validity and accountability of national elections by instituting rational and transparent procedures for voting, tabulation, and reporting of ballot results— played a pivotal role in the change process. In July 2000, following a hotly contested campaign, the opposition PAN (National Action Party) presidential candidate Vicente Fox defeated the PRI candidate Francisco Labastida. Most Mexicans and international observers credited IFE with a pivotal role in the outcome. Its head, José Luis Méndez, became a key advisor to President Fox.

Mexico had previously established civil service systems for certain occupations within several national government agencies, including the Ministry of Foreign Relations (established in 1922); the National Institute of Statistics, Geography and Informatics (1994); the National Water Commission (1995); teachers within the Ministry of Education (1992); the Internal Revenue Systems (2000); and the Federal Electoral Institute (1992, reformed in 1999) (Uvalle Berrones, 2000; Méndez Martínez, 2000). In April 2003, the Mexican national legislature approved a Professional Career Service Law (Ley de Servicio Profesional de Carrera, henceforth called the LSPC for its Spanish acronym), providing for the implementation of a career civil service system in the national government ministries directed through the office of the President (Ley, 2003). The LSPC is extraordinarily ambitious, particularly given the relative prior scarcity of merit systems in the national government. It requires that within two years each ministry will establish an advisory committee to develop and administer its own SPC, with the entire process coordinated by the Civil Service Agency within the Ministry of Public Function (Acuerdo, 2003). The LSPC has three major sections: a general introduction, a statement of the rights and responsibilities of career service employees, and a description of the system's structure. Most of the law comprises the third section, with subsections focused on planning, the national register of human resources, recruitment, professional development, training and certification, performance evaluation, and separation.

The national register, maintained centrally by this ministry, collects data on all employees and positions, to allow the matching of employees and applicants with existing and new positions. It is the basis for career development and training. Objective performance evaluation systems, and the possibility of discharge for poor performance based on them, are innovations causing some mixture of hope and trepidation among current employees in a culture that is not used to distinguishing between evaluation of performance and of persons. While it has been widely recognized that complete implementation of this system within two years is simply not possible, it is expected that ministries will develop elements of the system, share "best practices" with one another, and move incrementally but steadily toward a national professional service model.

The LSPC was followed by approval of similar laws in many of Mexico's 31 states, including the Federal District (DF), Sinaloa, Guanajuato, Mexico (the state surrounding the DF on three sides), and Quintana Roo (Ley, 2002). This is extraordinary in that Mexican public administration is highly centralized, and the LSPC applied only to federal ministries, not to state or local governments. It is as if regime change, the LSPC, and related transformations in political administrative culture gave state and local governments implicit permission to make similar advances (Mejía Lira, 2001; Moreno Espinosa, 2001; Moreno Espinosa, 2002; Cabrero Mendoza, et al., 2002).

Even more remarkably, the LSPC has led to an outpouring of professional, academic, and popular writing on Mexico's professional public service and its relation to more rational and accountable government. Contributors include experts from public universities (e.g., Uvalle Berrones, 2004); public-private "think tanks" (e.g., Arellano Gault, 2002, 2004); nongovernmental associations such as the Mexican Network for Professional Service [la Red Mexicana de Servicio Profesional] (Martínez Puón and López Cruz, 2004, Aguilera and Bohórquez, 2004); presidential advisors (e.g., Méndez Martínez, 2004; Pérez González, 2004); national government ministries (Mesta Delgado, 2004; Herrera Macías, 2004; Fócil Ortega, 2004; Muñoz García, 2004); the Federal District (Cedillo Hernández, 2004); and local governments (Acosta Arévalo, 2004). For example, one of the authors of this article is a visiting professor at UNAM who has taught an intensive course each summer since 1999 on "Professionalizing public human resource management: A comparative US–Mexican perspective" (based on Klingner and Nalbandian, 2001). Since 2002, he has taught similar courses and made related conference presentations (in the Federal District, Toluca, Culiacan, Chetumal, and internationally) on Mexican civil service reform (Klingner, 2003, 2004).

A cadre of professional public administrators, academicians, and civic reformers—many of them these authors' colleagues and protégées—have founded, published, and written for professional public administration journals that describe, assess, and contextualize these reforms (e.g., transparent government, corruption, nongovernmental organizations, decentralization, and career service systems) within the context of ongoing political, social, and economic transformations. These include *Prospectiva* (published by the Agrupación Política Nueva) and *Gestión y Política Pública* (published by CIDE). While Mexico's prestigious National Public Administration Institute (INAP) has remained relatively apart from these advances because some within the Fox administration consider it a stronghold of opposition party loyalists, similar state institutes conduct public administration research, training, and technical assistance (e.g., in Guanajuato, the Federal District, Quintana Roo, and Sinaloa) (Almada López, 2001).

Causality is too complex to resolve easily, and it is probable that civic organizations and public administration institutes arose simultaneously, spurred both by regime change and changes in political culture. The next section will take a closer look at these reforms and the underlying culture of governance and politics in Mexico.

GOVERNANCE, POLITICAL CULTURE, AND ADMINISTRATIVE REFORM IN MEXICO

Civil service is an indispensable democratic political institution. Neutral and professional bureaucracies enable government agencies to respond to the political agendas of elected and appointed officials while protecting long-term policies and programs, and avoiding the social costs of having politicians manipulate the bureaucratic structure with impunity. But it is not without cost (Frant, 1993). The price for avoiding a spoils system is the creation of a powerful group (civil servants) protected to some degree from political influence. The civil service is a centralized political institution, usually accompanied by rigid rules for hiring, for promoting, and for separating civil servants. It does not automatically make government more efficient.

This political dynamic affects the way political systems behave (Ackerman, 1999; Moe and Caldwell, 1994). During the seventy years that Mexico's political system was dominated by a powerful and authoritarian party, the bureaucracy was controlled through a "quasi-spoils system" (Arellano Gault, 2003, p. 169) that combined a semi-formal professionalization with patronage and loyalty to a strong chief executive. Typically, public employees were lower-level laborers, clerks, and technicians, or patronage employees (Arellano Gault and Guerrero Amparán, 2003, p. 154). Lower-level employees were, and still are, protected by contracts between the national government and powerful national unions with constitutional rights. They have permanent contracts and are very hard to fire. Patronage employees, often professional or managerial, were employed "at will." While this system did not promote individual merit or societal accountability, it did ensure tight control, management flexibility, and high loyalty to the party and its policies (Arellano Gault and Guerrero Amparán, 2003, p. 153).

The Fox administration's decision to propose the LSPC was not made lightly or without opposition. Many of his supporters advocated, at least privately, reducing the power of unions and avoiding the negative implications of civil service by progressing directly from patronage to performance contracting. But in the end, the benefits of a professional and politically insulated federal bureaucracy carried the day, even though it was acknowledged that it would limit the flexibility of his administration to control the administration's reform agenda. Congress passed the bill without too much opposition, and implementation began immediately. Clearly, however, there are enormous challenges to successful implementation of this civil service system. Resistance from some elements of the public sector and some powerful appointed public officials is making implementation slow, tortuous, and problematic.

First, there is a need to change the political culture of absolutist political control and administrative formalism, while still allowing political leadership and centralized policy direction to function effectively. In this context, absolutism is the centralization of political, economic, and social authority in the executive office of the President; and administrative formalism is the *sub rosa* functioning of absolute political authority under the trappings of a political and administrative system that, on paper, is decentralized and participative. Public officials are beginning to realize that the civil service reform law limits their power. For example, while two out of three positions on the technical committees responsible for implementing civil service in each ministry are appointed (per article 74 of the LSPC), some senior officials are resisting or blocking efforts to install strong technical committees in some ministries. This cultural change requires strong political support from the President and his ministers. Because this administration faces a range of pressing political issues, it is not surprising that civil service reform is not a top priority. As a partial solution, the administration continues to promote a managerial discourse of innovation and decision-making, without directly confronting the underlying issues of political culture and structural resistance.

Second, there is a need to develop a professional public administrative culture that clearly differentiates between political appointees and senior civil servants. Historically, the culture and practice of absolute political control made it difficult to hold individuals accountable. This meant a heavily politicized bureaucracy within which political appointees and professional administrators were almost indistinguishable, and whose accountability could not be clearly differentiated (Guerrero Amparán, 1999). Politically ambitious administrators were accustomed to using their positions to build political careers. However, a civil service system differentiates these two roles. Even politically appointed officials will be held accountable for their ministries' performance, given that these agencies have a public purpose beyond advancing the political careers of their appointed heads. Again, the risk here is administrative formalism. Some political appointees will seek to develop administrative systems that on their face resemble civil service, but in reality leave intact the traditional behavior and level of power a secretary and his/her team used to enjoy. Once again, political support from the President and his team is crucial, as is the support from public officials, media, and society in general for pushing the political and cultural transformation of the historical links between the political and administrative system.

Third, there is the dilemma of how to make the civil service system legitimate (strong and effective), but still responsive to needs for managerial flexibility and political oversight. This requires careful calibration of the balance between administrative and political perspectives, recognizing that each value, carried to extremes, will subvert the intent of the system. The danger, of course, is that political resistance will lead to limited implementation of the law by weak ministerial committees rather than strong and active ones. If reformers try to force the process, they encounter strong resistance. If they allow the implementation of weak committees in some ministries, they risk allowing the process to become a charade.

Fourth, strong oversight of civil service reform implementation of the civil service is crucial if Mexico is to face some of these challenges. The Civil Service Advisory Committee, supposedly the entity responsible for ensuring this, is actually composed of political and administrative appointees: nine from the Ministry in charge of the civil service (Secretaría de la Función Pública), one for each representative of the technical committees in the other ministries (about 15), three representatives from the Ministries of Labor, Treasury, and the Interior, and one representative from academic, private, and social communities (per article 70 of the Civil Service Law). Thus, only 3 out of about 30 members are not direct representatives of a particular ministry and its political leadership. Without the opportunity for open participation from groups and citizens with a more generalized interest in a professional public service, it is likely that the oversight function of the Advisory Board will be "captured" by more particular agency interests, resulting in a loss of autonomy and ability to exercise independent oversight of the system.

Fifth, the creation in law of a class of professional public managers by no means guarantees that they will develop the values or behaviors appropriate to effective and transparent management. In Mexico as in other countries, administrative formalism frequently masks corruption. While passage of the law and creation of an Advisory Committee is a good start, it does not in itself promote managerial flexibility or professionalism (Knott and Miller, 1987; Pacheco, 2003, p. 44). A civil service obsessed with neutrality and objective performance evaluation might implement a limited system that meets expectations. To build a system of performance evaluation requires time and political capacity in order to adjust administrative structures, to make the people confident of the application of the rules, to learn the difficulties of measuring performance in hundreds of different positions, and to understand the skills needed to manage a decentralized system with several different specialized entities (ministries, offices, and agencies). Simply promoting managerial discourse around these concepts or issues does not ensure that managers will learn and practice the complex behaviors required for the system to operate effectively. There is some difficulty separating evaluations of employee performance from evaluations of the employee as a person, making policies difficult to implement. But it is part of the business culture, and will become part of the public culture as business values spread, and as the professional public administration culture becomes more widespread. The most probable outcome is that by the end of the Fox administration's term of office in December 2006, Mexico will have a limited version of the system, dominated by top-level appointed officials, and minimally accountable to outside interests, with limited performance evaluation capability due to lack of time and expertise.

Sixth, implementation of the LSPC must confront the reality of corruption. The Ministry of Public Function (formerly termed the Comptroller) is the lead agency charged with fighting corruption. While its success in this area is generally considered limited (Rosenberg, 2003), this ministry is known for applying a hierarchical decision-making style based on rigid compliance with rules and procedures. Given that this ministry is also charged with implementing civil service reform, whether this culture can nurture the managerial flexibility and risk-taking required for a performance-based personnel system remains to be seen.

Seventh, implementation of the LSPC highlights power struggles between the executive and legislative branches in Mexican national politics. Legislative oversight is critical to effective implementation, particularly if the change in administration that will take place in December 2006 (Mexican presidents serve a six-year term and may not succeed themselves) is not to result in the loss of professional administrative capacity and organizational memory. But Mexico has a history of a strong executive and a weak legislative branch. Congress was not actively involved in developing the LSPC, and the executive branch understandably did not seek its involvement.

Eighth, the LSPC applies to only about 40,000 mid-level federal employees. Its coverage needs to be extended to the rest of the 2.5 million federal public employees. About 1 million of these are teachers with their own politically powerful union and relatively inflexible labor rules. About 600,000 are nurses and other medical professionals. The others (known as *de base* workers) are protected by membership in a politically powerful federation of unions (the FSTSE, or Federation of State Workers Unions) that, under Mexican law, is their only legitimate contractual representative and bargaining agent. Creating a general civil service system for all federal employees will require changes in at least two federal laws: the Federal Law for State Workers (to allow merit-based evaluations) and the Federal Work Law (to recognize productivity as a legitimate basis for employee evaluation). The first change is politically unlikely given the FSTSE's opposition. The second remains possible, but it is not clear whether the current political situation will allow the Fox administration to present these reforms to Congress.

In summary, there are clear signs of progress: a good law, flexible and decentralized administrative control, clear action items and implementation deadlines, and a dedicated implementation team with a clear vision beyond bureaucratic or managerial "business as usual" (no routine copying of "best practices" or "buzzwords" from the private sector). However, the challenges are great and support from society and civil servants is crucial if a true career system, flexible and capable of adapting to new situations, is to be successfully implemented. Because resistance by powerful interests is great, the forces that overcome resistance must be equally powerful and determined. Few Mexicans have a clear idea of the road ahead or the dangers to be faced. This is problematic, because civil service reform is crucial in the transformation of Mexico into a more accountable and legitimate democracy.

REFERENCES

Ackerman, B. 1999. "The New Separation of Powers." *Harvard Law Review* 113: 634–729.

Acosta Arévalo, J. 2004. "La Profesionalización del Servicio Público en Administraciones Municipales." *Servicio Profesional de Carrera* 1:1: 159–162.

Acuerdo que Establece los Lineamientos para la Instalación de los Comités Técnicos de Profesionalización y Selección en las Dependencias y Órganos desconcentrados de la Administración Pública Federal. *Diario Oficial de la Federación* September 18, 2003.

Adamolekun, L. 1990. "Institutional Perspectives on Africa's Development Crisis." *International Journal of Public Sector Management* 3:2: 5–16.

Aguilera, H. and Bohórquez, E. 2004. "Gobierno Profesional en México: Lo Deseable y Lo Posible." *Servicio Profesional de Carrera* 1:1: 111–122.

Almada López, C. March–April 2001. "Resumen de la Conferencia Magistral: Gobernabilidad y Políticas Públicas." *Eticadministrativa* 4: 3–12 (Instituto de Administración Pública del Estado de Quintana Roo).

Arellano Gault, D. 2004. "¿Porque un Servicio Profesional de Carrera es Importante para una Democracia?" *Servicio Profesional de Carrera* 1:1: 59–64.

Arellano Gault, D. 2003. "Profesionalización de la Administración Pública en México: ¿De un Sistema Autoritario a un Sistema Meritocrático Rígido?" In *Retos de la Profesionalización de la Función Pública*. Caracas: CLAD, pp. 161–212.

Arellano Gault, D. June 2002. "Nueva Gestión Pública: ¿El Meteorito que Mató al Dinosaurio? Lecciones para la Reforma Administrativa en Países como México." *Reforma y Democracia* 23: 8–40 (CLAD).

Arellano Gault, D. and Guerrero Amparán, J. P. 2003. "Stalled Administrative Reforms of the Mexican State." In B. Schneider, and B. Heredia, eds. *Reinventing Leviathan. The Politics of Administrative Reforms in Developing Countries*. Boulder, CO: North-South Center Press, pp. 161–180.

Cabrero Mendoza, E., García Del Castillo, R., García Vázquez, G., and Gómez Castro, L. November 2002. *Prácticas Municipales Exitosas*. Mexico: CIDE (Centro de Investigaciones y Docencia Económicas) and Fundación Ford (Ford Foundation). "Premio Gobierno y Gestión Local Edición 2002." *Innovación en Gobiernos Locales* 3:2: 4–5.

Cedillo Hernández, M. 2004. "Los Retos de la Reglamentación de la Ley de Servicio Profesional de Carrera en la Administración Pública Federal." *Servicio Profesional de Carrera* 1:1: 65–72.

Estatuto del Servicio Profesional Electoral y del Personal del Instituto Federal Electoral Aprobado por el Consejo General. Mexico: Instituto Federal Electoral, March 16, 1999.

Fócil Ortega, M. 2004. "El Servicio Profesional de Carrera en México: Las Implicaciones en la Operación del Nuevo Modelo de Administración del Personal Público." *Servicio Profesional de Carrera* 1:1: 73–94.

Frant, H. 1993. "Rules and Governance in the Public Sector: The Case of Civil Service." *American Journal of Political Science* 37: 25–57.

Guerrero Amparán, J. P. 1999. "Trabas y Oportunidades para el Servicio Civil en un México Democratizado." In R. Uvalle, and M. Ahuja, eds. *Visión Multidimensional del Servicio Público Profesionalizado*. Mexico City: UNAM, Plaza y Valdés, pp. 13–38.

Herrera Macías, A. 2004. "Algunas Consideraciones en la Implementación del Servicio Público de Carrera en México para Hacer frente a la Globalización." *Servicio Profesional de Carrera* 1:1: 95–110.

Klingner, D. 2004. "La Ética Pública y el Servicio Profesional de Carrera," 9th international conference of the Center for Latin American Development Administration, Madrid, November 5.

Klingner, D. 2003. "La Administración de Recursos Humanos y la Modernización del Estado," 8th international conference of the Center for Latin American Development Administration (CLAD), Panama City, Panama, October 30.

Klingner, D. December 2000. "South of the Border: Problems and Progress in Implementing New Public Management Reforms in Mexico Today." *American Review of Public Administration* 30:4: 365–373.

Klingner, D. July/August 1996. "Public Personnel Management and Democratization: A View from Three Central American Republics." *Public Administration Review* 56:1: 390–399.

Klingner, D. and Nalbandian, J. 2003. *Public Personnel Management: Contexts and Strategies*, 5th ed. Upper Saddle River: Prentice Hall, Simon & Schuster.

Klingner, D. and Nalbandian, J. 2001. *La Administración de Personal Público: Contextos y Estrategias*. Mexico: McGraw-Hill Interamericana.

Klingner, D. and Pallavicini Campos, V. 2002. "Human Resource Management Reform in Latin America and the Caribbean: What Works and What Doesn't." *Public Organization Review*, 2: 349–264.

Knott, J. and Miller, G. 1987. *Reforming Bureaucracy.* Englewood Cliffs, NJ: Prentice Hall.
Ley del Servicio Público de Carrera del Estado de Quintana Roo. Quintana Roo, January 31, 2002.
Ley del Servicio Profesional de Carrera en la Administración Pública Federal. *Diario Oficial de la Federación* April 10, 2003.
Martínez Puón, R. and López Cruz, A. 2004. "Alcances y Perspectivas del Servicio Profesional de Carrera en la Secretaría de Desarrollo Social." *Servicio Profesional de Carrera* 1:1: 163–190.
Mejía Lira, J. November–December 2001. "Nueva Gestión Pública: Nueva Cultura y Reforzamiento de Valores." *Eticadministrativa* 8: 3–15 (Instituto de Administración Pública del Estado de Quintana Roo).
Méndez Martínez, J. 2004. "Retos Inmediatos del Servicio Profesional de Carrera en México." *Servicio Profesional de Carrera* 1:1: 5–12.
Méndez Martínez, J. 2000. "The Next Step of the State Reform in Mexico: Professionalization of Public Servants." National Conference of the American Society for Public Administration, San Diego, March 2000.
Mesta Delgado, J. 2004. "Ley del Servicio Profesional de Carrera en la Administración Pública Federal." *Servicio Profesional de Carrera* 1:1: 13–26.
Moe, T. and Caldwell, M. 1994. "The Institutional Foundations of Democratic Government: A Comparison of Presidential and Parliamentary Systems." *Journal of Theoretical Economics* 150: 1: 171–195.
Moreno Espinosa, R. October 2002. "Profesionalización y Servicio Público de Carrera, Asignaturas Pendientes en el México del Siglo XXI." Congreso Latinoamericano de Administración para el Desarrollo (CLAD), International Conference, Lisbon, Portugal.
Moreno Espinosa, R. 2001. "Presentación del Libro." In D. Klingner and J. Nalbandian, eds. *La Administración de Personal Público: Contextos y Estrategias.* Mexico: McGraw-Hill Interamericana, pp. xi–xx.
Muñoz García, A. 2004. "La Evaluación del Desempeño del Servidor Público en el Servicio Profesional de Carrera." *Servicio Profesional de Carrera* 1:1: 123–158.
Pacheco, R. 2003. "Profesionalización y Reforma Gerencial en Brasil: Avances y Agenda Futura." In *Retos de la Profesionalización de la Función Pública.* Caracas: CLAD, pp. 25–95.
Pérez González, H. 2004. "Retos y Perspectivas del Servicio Público de Carrera en México." *Servicio Profesional de Carrera* 1:1: 27–40.
Rosenberg, T. August 10, 2003. "The Taint of the Greased Palm." *The New York Times Magazine,* pp. 28–33.
Sabet, G. and Klingner, D. April 1993. "Exploring the Impact of Professionalism on Administrative Innovation." *Journal of Public Administration Research and Theory* 3:2: 252–266.
Salgado, R. 1997. *Public Administration for Results: Choice, Design and Sustainability in Institutional Development and Civil Service Reform.* DPP Working Paper Series No. 106. Washington, DC: Interamerican Development Bank.
Uvalle Berrones, R. 2004. "Servicio Profesional y la Nueva Gestión Pública en México." *Servicio Profesional de Carrera* 1:1: 41–58.
———. 2000. *Institucionalidad y Profesionalización del Servicio Público en México.* Mexico City: Plaza y Valdes.

APPENDIX A: Employment Statistics

1. Federal Public Employees

	1992	1993	1994	1995	1996	1997	1998/P	1999/P	2000
Total for the Economy				27,347,482	28,270,286	29,346,956	30,635,319	31,406,543	0
Total Public Sector	4,533,410	4,477,065	4,557,432	4,595,218	4,626,535	4,727,178	4,804,973	4,810,586	0
Total Government	3,907,091	3,937,328	4,030,713	4,076,703	4,109,105	4,216,997	4,307,065	4,331,341	0
Central Government	2,434,901	1,399,977	1,431,289	1,428,964	1,419,434	1,357,000	1,382,370	1,369,195	0
Federal Government	2,065,859	1,028,105	1,055,348	1,046,473	1,033,613	960,567	966,778	952,905	
Federal District Government	146,493	149,318	151,468	153,444	156,741	159,960	175,388	176,940	
Decentralized Agencies	222,549	222,554	224,473	229,047	229,080	236,473	240,204	239,350	
Local Government	1,049,535	2,110,569	2,168,616	2,210,246	2,256,573	2,419,675	2,480,934	2,508,133	0
State Government	817,718	1,873,278	1,925,291	1,963,958	2,005,605	2,161,170	2,218,794	2,240,872	
Municipalities	231,817	237,291	243,325	246,288	250,968	258,505	262,140	267,261	
Social Security	422,655	426,782	430,808	437,493	433,098	440,322	443,761	454,013	
Public Enterprises	626,319	539,737	526,719	518,515	517,430	510,181	497,908	479,245	0
Directly Controlled	343,429	291,309	279,693	280,195	283,098	270,424	256,983	238,124	
Indirectly Controlled	282,890	248,428	247,026	238,320	234,332	239,757	240,925	241,121	0
Non-Financial	226,087	210,725	211,177	203,607	202,251	210,969	212,457	215,068	
Financial	56,803	37,703	35,849	34,713	32,081	28,788	28,468	26,053	

SOURCE: Income and Public Expenditures in Mexico (INEGI—Ingreso y el Gasto Público en México). Several Years

NOTE: These data represent not the number of persons employed in each activity, but the average number of positions required for production processes. Consequently, the same person could be occupying two or more positions in one or several economic activities at the same time, as do basic education teachers.

2. Federal Ministry Employees, by Agency and Level

Administrative and Agency Level	1992	1993	1994	1995	1996	1997	1998/P	1999/P	2000/P
Total at National Level				27,347,482	28,270,286	29,346,956	30,635,319	31,406,543	
Total	0	0	910,036	898,054	918,449	2,077,530	1,710,853	1,303,593	892,508
Government Branches and Electoral Bodies	0	0	66,211	33,761	39,691	60,072	45,619	48,130	52,635
Legislative			4,773	4,807	4,807	6,559	6,563	5,604	5,691
Judicial			14,955	15,626	16,876	19,557	19,483	21,475	27,756
Electoral Bodies[1]			45,287	11,122	15,794	31,644	16,902	18,118	13,868
Agrarian Court			1,196	1,347	1,336	1,348	1,520	1,527	1,528
Federal Fiscal Courts			—	859	878	964	1,151	1,406	1,709
Superior Federal Fiscalization Body									1,272
Human Rights National Commission									811
Central Administration	0	0	843,825	864,293	878,758	2,017,458	1,665,234	1,255,463	839,873
PRESIDENCIA			2,359	2,565	2,123	2,247	2,224	2,172	2,061
SEGOB			15,267	15,812	18,161	18,244	18,107	18,479	29,036
SER			3,703	3,716	3,690	3,747	3,912	3,912	3,957
SHCP			33,550	45,267	47,446	10,423	10,818	9,625	9,466
DEFENSA			169,689	172,072	163,638	177,018	183,788	181,708	181,944

SAGARPA	60,509	35,001	33,852	31,762	29,525	26,901	30,292
SCT[2]	44,115	42,350	75,335	1,337,572	1,013,720	709,396	298,682
SECOFI	6,042	6,204	5,535	5,407	5,308	5,121	5,071
SEP	243,975	241,566	250,234	251,847	255,444	156,032	129,153
SALUD	160,488	163,915	143,858	20,752	11,812	13,615	19,905
MARINA	48,170	53,128	53,128	54,247	53,566	54,972	55,223
STPS	6,107	6,033	5,984	5,882	7,057	6,079	6,102
SRA	11,245	11,436	11,571	10,158	3,189	2,662	2,655
SEMARNAP	4,436	34,150	34,681	58,741	36,469	36,028	36,923
PGR	14,201	15,839	15,132	15,573	15,806	15,753	14,538
ENERGIA	2,245	1,669	1,447	1,092	1,140	1,029	1,056
SEDESOL	13,601	9,404	8,608	8,345	8,336	7,239	9,307
SECTUR	2,373	2,410	2,271	2,321	2,338	2,249	2,212
SECODAM	1,750	1,756	2,064	2,080	2,675	2,491	2,290

[1]Since 1998, IFE is the only electoral body reported. The Electoral Court was separated and incorporated into the Supreme Court of Justice.
[2]Since 1997, includes the Temporal Employment Program.

SOURCE: Public Federal Treasury Accounts (different years)

3. Federal Public Salary Expenses ("Personal Services")

	1995	1996	1997	1998	1999	2000
NET FEDERAL PUBLIC SECTOR EXPENDITURES	**451,299.90**	**603,703.50**	**769,780.30**	**848,404.30**	**1,041,548.70**	**1,271,160.80**
Personal Services	**68,635.60**	**90,789.20**	**120,183.10**	**139,946.10**	**181,145.10**	**199,535.30**
Federal Government	322,955.30	423,247.60	563,711.80	630,077.20	789,600.50	974,024.00
Personal Services	34,374.60	46,526.40	47,634.40	57,049.20	69,691.10	84,375.60
Government Enterprises	128,344.60	180,455.90	206,068.50	218,327.10	251,948.20	297,136.80
Personal Services	34,261.00	44,262.80	72,548.70	82,896.90	111,454.00	115,159.70
AS A PERCENTAGE OF TOTAL EXPENDITURES						
NET FEDERAL PUBLIC SECTOR EXPENDITURES	**100.00%**	**100.00%**	**100.00%**	**100.00%**	**100.00%**	**100.00%**
Personal Services	**15.21%**	**15.04%**	**15.61%**	**16.50%**	**17.39%**	**15.70%**
Federal Government	100.00%	100.00%	100.00%	100.00%	100.00%	100.00%
Personal Services	10.64%	10.99%	8.45%	9.05%	8.83%	8.66%
Government Enterprises	100.00%	100.00%	100.00%	100.00%	100.00%	100.00%
Personal Services	26.69%	24.53%	35.21%	37.97%	44.24%	38.76%

SOURCE: Public Federal Treasury Accounts, different years (pesos, in current terms)

Chapter 4

Affirmative Action in the Twenty-First Century

Norma M. Riccucci

One of the most polemical and polarizing personnel issues of the last century was affirmative action. Scholars, practitioners, and policy makers have debated its appropriateness and potential effectiveness since its inception. After decades of legal wrangling and uncertainties, the U.S. Supreme Court issued a ruling in 2003 that paves the way for not only universities, but for public and private sector employers to rely on affirmative action policies not only to redress past discrimination but to promote or enhance diversity in the classroom and the workplace.

The purpose of this chapter is to provide a legal snapshot of the use of affirmative action in the workplace. It examines the U.S. Supreme Court's *Bakke* decision, as well as the Court's 2003 decisions in two University of Michigan cases. These decisions have major implications for the continued use of affirmative action not only in education, but in the workforce as well.

THE *BAKKE* RULING

First employed as a tool to promote equal employment opportunity (i.e., to prevent discrimination), affirmative action has evolved into a more proactive tool to not only redress past discrimination against persons based on such factors as race and gender, but to also correct racial and gender imbalances in the workplace. And, at least at the entry levels of employment, affirmative action has proved to be effective (see, for example, Riccucci, 2002; Kellough, 1997; Cornwell and Kellough, 1994; Rosenbloom and Featherstonaugh, 1977).

The U.S. Supreme Court issued its first substantive ruling on affirmative action in 1978 with its *Regents of the University of California v. Bakke* decision. The *Bakke* ruling upheld the general principle of affirmative action, but struck down its use by the University of California under the Fourteenth Amendment of the U.S.

Constitution and Title VI of the Civil Rights Act of 1964. A closely divided Court objected to the use of what it labeled "quotas" in admission decisions. The University of California's Davis Medical School was reserving 16 spaces out of a possible 100 for students of color. In actuality, the school was not operating on a strict "quota" system, but instead was setting a goal or benchmark for the admissions of students of color. A quota implies sanctions if not met; courts have the power to impose sanctions, but universities as well as employers do not sanction themselves with, for example, fines, if they don't meet their goals. The misuse of the term *quota* here has not only galvanized the debate over affirmative action, but, as will be seen later in this chapter, continues to serve as a yardstick in gauging the legality of affirmative action programs.

The Supreme Court's *Bakke* decision was so fractured that it created a split among lower federal courts over the use of affirmative action and in effect, whether the ruling could actually serve as legal precedent. The Court's decision in *Grutter v. Bollinger* (2003) reconciles this critical problem.

THE *UNIVERSITY OF MICHIGAN* RULINGS

In 2003, marking the twenty-fifth anniversary of the *Bakke* decision, the U.S. Supreme Court ruled on two affirmative action cases involving the University of Michigan. In one case, *Grutter v. Bollinger*, the Court was asked to rule on the constitutionality, under the Equal Protection Clause, of affirmative action at the University of Michigan Law School. In a 5–4 ruling, the Court majority opined that the racial diversity of a student body can be a sufficiently compelling interest on the part of a state university to warrant its use of racial preference in its admissions decisions. The Court ruled that the Fourteenth Amendment's Equal Protection Clause allows for the "Law School's narrowly tailored use of race in admissions decisions to further a compelling interest in obtaining the educational benefits that flow from a diverse student body" (*Grutter v. Bollinger*, 2003, p. 319).

Since *Bakke*, the courts have judged the constitutionality of affirmative action against the strict-scrutiny test. This two-pronged test asks 1) whether there is a compelling governmental interest for the program and 2) whether the program is sufficiently narrowly tailored to meet its specified goals (e.g., whether race is only one factor among many). In the context of *Grutter*, the U.S. Supreme Court ruled that the

> Law School's admissions program bears the hallmarks of a narrowly tailored plan. To be narrowly tailored, a race-conscious admissions program cannot "insulat[e] each category of applicants with certain desired qualifications from competition with all other applicants". . . . Instead, it may consider race or ethnicity only as a "'plus' in a particular applicant's file"; i.e., it must be "flexible enough to consider all pertinent elements of diversity in light of the particular qualifications of each applicant, and to place them on the same footing for consideration, although not necessarily according them the same weight". . . . It follows that universities cannot establish quotas for members of certain racial or ethnic groups or put them on sep-

arate admissions tracks. . . . Moreover, the program is flexible enough to ensure that each applicant is evaluated as an individual and not in a way that makes race or ethnicity the defining feature of the application (*Grutter v. Bollinger*, 2003, p. 322).

This decision, in effect, states that diversity, which is a goal of affirmative action, serves as a compelling government interest. And, if the programs are narrowly tailored, they can survive legal challenges. The program at the University of Michigan Law School met the two prongs of the strict-scrutiny test.

The second Supreme Court decision provides further clarification around what constitutes "narrowly tailored." In *Gratz v. Bollinger* (2003), the Supreme Court struck down the use of affirmative action in admissions at the University of Michigan's undergraduate programs in the College of Literature, Sciences, and Art. This program awarded 20 points on a scale of 150 for membership in an underrepresented group, such as African American, Latino, or Native American. An applicant could be automatically admitted with 100 points. The Court, in a 6–3 decision, ruled that the program was "not narrowly tailored to achieve the assertedly compelling interest in educational diversity [and] the admissions policy did not provide individualized consideration of each characteristic of a particular applicant" (*Gratz v. Bollinger*, 2003, p. 257).

In short, the Supreme Court would not support a point system such as the one used by the undergraduate program at the University of Michigan. This point system has been likened, even by the district court ruling in *Gratz*, to a quota system (see *Gratz v. Bollinger*, 2000).

Parenthetically, as many have argued, the assignment of 20 points for race is no different from awarding points for other "nonacademic" criteria. For example, under the undergraduate program in question at the University of Michigan, points were awarded for a variety of factors, including the following:

1. up to 20 points could be awarded at the Provost's discretion
2. up to 5 points could also be awarded to children or grandchildren of alumni
3. up to 5 points could be awarded for male students choosing to enroll in the nursing program
4. up to 10 points for residents of Michigan

Ultimately, the awarding of 20 points for race may not necessarily give students of color a "competitive" edge in the admissions process.

These two University of Michigan decisions form a critical basis of law around affirmative action. Moreover, they are significant not only in university admissions, but for public employment as well. As Naylor and Rosenbloom (2004, p. 151) point out: "Post-*Grutter*, there is greater reason to believe that narrowly tailored affirmative action to promote diversity in public employment can survive constitutional challenge." Thus, if government employers are seeking to promote diversity in the workplace, and the programs do not assign points based on such factors as race, affirmative action will be deemed legal.

Finally, it is worth noting that over 100 *amicus curiae* (friends of the court) briefs were filed in support of the University of Michigan's use of affirmative action including briefs from former President Gerald Ford, several state governments, elected officials, the military, major corporations, leading colleges and universities, civil rights organizations, and academic and research associations. The Bush Administration, however, filed a brief urging the Court to find the University of Michigan's use of affirmative action unconstitutional.

WHAT DOES THE FUTURE HOLD?

The *Grutter* decision in conjunction with previous Supreme Court precedents ensures the legality of affirmative action not only in university admissions, but also in hiring and promotions. Table 4.1 provides a summary of the Court's decisions around the use of affirmative action in employment. As can be seen, while affirmative action can be relied upon in hiring and promotion decisions, the Court has not upheld its use when layoffs are involved.

Layoffs and reductions-in-force (rifs) tend to be based on seniority, so that the last persons hired are the first fired. These systems are sometimes referred to as "last in, first out," or LIFO systems. Because women and people of color are systematically the last to be hired—due to, for example, past discrimination—they are generally the first in line to be fired when layoffs are instituted. In effect, layoff systems based on seniority tend to have a disproportionately harsh impact on women and people of color. The first U.S. Supreme Court case to examine this issue, albeit obliquely, was *Firefighters Local and Memphis Fire Department v. Stotts* (1984).

In 1980, the city of Memphis entered into a consent decree—to settle a lawsuit filed by Carl Stotts—to increase the representation of persons of color in uniformed jobs in the fire department. When fiscal problems ensued the following year and layoffs were necessary, reductions-in-force were made on the basis of a collectively bargained LIFO seniority system. Carl Stotts filed suit arguing that the layoffs would eviscerate the consent decree as well as any gains made pursuant to the decree. The *Stotts* Supreme Court did not make a ruling directly on affirmative action in this case, but rather on the legality of the seniority system. The Court opined that because the seniority system did not *intend* to discriminate against persons of color, it therefore was bona fide or legal under Title VII of the Civil Rights Act. The city's affirmative action efforts were effectively abrogated.

Two years after *Stotts*, the U.S. Supreme Court issued a ruling that squarely addressed the use of affirmative action in conjunction with layoffs. In *Wygant v. Jackson Board of Education* (1986), a local school district along with a labor union sought to maintain racial diversity in its workforce during a period of layoffs. The school district and union negotiated a layoff plan that required the use of seniority as well as preserving racial balance of the teaching faculty. Specifically, the contract stipulated that, in the event of layoffs, the most senior teachers would be retained

TABLE 4.1   Key U.S. Supreme Court Actions or Decisions on Affirmative Action

1978	*Regents of the University of California v. Bakke.* U.S. Supreme Court upholds the principle of affirmative action, but strikes down its operation by the University at California under the Fourteenth Amendment and Title VI of the Civil Rights Act of 1964.
1979	*United Steelworkers of America v. Weber.* U.S. Supreme Court upholds legality of voluntarily eveloped affirmative action plan under Title VII of the Civil Rights Act of 1964.
1980	*Fullilove v. Klutznick.* U.S. Supreme Court upholds constitutionality (under the Fifth and Fourteenth Amendments) of federal set-aside programs enacted by the U.S. Congress.
1984	*Firefighters Local Union and Memphis Fire Department v. Stotts.* U.S. Supreme Court upholds, under Title VII of the Civil Rights Act, as amended, the use of a seniority system in layoff decisions, despite its negative impact on affirmative action.
1986	*Wygant v. Jackson Bd. of Ed.* U.S. Supreme Court strikes down, under the Fourteenth Amendment to the U.S. Constitution, the use of affirmative action in layoff decisions.
1986	*Sheet Metal Workers' International Association v. EEOC.* U.S. Supreme Court upholds, under Title VII and the Fifth Amendment to the U.S. Constitution, a court-ordered affirmative action program to remedy past discrimination by a union and apprenticeship committee against people of color.
1986	*Int'l Assoc. of Firefighters v. City of Cleveland.* U.S. Supreme Court upholds, under Title VII, affirmative action consent decree that provided for the use of race-conscious relief in promotion decisions.
1987	*Johnson v. Transportation Agency, Santa Clara County.* U.S. Supreme Court upholds, under Title VII, voluntarily developed affirmative action program intended to correct gender and racial imbalances in traditionally segregated job categories.
1987	*U.S. v. Paradise.* U.S. Supreme Court upholds, under the Fourteenth Amendment to the U.S. Constitution, a court-ordered affirmative action plan aimed at remedying discrimination against African Americans in hiring and promotion decisions in Alabama Public Safety Department.
1989	*City of Richmond v. Croson.* U.S. Supreme Court strikes down the constitutionality, under the Fourteenth Amendment, of a local government's set-aside program because it could not satisfy the criteria of the strict-scrutiny test.
1989	*Martin v. Wilks.* U.S. Supreme Court allowed white firefighters to challenge, under Title VII, a consent decree, to which they were not a party, years after it had been approved by a lower court.
1995	*Adarand v. Peña.* U.S. Supreme Court rules that the Equal Protection Clause of the Fifth Amendment requires that racial classifications used in federal set-aside programs must undergo strict-scrutiny analysis.
1996	*Hopwood v. State of Texas.* U.S. Supreme Court let stand a ruling by the U.S. Court of Appeals for the Fifth Circuit, which struck down the constitutionality of an affirmative action program at the University of Texas Law School.
1999	*Lesage v. Texas.* U.S. Supreme Court throws out a reverse discrimination suit filed under the Equal Protection Clause of the Fourteenth Amendment against the University of Texas Department of Education.

(continued on the following page)

TABLE 4.1   *(continued from the previous page)*

2003	*Grutter v. Bollinger.* The U.S Supreme Court upheld affirmative action at the University of Michigan Law School under the Fourteenth Amendment, arguing that there is a compelling state interest in "racial diversity." Race was one factor considered among many other factors.
2003	*Gratz v. Bollinger.* The U.S. Supreme Court struck down the use of affirmative action in the University of Michigan's undergraduate program under the Equal Protection Clause of the Fourteenth Amendment and Title VI of the Civil Rights Act. The Court stated that the program was based on a formula or "quota" system, giving, extra points for race.

except that at no time will there be a greater percentage of minority personnel laid off than the current percentage of minority personnel employed at the time of the layoff (*Wygant*, 1986, p. 1845).

When it became necessary, layoffs were made in accordance with the collective bargaining provision. Consequently, persons of color with less seniority were retained and white teachers with greater seniority were laid off. White teachers affected by the layoffs challenged the constitutionality of the collective bargaining provision. The U.S. Supreme Court struck down the constitutionality of the layoff plan, on the grounds that the use of racial classifications in the layoff plan was not justified by a "compelling state interest." The Court began by stating that

[t]his Court never has upheld that societal discrimination alone is sufficient to justify a racial classification. Rather, the Court has insisted upon some showing of prior discrimination by the governmental unit involved before allowing limited use of racial classifications in order to remedy such discrimination (*Wygant*, 1986, p. 1847).

The Court went on to say that even if the school board's purpose was to remedy its own past discrimination, the means selected (i.e., the layoff plan) to achieve that goal were not "sufficiently narrowly tailored." The Court stated that "Other, less intrusive means of accomplishing similar purposes—such as the adoption of hiring goals—are available" (*Wygant*, 1986, p. 1852).

Finally, the Court argued that the use of affirmative action may not be appropriate in layoffs because of its impact on "innocent" parties. The Court argued, affirmative action is appropriate in hiring decisions, since the burden to be borne by "innocent parties" is diffused among society. In contrast, the *Wygant* Court stated, when affirmative action is employed during layoffs, the

entire burden of achieving racial equally [is placed on] particular individuals, often resulting in serious disruption of their lives. That burden is too intrusive (*Wygant*, 1986, pp. 1851–1852).

In summary, while the U.S. Supreme Court finds affirmative action legally permissible in hiring and promotions, it is unwilling to balance affirmative action against seniority rights.

CONCLUSION

The U.S. Supreme Court's ruling in the University of Michigan Law School has major implications for the continued use of affirmative action in the workplace. But, it should be noted that the ruling is based on a close 5–4 majority. The Court's conservative members, Justices Kennedy, Scalia, Thomas, and Chief Justice Rehnquist ruled against the use of affirmative action in admissions. With the victory of President Bush in the 2004 elections, and the certainty that some members of the Court will be replaced (e.g., Rehnquist), the victory around affirmative action may be short-lived.

But, for now, the University of Michigan decisions clearly support the continued use of affirmative action when, as outlined in this chapter, certain criteria are met.

REFERENCES

Cornwell, C., and Kellough, J. E. 1994. "Women and Minorities in Federal Government Agencies: Examining New Evidence from Panel Data." *Public Administration Review* 54:3: 265–270.

Firefighters Local Union No. 1784 and Memphis Fire Department v. Stotts. 1984. 467 U.S. 561.

Gratz v. Bollinger. 2003. 539 U.S. 244.

Gratz v. Bollinger. 2000. 122 F. Supp. 2d 811.

Grutter v. Bollinger. 2003. 539 U.S. 306.

Kellough, J. E. 1997. "Affirmative Action and Equal Employment Opportunity." *Review of Public Personnel Administration* 17:4, symposium.

Naylor, L. A. and Rosenbloom, D. H. 2004. "*Adarand, Grutter,* and *Gratz*: Does Affirmative Action in Federal Employment Matter?" *Review of Public Personnel Administration* 24:2: 150–174.

Regents of the University of California v. Bakke. 1978. 438 U.S. 265.

Riccucci, N. M. 2002. *Managing Diversity in Public Sector Workforces.* Boulder, CO: Westview Press.

Rosenbloom, D. H. and Featherstonhaugh, J. C. 1977. "Passive and Active Representation in the Federal Service: A Comparison of Blacks and Whites." *Social Science Quarterly* 57: 873–882.

Wygant v. Jackson Board of Education. 1986. 476 U.S. 267.

Chapter 5

Managing Diversity: Redux

Norma M. Riccucci

"It has taken my mother's time, my father's time, my brothers and my sisters' time, my nieces and my nephews' time. . . . How much time do you want for your progress?"

James Baldwin[1]

The terms *diversity* and *managing diversity* are, by now, well grounded in Americans' parlance. Virtually every organization, both public and private, has some form of program revolving around promoting and managing diversity. Yet, we know very little about the efficacy of these programs. Indeed, a study conducted by the National Urban League (2004) reveals that American workers believe diversity initiatives at their own organizations are ineffective. The study, which reports the survey findings of some 5,500 American workers, found that fewer than one-third of the workers believe their organizations have effective diversity programs.

A critical problem, then, is the lack of academic research on the implementation of diversity programs (Wise and Tschirhart, 2000). Decades after prescriptions were made for preparing for a more diverse workforce, research has yet to show whether and how diversity initiatives were implemented and whether they have been effective. And, while there is a well-established body of literature showing that most organizations, both public and private, have some type of diversity program, some of these programs are simply a continuance of affirmative action and equal employment opportunity policies (Riccucci, 2002a).

This chapter looks at the progress made around at least one key aspect of diversity initiatives: diversifying the upper, higher-paying ranks of public sector organizations. It begins with a brief look at the recommendations that organizations were expected to consider in light of predicted demographic changes in the labor force. It then focuses on one particular recommendation: the call to organizations to develop promotion policies to advance women and people of color upward in their hierarchies.

In an effort to discern whether the federal government has sought to promote diversity in the upper reaches of the federal bureaucracy, it provides a snapshot of the employment status of women and people of color over the past several years. It illustrates the lack of progress they have made in ascending to upper-level, policy-making positions in government, suggesting that the federal government may not have heeded the recommendations offered around managing diversity, specifically those to address the perduring problem of a "sticky ladder."[2]

EMPLOYMENT POLICIES AIMED AT PROMOTING DIVERSITY

A few decades ago, demographers began to predict major shifts in the racial and ethnic population of the U.S. These shifts, in turn, would affect the social composition of the labor force. The workforce changes that have already begun to occur include:

1. increases in the number of women
2. increases in the number of people of color
3. increases in the average age of workers
4. increases in foreign-born or immigrant workers
5. increases in the number of contingent workers (e.g., part-timers, temporary workers)[3]

Table 5.1 provides greater detail on important demographic changes that have implications for employment. It illustrates changes in the workforce based on gender, race, and ethnicity from 1978 to 1998, and projected changes to 2008. The table shows a decline in the participation of white men in the workforce, with an increase of white women (12.1 percent). In addition, the table shows remarkable increases of women of color in the workforce, while the projections for men of color show slight decreases in their workforce participation.

In response to these shifts, policy analysts and researchers offered a host of recommendations that public and private sector employers were encouraged to consider in order to prepare for increased diversity in the workplace (Gardenswartz and Rowe, 1993; Golembiewski, 1995; Wooldridge, Maddox, and Zhang, 1995; Wooldridge and Wester, 1991; *Civil Service 2000*, 1988; *Workforce 2000*, 1987; *Workforce 2020*, 1997; Selden and Selden, 2001; Riccucci, 2002a; Riccucci 2002b). Such recommendations included the following:

1. *Obtaining strong commitment and support for diversity initiatives from not only agency leaders, but also from government CEOs, such as mayors, governors, and the President.*

    If the top-level leaders communicate that a program to manage diversity is a critical goal for the agency and that it is integrated into the overall strategic goals of the organization, the stage is set for commitment by

TABLE 5.1 Workforce Participation Rates, 16 Years and Older, by Gender, Race, and Ethnicity, 1978, 1988, 1996, 1998, and Projected 2008

Group	Participation Rate (percent)					Percentage Point Change (percent)
	1978	1988	1996	1998	2008	1978–2008
White	63.3	66.2	67.2	67.3	67.9	4.6
Men	78.6	76.9	75.8	75.6	74.5	−4.1
Women	49.4	56.4	59.1	59.4	61.5	12.1
African American	61.5	63.8	64.1	65.6	66.3	4.8
Men	71.7	71.0	68.7	69.0	68.3	−3.4
Women	53.2	58.0	60.4	62.8	64.6	11.4
Asian and other[1]	64.6	65.0	65.8	67.0	66.9	2.3
Men	75.9	74.4	73.4	75.5	74.0	−1.9
Women	54.1	56.5	58.8	59.2	60.5	6.4
Hispanic origin[2]	—	67.4	66.5	67.9	67.7	0.3
Men	—	81.9	79.6	79.8	77.9	−0.4
Women	—	53.2	53.4	55.6	57.9	4.7

[1] The "Asian and other" group includes (1) Asians and Pacific Islanders and (2) American Indians and Alaska Natives. The historical data are derived by subtracting "black" from the "black and other" group; projections are made directly, not by subtraction.
[2] Data by Hispanic origin are not available before 1980. Percentage point change is calculated from 1988 to 2008.
SOURCE: Bureau of Labor Statistics (BLS) web site: stats.bls.gov/ (Participation refers to the percentage of a specific group participating in the workforce. So, by 2008, for example, 61.5 percent of all women will be participating in the workforce.)

lower-level managers, supervisors, and the employees themselves. The expression of commitment by leaders, however, must be backed by resources.

2. *Developing an organizational culture that supports and values diversity.*

A culture that is oriented toward change, acceptance, and openness is seen as crucial. Organizational cultures that don't require everyone to look alike, dress alike, talk alike, style their hair alike, and act alike may prove to be the most successful. And the efforts to bring about change in the culture, mission, and structure of the organizations must be *institutionalized.*

3. *Developing family-friendly benefits and policies.*

Employee benefits are extremely important to both public and private sector employees. And, for workers with dependents, benefits packages may be vital in their efforts to balance work and family responsibilities. Health care plans, day care, retirement plans, and disability benefits are among those that have provided some sense of security to workers and their families.

4. *Developing training and development programs.*

A key aspect of preparing managers, supervisors, and workers for diversity in the workforce lies in training and education. Managers and supervisors, for example, will need to possess the tools and skills necessary to address and respond to changes in work technology and demography. They will need to be attuned to the different values and expectations of various groups.

5. *Developing opportunities for promotion and advancement.*

A *glass ceiling*[4] or *sticky ladder*[5] has worked to prevent women and people of color from reaching upper-level, higher-paying jobs (Naff, 2001). One approach to breaking the glass ceiling is through management/professional development programs. Such programs may be aimed at preparing, over the course of two to four years, secretaries and clerical workers—predominately female occupations—for management positions. In addition, government officials may need to ensure that their "merit" exams for promotion are accurate, fair, and job-related. For example, governments would want to address the problem of cultural biases in exams.

In summary, a number of recommendations have been offered to assist employers in preparing for the major demographic shifts that have occurred in the labor force. However, the extent to which employers have adopted these recommendations is uncertain. Research is sorely lacking here. In an effort to address this shortcoming, this chapter looks at one critical aspect of managing and promoting diversity initiatives: diversifying the upper levels of government employment.

A SNAPSHOT OF THE DEMOGRAPHICS OF FEDERAL EMPLOYMENT

A good deal of research has illustrated that women and people of color have made some progress in terms of entry into government jobs. On the other hand, they have made few gains in terms of upward mobility in government service (Cornwell and Kellough, 1994; Naff, 2001). A review of federal employment data indicates that this picture has remained the same. It should be noted at the outset that data on the demographics of state and local government employment are virtually impossible to access. While the U.S. Bureau of Labor Statistics (BLS) provides summary data on the employment status of women and people of color in government, the BLS does not provide a breakdown by occupation, rank, or salary. The U.S. Equal Employment Opportunity Commission (EEOC) is the agency responsible for collecting state and local government employment data on women and people of color, but the agency's data are not up to date.[6] Thus, for the purposes of this chapter, only federal government data are relied upon. Of course, the lack of availability of data on the employment status of women and people of color makes it extremely difficult to study the progress, or lack thereof, that these groups are making in state and local government employment.

TABLE 5.2   Federal Executive Branch (Non-Postal) Employment, by Race and Ethnicity, 1992–2002

	1992	1994	1996	1998	2000	2002
TOTAL	**2,175,715**	**2,043,449**	**1,890,406**	**1,804,591**	**1,755,689**	**1,813,047**
RACE/ETHNICITY						
Non-Minority	1,570,812	1,462,185	1,341,157	1,269,790	1,224,836	1,255,941
% Non-Minority	*72.2*	*71.5*	*70.9*	*70.4*	*69.8*	*69.3*
Total Minorities	604,903	581,264	549,249	534,801	530,853	557,106
% Minority	*27.8*	*28.4*	*29.1*	*29.6*	*30.2*	*30.7*
African American	360,725	340,512	313,810	300,661	298,701	306,128
% African American	*16.6*	*16.7*	*16.6*	*16.7*	*17.0*	*16.9*
Latino	120,296	116,683	115,644	115,545	115,247	124,868
% Latino	*5.5*	*5.7*	*6.1*	*6.4*	*6.6*	*6.9*
Asian/Pacific Islander	81,522	82,833	81,851	81,028	78,969	86,425
% Asian/Pacific Islander	*3.7*	*4.1*	*4.3*	*4.5*	*4.5*	*4.8*
American Indian/ Alaska Native	42,360	41,006	37,944	37,567	37,936	39,685
% American Indian/ Alaska Native	*1.9*	*2.0*	*2.0*	*2.1*	*2.2*	*2.2*

SOURCE: U.S. Office of Personnel Management (OPM), www.opm.gov

Tables 5.2 and 5.3 provide summary data on the overall employment of women and people of color in federal government jobs. As the data show, between the periods of 1992 and 2002, there has been relatively little growth in the total employment of these groups. For example, African Americans increased their share of federal jobs from 16.6 percent to 16.9 percent over the ten-year period; women's employment increased from 43.5 percent to 44.6 percent.

TABLE 5.3   Federal Executive Branch (Non-Postal) Employment, by Gender, 1992–2002

	1992	1994	1996	1998	2000	2002
TOTAL	**2,175,715**	**2,043,449**	**1,890,406**	**1,804,591**	**1,755,689**	**1,813,047**
Women	945,546	896,117	831,840	801,250	790,169	808,435
% Women	*43.5*	*43.9*	*44.0*	*44.4*	*45.0*	*44.6*
Men	1,230,169	1,147,332	1,058,566	1,003,341	965,520	1,004,612
% Men	*56.5*	*56.1*	*56.0*	*55.6*	*55.0*	*55.4*

SOURCE: U.S. Office of Personnel Management (OPM), www.opm.gov

TABLE 5.4   Distribution of Federal Employees by Race, Ethnicity, and Gender, Pay Plan, and Grade, 2002 (Percentages)

	Women	Whites	African American	Latino	Asian/ Pacific Islander	American Indian/ Alaskan Native
Average Grade[1]	8.9	10.2	8.7	9.0	9.8	8.1
Senior Pay Levels[2]	24.7	86.4	6.8	3.3	2.7	0.8
Other White Collar	47.2	72.2	12.2	6.7	6.3	2.5

[1]Based on GS-01 to GS-15
[2]GS-16 and above

SOURCE: Data obtained from U.S. Office of Personnel Management (OPM), www.opm.gov

Tables 5.4 and 5.5 provide information on the pay grades and salaries of federal employees by race, ethnicity, and gender. As the data show, women and people of color are not well represented in the higher, "senior pay levels" (Table 5.4), and their average salaries are still far below that of men. As seen in Table 5.5, women's salaries continue to trail men's, and the annual average salaries of whites is higher than salaries for people of color. Only Asian/Pacific Islander's salaries are approximate to whites'.

A closer look at the representativeness of women and people of color in federal government employment shows another view of their employment status. *Representativeness ratios* generally compare the percentage of a group's employment with the percentage of that group in the general population (see Dolan, 2000; Meier, 1993). The equation looks like this:

$$\text{Women's Representativeness Ratio} = \frac{\text{\% Women in Federal Employment}}{\text{\% Women in General Population}}$$

The ratio equals 1.0 when women's representation in employment equals their representation in the general population (Sigelman, 1976; Dometrius, 1984). The ratio, which has its roots in representative bureaucracy, seeks to determine the

TABLE 5.5   Average Salary by Race, Ethnicity, and Gender, Federal Civilian Employment, 2002

	Average Salary
Women	$49,919
Men	$63,005
Whites	$59,569
African American	$48,303
Latino	$49,104
Asian/Pacific Islander	$58,128
American Indian/Alaskan Native	$44,587

SOURCE: Data obtained from U.S. Office of Personnel Management (OPM), www.opm.gov

TABLE 5.6   Representativeness Ratios[1] for Women and People of Color in Federal (Non-Postal) Employment, 1998 and 2002

	1998	2002
Gender and Ethnic Group		
Women	0.9	0.9
Men	1.1	1.1
White	1.0	1.0
African American	1.2	1.3
Latino	0.6	0.6
Asian/Pacific Islander	1.2	1.2
American Indian/Alaska Native	1.3	1.3

[1]Representativeness ratios are calculated by dividing the percentage of the group employed by the federal government by the percentage of the group in the general population.

SOURCE: Data obtained from U.S. Office of Personnel Management (OPM), www.opm.gov

degree to which the social characteristics of the bureaucracy reflect the social characteristics of the populations the bureaucracy serves. In a broader sense, the theory of representative bureaucracy asks whether and how bureaucrats mirror the preferences of their counterparts in the general public (Sigelman, 1976; Dometrius, 1984; Meier, 1993; Dolan, 2000).[7]

Table 5.6 provides representativeness ratios for women and people of color in federal employment for 1998 and 2002. As the data show, most groups have achieved full representation in government jobs, in terms of total employment for both time periods. That is to say, they have achieved federal employment in proportion to their share of the general population. However, women are slightly under full representation, and Latinos relative to the other groups, are extremely underrepresented in federal employment.

The representativeness ratio, as noted, captures the total employment picture for women and people of color. However, it does not tell us the degree to which they are well represented in upper-level, higher-paying, policy-making positions. A *stratification ratio* indicates the degree to which women and people of color are distributed throughout the various grade levels (Sigelman, 1976; Dometrius, 1984). The equation looks like this:

$$\text{Latino's Representativeness Ratio} = \frac{\%\ \text{Latino in Upper-Level Posts}}{\%\ \text{Latino in Lower-Level Posts}}$$

The ratio equals 1.0 if a group is represented in the two employment levels equally.

As Table 5.7 shows, women and people of color are disproportionately concentrated in lower-level jobs in the federal government. Although there is slight progress between the two time periods, women and people of color have not been promoted to upper-level jobs. The data in Table 5. 7 also show that whites have been very successful in reaching higher job posts in the federal government, and

TABLE 5.7 Stratified Representativeness Ratios[1] for Women and People of Color in Federal (Non-Postal) Employment, by Job Level, 1998 and 2002

Gender and Ethnic Group	1992	2002
Women	0.25	0.46
White	1.55	1.44
African American	0.19	0.34
Latino	0.35	0.43
Asian/Pacific Islander	0.84	0.91
American Indian/Alaska Native	0.18	0.21

[1]Stratified representativeness ratios are calculated by dividing percentage of the group in upper-levels (GS 14-15) by percentage of the group in lower levels (GS 1-4). See Sigelman (1976) and Dometrius (1984).

SOURCE: Data obtained from U.S. Office of Personnel Management (OPM), www.opm.gov

Asian/Pacific Islanders are also distributed almost evenly between upper- and lower-level positions, as the stratified representativeness ratio of .91 for 2002 indicates. Women, as well as African Americans, Latinos, and American Indians/Alaska Natives continue to lag behind in terms of promotions to high-level, policy-making positions in the federal government.

DISCUSSION

A study conducted by the National Urban League in 2004 found that:

> For more than 40 years, corporations across the nation have invested a great deal of energy and resources in the area of diversity. Today diversity is not only part of the culture of many corporations but a core business strategy as well. Yet the business community has struggled to develop a meaningful measure of the effectiveness of diversity and inclusion programs (National Urban League, 2004, p. ii).

To be sure, one measure of the success of diversity programs is the extent to which organizations are moving women and people of color into upper-level positions of power. Diversifying in the upper echelons of hierarchies is critical. First, it creates channels of upward career mobility for women and people of color. Upper-level jobs carry greater power, prestige, and monetary rewards. In addition, women and people of color in high-level positions of power can serve as role models for everyone in the organization. Moreover, diversity in the upper levels of public bureaucracies helps in terms of making progress toward active representation. Addressed earlier in this chapter, the concept of representative bureaucracy refers to the degree to which women and people of color are able to serve their counterparts in the general population. In addition to the importance of active representation, the simple question remains: *How can organizations continue to tout the importance of diversity, when the upper echelons (and those doing the touting) are mostly white, and mostly male?*

As the research presented here indicates, aside from Asian/Pacific Islanders, women and people of color continue to be disproportionately concentrated in lower-level federal government jobs, which carry no power, status, prestige, or salary advantages. If women and people of color are to make real employment gains, programs and policies must be more aggressively pursed around promotion and upward mobility. This mandate has been repeatedly made to both public and private sector employers. As a frustrated James Baldwin asks: "How much time do you want for your progress?"[8]

CONCLUSIONS

Diversity is a concept that has become integral to human resource management practices and more broadly, to the governing of our public and private sector institutions. Yet, for all the hype and self-promotion around organizational diversity efforts, the progress that public and private sector employers are making toward managing diversity initiatives is sketchy at best.

However, one thing remains clear: The social composition of this nation is shifting as we move into the twenty-first century. Demographers as a corollary promised that the employment landscape for women and people of color would be auspicious. Yet, progress toward real employment gains remains illusive to the extent that women and people of color continue to be concentrated in lower-level, lower-paying jobs in the public and private sectors. If organizations are genuinely interested in promoting and managing diversity in the workplace, they would strengthen their efforts to move women and people of color into higher-level jobs. Until there is greater commitment and stronger leadership on this critical issue, progress toward real employment gains for women and people of color will remain unattainable. This has implications for the continued health, productivity, and competitiveness of public organizations.

An analogy can be drawn with the American labor movement. Private sector unions were repeatedly warned that unless they made significant changes to adapt to the shifting economy (from manufacturing to industrial), as well as to increased automation and globalization, they would be decimated in terms of union membership. By failing to adapt, union membership has in fact plummeted in the private sector over the past several decades. In the 1950s, labor unions represented about 35 percent of the nation's workforce. By 2004, only 12.5 percent were union members.[9] Instead of turning to service occupations and those heavily employed in these industries—predominately women and people of color—big labor chooses to raid one another's industries, diluting power for themselves and their workers. Flight attendants, for example, are now divided among several different unions, making leverage over the airlines virtually impossible (Bai, 2005).

The unions that consciously decided to adapt to the economic and social changes underway in our society are those that began to unionize a population of workers heretofore wholly ignored by American labor: women and people of color in service industries, including public-sector workers. Indeed, public employees now represent the greatest share of unionization in this country; today 41.5 percent of public employees at all levels of government are represented by unions.[10]

The Service Employees International Union (SEIU) has been one of the most successful unions in the past few decades, because of its foresight to organize janitors, nurses, and home health care aides, a third of whom are women, Latino, African American, or Asian. The SEIU is now the largest and fastest-growing union in North America (Bai, 2005).

In short, the organizations that fail to adapt to predicted, foreseeable economic and social changes will not be successful in competing for quality employees. At a time when this nation is challenged to recruit the best possible employees for public service, government employers are encouraged to take positive steps to fully embrace and effectively manage diversity in their workforces.

NOTES

1. This was acclaimed author James Baldwin's response to a television reporter who made a statement, one generally attributed to well-meaning white liberals, that "racial progress takes time."
2. The *sticky ladder* is a term employed by David Brooks (2005) in a *New York Times* Op-Ed column in reference to the problem of declining social mobility in this country. It is used here as a reference to barriers preventing upward mobility in organizations.
3. See, for example, Gardenswartz and Rowe, 1993; Wooldridge, Maddox, and Zhang, 1995; Wooldridge and Wester, 1991; Loden and Rosener, 1991; *Civil Service 2000*, 1988; *Workforce 2000*, 1988; *Workforce 2020*, 1997.
4. The *glass ceiling* is a concept that refers to the artificial barriers that keep women from reaching upper-level management positions in public and private sector organizations. See Naff, 2001.
5. *Supra* note 2.
6. The last issue of *Job Patterns for Minorities and Women in State and Local Government* was published by the EEOC in 1999. This document is not available online, and repeated efforts to contact the agency have been met with voice recordings and answering machines. To date, no calls have been returned. It is not available through EEOC field offices, and university libraries tend not to have the latest issue.
7. A distinction is drawn between *passive* representation, where the bureaucracy has the same demographic origins as the population it serves, and *active* representation, where bureaucrats act on behalf of their counterparts in the general population. Active representativeness theory holds that values which are linked to demographic origins will be translated into programs, policies, or decisions that benefit individuals of similar origins (Rosenbloom and Featherstonhaugh, 1977; Mosher, 1982; Meier, 1993; Seldon, 1997).
8. *Supra* note 1.

9. U.S. Bureau of Labor Statistics, www.bls.gov/news.release/union2.nr0.htm, date accessed, February 2, 2005.
10. U. S. Bureau of Labor Statistics, www.bls.gov/news.release/union2.t03.htm, date accessed, February 2, 2005.

REFERENCES

Bai, M. 2005. "The New Boss." *The New York Times Magazine* January 30: 38–45, 62, 68, 71.

Civil Service 2000. 1988. Indianapolis, IN: Hudson Institute.

Cornwell, C. and Kellough, J. E. 1994. "Women and Minorities in Federal Government Agencies: Examining New Evidence from Panel Data." *Public Administration Review* 54:3: 265–270.

Brooks, D. 2005. "The Sticky Ladder." *New York Times* January 25: A19.

Dolan, J. 2000. "The Senior Executive Service: Gender, Attitudes and Representative Bureaucracy." *Journal of Public Administration Research and Theory* 10:3: 513–529.

Dometrius, N. C. 1984. "Minorities and Women Among State Agency Leaders." *Social Science Quarterly* 65:1: 127–137.

Gardenswartz, L. and Rowe, A. 1993. *Managing Diversity: A Complete Desk Reference and Planning Guide*. Homewood, IL: Business One Irwin.

Golembiewski, R. T. 1995. *Managing Diversity in Organizations*. Tuscaloosa, AL: University of Alabama Press.

Loden, M. and Rosener, J. B. 1991. *Workforce America!* Homewood, IL: Business One Irwin.

Meier, K. J. 1993. "Representative Bureaucracy: A Theoretical and Empirical Exposition." In J. Perry, ed. *Research in Public Administration*, Greenwich, CT: JAI Press, Inc, pp. 1–35.

Mosher, F. C. 1982. *Democracy and the Public Service*, 2nd ed. New York, NY: Oxford University Press.

Naff, K. C. 2001. *To Look Like America*. Boulder, CO: Westview Press.

National Urban League. 2004. *Diversity Practices That Work: The American Worker Speaks*. Washington, DC: National Urban League.

Riccucci, Norma M. 2002a. *Managing Diversity in Public Sector Workforces*. Boulder, CO: Westview Press.

Riccucci, N. M. 2002b. "Managing Diversity in the Government Workplace." In C. Ban and N. M. Riccucci, eds. *Public Personnel Management: Current Concerns, Future Challenges*, 3rd ed. New York, NY: Longman Publishers.

Rosenbloom, D. H. and Featherstonhaugh, J. C. 1977. "Passive and Active Representation in the Federal Service: A Comparison of Blacks and Whites." *Social Science Quarterly* 57:x: 873–882.

Selden, S. C. 1997. *The Promise of Representative Bureaucracy: Diversity and Responsiveness in a Government Agency*. Armonk, NY: M.E. Sharpe.

Selden, S. C. and Selden, F. 2001. "Rethinking Diversity in Public Organizations for the 21st Century: Moving Toward a Multicultural Model." *Administration & Society* 33:3: 303–329.

Sigelman, L. 1976. "The Curious Case of Women in State and Local Government." *Social Science Quarterly* 57:4: 591–604.

Wise, L. R. and Tschirhart, M. 2000. "Examining Empirical Evidence on Diversity Effects: How Useful Is Diversity Research for Public-Sector Managers?" *Public Administration Review* 60:5: 386–394.

Wooldridge, B., Maddox, B. C., and Zhang, Y. 1995. "Changing Demographics of the Work Force: Implications for the Design of Productive Work Environments: An Exploratory Analysis." *Review of Public Personnel Administration* 15:3: 60–72.

Wooldridge, B. and Wester, J. 1991. "The Turbulent Environment of Public Personnel Administration: Responding to the Challenge of the Changing Workplace of the Twenty-First Century." *Public Personnel Management* 40:2: 207–224.

Workforce 2000. 1987. Indianapolis, IN: Hudson Institute.

Workforce 2020. 1997. Indianapolis, IN: Hudson Institute.

Chapter 6

Lesbians and Gay Men in the Public-Sector Workforce

Charles W. Gossett

Most public-sector organizations already have a diverse work force with respect to the sexual orientation and gender identity of their employees; however, they are often unaware of this fact or unwilling to acknowledge it. Ironically, although many government agencies struggle to increase the representation of historically underrepresented racial and ethnic groups and women, many have, until very recently, actively sought to prevent lesbian, gay male, bisexual, and transgendered (LGBT) job applicants from being hired or to remove such employees from their jobs. This contradictory situation—success in recruiting and promoting personnel that the organization, in many instances, would prefer not to have—makes the issue of LGBT employees in the public workplace quite different from the problems faced by historically underrepresented groups. At the same time, however, advocates and opponents of laws that would provide legal protection against discrimination on the basis of sexual orientation make remarkably similar use of the strategies and rhetoric of the supporters and enemies of the civil rights movement of African Americans and the women's movement. Thus, personnel administrators, who will inevitably face questions concerning sexual orientation and employment, need familiarity with the historical experience of LGBT people employed in the public sector, the current status of legal protections (or lack thereof) for LGBT employees, and some of the ways that traditional aspects of personnel administration are affected by their increasingly open presence of in the workforce.

TERMINOLOGY

Before proceeding, a brief word about terminology may be useful. When talking about lesbians, gay men, and bisexuals, we are identifying people on the basis of

70

what is usually called *sexual orientation*. Homosexuality, bisexuality, heterosexuality, and asexuality are generally included whenever reference is made in laws to a person's sexual orientation. In the 1970s and 1980s, it was not unusual to encounter comments and laws that used the term *sexual preference* or *affectional preference* rather than sexual orientation. Advocates for gay rights, however, object to the use of the word "preference" because it represents a conclusion that one's sexual orientation is a choice. Since they see the question as to the nature and origins of homosexuality, and for that matter of heterosexuality, as one that is still unresolved, they prefer the term "orientation," which may or may not be the result of a conscious choice.

Opponents of laws that prohibit discrimination on the basis of sexual orientation often claim that pedophilia and bestiality are also sexual orientations, and historically many state laws grouped homosexuality with those behaviors. However, in recent decades, and especially since 1973 when the American Psychiatric Association removed homosexuality from its list of mental disorders (Bayer, 1987), the common use of the term "sexual orientation" has not included behaviors still classified as mental or psychological disorders.

In many older works on the topic, the word "gay" is used as a universal term denoting all persons with a homosexual orientation. It is still commonly used as an adjective in phrases like "gay rights" or "gay politics." Most activists, however, use the term "gay and lesbian" since the word "gay" on its own tends to conjure up images of only gay men. "Lesbian" is a term that has been used to denote sex between two women since at least 1732, deriving from the word "Lesbos," the Greek isle on which the poet Sappho lived in ancient times (Stewart, 1995). Other terms that have emerged in recent years to identify homosexual people include "same gender loving" (principally used by African American men concerned that the term "gay" is too specifically identified with white male homosexuals); "two spirit" (principally used by Native Americans who believe that it better captures the meaning of homosexuality within Native American cultures); and "queer" (a term that was "reclaimed" by gay and lesbian activists in the 1990s and often refers to anyone engaged in unconventional adult sexual relationships). In the development of outreach efforts by public health officials concerned with stopping the spread of AIDS, one is likely to encounter the abbreviation MSM which stands for "men who have sex with men." This term is used to refer to men who engage in homosexual behavior but who do not identify themselves as gay men. Many of these men are on the "down low," a recently popularized term to describe MSM. In this chapter, however, we will use just the terms "gay men" and "lesbians" as they have a wider usage in public discourse.

Another term is "transgendered persons," namely those persons whose biological sex at the time of birth does not match their psychological gender identity which emerges subsequently. This group includes transsexuals (i.e., persons who have had or are preparing to have surgical alteration of their biological sex to match their gender identity or, occasionally, persons who have decided not to have surgery, but rely on hormone therapies and live their lives in a manner consistent with their gender identity) and cross-dressers or transvestites (i.e., persons who choose to dress as a member of the opposite sex, either on a regular basis or only occasionally, but do not plan to surgically alter their bodies) (Bornstein, 1995; Califia, 1997; Garber, 1992; Green, 2000; Currah and Minter, 2000). Transgendered persons may or may not also be lesbians or gay males. If so, they face many of the same problems as other lesbians and gay men. If they are heterosexual in their sexual orientation, they are still likely to face discrimination in the workplace (Green, 2000).

Unlike homosexuality, however, transgendered individuals are still considered to be suffering from a mental disorder by the medical profession. Gender Identity Disorder (GID) or "gender dysphoria" are terms with which the American Psychiatric Association characterizes the illness of those who are transgendered (American Psychiatric Association, 2000). It is important to note that, although transgenderism remains classified as a medical disorder and homosexuality is no longer classified as such, the principal legal tool for protecting people with physical or mental impairments, the Americans with Disabilities Act, specifically *excludes* use of the Act to protect their rights. On the other hand, some state laws prohibiting disability discrimination, like New Jersey, have found that transgendered people are covered (*Enriquez v. West Jersey Health Systems*, 2001).

HISTORICAL OVERVIEW

Although the written record of sexual relations between persons of the same sex indicates that such practices are hardly a new phenomenon, the concept of such persons as a "class" different from persons who have sexual relations with persons of the opposite sex is usually traced to the latter half of the nineteenth century. At that time, homosexual behavior moved from being a "sinful" act to being viewed as an "illness," more specifically a psychiatric abnormality (Katz, 1995). Despite the characterization of homosexuality as a disease, however, it retained an identity as a sin as evidenced by the fact that, in the United States, all states had laws that criminalized sexual relations between persons of the same sex for most of this century (Nice, 1994), though between 1960 and 2000, 34 states and the District of Columbia decriminalized such behaviors. In 2003, however, the U.S. Supreme Court ruled, in *Lawrence v. Texas*, that states could not criminalize private and consensual homosexual activity.

Recently, scientific investigations into a biological origin for homosexuality have become prominent in discussions of whether sexual orientation is a personal characteristic more appropriately compared to race, ethnicity, or gender or whether comparison to some voluntary behaviors like religious choice is more suitable. The very fact that the term "sexual orientation" has replaced "sexual preference" in the discussion of this topic suggests that the arguments in favor of at least a partial biological explanation have gained fairly wide acceptance (Burr, 1993; LeVay, 1993; Hamer & Copeland, 1994). This brief discussion of how homosexuality has been conceptualized is important because, as in all policy matters, how the "problem" is stated has great influence on how "solutions" are developed.

In the United States, there is evidence that from its founding, persons engaging in sexual activity with persons of the same sex have been dismissed from public service (Shilts, 1993). For the most part, such dismissals were focused on the acts allegedly committed and not because the accused was a particular "type" of person. With the development of the concepts and terms of "homosexual" and "heterosexual" in the late 1800s and early 1900s, shorthand labels that purported to predict everything from sexual desires to fitness for particular types of employment became available to society. Public employers now had available scientifically-defined "groups" that could be favored (heterosexuals) or discriminated against (homosexuals) (Katz, 1995).

THE MILITARY

Perhaps the best known efforts at using the criterion of homosexuality to make employment decisions are in the military. Several writers (Shilts, 1993; Berube, 1990; Meyer, 1996) have recounted the history of "gays in the military," but Shilts' story clearly demonstrates that the use of "homosexual" as a classification tool for personnel management really accelerated during World War II. Until 1993, the question as to whether a person was a homosexual appeared on military application forms; it was dropped only as part of a compromise between the President and the Congress over the issue of officially allowing lesbians and gay men to serve in the armed forces (Aspin, 1993). This "Don't Ask, Don't Tell" compromise policy says that homosexual conduct, including the mere statement that one is a gay male, lesbian, or bisexual, is still grounds for discharge from military service, regardless of performance. The rationale offered in defense of this policy, given that several studies have demonstrated no perceptible differences in ability or performance between homosexual and heterosexual military personnel (Dyer, 1990; Wolinsky and Sherrill, 1993), is that military readiness is harmed by the fact that many military personnel are made uncomfortable by the knowledge that homosexuals are serving with them. This argument is strikingly similar to the arguments raised when President Truman ordered the integration of armed forces units rather than continuing to segregate different races in separate units (Keen, 1995, 1992; Kauth and Landis, 1996). In the current case, however, gay male and lesbian soldiers are already integrated into all units, which makes it not surprising that some opponents of homosexuals serving openly in the military proposed segregation of homosexuals and heterosexuals as a compromise solution. To date, however, federal courts have not found discrimination against homosexuals by the branches of military service to violate any constitutionally protected rights (*Able v. United States*, 1998) and the number of military personnel discharged for homosexuality has increased since the "Don't Ask, Don't Tell" policy went into effect (D'Amico, 2000; Lehring, 2003).

FEDERAL CIVILIAN EMPLOYMENT

In the post-World War II period, especially during the early years of the Cold War, civilian government employees who were lesbians and gay men were also targeted for removal from public employment. Although the early 1950s are better known for the McCarthy hearings that sought to identify and remove alleged Communist Party members and sympathizers from government positions, homosexuals were also a major target of Congressional investigating committees (Johnson, 2004; Lewis, 1997; Katz, 1992, 91–105). Despite a variety of epithets and accusations of moral weakness, the "official" reason given as to why homosexuals were unfit for public service was that they posed a "security risk" to the nation. The logic behind this claim was that lesbian and gay male employees, being members of socially despised groups and, almost by definition, engaged in criminal acts every time they had sexual relations, would not want their employer or family members to know of their homosexuality. Thus, according to this logic, homosexual employees were highly susceptible to blackmail by foreign agents who would either threaten exposure or simply prey on the fact that they were morally weak. That there was no evidence of any homosexual American government employee having engaged in espionage or betrayal of government secrets was irrelevant. Nor did the circularity of the argument—homosexuals must be dismissed from employment because they could be blackmailed because they would lose their jobs if it was known that they were homosexuals—have any affect on the policy. Not surprisingly, given the nature of the "security risk" argument, most of the dismissals of homosexual employees occurred in the State Department and among civilian employees in defense agencies (Lewis, 1997). It wasn't until August 1995 that President Clinton issued an executive order prohibiting government agencies from denying security clearances simply because the person is a lesbian or gay man (Chibbaro, 1995; Lewis, 2001).

While specific numbers are hard to come by, it appears that during the late 1950s and throughout the 1960s, the number of dismissals of lesbian and gay male employees seems to have declined from the heights reached during the McCarthy era. In addition to the security risk argument, Lewis (1997) identifies three other reasons used to justify the dismissal of homosexual employees from civilian federal service: (1) homosexuality is an example of the "criminal, infamous, dishonest, immoral, or notoriously disgraceful conduct" that always justifies a refusal to hire or a dismissal; (2) the presence of homosexuals impaired "the efficiency of the service" because some employees would be so upset working with known homosexuals that they could not perform their own jobs; and (3) employing homosexuals would "embarrass" the agency and impair its standing in the public's eyes. Over the years, the courts struck down each of these reasons for dismissing or refusing to hire openly lesbian and gay male personnel, although never completely closing the door to the possibility that in some circumstances a dismissal or refusal to hire on the basis of sexual orientation might be legitimate. Relying on the "nexus" arguments developed during the 1960s and 1970s, absent a clear connection between a person's sexual orientation and the ability to perform a particular job, discrimination against lesbians and gay men is not permissible. Of course, whether there is a connection is left to the judge reviewing the discriminatory claim.

As the social climate changed, particularly in the period following the historic Stonewall rebellion, which is often cited as the beginning of the current press for equal rights for lesbians and gay men (Duberman, 1993), the former Civil Service

Commission (CSC) began to modify its official policies in response to both court decisions and political pressure. In the mid-1970s, the CSC advised agencies that "merely" because a person is a homosexual, absent a showing that conduct affects ability to perform the job, there were insufficient grounds for a finding of "unsuitability." In 1980, the first Director of the Office of Personnel Management, Alan Campbell, reemphasizing the importance of a nexus between off-duty behavior and job performance, issued a memorandum that stated "applicants and employees are to be protected against inquiries into, or actions based upon, non-job-related conduct, such as religious, community or social affiliations, or sexual orientation" (Lewis, 1997). This policy was also consistent with language in the 1978 Civil Service Reform Act that outlined "merit principles" that required selections to be made "solely on the basis of relative ability, knowledge, and skills" and that employee retention should be based only on "the adequacy of their performance" (P.L. 95–454, §2301(b)(1) and (6), 1978). Despite a change in administration, this policy remained in effect throughout the 1980s.

In the 1992 election campaign, the question of lifting the ban on "gays in the military" was a clear policy difference between the Democratic and Republican candidates. And while the victory of Bill Clinton did not lead to a repeal of this particular prohibition, there was hope that a presidential order prohibiting employment discrimination on the basis of sexual orientation in the civilian branches of government would be issued. However, a different strategy emerged based on concerns that the anti-gay frenzy that had been whipped up over the military debate would lead to Congressional action overturning an executive order covering civilians. Instead of a single order, the White House encouraged each cabinet department and independent agency to issue its own nondiscrimination policy. By mid-1995, 13 of 14 cabinet departments and more than 15 agencies had issued such statements. In 1998, President Clinton amended the executive branch's equal employment policy statement originally issued in 1969, Executive Order 11478, by adding the words "sexual orientation" to the list of categories protected from discrimination in federal civilian agencies (Executive Order 13087). Some members of Congress sought to overturn this executive policy legislatively, but were unsuccessful.

Following the election of George W. Bush as President in the 2000 election, many gay rights advocates were concerned that he would rescind Executive Order 11478, but that didn't happen. And although President Bush has not been an advocate for gay rights, he has continued the practice of appointing openly gay men and lesbians to senior positions in his administration, including an ambassador and White House aides. Even position descriptions for positions in the Executive Office of the President include "sexual orientation" in the equal employment opportunity statement.[1]

CURRENT FEDERAL ACTIVITY

In 1995, a bill known as the Employment Non-Discrimination Act (ENDA) was introduced into the U.S. Congress. Beginning in 1974, Congressional supporters of equal rights for gay men and lesbians had simply tried to amend the Civil Rights

Act of 1964 to prohibit discrimination on the basis of sexual orientation. Gay activists changed strategies with the election of Bill Clinton and decided to focus exclusively on the issue of employment discrimination and developed ENDA as the legislative tool for doing so (Feldblum, 2000). The bill was reintroduced in each subsequent Congress with more sponsors each time (44 Senators and 181 Representatives in 2004). This bill would prohibit employment discrimination in the public and private sectors on the basis of sexual orientation in a manner similar to, but more restricted than, the way such discrimination is prohibited by the Civil Rights Acts of 1964 and 1991 for the categories of race, color, national origin, religion, and sex. In addition to exemptions for small employers and religious organizations that can be found in other civil rights laws, ENDA also includes some unique features designed to disarm potential critics, but of great importance to personnel managers who would be responsible for seeing that the law was followed in their organizations. First, the Act does not apply to the provision of employee benefits to an individual for the benefit of his or her partner, an issue discussed later in greater detail. Other sections of the proposed law forbid both the use of statistics to establish disparate impact as *prima facie* evidence of discrimination and establishment of quotas or preferential treatment for lesbians or gay men. Also, the law makes clear that the nondiscrimination requirement does not apply to the armed forces nor will it "repeal or modify any Federal, State, territorial, or local law creating special rights or preferences for veterans." The latter statement recognizes that the issue of veterans' preference, a policy employed by many government jurisdictions becomes problematic if the military is allowed to arbitrarily exclude lesbians and gay men. In *Personnel Administrator v. Feeney* (1979), the Court found that providing veteran's preference in employment decisions did not constitute illegal sex discrimination because women could join the military. Lesbians and gay men prohibited from serving in the armed forces will be unable to earn veterans' preference. Without this specific protection guaranteeing "special rights and preferences for veterans," a decision quite different from *Feeney* would be likely should the bill become law.

In the most recent controversies concerning ENDA, pressure has been brought to bear on those gay rights advocacy organizations lobbying most heavily for the law to include the phrase "gender identity" along with "sexual orientation" when talking about the bases for prohibiting discrimination. Concern that inclusion of "gender identity" in the bill's language will make it even more difficult to achieve passage has kept it out of the bill through 2004, although it appears that advocates may be ready to include it the next time the bill is introduced.

State and Local Government

Although no legal protections against discrimination based on sexual orientation have been enacted at the federal level, 140 local governments had passed laws or adopted personnel policies covering public employees by 1994 (Riccucci and Gossett, 1996) and over 200 local jurisdictions had such policies in place by 2005 (Cahill, 2005). By the end of January 2005, there were 15 states and the District of

Columbia with sexual orientation anti-discrimination laws, of which five states and D.C. also prohibited discrimination on the basis of gender identity. Another 11 states had executive orders issued by the governor protecting state employees from sexual orientation discrimination, of which three also included gender identity protection (Cahill, 2005).

The forms and types of discrimination against lesbian and gay male public employees historically practiced by the federal government were often repeated at the state levels, as well. Even the Congressional hearings of the 1950s attempting to root out homosexuals from federal service had their counterparts in state legislatures, the best known being the Johns Committee hearings in Florida in the 1960s (*Government versus Homosexuals*, 1975). However, because one consequence of American federalism is that the national and state levels of government have somewhat different responsibilities, the concerns of state and local governments about homosexuality were not exactly the same as the concerns of political leaders in Washington, D.C. Rather than using "national security" as the core element of an anti-homosexual campaign, state and local leaders focused on the issue of education and an alleged danger to children from lesbian and gay male teachers. As was true with fear of the national security risk, fear of teachers molesting or "recruiting" students was based less on evidence than on emotion. The articulation of specific fears about homosexual teachers is a development of the post-World War II era when courts began demanding that public employers show a "nexus" between an employee's behavior off duty and job performance. Courts were somewhat lenient in accepting evidence of a nexus when cases involved school board decisions to dismiss lesbian and gay male teachers, largely because of the traditional "role model" responsibilities of teachers and acceptance of the unsupported claim that homosexual teachers pose a danger to children (Harbeck, 1992; Rienzo, Button, & Wald, 1999). Although teachers were the primary focus of anti-gay discrimination at the state and local levels, the general negative climate affected employees in other types of jobs as well.

As indicated earlier, however, some state and local governments have decided to treat sexual orientation as a category similar to race, sex, and religion in laws prohibiting employment discrimination. Unlike the approach being used at the national level, however, most jurisdictions have not set about writing special legislation in the style of ENDA. Instead, where such laws have been adopted, the terms "sexual orientation," "sexual preference," or "affectional preference" and, in some cases, "gender identity" were simply added to the list of all protected categories in existing civil rights laws. The city first credited with adopting a sexual orientation nondiscrimination law was East Lansing, Michigan in 1972; the first territory was the District of Columbia in 1973; the first county was Santa Cruz, California in 1975; and the first state was Wisconsin in 1983 (Singer and Deschamps, 1994).

Although there is great variety in exactly what is covered by such laws, where they do exist, public employment, at a minimum, is covered. However, due to the nature of multiple types of governments found in American states, laws passed by one jurisdictional unit do not always apply to other overlapping jurisdictions. For example, although a city council may have passed a sexual orientation nondiscrimination ordinance, such a law may not apply to the employees of that town's school system, which is under the authority of a separately elected school board. Obviously, personnel specialists must be aware of whether the jurisdiction in which they work provides such protections in order to effectively perform their jobs. Several gay rights advocacy organizations maintain web-based listings of such localities including the Human Rights Campaign (www.hrc.org/), Lambda Legal Defense and Education Fund (www.lldef.org/), and the National Gay and Lesbian Task Force (www.ngltf.org/). The Transgender Law and Policy Institute maintains a similar list of employers who provide protections on the basis of gender identity (www.transgenderlaw.org/).

IMPLICATIONS OF NONDISCRIMINATION LAWS FOR PERSONNEL FUNCTIONS

If a jurisdiction adopts a law that prohibits discrimination on the basis of sexual orientation and/or gender identity—especially if that protection is achieved by adding the terms to the list of other criteria in existing laws rather than developed as a separate law similar to ENDA with a series of exceptions to the traditional interpretations of such laws—there are a number of corollary issues that must be faced by personnel administrators. These include issues involving recruitment, selection, and affirmative action; discrimination complaints; terminations; sexual harassment; diversity training; compensation and employee benefits; and several miscellaneous related tasks.

RECRUITMENT, SELECTION, AND AFFIRMATIVE ACTION

For many people, two of the most important contributions to personnel management coming out of the movements for civil rights for African Americans and women have been the focus on (1) expanding the number and variety of sources from which job applicants are recruited, and (2) improving personnel selection methods by insisting that jobs be carefully defined and that the methods for selecting people be validly related to identifying the necessary skills for each job. Expanded outreach helps organizations attract previously underutilized or overlooked talent while better selection tools are supposed to weed out "irrelevant" considerations such as race or sex or religion in determining whether a person was qualified for a particular job. In jurisdictions that prohibit sexual orientation discrimination, that characteristic is also to be treated as irrelevant.

As noted earlier, because the sexual orientation of a job applicant or an employee is not usually apparent, it is probable that most lesbians and gay men do not face the blatant discrimination faced historically and currently by persons of color and women. This is particularly true with respect to recruitment and access to job information since sexual orientation is a characteristic that overlays other demographic (and legally protected) characteristics such as race, ethnicity, sex, and religion. To the extent that information and recruitment activities are targeted toward one of those groups, many lesbian and gay men will receive the information as well. However, organizations that have historically discriminated against lesbians and gay men may find, just as agencies that discriminated against African Americans or women have found, that positive, specifically targeted, and sustained recruitment efforts are necessary to overcome the resistance to working for previously hostile organizations. Thus, police departments in some cities have set up recruitment booths at lesbian and gay male festival sites or established community liaisons to overcome negative perceptions earned after years of anti-gay harassment.

There are two specific situations in which discrimination against homosexuals may occur at the selection stage also. One is that popular stereotypes often associate certain physical and behavioral characteristics with homosexuality, for example men who exhibit mannerisms society views as feminine and women who exhibit mannerisms considered masculine. Such a person may or may not be a homosexual but is much more likely to face discrimination based on perceived sexual orientation than lesbians and gay men who exhibit socially defined gender-appropriate behaviors. While there are no federal court decisions specifically on this issue, the principle identifying gender stereotyping as a basis for employment decisions as illegal discrimination in *Price Waterhouse v. Hopkins* (1989) may become the basis for such claims (Harvard Law Review Association, 1989).

The second exception is for lesbians, gay men, and bisexuals who make known their sexual orientation to potential employers. For a variety of reasons, more and more lesbians and gay men and bisexuals are choosing to publicly identify their sexual orientation and do so in a variety of ways. Application forms provide a number of opportunities for people to reveal their sexual orientation. Perhaps the most obvious is when application forms ask about organizational memberships. Required listings of organizational memberships have been used by public employers to screen out certain job applicants (*Shelton v. Tucker*, 1960). Failure to list a particular organizational membership became grounds for dismissal on the basis of having submitted a fraudulent application. This Catch 22 scenario has been replicated with respect to the hiring of lesbians and gay men (*Acanfora v. Board of Education of Montgomery County*, 1974), although in the absence of a nondiscrimination law this method of identifying and discriminating against people may still be used.

A second feature of the application form that is relevant here is the marital status box. Many jurisdictions prohibit discrimination on the basis of marital status, but some do not, including several that prohibit discrimination on the basis of sexual orientation. Marriage is both a legal and a religious ceremony and, until 2004, no American jurisdictions legally recognized marriages between two people of the same sex,[2] although some religious denominations do perform such unions (Sherman, 1992; Sullivan, 1997). In any event, a person who considers him- or herself married to someone of the same sex, may very well choose to indicate that by checking the "Married" box on an application form as the most honest representation of his or her relationship status (*Shahar v. Bowers*, 1993). In a similar manner, lesbian and gay male employees may reveal their sexual orientation informally, though not inadvertently, in the course of an interview (Woods, 1993; McNaught, 1993).

The issue of affirmative action in the context of sexual orientation is somewhat more complex than it is in the case of race or gender. First, there is no reliable statistical way to determine whether lesbians and gay men are proportionally represented, overrepresented, or underrepresented in a particular type or level of a government job. This is not surprising given that there continues to be a dispute over what proportions of the total population should be classified as homosexual, bisexual, and heterosexual (Singer and Deschamps, 1994). And while there have been very few people calling for affirmative action programs similar to those in place for historically underrepresented groups, there have been regular calls by activists for the appointment of "openly gay" officials at the highest levels of each political jurisdiction.

Issues of recruitment and selection for transgendered persons share some similarities with and a few differences from those faced by gay men and lesbians. Again, an employer may or may not realize that he or she is interviewing or reviewing the application of a transgendered person. Depending on where a person is in the sexual reassignment program, a job applicant may still present physical features associated with the sex they were born with rather than the sex to which they are changing. Again, depending where the individual is in the process of change, various official documents, such as a driver's license, may not comport with the physical appearance of the job applicant. This may present a problem for the applicant when asked to respond to an item about their sex. Most would prefer to respond in terms of their gender identity rather than their biological sex, but in some states transgendered people may not change legal documents indicating their sex until surgery has been completed and other states do not allow any alteration to legal records that accurately characterized the person's sex at the time they were issued (e.g., a birth certificate). Job application forms usually request other names that a person may have used in order to complete background checks or follow up on references. Transgendered persons will often have both a male and a female legal name that might cause confusion, and possible discrimination by an employer.

Also, the number of transgendered persons in the United States is unknown and such information is not collected by any government agencies. Thus, while public employers who wish to specifically recruit the transgendered will find organizations that can help them reach such people, there is little concern about developing affirmative action programs. But again, publicly recognized transgendered public officials do serve as role models for others and some employers are concerned if their workforce does not include some visible representation of members of this group of people.

DISCRIMINATION COMPLAINTS

For most employees, bringing a complaint of discrimination to the attention of the appropriate authorities is not easy. Such a complaint formalizes a conflict by bringing in a third party, often from the personnel department in the form of an employee relations specialist or an equal employment opportunity officer. Employees who believe they are being treated in a discriminatory manner because of their race, gender, age, or disability must reach a point where the personal, psychic, and physical costs of the discriminatory behavior outweigh the costs of the tension in the work environment that are likely to result from filing a formal complaint. But for many lesbian and gay male employees, particularly those who have not discussed their sexual orientation in the workplace but who receive discriminatory treatment based on people's perceptions that they are gay, the decision also involves making a public record of their sexual orientation. This is an additional cost not usually borne by people for whom the discriminatory treatment is based on a visible characteristic such as skin color or gender or on a less visible, but also socially stigmatized, characteristic such as certain physical disabilities or religion. As a consequence, it is not surprising that even when jurisdictions adopt nondiscrimination laws that include sexual orientation, the use of such protective provisions is relatively low (Riccucci and Gossett, 1996; Button, Rienzo, and Wald, 1997). While several explanations are possible for the low number of complaints, the stigma still given to homosexuality in American society remains the most likely factor leading to reluctance to file a complaint.

Transgendered employees are also often subject to discrimination in the workplace. Far fewer workplaces provide protection from such discrimination than provide it for gay men and lesbians (Cahill, 2005) and the transgendered may be as reluctant as they are to file complaints. However, transgendered employees have found that the *Price Waterhouse* (1989) case has much more immediate relevance to them since by definition they are not acting in accordance with stereotypical expectations of their biological sex. This argument has successfully been used in the case of *Smith v. City of Salem* (2004). These cases can be made even in the absence of specific laws prohibiting discrimination against gender identity, because some courts have found that the discrimination is on the basis of sex as covered in Title VII of the 1964 Civil Rights Act.

An important difference, however, is determining what constitutes discrimination against the transgendered and this often comes down to some rather mundane issues of office policy. If there is a dress code, are transgendered persons required to dress in accordance with their biological sex or their gender identity? Which toilet facilities should a transgendered person use? Are there positions with bona fide occupational qualifications related to gender (e.g., a prison guard who conducts body searches) and how do those apply to transgendered employees? And if the employer makes a decision that is different from the decision the transgendered person would like to have made, is it discrimination? The response depends on where the actions took place (Harris and Minter, 2002).

In the past few decades, as noted earlier, the courts have been forcing public employers to demonstrate how any particular off-duty behavior has an impact on the job performance of an individual employee before using that off-duty behavior as justification for a termination of employment. At the federal level, *Norton v. Macy* (1969) was the first case involving homosexual activity to apply this standard in a way that overturned the agency's decision to terminate. Although this standard is now fairly well-entrenched, application of the standard does not automatically lead to a finding of no relationship between sexual orientation (or a related aspect, such as a declaration of sexual orientation) and the requirements of a particular job. Several cases, for example, *Singer v. United States Civil Service Commission*, 1976, and *Shahar v. Bowers*, 1995, have found that an individual could be denied a job because of some factor closely related to his or her sexual orientation. With the decision in the *Lawrence* case, however, such cases are much less likely to find the courts upholding the denials or terminations of employment.

Sexual Harassment

The distinction that courts make between *quid pro quo* sexual harassment and harassment created by a "hostile environment" is proving to be particularly important to lesbians and gay men as the federal courts develop case law in this area. In *Oncale v. Sundowner Offshore Services* (1998), the U.S. Supreme Court unanimously found that Title VII of the Civil Rights Acts of 1964 and 1991 included protection against being sexually harassed by a person of the same sex. Previously, lower courts had been divided with some saying same-sex sexual harassment was not covered, some saying it was covered only if the harasser were a homosexual, and others saying that the issue was the sexual nature of the harassment regardless of the orientation of the harasser (Turner, 2000; Paetzold, 1999). The *Oncale* case was ultimately settled out of court, so whether the alleged victim could have established that he had been harassed in violation of Title VII was not finally decided.

Even though the Supreme Court has made clear that same-sex sexual harassment is possible, federal courts have been equally clear that the discrimination must be on the basis of sex and not the sexual orientation of the victim (Zalesne, 2001). Specific claims of sexual orientation discrimination in the U.S. Postal Service were rejected by the U.S. Court of Appeals (*Simonton v. Runyon*, 2000). Applying the principle from *Price Waterhouse*, however, a different U.S. Court of Appeals has found that sex stereotyping of male appearances and behaviors may have led to the sexual harassment of a summer youth employee (he wore an earring) in a municipal public works program (*Doe v. City of Belleville*, 1997). On the other hand, establishing that the person accused of sexually harassing someone of the same sex was a homosexual could be used to support a charge of sexual harassment in such cases (Zalesne, 2001).

In what many consider a rather bizarre twist, federal courts have created what amounts to a "bisexual safe harbor" when the person accused of harassment harasses men and women equally, or, in the words of the court, the victims are subject to an "equal opportunity harasser" (*Holman v. Indiana*, 2000). The reasoning is that because both sexes suffer ill treatment there is no discrimination against one sex or the other, hence no violation of Title VII. It should be noted, however, that discrimination *against* an employee because of his or her bisexuality is not prohibited by Title VII (Colker, 1993).

Some state and local governments prohibit discrimination in employment based on sexual orientation and gender identity, however, and state courts are making different decisions because, if sexual orientation or gender identity discrimination is prohibited and if creation of a hostile environment is a form of discrimination, then an anti-gay or anti-transgendered hostile environment would not be defensible (*Murray v. Oceanside Unified School District*, 2000). Similarly, New York state courts have interpreted the term "sex" more broadly than have the federal courts and found that transgendered employees who are harassed are protected by state nondiscrimination laws, even when they don't specifically mention gender identity (*Maffei v. Kolaeton Industry*, 1995).

COMPENSATION AND EMPLOYEE BENEFITS

Government entities, like private businesses, are governed by the Equal Pay Act of 1963. Lesbians, gay men, bisexuals, and the transgendered are not paid different wages or salaries based specifically on their sexual orientation or gender identity, though there is some evidence that earnings of gay men are somewhat lower than comparable heterosexual men in society at large (Badgett, 1995). Of more immediate relevance, however, is the fact that the concept of "compensation" has, in recent years been broadened beyond the idea of base pay and take-home pay to an idea called "total compensation" (McCaffery, 1992). Total compensation attempts to recognize that the value an employee receives from his or her employer in exchange for work includes more than just wages and salary, but a variety of monetary and non-monetary benefits as well. While thirty or forty years ago, such benefits made up a relatively small proportion of total payroll expenses, by the 1980s, such benefits comprised up to 40 percent of payroll costs (Gossett, 1994). Unlike actual wages and salaries, however, many employers distribute benefits of different value to different types of employees. The most common distinction made that results in differential benefit treatment is between married and unmarried employees. While technically this is a distinction between single and married employees, the fact that gay male and lesbian employees are prohibited in most states from marrying a same-sex partner whom they see as the equivalent of a legal spouse, makes this an issue of particular concern to them. Differences in treatment can be seen in a wide variety of benefits including sick leave, bereavement leave, life insurance, health insurance, disability compensation, and retirement benefits.

Leave benefits are important because they usually include allowances for an employee to take leave to care for an ill family member or to attend the funeral of a deceased family member. "Family member," however, is usually defined as a blood relative or someone related by marriage. Even when lesbian and gay male employees are willing to make known to their employers that they are in a relationship with someone of the same sex, a person who is their family, existing rules generally do not enable an employee to take leave to care for or grieve for such partners (or the children or the parents of such partners). Employee life insurance programs many times permit employees to purchase additional group coverage on the lives of their spouses and children, a benefit denied to unmarried employees. Disability (or workers') compensation in some jurisdictions provides different levels of benefits for employees with a spouse and/or dependent children than it provides for "single" employees. And pension programs, particularly defined benefit programs, usually include an option for an employee to elect a reduced annuity in order to provide a survivor's annuity for his or her spouse or minor children, another benefit denied to unmarried employees except in unusual circumstances (District of Columbia, 1990).[3]

For gay male and lesbian activists, equal access to health benefits for the same-sex partners of homosexual employees is often sought once legal protection against employment discrimination has been obtained. In the United States, access to health insurance for adults is, for all practical purposes, tied to employment. Most government employers offer their permanent employees the opportunity to purchase subsidized health insurance for themselves and for certain members of their family, namely their legal spouse and their own minor children and any minor children of their spouse. Given that employers may subsidize family health benefit plans at a higher dollar value (even if it is at the same percentage rate of the premium cost) than the subsidy given to single employees, an argument can be made that single and married employees are receiving unequal pay for equal work. More common, however, are complaints that the partners of heterosexual employees are being treated differently from the partners of homosexual employees. Technically, however, courts and human relations commissions that receive such complaints in a formal manner usually rule that the distinction made is not on the basis of sexual orientation but on the basis of marital status. That is, the difference in treatment is not because the employee is homosexual, but because he or she is not legally married to his or her partner; the fact that the law prevents the homosexual partners from marrying is not a concern of the employer (Riccucci and Gossett, 1996). An exception to this trend occurred in Oregon where state courts found that the denial of health benefit coverage for the domestic partners of gay men and lesbian state employees violated the state constitution's guarantee of equal treatment of all citizens (*Tanner v. Oregon Health Sciences University*, 1998).

In addition to seeking redress through the legal system, lesbians and gay men have also used the political process to secure such benefits. In many local governments (municipalities, counties, school boards, special districts), laws have been passed, collective bargaining agreements negotiated, or executive orders issued that provide for access to health benefits and various leave benefits by employees with same-sex partners on the same or similar terms available to employees who have opposite-sex partners (Gossett, 1994). These programs are usually referred to as "domestic partnership" benefit programs. Opposition to such programs often turns on the fear of significant increases in costs to the employer, although in practice cost increases have been very limited (Hostetler and Pynes, 1995; Badgett, 2000).

Although most of the jurisdictions adopting the domestic partnership benefit programs treat unmarried opposite-sex partnerships the same way that they treat same-sex partnerships, a few have proposed limiting access to benefits only to same-sex partners on the theory that opposite-sex partners have the option of marriage while same-sex partners do not. Private corporations that offer domestic partnership benefits to their employees often limit such benefits to only same-sex couples. While there is some logic in this latter position, a public entity that adopts it is open to criticism as discriminating against heterosexuals and creating "special rights" for homosexuals alone. Of course, this argument can be countered by saying that this different treatment is only offered because civil marriage is a "special right" available only to opposite-sex partners (Horne, 1994; Donovan, 1998). As the number of private-sector companies offering such benefits increases, whether a public-sector employer offers them may also become an issue in the competition for the best employees (Herrschaft, 2000).

In recent developments, following the decision to allow same-sex marriages in Massachusetts, employers in that state are wrestling with the question of whether to continue providing benefits to domestic partners who choose not to marry or to require that any couple, opposite sex or same sex, must be married in order to receive benefits. While a decision to condition benefits solely on marriage may seem reasonable in these circumstances, others have pointed out that the decision to marry may not be practical for all same-sex couples since a variety of federal laws and rules might disadvantage them in a way that heterosexual couples are not disadvantaged. For example, the military career of someone who married a partner of the same sex would most likely be ended, which would not be the case for a soldier or sailor who married someone of the opposite sex. Also, not all employees in an organization necessarily live in a state that allows same-sex couples to marry and currently Massachusetts does not allow non-residents to marry (Blanton, 2004).

There is one benefits issue that is of special concern to transgendered employees. Such employees often have extensive and expensive medical needs as a result of their transgendered status and many employer-sponsored health plans have excluded coverage for the psychological, medical, surgical, and prescription services needed. San Francisco gained a great deal of attention when, in 2002, in response to a recommendation of its Human Rights Commission, it specifically incorporated into its health plan the medical benefits needed by transgendered employees (Gordon, 2001).

DIVERSITY TRAINING

In recognition of the changing composition of the American workforce, a number of employers, public as well as private, have begun to focus on ways of utilizing workforce diversity to facilitate achievement of the organization's goals. "Diversity training" is one approach that employers take to teach workers and supervisors to deal with cultural and value differences among their co-workers and subordinates. Such training hopes to eliminate dysfunctional friction at the worksite and to train supervisors to recognize, avoid, or properly handle discriminatory treatment so as to minimize legal actions against the employer. Sexual orientation and gender identity, however, are topics ignored in many discussions of diversity (Cox, 1993; Caudron, 1995).

In organizations governed by laws or policies that prohibit discrimination on the basis of sexual orientation and/or gender identity, inclusion of these issues in diversity training courses flows naturally from the official policy. This does not mean, however, that sexual orientation or gender identity will be a particularly comfortable or easy topic to address in such training. When there is no protection against discrimination, handling these issues can be quite explosive and even threatening given that self-revelation by lesbians, gay men, bisexuals, or the transgendered may lead to dismissal or harassment. On the other hand, avoiding the topic may defeat the purpose of much diversity training that is aimed at making people tolerant and understanding of important differences among co-workers which, in turn, builds trust and facilitates the work of the organization (McNaught, 1993; Winfeld and Spielman, 1995; Zuckerman and Simons, 1996).

OTHER ISSUES

Personnel offices are frequently assigned responsibility for addressing a variety of other workplace-related issues in addition to the core personnel functions. Many of these tasks can be grouped under the very broad heading "Quality of Work Life" (QWL). The presence of lesbian, gay male, and bisexual employees in the workforce is not often addressed in the existing QWL literature, but personnel officials who wish to ensure inclusive work environments need to be aware of how certain actions affect non-heterosexual employees.

Lesbians and gay men are often accused of "flaunting" their sexuality whenever it becomes known to other workers; they have violated the presumption of heterosexuality that pervades most organizations. Whether the employee simply made a statement about his or her sexual orientation, discussed his or her social activities over the weekend, displayed a picture of his or her family on the desk, or appeared at an office function with the person he or she lives with, many employees are scandalized and find such behavior inappropriate in a work setting. Yet, if any of these situations had involved a heterosexual employee, no notice would have been taken. If the organization is committed to equal treatment regardless of sexual orientation, managers and their advisers in the personnel office must be able to distinguish unacceptable behavior from unexpected behavior. Standards concerning appropriate levels of discussion or knowledge about an individual's life outside the office need to be consistent, although, of course, every employee is entitled to determine the amount of personal information shared for him- or herself.

"Celebrating diversity" is a somewhat recent addition to the responsibilities of the personnel office and is considered part of maintaining organizational morale. In the public sector, events such as Black History Month may be even more important than in the private sector because they also reinforce the idea that the government is there to serve all of the people. Activists are working to establish a "Gay, Lesbian, and Bisexual History Month" in October (Jennings, 1994). For the past several years, October 11 has been celebrated as "Coming Out Day" when lesbians, gay men, and bisexual people are encouraged to identify themselves in some way to their families, friends, and co-workers (www.hrc.org/ncop/). Late June is traditionally the time for Gay Pride celebrations. Again, to the extent that personnel offices are responsible for making all employees feel that the organization respects and values the contributions any group makes, they must be knowledgeable about events and times of the year that have special meaning to each particular group.

Employee recognition is often an important part of an organization's traditions. Annual award dinners, employee appreciation picnics and parties, holiday parties, and other similar activities frequently fall to the personnel office to organize. Many times these events are designed to include family members in appreciation of the important role that family life plays in support of the productivity of each worker. Invitations to "husbands" and "wives" are likely viewed as limited to only legally married partners of employees; more inclusive invitations to "your guest" or "your partner" will indicate that the partners and family members of lesbian and gay male employees are welcome.

Occupational safety and health is another responsibility often assigned to the personnel office. Although there are no occupational injuries or diseases that are unique to lesbian and gay male employees, the public association of Acquired Immune Deficiency Syndrome (AIDS) with gay men has created a volatile workplace issue that must be addressed by personnel officers. (See Chapter 7 in this volume.) Effective education about how AIDS is and is not transmitted has become one of the most important occupational safety issues during the last ten years.

A related, but important health issue for transgendered employees concerns access to proper toilet facilities while on the job. This is one of the first issues raised by co-workers of a transgendered person and one that managers have to resolve immediately in order to prevent unnecessary disruptions in the workplace. Most transgendered employees would prefer to use the restroom facilities consistent with their gender identity, but non-transgendered employees are often extremely uncomfortable in such situations (Smith, 2003; *Goins v. West Group*, 2001). Some employers have resolved this dilemma by designating at least one facility as a "unisex" facility, a practice that is not uncommon in very small offices even when there are no transgendered employees.

Many organizations have anti-nepotism provisions in their personnel policies and the question of how these policies apply to lesbian and gay male partners who work for the same organization presents a quandary. In organizations that provide for the registration of domestic partners and treat such partnerships in a manner similar to the way marital partnerships are treated with respect to employee benefits, for example, application of anti-nepotism rules to homosexual partners would seem to be appropriate. But if the organization does not recognize such partnerships in any other way, "legitimizing" the relationship through the application of anti-nepotism rules would undercut the rationale for not recognizing the partners for other purposes.

CONCLUSION

Public-sector organizations in the new century have three options available for addressing issues pertaining to lesbians, gay men, bisexuals, and the transgendered who currently, or may potentially, work for them. Historically, government agencies actively sought to identify and remove such employees; to some extent, this is still the policy of the United States military. A second option is to simply ignore the fact that the organization has non-heterosexual employees and trans-gendered employees and omit these issues from personnel policies or practices. This probably describes the current situation in most public-sector organizations. Finally, governments can choose to recognize, appreciate, and attempt to find advantages in the diversity of sexual orientations and gender identities to be found in its workforce. A small, but increasing, proportion of the 83,000 govern-mental units found in the United States have chosen this strategy. Though only a few cities and counties have adopted this approach, those that have include some of the country's largest municipal jurisdictions so, in practical effect, many public employees work in places that officially forbid discrimination on the basis of sexual orientation and/or gender identity (van der Meide, 2000; Cahill, 2005).

Regardless of which strategy any particular organization currently applies to the issue of sexual orientation and the workplace, the pressures for a policy change will confront every public-sector organization in the next few years. Whether it is to remove a policy of automatic exclusion of homosexuals as in the military, or to provide the protection of a nondiscrimination law, or to treat domestic partnerships in the same way that marriages are treated for employee benefits, or to make health benefit plans inclusive of the services needed by trans-gendered employees, the demands for change are unlikely to subside.

NOTES

1. See, e.g., www.whitehouse.gov/oa/jobs/OA-03-33-RM_PersAsst_bob_.pdf
2. In 2003 (*Goodridge v. Department of Public Health*), the highest state court of Massachu-setts found that there was no state constitutional basis for denying marriage rights and benefits to two people just because they were the same sex. In 2000 (*Baker v. State of Vermont*), the Vermont Supreme Court ruled that same-sex couples should be eligible to receive the same state-provided benefits available to opposite-sex couples.
3. The federal Civil Service Retirement System, for example, allows an unmarried employee to show that a third party is financially dependent on the retiree and provision for a sur-vivor annuity can be made for that person. However, if the employee died before actually retiring, such a dependent third party, unlike a spouse and/or minor children, would not be eligible for an annuity. There is no requirement that spouses or children actually be financially dependent on the retiree in order to receive a survivor's annuity.

REFERENCES

Able v. United States. 1998. 155 F. 3d 628; 1998 U.S. App. LEXIS 23359.
Acanfora v. Board of Education of Montgomery County. 1974. 491 F. 2d 498.
American Psychiatric Association. 2000. *Diagnostic and Statistical Manual of Mental Disorders*. 4th ed. Arlington, VA: American Psychiatric Association.

Aspin, L. 1993. Memorandum to Secretaries of the Army, Navy, Air Force, and Chairman of the Joint Chiefs of Staff, July 19.

Badgett, M.V. L. 1995. "The Wage Effects of Sexual Orientation Discrimination." *Industrial & Labor Relations Review* 48:4: 726–739.

Badgett, M.V. L. 2000. "Calculating Costs with Credibility: Health Care Benefits for Domestic Partners." *Angles: Journal of the Institute for Gay and Lesbian Strategic Studies* 5:1: 1–8. www.iglss.org/media/files/Angles_51.pdf.

Baker v. State of Vermont. 2000. 170 Vt. 194.

Bayer, R. 1987. *Homosexuality and American Psychiatry: The Politics of Diagnosis.* Princeton, NJ: Princeton University Press.

Berube, A. 1990. *Coming Out Under Fire: The History of Gay Men and Women in World War Two.* New York, NY: Penguin Books.

Blanton, K. 2004. "Benefits for Domestic Partners Maintained." *Boston Globe.* August 22.

Bornstein, K. 1995. *Gender Outlaw: On Men, Women, and the Rest of Us.* New York, NY Vintage Books.

Burr, C. 1993. "Homosexuality and Biology." *The Atlantic Monthly*, March: 47–65.

Button, J. W., Rienzo, B. A., and Wald, K. D. 1997. *Private Lives, Public Choices: Battles Over Gay Rights in American Communities.* Washington, DC: Congressional Quarterly Press.

Cahill, S. 2005. *The Glass Nearly Half Full.* Washington, DC: The National Gay and Lesbian Task Force Policy Institute. www.thetaskforce.org/downloads/GlassHalfFull.pdf.

Califia, P. 1997. *Sex Changes: The Politics of Transgenderism.* San Francisco, CA: Cleis Press.

Caudron, S. 1995. "Open the Corporate Closet to Sexual Orientation Issues." *Personnel Journal* 74: August: 42–55.

Chibbaro, Jr., L. 1993. "Sodomy Law Repealed." *The Washington Blade* [Washington, DC], September 17, p. 1+.

Chibbaro, Jr., L. 1995. "Clinton: Being Gay Is 'Not a Security Risk'." *The Washington Blade* [Washington, DC], August 4, p. 1+.

Colker, R. 1993. "A Bisexual Jurisprudence." *Law & Sexuality* 3: 127–137.

Cox, Jr., T. 1993. *Cultural Diversity in Organizations: Theory, Research & Practice.* San Francisco, CA: Barrett-Koehler Publishers.

Currah, P. and Minter, S. 2000. *Transgender Equality.* Washington, DC: National Gay and Lesbian Task Force. www.thetaskforce.org/downloads/transeq.pdftranseq.pdf.

D'Amico, F. 2000. "Sexuality and Military Service." In C. A. Rimmerman, K. D. Wald, and C. Wilcox, eds. *The Politics of Gay Rights.* Chicago, IL: University of Chicago Press.

District of Columbia. 1990. "Human Resources Policy."

Doe v. City of Belleville. 1997. 119 F. 3d 563; 1997 U.S. App. LEXIS 17940.

Donovan, J. M. 1998. "An Ethical Argument to Restrict Domestic Partnerships to Same-Sex Couples." *Law & Sexuality* 8: 649–670.

Duberman, M. 1993. *Stonewall.* New York, NY: Dutton.

Dyer, K., ed. 1990. *Gays in Uniform: The Pentagon's Secret Reports.* Boston, MA: Alyson Publications.

Enriquez v. West Jersey Health Systems. 2001. 342 N.J. Super. 501; 777 A.2d 365; 2001 N.J. Super. LEXIS 283.

Feldblum, C. 2000. "The Federal Gay Rights Bill: From Bella to ENDA." In J. D'Emilio, W. B. Turner, and U. Vaid, eds. *Creating Change: Sexuality, Public Policy and Civil Rights.* New York, NY: St. Martin's Press.

Garber, M. 1992. *Vested Interests: Cross-Dressing and Cultural Anxiety.* New York, NY: HarperPerennial.

Goins v. West Group. 2001. 635 N.W.2d 717; 2001 Minn. LEXIS 789.

Gordon, R. 2001. "S.F. to Finance Staff Sex Changes." *San Francisco Chronicle* May 1, p. A1.

Goodridge v. Department of Public Health. 2003. 440 Mass. 309.

Gossett, C. W. 1994. "Domestic Partnership Benefits: Public Sector Patterns." *Review of Public Personnel Administration* 14 Winter: 64–84.

Government versus Homosexuals. 1975. New York, NY: Arno Press.

Green, J. 2000. "Introduction to Transgender Issues." In P. Currah and S. Minter. *Transgender Equality.* New York, NY: National Gay and Lesbian Task Force.

Harbeck, K. M. 1992. "Gay and Lesbian Educators: Past History/Future Prospects." In K. M. Harbeck, ed. *Coming Out of the Classroom Closet.* New York, NY: Harrington Park Press, pp. 121–140.

Hamer, D. and Copeland, P. 1994. *The Science of Desire.* New York, NY: Simon and Schuster.

Harris, S. I. and Minter, S. 2002. "Employment Rights for Transgendered People." *Bay Area Reporter*, July 11. www.las-elc.org/arch-020711-transgender.html.

Harvard Law Review Association (Editors). 1989. *Sexual Orientation and the Law.* Cambridge, MA: Harvard University Press.

Herrschaft, D. 2000. "A Trend Towards Fairness." *HRC Quarterly* Winter: 16–17.

Holman v. Indiana. 2000. 211 F. 3d 399; U.S. App. LEXIS 8532.

Horne, P. S. 1994. "Challenging Public- and Private-Sector Schemes Which Discriminate against Unmarried Opposite-Sex and Same-Sex Partners." *Law & Sexuality* 4: 35–52.

Hostetler, D. and Pynes, J. E. 1995. "Domestic Partnership Benefits: Dispelling the Myths." *Review of Public Personnel Administration* 15:Winter: 41–59.

Human Rights Campaign. 2000. Worknet-Discrimination-State and Local Governments. www.hrc.org/.

Jennings, K. 1994. "Why We Need a Lesbian and Gay History Month." *TWN* [Miami, FL], October 19, p. 6.

Johnson, D. K. 2004. *The Lavender Scare: The Cold War Persecution of Gays and Lesbians in the Federal Government.* Chicago, IL: University of Chicago Press.

Katz, J. N. 1995. *The Invention of Heterosexuality.* New York, NY: Dutton.

Katz, J. N. 1992. *Gay American History: Lesbians and Gay Men in the U.S.A.* Revised Edition. New York: Meridian.

Kauth, M. R. and Landis, D. 1996. "Applying Lessons Learned from Minority Integration in the Military." In G. M. Herek, J. B. Jobe, and R. M. Carney, eds. *Out in Force: Sexual Orientation and the Military.* Chicago, IL: University of Chicago Press.

Keen, L. 1992. "Military History: Blueprint for Bias." *The Washington Blade* [Washington, DC], December 11, p. 1+.

Keen, L. 1995. "Despite Setbacks, Sodomy Law Challenges 'on a Roll.'" *The Washington Blade* [Washington, DC], June 30, p. 1+.

Lawrence v. Texas. 2003. 539 U.S. 558.

Lehring, G. L. 2003. *Officially Gay: The Political Construction of Sexuality by the U.S. Military.* Philadelphia, PA: Temple University Press.

LeVay, S. 1993. *The Sexual Brain.* Cambridge, MA: MIT Press.

Lewis, G. B. 1997. "Lifting the Ban on Gays in the Civil Service: Federal Policy Towards Gay and Lesbian Employees since the Cold War." *Public Administration Review* 57:5: 387–395.

Lewis, G. B. 2001. "Barriers to Security Clearances for Gay Men and Lesbians: Fear of Blackmail or Fear of Homosexuals?" *Journal of Public Administration Research and Theory* 11:4: 539–557.

McCaffery, R. M. 1992. *Employee Benefit Programs: A Total Compensation Perspective,* 2nd ed. Boston: PWS-Kent Publishing Company.

McNaught, B. 1993. *Gay Issues in the Workplace*. New York, NY: St. Martin's Press.

Maffei v. Kolaeton Industry. 1995. 164 Misc. 2d 547; 626 N.Y.S.2d 391; 1995 N.Y. Misc. LEXIS 115.

Meyer, L. D. 1996. *Creating GI Jane: Sexuality and Power in the Women's Army Corps During WW I*. New York, NY: Columbia University Press.

Murray v. Oceanside Unified School District. 2000. 79 Cal. App. 4th 1338; 2000 Cal. Appl LEXIS 298.

Nice, D. C. 1994. *Policy Innovation in State Government*. Ames, IA: Iowa State University Press.

Norton V. Macy. 1969. 417 F. 2d 1161.

Oncale v. Sundowner Offshore Services. 1998. 479 U.S. 806.

Paetzold, R. 1999. "Same-Sex Sexual Harassment Revisited." *Employee Rights and Employment Policy Journal* 3: 251.

Personnel Administrator v. Feeney. 1979. 422 U.S. 256.

Price Waterhouse v. Hopkins. 1989. 490 U.S. 228, 104 L. Ed. 2d 268, 109 S. Ct. 1775.

Riccucci, N. M. and Gossett, C. W. 1996. "Employment Discrimination in State and Local Government: The Lesbian and Gay Male Experience." *American Review of Public Administration* 26:2: 175–200.

Rienzo, B. A., Button, J. W., and Wald, K. D. 1999. "Conflicts over Sexual Orientation Issues in the Schools." In E. B. Sharp. *Culture Wars & Local Politics*. Lawrence, KS: University Press of Kansas.

Shahar v. Bowers. 1993. 836 F. Supp. 869.

Shahar v. Bowers. 1995. 70 F. 3d 1218.

Shelton v. Tucker. 1960. 364 U.S. 479.

Sherman, S., ed. 1992. *Lesbian and Gay Marriage*. Philadelphia, PA: Temple University Press.

Shilts, R. 1993. *Conduct Unbecoming: Lesbians and Gays in the U.S. Military: Vietnam to the Persian Gulf*. New York, NY: St. Martin's Press.

Simonton v. Runyon. 2000. 232 F. 3d 33; 2000 U.S. App. LEXIS 21139.

Singer v. United States Civil Service Commission. 1976. 530 F.2d 247; *vacated*, 429 U.S. 1034.

Singer, B. L. and Deschamps, D., eds. 1994. *Gay and Lesbian Stats: A Pocket Guide to Facts and Figures*. New York, NY: The New Press.

Smith v. City of Salem. 2004. 378 F.3d 566; 2004 U.S. App. LEXIS 16114. (Amended Opinion)

Smith, J. 2003. "Employee Sues over Transgender Bathroom Use." *Southern Voice*. July 4. www.sovo.com/2003/7-4/news/localnews/transbath.cfm.

Stewart, W. 1995. *Cassell's Queer Companion*. New York, NY: Cassell.

Sullivan, A. Ed. 1997. *Same Sex Marriage: Pro and Con*. New York, NY: Vintage Books.

Tanner v. Oregon Health Sciences University. 1998. 157 Ore. App. 502; 971 P.2d 435; 1998 Ore. App. LEXIS 2183.

Turner, R. 2000. "The Unenvisaged Case, Interpretive Progression, and Justiciability of Title VII Same-Sex Sexual Harassment Claims." *Duke Journal of Gender Law and Policy* 7: 57.

van der Meide, W. 2000. *Legislating Equality*. New York, NY: National Gay and Lesbian Task Force.

Winfeld, L. and Spielman, S. 1995. *Straight Talk about Gays in the Workplace*. New York, NY: American Management Association.

Wolinsky, M. and Sherrill, K. 1993. *Gays and the Military: Joseph Steffan versus the United States*. Princeton, NJ: Princeton University Press.

Woods, J. D. 1993. *The Corporate Closet*. New York, NY: The Free Press.

Zalesne, D. 2001. "When Your Harasser Is Another Man." *The Gay and Lesbian Review* 8:1: 19–21.

Zuckerman, A. J. and Simons, G. F. 1996. *Sexual Orientation in the Workplace*. Thousand Oaks, CA: Sage Publications.

Chapter 7

Chronic Health Challenges and the Public Workplace

James D. Slack

In both the public and private sectors, the American workplace currently faces two kinds of health care challenges.[1] The first kind can be described as "acute," and these include routine health issues such as colds and influenza as well as such reparable damages to the body as broken bones, ergonomics, and migraine headaches. Although acute health issues are problematic, chronic health issues represent far greater challenges to the workplace. The chronic health issues include long-term and reoccurring health conditions that, in many cases, are either irreparable or terminal. These include physical impairments such as cancers, dysfunctional organs, and paralysis, as well as such mental impairments as depressive disorders, schizophrenia, and anxiety disorders.

Because chronic health issues do not always present a healing remedy, they tend to place a greater burden on the organization's benefit package. They also require greater investments in thought and resources in finding remedies to the resulting disruption to the workflow. Moreover, the challenge of chronic health issues is that management must find ways to protect the workplace rights of affected employees as well as maintain the collective health rights of the entire workforce. As a result, chronic health issues tend to be subject to increasing litigation and this represents the greatest cost to the workplace. This chapter focuses on what public personnel managers need to know about the challenges surrounding chronic health issues that affect the workplace.

THE COST OF POOR HEALTH IN THE AMERICAN WORKPLACE

As a result of government regulations and oversight, the American workplace remains reasonably safe. In 2003, "only" 5,027 private-sector employees and "only" 532 civilian public-sector employees died as a result of workplace accidents. Of the fatalities in the public workplace, 98 were federal employees, 102 were state employees, and 332 were county and municipal employees (U.S. Department of Labor, Sept. 14, 2004). The rate of fatalities (per 100,000 workers) between 1992 and 2002 fell from 5.5 to 4.2, in the private sector, and from 3.7 to 2.7 in the public sector (U.S. Department of Labor, 2004).

In both the public and private sectors, however, the human resource cost of poor health is vast and growing. Between 1991 and 2004, the health insurance cost for compensation per employee increased from $15.40 to $23.29. State and local governments experienced the highest costs for health insurance compensation per employee during this time, increasing from $22.31 to $34.21 (U.S. Department of Health and Human Services, September 2004). As shown in Table 7.1, productivity costs associated with chronic health conditions are approaching one-half trillion dollars annually. Moreover, the annual productivity costs arising from chronic risk factors are also staggering: $80 billion from smoking; $76 billion from physical inactivity; $9 billion from poor nutrition (U.S. Department of Health and Human Services, 2003).

Obesity, as defined by greater than 30 percent body fat (or approximately 30 pounds overweight) is one catalyst to a variety of chronic illnesses, including hypertension, heart disease, diabetes, and arthritis. It can also lead to, and be symptomatic of, mental health problems. According to the Centers for Disease Control and Prevention (2005), 34 percent of American adults are overweight and another 30 percent are obese. Table 7.2 demonstrates that the threat of obesity to the American worker exists regardless of geographic variation.

While estimates vary, workplace costs associated with chronic mental health issues are staggering. Peter Greenberg et al. (2003) estimates that poor health taxes the American workplace by approximately $52 billion annually, including over

TABLE 7.1 Productivity Costs of Selected Diseases, 2003

Disease	Costs (in $billions)
cardiovascular disease/stroke	$142.5
cancer	$110.7
arthritis	$ 60.0
obesity	$ 56.0
diabetes	$ 39.8

SOURCE: U.S. Department of Health and Human Services, Centers for Disease Control and Prevention, "The Power of Prevention." April 2003.

TABLE 7.2   Average Body Fat by State

< 10%	10–14.9%	15–19.9%		>20%	
none	Colorado	Arizona	California	Alabama	Alaska
		Connecticut	Delaware	Arkansas	Georgia
		Florida	Hawaii	Illinois	Indiana
		Idaho	Maine	Iowa	Kansas
		Maryland	Mass.	Kentucky	Louisiana
		Minnesota	Montana	Michigan	Mississippi
		New Hampshire		Missouri	Nebraska
		New Jersey	New Mexico	No. Carolina	Ohio
		New York	Nevada	Oregon	Pennsylvania
		No. Dakota	Oklahoma	So. Carolina	Tennessee
		Rhode Island	So. Dakota	Texas	
		Utah	Virginia		
		Vermont	Washington		
		Wisconsin	Wyoming		

SOURCE: U.S. Department of Health and Human Services, Centers for Disease Control and Prevention, "The Power of Prevention." April 2003.

$36 billion in absenteeism. The National Mental Health Association (2005) estimates the cost of absenteeism at $43.7 billion, and the University of Michigan Health System's Depression Center estimates absenteeism at $52 billion (Carli, 2004).

Other costs are also associated with chronic mental health challenges. The National Mental Health Association (2005) estimates that more than 200 million sick days per year are consumed by mental health symptoms, and that nearly 75 percent of workers experiencing mental health challenges are women. Surveys conducted by the Depression Center at the University of Michigan Health System (Carli, 2004) indicate that over 80 percent of employees suffering from depression lack motivation and have difficulty in concentration, while nearly one in four experience chronic physical pain. According to Greenberg et al. (2003), these symptoms exacerbate the costly phenomenon of "presenteeism"—being present at work but not fully functional—by more than $15 billion annually.

CHRONIC HEALTH CONDITIONS AMONG AMERICAN EMPLOYEES

Chronic health conditions are disabilities. In the United States and other developed countries, they are caused by a wide variety of physical and mental factors as well as by adverse behavioral patterns. Although chronic health conditions have a direct impact on the ability to work, the top causes of disabilities do not stem necessarily from workplace accidents or workplace conditions but from the

TABLE 7.3 Most Common Causes of Disabilities in the United States

Ranking	Cause of Disability
1	arthritis or rheumatism
2	back or spine problems
3	heart disease
4	lung or respiratory problems
5	deafness or hearing
6	limb/extremity stiffness
7	mental or emotional problems
8	diabetes
9	vision problems
10	stroke

SOURCE: U.S. Department of Health and Human Services, Centers for Disease Control and Prevention, "The Power of Prevention." April 2003 (www.nimh.nih.gov).

employee's personal environment. The most common causes for disabilities are reported in Table 7.3.

In the United States, there are more than 86 million disabled persons—31 percent of the total population. According to the U.S. Centers for Disease Control and Prevention (2001), there are approximately 42 million people with physical impairments. More than 7 million use assistive technology devices (ATD) because of mobility impairments, and almost five million use ATDs for orthopedic impairments. Although younger workers can develop chronic diseases, Table 7.4 reports that these illnesses are much more prevalent in more mature employees. Table 7.5 reports that these disabilities significantly affect both men and women, as well as European and African Americans.

The National Institute of Mental Health (2005) estimates that approximately 22 percent of adult Americans suffer from at least one form of mental impairment.[2] Within this total, 13.3 percent suffer from anxiety disorders, 5.4 percent suffer

TABLE 7.4 Percentage of Selected Chronic Diseases by Age

Disability	18–44 Years of Age	45–64 Years of Age
diabetes	1.9	9.5
prostate disease	0	7.5
heart disease	4.0	12.7
high blood pressure	7.4	29.0
arthritis	7.8	28.8
visual impairment	5.7	11.0
hearing impairment	6.7	17.5

SOURCE: U.S. Center for Disease Control and Prevention, National Centers for Health Statistics, January 2005 (www.cdc.gov/nchs/fastats).

TABLE 7.5 Percentage of Selected Reported Chronic Diseases by Race and Gender

Disability	Race		Gender	
	White	**Black**	**Male**	**Female**
diabetes	6.1	10.1	7.3	6.1
prostate disease	1.8	2.0	1.8	——
heart disease	11.5	9.9	12.2	10.5
high blood pressure	20.4	29.8	20.9	21.4
arthritis	21.3	22.2	17.8	23.7
visual impairment	9.0	11.7	8.1	10.4
hearing impairment	16.2	8.8	19.1	11.8

SOURCE: U.S. Centers for Disease Control, National Center for Health Statistics, January 2005 (www.cdc.gov/nchs/fastats).

from dysthymic disorders, 2.3 percent from obsessive-compulsive disorders, and 1.2 percent from bipolar disorders. By the year 2020, major depressive disorders are expected to become the number one cause of disabilities among adults in the U.S. and other developed nations (Murray and Lopez, 1996). Work-related factors, such as economic hardship, role conflict, work overload, and stress, are expected to contribute greatly to the rise in depressive disorders among adult men and women (McCurry, 2000; U.S. Department of Health and Human Services, 1999).

Disabled Americans can be found in all segments of society; they are rich and poor, Anglo and non-Anglo, men and women. Some have chronic conditions that are very apparent to everyone, and others suffer from conditions that are not so immediately apparent; still others have disabilities that may not be evident at all. Regardless of whether one can actually see the affliction, people with chronic physical or mental impairments are considered to be disabled.

PROTECTING DISABLED WORKERS

Disabled Americans need protection because society makes them vulnerable in at least three ways. First, historically we have neglected the needs of disabled people. It was not until the early 1970s that the first piece of legislation was enacted in the U.S. that actually dealt with the issue of providing disabled people with access to fundamental social and community activities, such as entering public buildings or using the bathrooms in those buildings. By ignoring their needs for nearly 200 years, we also denied them meaningful participation in society. Second, various disabilities are often misunderstood and, as a result, the capabilities of disabled individuals are frequently underestimated. Our initial tendency is to assist the paraplegic person in the wheelchair, or to refrain from directing too many questions to the person with a speech impairment. By wanting to help them in this fashion, we often make the assumption that disabled people cannot participate meaningfully in our society. Third, disabilities can make us feel uncomfortable, and therefore we tend not to want disabled individuals around us. The history of cancer certainly reflects this feeling. Discomfort is sometimes pronounced when it comes to being around people with contagious diseases, such as hepatitis or the human immunodeficiency virus (HIV) that causes Acquired Immunodeficiency Syndrome (AIDS). Our own fears about disabilities can block opportunities for meaningful participation on the part of the disabled person.

Two pieces of federal legislation, the 1973 Rehabilitation (Rehab) Act and the 1990 Americans with Disabilities Act (ADA) protect the workplace rights of disabled employees. While the two laws have many similarities, there are four factors that separate them (Slack, 1998). The first difference is jurisdiction. Rehab protects individuals who are employed in federal programs, or those who are employed in agencies that either receive federal contracts or direct federal funding. Hence, state and local governments, as well as many nonprofit organizations, are covered by Rehab. The ADA, on the other hand, is much broader in jurisdiction because it covers organizations that affect commerce and that do not receive federal funding. Congress defined "affecting commerce" broadly to include the public and private sectors. While the vast majority of businesses are covered under ADA—organizations that employ 15 or more full-time employees for most of the year—state and local governments and nonprofit organizations may also fall under the jurisdiction of the ADA if they have programs that do not receive federal funding.[3] Hence, public human resource specialists must be aware that employees in their organizations may be protected by both Rehab and the ADA.

The second difference deals with selection expectations. Rehab requires management to be "disability sensitive." It requires managers to take affirmative action with disabled individuals in the hiring, promotion, and retention processes. The ADA, on the other hand, requires management to be "disability-blind" when it comes to these matters. It prohibits managers from using affirmative action practices in selecting disabled individuals. Public and nonprofit human resource specialists must, therefore, be aware as to which law applies to which selection process because Rehab can invite litigation from disabled persons and the ADA can invite litigation from those who are not.

The third difference between Rehab and ADA deals with enforcement mechanisms. Seeking remedy against an employer is a bit more complex under Rehab, requiring the involvement of the EEOC, the federal department responsible for funding the particular program, and the U.S. Department of Justice. The ADA, however, simply requires notification through the EEOC.

Fourth, the laws differ in terms of permanent physical modification expectations, with architectural requirements being much stricter under Rehab. Employers "must accommodate" the disabled in removing office barriers. Hence, the organization is expected, regardless of cost and inconvenience, to do such things as install wheelchair ramps, provide braille instructions in elevators, and make restrooms handicap-accessible.[4] In contrast, the ADA requires permanent structural modifications to be made only when those accommodations are "readily achievable" in terms of expense and effort.

From all other perspectives, Rehab and the ADA are identical. Each is designed to protect the workplace rights of disabled Americans or, in the case of Rehab, "handicapped-Americans."[5] An employer cannot discriminate against a disabled employee if the employee is otherwise qualified to perform the essential functions of the job with or without reasonable accommodations. In providing protection from workplace discrimination, both Rehab and the ADA use the same three-pronged definition of "disability." A person can claim to be protected under either law if he or she:[6]

1. has a physical or mental impairment that substantially limits one or more of the major life activities; or
2. has a record of such an impairment; or
3. is regarded as having such an impairment.

The second and third prongs of the definition are intended to prevent speculation on the part of the employer as to what employee-related costs the future might bring to the organization. They are especially important in combating subtle and clever disability-based discrimination in the workplace. The second prong protects a person from either being denied employment or being terminated from employment as a result of fear that additional costs might be borne at the end of the impairment's remission. *Cleveland v. Policy Management Systems* (1999) and *Sheehan v. Marr* (1st Cir. 2000) underscore that, while an employee may be deemed as "totally disabled" through another law (such as, the Disabled Veterans Act), management is prevented from presuming automatically that the employee cannot perform the essential functions of the job and, hence, is unprotected under Rehab and the ADA.

The third prong protects those individuals with impairments that might never manifest, yet present the possibility of someday adding to the organization's health care and workplace expenses. A series of court decisions *(School Board of Nassau County v. Arline*, 1987; *Murphy v. United Parcel Services, Inc.*, 1999; and *Sullivan v. River Valley School District*, 1999), make it very clear that employees must be judged on actual abilities to perform the essential functions of the job. They cannot be judged on the basis of financial fears or social bigotry.

DISABILITIES COVERED AND NOT COVERED

While all chronic health conditions are viewed as disabilities, the federal government has been relatively careful in delineating specifically which disabilities are protected under the ADA and Rehab. Physical impairments include physiological disorders, cosmetic disfigurements, and anatomical losses or dysfunctions that affect at least one of the major body systems.[7] Mental impairments include psychological disorders such as emotional or mental illness, specific learning disabilities, mental retardation, and organic brain syndrome.[8] Asymptomatic chronic conditions, especially workers with HIV are protected under both Rehab and the ADA, as affirmed in *Bragdon v. Abbott* (1998).

Some physical and mental impairments are not protected. For instance, EEOC guidelines do not recognize certain physical characteristics, such as age, pregnancy, normal ranges of weight and muscle tone, height, and hair color. Personality traits, such as poor judgment and hot tempers, are also not considered impairments.[9] Congress made it very clear that certain lifestyles and behaviors are not protected under either Rehab or the ADA: homosexuality, transsexualism, transvestism, pedophilia, exhibitionism, voyeurism, kleptomania, compulsive gambling, and pyromania, to name a few.[10]

Past abuse of addictive drugs and alcohol is considered a protected disability, but *current* abuse is not protected under either Rehab or the ADA. In *Collings v. Longview Fibre* (9th Cir. 1995), "current" use of addictive drugs was defined as being a matter of months prior to detection and discharge. In *Conley v. Village of Bedford Park* (7th Cir. 2000), the court ruled that recovering alcoholics are protected under Rehab and the ADA as long as they are actually "recovering" and as long as they can perform the essential functions of the job. The reason for distinguishing between "past" and "current" problems with drugs and alcohol is that Congress acknowledges the right of employers to maintain a safe workplace. Employers can demand that employees' blood and urine be free from drugs and alcohol at the workplace (Colbridge, 2000). In *Newland v. Dalton* and *Williams v. Widnall (9th Cir. 1996)*, the courts ruled that employers do not have to tolerate disruptive behavior or insubordination of recovering addicts (drugs or alcohol) even if the behavior is the result of the addiction.

Finally, the courts have also limited correctable chronic health conditions that are protected under the ADA and Rehab. *Sutton v. United Airlines* (1999) and *Murphy* (1999), the Supreme Court determined that many correctable impairments, such as poor eyesight or high blood pressure, are not protected and are therefore considered "mitigating measures." As Justice Sandra Day O'Connor noted in *Sutton*, "If the impairment is corrected it does not 'substantially limit' a major life activity."

Substantially Limiting Major Life Activities

As affirmed in *Sutton* (1999) and *Murphy* (1999), disabilities covered by both Rehab and the ADA must substantially limit major life activities. Rehab and the ADA take a broad view on what constitutes "major life activities": walking, seeing, hearing, performing manual tasks, or caring for oneself. All or a combination of these activities are central to performing anyone's job. In *Bragdon* (1998) the court underscored that protection under these two laws do not necessitate a "total" limitation but only a "substantial" limitation. However, in *Sutton* (1999) the court ruled that decisions regarding substantial limitations must be made on a case-by-case basis and not simply on a diagnosis of an impairment. In order to be deemed "substantially limiting," Rehab and the ADA require the disability to be severe in nature, long-term in duration, and permanent in terms of impact on major life activities.

NOTIFICATION AND DOCUMENTATION REQUIREMENT

The ADA and Rehab are similar to other pieces of civil rights legislation in that the burden of proving membership within the protected class belongs solely to the individual seeking protection. Hence, it is the responsibility of the disabled employee to provide management with clear notification and accurate documentation about the chronic health condition. Because many kinds of disabilities are not readily apparent, this requirement typically means the submission of a note or report from either a physician or a mental health counselor.

While the notification and documentation requirement may seem benign albeit "bureaucratic," it can have serious impact on persons with certain kinds of disabilities. People tend not to want to "publicize" personal health conditions and, given the social stigma attached to some chronic illnesses, many employees are afraid of ridicule or retribution. Mental depression or past drug abuse, for instance, may not be issues about which one wants to talk with a supervisor. And given the stigma that still surrounds HIV/AIDS, providing documentation remains risky business for many people infected with the retrovirus (Slack, 2001, 2002). For employees with HIV/AIDS, the requirement means presenting *official* documentation that directly links the retrovirus to him- or herself. An anonymous blood test will not satisfy the notification requirement.

The fact is that Rehab and the ADA make the topic of chronic health conditions far less personal and changes the very nature of confidentiality in the workplace (Slack, 1998, 1996). Especially in circumstances where reasonable accommodations are requested, the circle of entities that may need to know *something* (yet *not necessarily everything*) about an employee's health condition may extend well beyond the confidence of the immediate supervisor: human resource specialists, other supervisors (in case of job transfer), co-workers and union stewards (in case of job modifications), the legal staff (for guidance on applying Rehab and the ADA), the insurance staff (for purposes of benefit consultation and processing pharmaceutical claims), the organization's first-aide staff (in case of emergencies), the medical staff (for purposes of verifying the disability), and the Employee Assistance Program (EAP) staff (for counseling, intervention, and crisis management). Confidentiality remains, but the need-to-know boundaries are expanded significantly.

Ultimately the employee is faced with the dilemma of either not notifying the employer—out of fear of ridicule, ostracization, or discrimination—or trusting that the employer will comply with the tenets of either law and be sensitive to the changing nature of confidentiality as well as reactions to social stigmas that may be attached to specific chronic conditions. In both the private (Scheid, 1998) and public (Slack, 1998) sectors, management's compliance *with* the law tends to come part and parcel with understanding *of* the law. Similarly, it appears that disabled employees' tendency to exercise rights covered by both laws increases with added education and training about protections provided by the laws (Granger, 2000). Without proper notification and documentation, however, disabled workers cannot make claims and management bears no responsibility in protecting workplace rights.[11]

MANAGEMENT'S RESPONSIBILITIES

Chronic health conditions present tremendous challenges to workplace and personnel managers. Some of the more critical issues include (1) redefining job descriptions, (2) determining the agency's capacity to provide reasonable accommodations, (3) controlling costs, and (4) acquiring information and developing strategies to train staff and employees to better prepared them to handle effectively situations involving disabilities.

JOB DESCRIPTIONS

Rehab and the ADA protect disabled workers as long as they can perform the essential functions of their jobs. Although required in neither Rehab nor the ADA, it is wise to re-analyze each job description within the organization so that tasks deemed to be "essential" in nature can be distinguished from tasks that are "marginal." Doing so permits management to determine—and document in court, if necessary—whether a disabled job applicant or employee is otherwise qualified to perform the essential functions of a job. It is especially important to modify job descriptions prior to beginning the selection process, since they are the basis for most job announcements and will be central to counter litigation.

REASONABLE ACCOMMODATIONS

Federal courts have placed limitations on what employers are expected to do on behalf of disabled workers and disabled applicants. In *Board of Trustees of University of Alabama v. Garrett* (2001), the court ruled that state employees cannot sue the state in federal court for violations of Title I of Rehab and the ADA. This ruling was affirmed in *Tennessee v. Lane* (2004). In *Raytheon Co. v. Hernandez* (2003), the court ruled that organizations do not have to consider rehiring former disabled workers who were discharged for violating workplace conduct rules.

Nevertheless, Rehab and the ADA require management to provide reasonable accommodations to otherwise qualified employees and job applicants with disabilities if such accommodations are needed in performing the essential functions of the job. Both laws also require management to do so only in response to requests by the employees for such accommodations. Although management cannot impose reasonable accommodations on employees or job applicants, it should be prepared to enter into a discussion about specific workplace accommodations.

What Is Reasonable Accommodation?   From management's point of view, it is important to provide disabled employees with reasonable accommodations for at least two reasons. First, reasonable accommodation constitutes a significant form of health intervention. Early intervention can keep disabled employees healthier and, therefore, more productive for a longer period of time. Second, adoption of reasonable accommodation strategies can be submitted in court as evidence that the organization is attempting to comply with both the letter and spirit of Rehab and the ADA.

But what constitutes a reasonable accommodation? Reasonable accommodations can and should take a variety of forms. Recognizing that reasonable accommodation is very much in the eye of the beholder, Congress suggests three types: (1) physical or structural changes, such as modifying buildings to ensure wheelchair accessibility; (2) job modification, such as removing marginal tasks from the job description, acquiring assistive technology devises (ATDs), flextime utilization, job transfer, or filling of vacancies; and (3) modification of selection and training materials and processes, such as using special readers or interpreters, or changing the size of print on examinations.

Management must recognize that each worksite—indeed, each set of essential functions, type of disability, stage and level of disability, and individual capability—constitutes a unique situation and, thereby, calls for unique accommodations. Hence, what is needed for one disabled American to perform the essential functions of a particular job in a specific workplace will not be identical to what is needed for another disabled American in either the same or different place of employment. A case-by-case approach is required, and this means that human resource specialists and workplace supervisors must gain familiarity with chronic health conditions present in the particular workforce.

In many ways, devising reasonable accommodations for physical disabilities is more straightforward than building strategies to deal with employees with mental disabilities. Certainly there are exceptions; some physical disabilities, especially those with few outward manifestations, can be very problematic in finding accommodations that are acceptable and reasonable. Contagious physical illnesses, such as hepatitis or HIV-related illnesses, are causes for concern especially in improperly trained workforces or ill-equipped workplaces. For the most part, however, it is somewhat simpler to deal with an employee who is paraplegic, or perhaps one who has a hearing or sight loss. Assuming the necessary re-examination of job descriptions, one can determine if the employee is otherwise qualified to perform the essential functions of the job. One can also determine whether reasonable accommodations are needed to enable the employee to perform the essential functions.

Providing reasonable accommodations for mental impairments is a much harder task, one that workplace supervisors and human resource specialists least understand (Schwartz and Post, 2000; Wimbiscus, 1996-1997; Meltsner, 1998). This has led to a growing number of lawsuits. One employee with a mental impairment was denied the use of accrued paid leave time, as well as unpaid leave, to deal with psychiatric problems (*Schmidt v. Safeway, Inc.,* 1994). Another was called derogatory names by supervisors (*Owens v. Archer Daniels Midland Co.,* 1999), and another suffered from a hostile work environment (*Disanto v. McGraw-Hill,* 1998). One organization denied a mentally disabled employee's request for accommodations in the form of medication breaks, restroom breaks, and technical assistance during training sessions (*Barton v. Tampa Electric Co.,* 1997). In each of these instances, the organization lost in litigation and was directed to compensate the employee with millions of dollars.

Stephen Sonnenberg (2000a, 2000b) offers a variety of suggestions on how to deal effectively with employees who suffer from mental disabilities. Five of his suggestions are given here:

1. "Review and revise job descriptions to include references to employees' ability to cope with stressful circumstances."

   The job description should protect both the organization and the employee. If stressful activities are central to the job, coping with stress should be listed as an essential function.

2. "If an employee appears or claims to have a mental impairment, scrupulously avoid generalizations or stereotypes about mental illness. Resist the temptation to play armchair psychologist."

   Much of the litigation pertinent to mental impairments results from managers and human resource specialists attempting to solve mental health problems on their own. Management should have in place a referral system to handle these issues.

3. "If an employee complains that working with his supervisor is too stressful and causes emotional problems, elicit a written admission that he will be able to perform essential job duties only if he has a different supervisor or works in a different location."

   This will help protect the organization from litigation. Neither Rehab nor the ADA require reasonable accommodations, in this case a job transfer, simply because of difficulty in working with either a supervisor or coworker (Goldman, 1999). Reasonable accommodation is permitted only in cases where the employee is substantially limited in his or her ability to perform the essential functions of the job. The organization is further protected if the job description includes the statement of "ability to work in stressful conditions" as an essential function.

4. "Consider even vague requests for accommodation from employees, their family members, or their representatives as triggering a duty to engage in an interactive process with the employee."

   The request for reasonable accommodation may not always be clear and precise. This is especially true in the case of employees with mental health conditions (Noe, 1997). Because reasonable accommodations are always on a case-by-case basis, the employee may not even know what is needed to keep him or her able to perform the essential job tasks. Management must listen closely.

5. "A psychiatric diagnosis is not determinative."

   The decision to provide reasonable accommodation is never a function of a medical opinion. It is always a function of law. Rehab and the ADA, and subsequent court decisions, are the basis for determining who is protected and who is accommodated. The psychiatric diagnosis is only the first step in making these determinations.

Controlling Costs

If employers dislike Rehab and ADA, it is primarily because of a fear of cost. With few exceptions, however, providing individualized and reasonable accommodations prove to be one of the least expensive activities. The Job Accommodation Network (2005) estimates that most reasonable accommodations will typically cost under $500 per case. Some examples of relatively inexpensive accommodations might include flextime for medical appointments or work breaks to apply medication. For employees with suppressed immune systems or mental disabilities, a relatively inexpensive accommodation might involve an occasional five-minute "stress break." For employees with special dietary needs, especially diets needed for specific medication, vendors can provide specialized machine foods at no cost to the employer.

But the expense of accommodation is a legitimate concern for the work organization and so the question remains: How far do you have to go to provide reasonable accommodation? In *Alexander v. Choate* (1985), the court underscored the need for accommodations to be *reasonable*. Organizations do not have to endure undue hardships in providing accommodations. They do not have to operate in the red, nor do they have to lay off employees. Private businesses are expected to make a profit, and public and nonprofit organizations are expected to continue service productivity.

What determines undue hardship? As in the case of accommodations, undue hardship is seen through the eye of the beholder and is determined on a case-by-case basis. Rehab and the ADA provide the following guidelines to assist organizations and the courts in determining whether specific accommodations are "reasonable" in particular work organizations: (1) the nature and cost of the specific accommodation, (2) the financial resources of the specific organization, (3) whether the organization is a part of a larger organization with greater financial resources, and (4) the nature (indoor/outdoor, temporary/permanent) of the worksite.[12]

The cost of group insurance packages is a continuing concern of employers and is a primary issue in the area of undue hardship. Unlike other kinds of accommodations, the group health package represents a "collective" accommodation and, therefore, the cost of which is not eased terribly by the size of the organization. In a series of decisions (*Chrysler v. DILHR*, 1976, *Western Weighing Bureau v. DILHR*, 1977, *McDermott v. Xerox*, 1985) rendered even before the passage of the ADA, the courts have ruled consistently that a work organization cannot discriminate against employees based on either knowledge about current costs or speculation about future costs. Yet the courts have also recognized the right of work organizations to consider the issue of expense in purchasing insurance policies and health care packages for employees. This seems especially true in the case of mental impairments (Serritella, 2000). In *Weyer v. Twentieth Century Fox Film Corp.* (2000), the court held that a more limited plan of coverage, specifically a shorter term of coverage, for mental disabilities was permissible to help reduce costs and thereby avoid undue hardship. In *Hess v. Allstate Ins. Co.* (2000), the court found that work organizations and insurers cannot be held liable for offering less health care coverage for mental disabilities than they do for physical disabilities. In essence, federal courts are continually searching for balance between protecting disabled Americans in the workforce and ensuring that the workplace does not suffer unduly. Debate over group health insurance is central to the search for balance.

INFORMATION AND TRAINING

It is quintessential for management to acquire current and realistic information regarding medical, legal, and application dimensions of chronic health issues facing the workplace. For instance, a fundamental fear is the transmission of contagious physical impairments, particularly blood-borne pathogens like HIV and hepatitis, through workplace activities. The Occupational Safety and Health Administration (OSHA) and the National Institute for Occupational Safety and Health (NIOSH) provide employers with both procedural regulations and technical assistance in meeting this responsibility.[13] General updates on disability issues can be found in *Report on Disability Programs*.[14] The website for the Job Accommodation Network (JAN) provides a wide variety of information, including the Searchable Online Accommodation Resource (SOAR), which can be helpful in developing reasonable accommodations for specific chronic impairments. The Disability Rights Section of the Department of Justice's Civil Rights Division offers a variety of documents designed to assist state, county, and municipal governments in complying with the ADA. These documents can be accessed through the JAN website.[15] Routine staff meetings should include relevant topics, such as updates on pertinent court cases, web-based information, and circulation of relevant information.

It is also management's responsibility to develop and implement strategies to train staff and employees in order to better prepare the workplace to handle effectively situations involving chronic health conditions. This involves training on how to implement Rehab and ADA, as well as on how to protect the health of all employees. It also entails acquiring a basic and preliminary understanding of the types of mental and physical impairments found in the particular workplace. Not providing such training simply increases vulnerability to litigation as a result of inappropriate workplace actions and behavior. Litigation is always the most expensive workplace cost.

Especially in the public sector, employee and staff training tends to take a back seat to other budgetary priorities. Richard L. Schott (1999) notes that this is especially true when it comes to providing training programs in the area of mental health. Stephen Sonnenberg (2000a, 2000b) reminds us that the effectiveness of mental health training depends on developing relationships with mental health professionals. In order to gain a better understanding of both physical and mental impairments, it is quintessential to incorporate a variety of external expertise into the training strategy.

For management to send an unambiguous message as to the importance of employee disabilities, training must be mandatory, workplace-specific, and periodic. It should include such topics as (1) Rehab, ADA, and OSHA regulations; (2) workplace-specific procedures that management will follow when an employee seeks to provide notification and documentation about a disability; (3) the changing nature of confidentiality under Rehab and the ADA, and its application to the specific workplace; (4) services provided by the organization, including concrete but preliminary sketches of possible "individualized" reasonable accommodations; (5) undue hardship issues pertaining to the specific workplace; and (6) with the help of external experts, familiarization with disabilities and health issues potentially facing the organization.

CONCLUSION

One thing is abundantly clear about the American workplace: Healthy people are less expensive and more productive than sick people. Two things are equally evident about the American workforce: Individually, we are aging and thereby incrementally becoming less healthy; collectively, we are facing a greater number (and a wider variety of kinds) of chronic health challenges. Since Rehab and the ADA prohibit the exclusion of persons with many types of mental and physical impairments from the workplace, management must do whatever it can to keep them healthy and productive. Whether it is a result of humanitarian feelings of compassion for the employee or businesslike concerns about profit and productivity, it is in management's best interest to develop a workplace environment that supports the needs of disabled employees as well as that guards the health of all employees. Building a positive workplace environment—one where employees with chronic health conditions feel comfortable in exercising their rights under the law and where supervisors feel encouraged in the application of those rights—remains a challenge for management and human resource specialists in this new century.

NOTES

1. I want to thank William A. Anderson, a graduate assistant in the Department of Government at the University of Alabama at Birmingham, for his help in data and information collection. I also want to thank Sarah A. Slack and Samuel D. D. Slack, my children, for special assistance given in the preparation of this manuscript.
2. Diagnoses of mental illness in the United States are based on standards set by the American Psychiatric Association. See American Psychiatric Association, Diagnostic and Statistical Manual for Mental Disorders, fourth edition (DSM-IV), Washington, DC: American Psychiatric Press, 1994.
3. Several types of organizations are exempt from both pieces of legislation: the federal government, Native American tribes, private clubs, and in certain situations, religious organizations.
4. The laws also differ in terms of appropriate references to chronic health conditions. Rehab refers to persons with chronic health conditions as being "handicapped." ADA

refers to these persons as being "disabled." Hence, public human resource specialists should use to term "handicap" in referring to Rehab and "disability" when referring to the ADA.

5. For the sake of clarity throughout the rest of this chapter, only the term "disability" will be used.
6. 29 CFR section 1630.2(h)(1).
7. 29 CFR section 1630.2(h)(2).
8. 29 CFR section 1630.2(h)(2) and 29 CFR section 1630, App., 1630.2(h).
9. 42 USCA section 12211(b).
10. 56 Fed. Reg. 35,748, July 26, 1991.
11. *Ibid.*
12. 42 U.S.C. 12111 section 101(10)(B) (1995).
13. The website for OSHA is www.osha.gov. The website for NIOSH is www.cdc.gov/niosh.
14. *Report on Disability Programs* is a newsletter published by Business Publishers, Inc., 8737 Colesville Road, Suite 1100, Silver Spring, MD 20910-3928. (301) 589-5103. www.bpinews.com. It is published 25 times a year.
15. For instance, see "ADA Guide for Small Local Governments, including Towns, Townships, and Rural Counties," "Cites and Counties: First Steps Toward Solving Common ADA Problems," and "ADA Guide for Local Governments," all produced by the U.S. Department of Justice, Civil Rights Division, Disability Rights Section

REFERENCES

Alexander v. Choate. 1985. 469 U.S. 287.

Barton v. Tampa Electric Company. 1997. 6 AD Cases 1179. M.D. Florida.

Board of Trustees of University of Alabama v. Garrett. 2001. 531 U.S. 356.

Bragdon v. Abbott. 1998. 524 U.S. 624.

Carli, T. 2004. "Depression-in-the-Workplace-Survey." University of Michigan Health System, Depression Center. www.med.umich.edu/opm/newspage/2004.

Chrysler v. DILHR. 1976. 14 Fair Empl. Prac. Cases (BNA) 344. Wis.Cir.Ct. 1976.

Cleveland v. Policy Management Systems, et al. 1999. 526 U.S. 795.

Colbridge, T. D. 2000. "Defining Disability Under the Americans with Disabilities Act." *FBI Law Enforcement Bulletin* 69:10: October: 28–32.

Collings v. Longview Fibre. 1995 and 1996. 63 F 3d 828 (9th Cir. 1995), cert. denied, 116 S. Ct. 711 (1996).

Conley v. Village of Bedford Park. 2000. 2000 WL703806. 7th Cir. Ill.

Disanto v. McGraw-Hill. 1998. 8 AD Cases 1147. S.D. New York 1998.

Goldman, C. 1999. "Recognizing When Stress Results from Covered Disability." *ADA Compliance Guide* July.

Granger, B. 2000. "The Role of Psychiatric Rehabilitation Practitioners in Assisting People in Understanding How to Best Assert Their ADA Rights and Arrange Job Accommodations." *Psychiatric Rehabilitation Journal* 23:3: Winter: 215–214.

Greenberg, P. E., Kessler, R. C., Birnbaum, H. G., Leong, S. A., Lowe, S. U., Berglund, P. A., and Corey-Lisle, P. K., 2003. "The Economic Burden of Depression in the United States." *Journal of Clinical Psychology* 64:12: December: 1465–1475.

Hess v. Allstate Ins. Co. 2000. 19 NDLR 28. D. Me. 2000. No. 99-384-P-C.

Job Accommodation Network. 2005. www.janweb.icdi.wvu.edu. 918 Chestnut Ridge Road, Suite 1, Morgantown, WV 26506-6080. phone: (800) ADA-WORK. Email: mailto:jan@jan.wvu.edu.

McCurry, P. 2000. "Disabling Depression." *Director* 54:2: September: 34–38.

McDermott v. Xerox. 1985. 65 N.Y.2d 213, 480 N.E. 2d 695,491 N.Y.S. 2d 106.

Meltsner, S. 1998. "Psych. Disabilities: What's Real, What's Protected." *Business and Health* June: 46–53.

Murphy v. United Parcel Service, Inc. 1999. 527 U.S. 516.

Murray, C. J. L. and Lopez, A. D., eds. 1996. *Summary: The Global Burden of Disease: A Comprehensive Assessment of Mortality and Disability from Diseases, Injuries, and Risk Factors in 1990 and Projected to 2020.* Cambridge, MA: Harvard School of Public Health, Harvard University Press.

National Institute of Mental Health, U.S. National Institutes of Health. January 2005. www.nimh.nih.gov.

National Mental Health Association. 2005. www.nmha.org/infoctr/factsheets/ depressionworkplace.cfm.

Newland v. Dalton. 1996. 81 F.3d 904. 9th Cir.

Noe, S. R. 1997. "Discrimination Against Individuals with Mental Illness." *Journal of Rehabilitation* January–March: 20–26.

Owens v. Archer Daniels Midland Co. 1999. 30 F. Supp.2d. 1802. C.D., Illinois.

Raytheon Co. v. Hernandez. 2003. 9th Cir. No. 02-749.

Scheid, T. L. 1998. "The Americans with Disabilities Act, Mental Disability, and Employment Practices." *Journal of Behavioral Health Services and Research* 25:3: 312–325.

School Board of Nassau County v. Arline. 1987. 480 U.S. 273 at 284.

Schmidt v. Safeway, Inc. 1994. 561 F. 3d. 302. C.D., Illinois.

Schott, R. L. 1999. "Managers and Mental Health: Mental Illness and the Workplace." *Public Personnel Management* 28:2: Summer: 161–184.

Schwartz, R. H. and Post, F. R. 2000. "The ADA and the Mentally Disabled: What Must Firms Do?" *Business Horizons* 43:4: July/August: 52–56.

Serritella, D. 2000. "Disability and ADA: Employers and Insurers Not Obligated by the ADA to Provide Equal Benefit Plans for Physical and Mental Disabilities." *American Journal of Law and Medicine* 26:4: 112–115.

Sheehan v. Marr. 2000. 207 F.3d 35. 1st Cir.

Slack, J. D. 2001. "Zones of Indifference and the American Workplace: The Case of Persons with HIV/AIDS." *Public Administration Quarterly* 25.

Slack, J. D. 2002. "The Americans with Disabilities Act and Reasonable Accommodations: The View From Persons with HIV/AIDS." *Policy Studies Journal* 29.

Slack, J. D. 1998. *HIV/AIDS and the Public Workplace: Local Government Preparedness in the 1990s.* Tuscaloosa, AL: University of Alabama Press.

Slack, J. D. 1996. "Workplace Preparedness and the Americans with Disabilities Act: Lessons from Municipal Government's Management of HIV/AIDS." *Public Administration Review* 56:2: March/April: 159–167.

Sonnenberg, S. P. 2000a. "Coping with Mental Disabilities in the Workplace: Tips for Employers." *Employee Benefit News* 14:7 June: 78–81.

Sonnenberg, S. P. 2000b. "Mental Disabilities in the Workplace." *Workforce* 79:6: 142–144.

Sullivan v. River Valley School District. 1999. 194 F.3d 1084. 10th Cir.

Sutton v. United Airlines, Inc. 1999. 527 U.S. 471.

Tennessee v. Lane et al. 2004. 6th Cir. No. 02-1667.

U.S. Department of Health and Human Services, Centers for Disease Control and Prevention. 2005. www.cdc.gov/nchs/fastats/overwt.htm.

U.S. Department of Health and Human Services, Centers for Disease Control and Prevention, National Center for Health Statistics. September 2004. Publication No. 20004-1232.

U.S. Department of Health and Human Services, Centers for Disease Control and Prevention. 2003. "The Power of Prevention."

U.S. Department of Health and Human Services, Centers for Disease Control and Prevention. January 2001. National Center for Health Statistics. www.cdc.gov/nchs/fastats/disable; and www.cdc.gov/nchs/fastats/aids-hiv.

U.S. Department of Health and Human Services. 1999. *Mental Health: A Report of the Surgeon General*, Rockville, MD: U.S. Department of Health and Human Services, Substance and Mental Health Services Administration, Center for Mental Health Services, National Institutes of Health, National Institute of Mental Health. See especially Chapter 4, "Adults and Mental Health."

U.S. Department of Labor, Bureau of Labor Statistics. September 14, 2004. "Workplace Injuries and Illness in 2003." www.bls.gov/iif/home.htm.

U.S. Department of Labor, Bureau of Labor Statistics, Census of Fatal Occupational Injuries, 2004.

Western Weighing Bureau v. DILHR. 1977. 21 Fair Empl. Prac. Cases (BA) 344. Wis.Cir.Ct.

Weyer v. Twentieth Century Fox Film Corp. 2000. 198 F.3d 1104. 9th Cir.

Williams v. Widnall. 1996. 79 F. 3d 1003. 10th Cir.

Wimbiscus, M. 1996-1997. "Responsibilities of Employers Toward Mentally Disabled Persons Under the Americans with Disabilities Act." *Journal of Law and Health* 11: 173–193.

Chapter 8

The Demise of Public Employee Unionism?

T. Zane Reeves

The widespread perception is that unions are dying.
The reality is that unions are being murdered.

Frank Joyce, 2005

Much has been written about the phenomenon of public employees and their unions. Questions abound: Why did so many government employees in the United States either join unions or find themselves represented by unions in the period roughly from 1960 to 1980? Why has the movement stagnated overall since that time? What is the future of public employee unions in a post-9/11 world?

BACKGROUND

On the surface, it appeared that government employees were unlikely candidates for union converts in the 1960s and 1970s; even now compared to their private-sector counterparts, they are better paid, have excellent pension plans, and relatively stable job security. Government workers also are protected by merit systems and have access to grievance appeal procedures should they ever face disciplinary actions by their bosses. Yet, join unions they did, and no one predicted it would happen beforehand. This chapter explores why this phenomenon occurred, why it has seemingly lost momentum (especially among federal employees), and what we can expect of the future.

When comparing unionization in the public and private sectors, it's clear that the reasons workers vote for unions to represent them are quite different in the public sector. Keep in mind that the public sector includes government employees who work for federal, state, municipalities, counties, and special jurisdictions, while private-sector employees are employed by corporate, business, not-for-profit, and even tribal enterprises such as casinos. The world of industrial relations in the private arena was finalized by national legislation during with the New Deal of Franklin Roosevelt. By contrast, public-sector unionization happened like a surprise attack in the 1960s and 1970s and the battleground is still being fought state by state. The first obvious question is why were public employees so susceptible to the union message (and why didn't we see it coming)?

One clue is to consider how public employees are different from their private-sector counterparts. Go back to the Great Depression in America. It's not too difficult to imagine why a massive number of private-sector employees joined unions under those horrific working conditions. Union membership went from approximately 2 million to 12 million in this country following passage in 1935 of the National Labor Relations Act (NLRA). And that core of union support is the only remaining pillar of the Democratic Party, to which we will return when looking at the current struggle between federal employee unions and the Republicans in Congress and the White House.

Who are these public workers who joined unions? Unlike their private-sector brothers and sisters, they don't work in mines or in sweatshops, nor do they build automobiles or work in factories. Think about them. Public employees look like most students studying public administration, although perhaps slightly older versions. They are overwhelmingly professionals, technicians, or support staff, as opposed to blue-collar miners, automobile workers, meat packers, and truck drivers, even though there are those in the public sector as well. Moreover, they are covered by merit systems that are supposed to protect individual employees from abuses. Remember, if you worked for one of the big three automobile manufacturers in the 1930s and 1940s, or steel mills, or mines there were no job protections. Life was in Hobbesian terms, "short, brutish, and nasty."

Not only was work pure drudgery during the Depression, one could be fired for no reason whatsoever. That's not true for most public employees, who have much more job security and due process rights. There have always been merit systems in place along with grievance appeal procedures. The myth that public employees can't be fired is patently false, as thousands at all levels of government are discharged every year. In large part, thanks to unions who protect employees from unjust disciplinary action, employers can't arbitrarily and capriciously fire most public employees and get away with it. These employees have grievance rights and their unions are only too willing to represent them upon appeal, in many cases even when the preponderance of evidence supports their termination. Unless they're an at-will employee at the very top of the organization or a probationary employee at the very lowest level, public employees can't be fired without just cause or if someone does fire them without cause, they can appeal through the union.

Thus, the merit system ought to be a factor that would help keep unions out of the government workplace by persuading public employees not to join unions.

That has not been the case. Even though promises of just cause employment protection should work against union organizing in the public sector, it has done the opposite. The collective bargaining agreement between public management and the union almost universally includes a clause providing disciplinary action only for "demonstrable just cause," demonstrated in an evidentiary hearing through evidence and testimony of witnesses. Who typically represents public employees in these grievance hearings—union representatives! So, even though the merit system would seem to be a disincentive to join a union, ironically the merit system's provision of a due process appeal of unfair disciplinary actions is a strong recruiting tool for public employee unions. Even more attractive is the union's unwritten promise to represent employees who are disciplined or discharged for just cause and wish to appeal that decision. In either situation, most unions will "stand by their man/woman."

Thus, starting in the 1960s, massive numbers of public employees joined unions and/or were organized by unions into bargaining units. If one could envision these trends graphically, the private sector saw a sharp increase in unionization starting in 1935, leveling off during the war years, continuing to increase until about 1948, when there starts a decline that is still spiraling downward. Private-worker unions are greatly alarmed by this trend and are searching for answers. Unless unions do a much better job of "organizing the unorganized" in service and technological fields, they will never recapture a growth trend. Controversial union leaders such as Andy Stern, president of "the largest and fastest growing union in the country" Service Employees International Union (SEIU), is determined to reform the labor movement and the Democratic Party to reform labor organizing (Bai, 2005). Other more traditional labor leaders are advocating cutting their contributions to the AFL-CIO in order to free up more money for organizing untapped employee groups (Greenhouse, 2005). These are signs that may change, but the current state of unionization in the private sector is still in rapid decline as they lose more members than they gain.

Compare this decline to the public sector. There was very little union growth throughout the 1940s and 1950s, in fact almost none. Beginning in about 1960, unionization among state, federal, and local employees sky-rocketed dramatically and increased very sharply throughout the 1960s and most of the 1970s, when it started leveling off. Today it remains in a homeostatic state of slight growth over all. It has peaked. Nonetheless, depending on whose figures you read and these figures aren't easy to come by, about 40 percent of public employees belong to unions or are represented by unions. So, union growth among government workers really went from zero to about 40 percent in a 20-year period.

Why did this improbable phenomenon happen? One theory is that job insecurity or fear of RIF or layoff among government workers led to unionization. Were there a lot of public employees being RIFed? Not during the 1960s. Those were fat times, it was John F. Kennedy's New Frontier and later Lyndon Johnson's Great Society and war on poverty. And with the Vietnam War, the civilian employment in defense grew even more. Those were not times of RIF. As far as trying to explain that initial surge, fears of layoff or RIF aren't plausible. For one thing, throughout the 1940s, 1950s, 1960s, one reason people went into public employment (government employment) was because of job security. This was the big advantage that public employment had over private employment. You knew you wouldn't be laid off. Now, that's no longer as true, even though in times of Enron and WorldCom, government is still a much more secure place to work than the private sector.

What about the possibility that public employee unionization was caused because the United States experienced very turbulent times during the 1960s and 1970s? Let's explore that option. It was a period of unrest and dissent more than at any time since the Civil War. The nation was wracked by an increasingly divisive war in Vietnam, civil rights movement, urban uprisings, feminist advocacy, and counter culture challenges. All converged during this era, but why would this cause government workers to join labor unions? There is no apparent nexus between public employee unionization and politicization during the 1960s and 1970s. What about other possible causes of the rapid unionization during this era? Another theory was that unions dangled the lure of higher wages. Join the union and you'll make more money. Sounds reasonable, except for the fact that elected legislators set the parameters of public employee compensation, not negotiators at the bargaining table.

What we're trying to understand is a phenomenon in which millions of American public employees unexpectedly joined unions. Let's assume that basically human beings are rational in the decisions they make. Sometimes with a little alcohol or when they fall in love, they become irrational, but for the most part when they're sane and sober, they're rational. Ask yourself, would you join a union if someone said, "Oh, by the way, your union dues are $35 a month?" No one is looking for ways to waste money. As a teacher or nurse, you don't say, "I've got an extra $35 a month. I think I'll join a union." No, the reason teachers, police officers, firefighters, and nurses join unions as well as city, county, state, and particularly federal employees is because they believe it is worth their dues; they receive a direct benefit—job security through protection against layoff and arbitrary and capricious actions by bosses.

The federal sector presents an excellent case study for analyzing the lure of unionization and reasons why federal employee unionization may be posed for a growth surge.

EVOLUTION OF FEDERAL LABOR-MANAGEMENT RELATIONS

Labor-management relations at the federal level have evolved through three phases and, as actor Jack Pallance said in the film, *City Slickers*, "The day ain't over yet." As an overview, the three stages are summarized in the following discussion:

Policy Formulation Through Executive Order (1962–1978)

Accepting the conclusions of a presidential task force on January 17, 1962, President John F. Kennedy issued Executive Order 10988, which established the first guidelines for *federal* employee collective bargaining. Even though it was a precedent-setting "stroke of the presidential pen," reactions were mixed. President Kennedy (1962:, p. 551) proclaimed that his order would "foster efficiency and democracy." Felix Nigro (1969:, p. 80) later called the order "an affirmative statement of the desirability of employee-management cooperation" while some unions criticized it because "the determination of bargaining units and judgments regarding labor practices were left in the hands of the employing department" (Spero and Capozzola, 1973:, p. 139). The order was viewed by union leaders as a glass "half empty rather than half full" because it limited the scope of bargaining, offered no substitute for the right to strike, lacked either a central administering or adjudicatory agency, and failed to specify dispute resolution procedures (Bureau of National Affairs, 1971).

Following recommendations of a Civil Service Commission advisory panel, President Richard Nixon issued Executive Order 11491 in 1969, which greatly expanded the earlier Kennedy order by providing secret ballot certification elections and dispute resolution procedures to be administered by the Federal Labor Relations Council. Both Kennedy and Nixon executive orders made federal labor-management relations policy more closely parallel to those in the private sector and provided a modicum of collective bargaining for federal employees. Another major criticism leveled by some unions was that the orders did not provide what they viewed as an essential element given by the NLRA to private-sector unions: the right to call a strike if bargaining reached an impasse (Bureau of National Affairs, 1971).

In 1971, President Nixon expanded the scope of his previous order by issuing Executive Order 11616, which required negotiated grievance procedures in all subsequent agreements and strengthened the role of union negotiators. It is fascinating to realize that Republican President Richard Nixon, during the mid-point of the Vietnam War would sign an executive order strengthening union influence among federal employees; it is particularly remarkable when we compare it to measures cutting those privileges during the second George W. Bush administration. For example, Executive Order 11616 permitted an employee involved in a grievance proceeding the following guarantees (Nixon, 1972):

- Time off to prepare his or her own grievance case.
- Hearings conducted by qualified hearing officers.
- Exhibits to be used by the agency must be made available in discovery to an employee or his or her union representative prior to the hearing.
- Documents not provided to the union or grievant in advance would not be admissible evidence.
- Verbatim transcripts of the hearing must be made available to the grievant or union afterwards.

The scope of collective bargaining in the federal sector was further expanded in 1975 by another Republican President, Gerald Ford who signed Executive Order 11838 (Ford, 1976), which essentially made all federal agency regulations negotiable unless the agency could show a *"compelling need"* not to negotiate. Furthermore, any proposed changes in personnel policies were designated as mandatory bargaining subjects, even when a collective bargaining agreement was already in force. Finally, the Ford order also expanded the scope of grievance procedures to include the interpretation and application of agency regulations as well as negotiated agreements.

The importance of these presidential executive orders lay not in their *substantive* reshaping of federal labor-management relations; rather, they were a *symbolic* encouragement of public employee unionism at all levels of government. Coincidentally, executive orders during the presidencies from Kennedy to Ford corresponded with a period when unions at all levels were organizing rapidly and frequent strikes and job actions in the public sector were a common consequence. By the end of this period, a new and evidently more predictable era had emerged in labor-management relations, one of "growing up, settling down" (Stanley, 1972).

The symbolism of executive orders during the 1960s and 1970s is evidenced by the fact that Congress retains sole constitutional authority to determine wages and benefits. These orders did not, as Beal, Wickersham, and Kienast noted at the time (1976):

> "change from the historic exclusion from negotiated grievance/arbitration procedures matters subject to statutory appeals such as discharge, demotion, or discrimination based on race, sex, etc. Neither did the new amendments . . . repeal its ban on union or agency shops or the requirement that the management rights clause . . . be part of all negotiated agreements."

Executive orders from Republican and Democratic presidents during this era gave symbolic encouragement for federal employees and managers to organize and negotiate in good faith concerning issues of concern to both sides.

EQUILIBRIUM THROUGH LEGISLATION (1978–2000)

In 1978, President Jimmy Carter pushed through perhaps the most important legislation of his otherwise troubled presidency: the Civil Service Reform Act (CSRA), which abolished the Civil Service Commission, created the Office of Personnel Management (OPM), and Senior Executive Service (SES). Thus, Title VII of CSRA became the first federal legislation defining collective bargaining in the federal sector of employment. The CSRA authorized a new Federal Labor Relations Authority (FLRA) with the intent of separating the *labor-management adjudication* function from the *management advisory* role to federal agencies that would be handled by an Office of Labor-Management Relations (OLMR) in OPM. Clearly, the independent FLRA was intended to play the pivotal role in shaping the nature of labor-management relations at the federal level. Modeled after the National Labor Relations Board (NLRB) in the private sector, the FLRA's three-member board, appointed by the president to serve five-year terms, was removable only for cause. Their responsibilities subsumed most functions previously performed by the Federal Labor Relations Council and the Labor Department in areas such as determining appropriate bargaining units, supervision of certification elections, deciding unfair labor practices, ruling on negotiability issues, and on exceptions filed to arbitration awards.

Three other units within the FLRA were delegated responsibility for mediating disputes, settling impasses, and prosecuting unfair labor practices (ULP): (1) the independent Federal Service Impasses Panel (FSIP) retained authority to direct terms of settlement when alternative dispute resolution efforts failed; (2) the Federal Mediation and Conciliation Service (FMCS) was continued to assist parties who requested assistance with arbitration or mediation services in labor-management disputes; and (3) the General Counsel was empowered to investigate charges of unfair labor practices and either dismiss them or issue and prosecute a complaint from unions or agencies.

Overall, management rights in federal-sector collective bargaining were reinforced and expanded by the CSRA, by reserving to federal managers the authority to make decisions and take actions not subject to the negotiation process The parties were prohibited from bargaining on federal pay, benefits, and involuntary fees paid to unions by non-union members of the bargaining unit, i.e., agency shop, or fair-share arrangements. Furthermore, management rights were reaffirmed through the prohibition against bargaining on mission, budget, organization, number of employees, internal security issues, contracting out determinations, and management's right to select promotional candidates from properly ranked and certified employees. Even so, the CSRA permitted voluntary, in no way mandatory, negotiations over the methods, means, and technology of conducting agency operations. It is critical to note, in light of what was to come during the Bush administration that management's right to determine whether staffing selections, either internally or externally, was specifically guaranteed.

Thus, CSRA ushered in a new phase of federal labor-management relations, one in which unions were seemingly legitimized as key participants in personnel policy making (McCabe, 1982); this was particularly true in issues subject to negotiated grievance and arbitration procedures. The CSRA expanded the scope of collective bargaining in two important respects. First, the methods and means by which work is performed became a permissible topic of bargaining. Secondly, federal agencies such as OPM, GSA, and OSHA, which issue government-wide personnel regulations, were required to consult with unions regarding any proposed changes that affect a substantial number of workers. However, agency-wide and government-wide regulations issued during the life of the collective bargaining agreement could not override the exigent contract provisions and must be brought into conformity during renegotiation. Finally, binding arbitration, once an option for negotiated grievance procedures, was mandated by CSRA's Title VII as the final stage of grievance resolution.

As noted elsewhere (Hays and Reeves, 1984:, p. 342), CSRA's creation of the FLRA was predicated upon an *equilibrium model*, which assumes that:

> . . . the key to labor peace is strong collective bargaining legislation and union security. In effect, the union plays the watchdog role, keeping management practices honest while providing workers with a sense of participation in policy determination. Thus, strong labor and responsive management equalize each other and they are compelled to work cooperatively for more harmonious relations.

This equilibrium model, as with the *symbolic phase* of federal labor-management relations that preceded it, was accepted and strengthened by both Republican and Democratic administrations during Presidents Ronald Reagan, George H. Bush, and Bill Clinton. Not even President Reagan following the calamity of the air traffic controller's illegal strike attempted to reverse the equilibrium adhered to by federal unions and their managers.

The equilibrium model was modified during the Clinton presidency under the particular aegis of Vice President Al Gore's National Performance Review (NPR), which advocated what Rosenbloom and Kravchuk (2002:, p. 270) have termed as *codetermination* of policy as a model of collective bargaining and Labor-Management Partnerships (LMP). Codetermination's mission was proclaimed by Vice President Gore (1993) as, "We can only transform government if we transform the adversarial relationship that dominates federal union-management interaction into partnership for reinvention and change" (Gore, 1993:, p. 15). Thus, the NPR envisioned labor-management relations as a partnership of two equals, rather than an unrelenting struggle between adversaries.

To reach this goal, President Clinton appointed a National Partnership Council (NPC) in 2000, which in addition to management representatives included the presidents of three federal employee unions (AFGE, NTEU, and NFFE) and a representative of the Public Employee Department of the AFL-CIO. The NPC's mandate was to ". . . propose the statutory changes needed to make the labor-management partnership a reality" (Gore, 1993:, p. 15). President Clinton's Executive Order-12871 (October 1, 1993) promised a new era of labor-management relations:

> Only by changing the nature of Federal labor-management relations so that managers, employees, and employees' elected union representatives serve as partners will it be possible to design and implement comprehensive changes necessary to reform government.

Certainly, federal employee unions were quite willing partners in the Clinton administration's plan to reform procurement procedures or reduce rigid personnel policies and procedures, but plans to cut 272,000 federal jobs by 1998 did not have similar appeal.

Partnership in Cutback. Quite surprisingly, union participation as partners in the process of decreasing the number of federal employees was precisely what occurred as 75,000 federal jobs were eliminated during 1994, the first year of the labor-management partnership (Carroll, 1995). For example, two federal unions and agencies entered into partnership agreements as follows:

- National Treasury Employees Union (NTEU) and the Customs Service agreed to a partnership that NTEU President Robert Tobias commented was essential because, ". . . agency reorganizations or reinventions cannot be implemented without the cooperation and involvement of the union. Union and management need each other in order to succeed" (Tobias, 1994). The agreement seeks organizational "transformation . . . participation as an equal partner in meetings . . . appointment to all task forces and groups for the purposes of changing work processes" and "treating each other with dignity and respect, sharing ideas, proposals, information and concerns with each other" (Hyde, 1994).
- American Federation of Government Employees (AFGE) and the Office of Personnel Management (OPM) reached a partnership agreement, which survived a massive reduction in a force (RIF) in the agency's administration group. AFGE President John Sturdivant cited local 2302 in Kentucky, as an example of "successful experiences in partnership" where, evidently, the local's payroll was reduced by 16 percent in 14 months—4 percent more than required over 5 years in the NPR (Parker and Slaughter, 1994). Remarkably, OPM laid off almost 20 percent of its employees in 1994 (Causey, 1994).

President Clinton's executive order directed the National Partnership Council (NPC) to reform the adversarial state of federal labor law. Accordingly, the NPC moved to broaden the scope of collective bargaining by directing agencies to negotiate over issues; e.g., agency shop and performance appraisals that were previously voluntary. Finally, the NPC directed federal agency heads to develop labor-management partnerships at appropriate levels throughout their respective agencies. However, those proposed agency agreements were never passed by Congress nor approved by President Clinton.

In order to entice union participation in a partnership venture, the following promises were made to federal employee union leaders by the Clinton administration (Ban, 1995):

- that many cuts in jobs would accrue through attrition and buyouts;
- that many of the jobs eliminated would be held by middle management, labor specialists, classification positions, and personnelists (positions not included within collective bargaining agreements);
- that partnership participation with the union would extend throughout civilian federal agencies, from top to bottom;
- that legislation would be sought to require management to negotiate certain issues that were not previously permissible items for bargaining; e.g., agency shop and fair share representation fees, classification, and performance evaluation.

As indicated, none of the aforementioned promises were ever honored. Without obtaining agency shop provisions, federal employee unions simply lacked the capability and finances to serve as strong federal partners.

Federal employee unions also were greatly weakened by prohibitions against collective bargaining for *supervisors* as well as the ban prohibiting union security clauses in collective bargaining agreements. As a result, even though almost two-thirds of federal employees were included within bargaining units, less than one-third voluntarily joined a union (Masters and Atkin, 1995). By July 1995, not only did the proposed legislative changes languish in a hostile Republican-dominated Congress, there was growing criticism from labor observers that the highly touted partnership was merely a facade ". . . it is being driven from the top down by the White House along the rigid vertical structure of each agency" (Anglin, 1994). Others characterized the downsizing as a subterfuge for, "putting the AFGE label on your pink slip" (Parker and Slaughter, 1994:, p. 10). Finally, union leaders began to feel "estranged" because the Clinton administration dropped proposed labor law reforms from the draft civil service reform bill (Ban, 1995).

Thus, the codetermination and equilibrium models ended in disarray with termination of the Clinton presidency in January 2001 and the shape of federal labor-management relations, along with so many other things in American society and politics were to dramatically change with the horrific terrorist attacks of September 11, 2001.

Policy Change and Retrenchment (2000–Present)

In response to the events of 9/11, Congress approved and President Bush signed the Aviation and Transportation Security Act (ATSA) on November 19, 2001, which among other things, created a new federal agency, the Transportation Security Administration (TSA) with primary responsibility for airport and aviation security. TSA would grow from 13 employees in January 2002 to well over 64,000 two years later; most of whom were airport screeners earning from $23,000 to $35,400 per year plus locality pay. Not surprisingly, the American Federation of Government Employees (AFGE), the largest federal employee union, filed petitions with the FLRA that asked for certification elections to designate their union as the exclusive representative of TSA security screeners at New York LaGuardia and Baltimore-Washington airports.

The Bush administration's response was immediate. Admiral James Loy, Under Secretary of Homeland Security, exercising his legal authority under ATSA issued an order on January 9, 2003 precluding collective bargaining by TSA screeners after determining, "mandatory collective bargaining is not compatible with the flexibility required to wage the war against terrorism" (U.S. Transportation Security Administration, 2003:, p. 1). Admiral Loy (2003) offered the following rationale for his decision:

> Fighting terrorism demands a flexible workforce that can rapidly respond to threats. That can mean changes in work assignments and other conditions of employment that are not compatible with the duty to bargain with labor unions.

Admiral Loy suggested that unions could be replaced by enlightened managers and besides, screeners already enjoyed many of the same protections as other federal employees, including equal employment opportunity and whistleblower protection. Loy affirmed his commitment to a model workplace and directed the establishment of a Model Workplace Group (MWG), whose mandate would be to design a plan for how best to address workplace issues. MWG would be headed by TSA's office of civil rights human resources training and a new ombudsman. The group's mission was to "look for ways to promote high performance and good management practices and propose strategies to prevent and resolve conflicts" (U.S. Transportation Security Administration, 2003:, p. 1). Admiral Loy's vision of a union-free workplace at TSA was touted to be "world-class":

> With our employees' help we have put in place a new agency that is delivering *world-class* security and *world-class* customer service. Now we will work together to create a *world-class* workplace.

Carol DiBattiste (2003:, p. 6), TSA Chief of Staff in an address to the Diversity Best Practices in 2003 lauded Admiral Loy's changes:

> Acceptance of change is dependent on trust. Explain the justification for change and if there's trust there's the ready acceptance. I know from personal experience that trust goes a long way when it comes to acceptance of management decisions, whether the decision brings changes painful or pleasurable.

On March 1, 2003, the "union-free" TSA was transitioned into the new Department of Homeland Security (DHS), which already encompassed 21 other established federal agencies. Most had long histories of labor-management relations and the original Homeland Security Act of November 25, 2002 had included a provision calling for "meaningful collective bargaining" at the DHS. How would a union-free TSA fit into the emerging organizational culture at DHS and how "meaningful" would collective bargaining be in the second administration of President Bush? The answer was not long in coming.

On January 27, 2005, the Department of Homeland Security and Office of Personnel Management jointly issued a new Human Resource Management System (HRMS) that covered most of its 110,000 civilian employees, excluding TSA from all elements of the system. HRMS brought about significant changes in classification, compensation, performance management, adverse actions, appeals, and labor relations, but its most controversial elements were in two areas: (1) "reducing the number of situations where collective bargaining is required" and (2) "streamlining adverse actions and appeals processes." Specifically, within collective bargaining, the HRMS provided changes such as (U.S. Department of Homeland Security, 2005:2):

- Non-negotiable management rights were expanded (to assure ability to act);
- Bargaining on procedures was prohibited (but management required to confer);

- Limited bargaining on the impact of a management action;
- Expedited collective bargaining with impasse resolution;
- Homeland Security Labor Relations Board (HSLRB) established (to ensure mission focus, provide one-stop dispute resolution).

It is interesting that these regulations were formulated jointly with OPM, the executive branch's "personnel office," rather than the independent Federal Labor Relations Authority created to oversee federal collective bargaining under the Civil Service Reform Act.

Predictably, reaction from the affected federal employee unions was swift and vociferous. On the same day, January 27, the American Federation of Government Employees (AFGE), National Treasury Employees Union (NTEU), National Federation of Federal Employees (NFFE), and National Association of Agriculture Employees (NAAE) filed suit challenging DHS's new HRMS on statutory and constitutional bases.

The new regulations for DHS personnel compelled employees to take their concerns to HSLRB, an internal board appointed by the DHS secretary, with no requirement for Senate confirmations as required by other federal labor relations entities. As noted, employee and union complaints regarding negotiability disputes and exceptions to arbitral awards previously had been handled by the independent FLRA.

AFGE General Counsel Mark Roth (2005) denounced the HRMS provision for an internal board:

> This violation of the constitutional right to due process shortchanges the American taxpayer. Without due process, managers will have free rein to retaliate against employees who challenge management decisions. The narrowed scope of bargaining in the new regulations allows management to implement transfers and shift changes with impunity. To see how this would work, one need only to look at the Office of Special Counsel, where career employees who spoke out against management decisions suddenly find themselves transferred to offices thousands of miles away from their homes. Who will be held accountable if the DHS fails its mission?

T. J. Bonner (2005), president of AFGE's National Border Patrol Council complained, "the new system allows for the same sort of cronyism that nearly destroyed our nation's civil service a century ago." NTEU President Colleen Kelley (2005:, p. 1) was equally emphatic:

> The employees losing their basic rights are the same men and women who guard our borders every single day. There is absolutely no basis for stripping them of their rights while asking them to help keep America and our way of life intact. The longstanding rights are being replaced with a one-sided regime under which the majority of important conditions of employment are not subject to negotiation— even on the impact and implementation of management-initiated changes on such working conditions.

Thus, the line was drawn between DHS and its employees' unions over the future of collective bargaining in a post-9/11 era. "We, the unions, had earnestly sought to design a new, efficient personnel system in collaboration with DHS managers," said AFGE national president John Gage (2005:, p. 1). "With our efforts rebuffed and our gravest concerns ignored, we now, unfortunately, have no choice but to pursue a remedy through the federal courts."

Nor was DHS the only agency battleground in federal employee collective bargaining. A coalition of 36 unions, which represented a majority of the Department of Defense's (DOD) 770,000 civilian employees banded together as the United DoD Workers' Coalition (UDWC) to fight new DOD personnel system they believed would take away federal employee rights (2005). In its new National Security Personnel System (NSPS), also known as the Rumsfeld Plan, unions claimed that DOD "significantly narrowed employee rights to collective bargaining and all but eliminated due process rights that enable employees to speak with confidence when they see wrongdoing or mismanagement" (American Federation of Government Employees, 2005). AFGE National President Gage (2005) announced, "To call this a 'National Security' system is a joke; if anything, the Rumsfeld plan makes the nation less secure."

Specifically, the UDWC challenged the NSPS as a statutory violation of work rules because of DOD's refusal to consult with unions representing its employees, as called for in the defense authorization legislation that authorized the creation of a new personnel system, and went ahead in issuing its rule changes in violation of section 9902(m) of the Defense Authorization Act for FY 2004 (American Federation of Government Employees, 2005). National Federation of Federal Employees (NFFE) President Richard N. Brown (2005) lamented at a Coalition press conference, "Brothers and Sisters, unions didn't just appear one day. They were voted in by workers in order to ensure that they would have a united voice in the workplace. . . . NSPS attempts to silence that voice." John Sweeney (2005), president of the AFL-CIO, asserted that "The Bush Administration is now stepping out way beyond any appropriate flexibility in work rules and into radically undermining good pay, decent workplace standards and workers rights throughout the federal workforces. We are here to tell the Bush Administration that the attack on workers' rights ends here."

FUTURE OF FEDERAL EMPLOYEE COLLECTIVE BARGAINING

With all due respect to John Sweeney of the AFL-CIO and federal employee union leaders, the world of public employee collective bargaining has changed dramatically and probably irrevocably since John Kennedy signed Executive Order 10988 in 1962 and the change is not good news for unions. First, rates of unionization continue to decline from a high of 20.1 percent in 1983 (the first year for which comparable union data was available) to 12.5 percent in 2004 (Bureau of National Affairs, 2004:, p. 2). Even more revealing is that the percentage of private-sector workers in unions was down to 7.9 percent in 2004 (Joyce, 2005:, p. 1). In many cases this decline did not reflect large numbers of union decertification votes, but rather the loss of employment in industries that were traditionally unionized, such as steelmaking and automobile manufacturing. Secondly, the freer movement of capital and trade around the world, "globalization," has resulted in more goods being produced overseas for the American market. At the same time, massive immigration by workers in search of better economic conditions has become a second type of globalization (Nissen, 2002).

Finally, many union leaders seemingly do not appreciate the changed nature of partisan politics following 9/11 and the 2004 presidential election. Although union support was a major factor in Kennedy's narrow defeat of Richard Nixon in 1960, it was private-sector unions that made the essential difference in the outcome, not public employees. By comparison, public employee unions, including AFSCME at state and local levels and AFGE at the federal level endorsed and its members worked hard for Al Gore in 2000 and John Kerry in 2004, which emphasized a decidedly anti-Bush message. Labor is thought to have spent at least $140 million in hard cash in the 2004 presidential campaign, not including staff time and other resources (Joyce, 2005). This continued involvement in the political arena is occurring even though unions have "repeatedly failed to elect labor-friendly candidates . . . or get meaningful results when they did, more politics is the one thing that virtually all union leaders agree on (Joyce, 2005:, p. 1)."

Not surprisingly, following the 2004 election, Republican strategist Grover Norquist proclaimed a broad campaign to further decimate organized labor as its highest priority (Joyce, 2005). The Republican advantage in fighting unions is the war on terrorism, which has irrevocably heated the debate surrounding strategies for improving national security. The Bush administration's Rumsfeld plan, non-union stance at TSA, and restructuring of collective bargaining at DHS and DOD allow the outward cry for national security to cloud a political counter-attack on a system of labor-management relations that has evolved over the preceding forty-five years. Rather than engage the Republicans in a political battle over national security they probably cannot win, a few labor reformers are urging unions to return to what worked best during the era of rapid growth—organizing unorganized workers (Bai, 2005; Greenhouse, 2005; Joyce, 2005). Rather than "circling the wagons around the needs of current union members"; they contend that union leaders would be better advised to consider the model advocated by SEIU National President Andy Stern (Bai, 2005) to recruit a new mass of public- and private-sector employees.

REFERENCES

American Federation of Government Employees. 2005. "Defense Workers' Unions to Sue Pentagon." *News Release*, Washington, DC: February 10. www.afge.org/Index.

Anglin, G. 1994. "Federal Sector Partnerships: Boon or Boondoggle?" *Labor Notes* September: 10.

Bai, M. 2005. "Is There a Place for Unions in the 21st-Century Economy?" *The New York Times Magazine* January 30: 37–45; 62–63.

Ban, C. 1995. "Unions, Management and the NPR." In Donald F. Kettl and John DiIulio Jr., eds. *Inside the Reinvention Machine: Appraising Government Reform*. Washington, DC: Brookings Institution.

Beal, E., Wickersham, E., and Kienast, P. 1976. *The Practice of Collective Bargaining*, 5th ed. Homewood, IL: Richard D. Irwin.

Bonner, T. J. 2005. Quoted in "Homeland Security Unions Plan to Sue DHS," American Federation of Government Employees, *News Release* January 26, Washington, DC.

Brown, R. N. 2005. "President Brown Speaks at United DoD Workers Coalition Press Conference." *NFFE News* February 9. www.nffe.org.

Bureau of National Affairs. 1971. *Labor Relations Yearbook: 1970*. Washington, DC.

Bureau of National Affairs. 2004. *Labor Relations Yearbook: 2004*. Report of Cornell University Conference, Washington, DC.

Carroll, J. D. 1995. "The Rhetoric of Reform and Political Reality in the National Performance Review." *Public Administration Review* May–June: 302–312.

Causey, M. 1994. "The OPM Blues." *Washington Post* July 7: B2.

DiBattiste, C. 2003. "The Human Side of Human Capital." Speech given to *Diversity Best Practices Conference*, St. Regis Hotel, Washington, DC. April 22. www.tsa.gov/public/display.

Ford, G. R. 1976. *Public Papers of the President: 1975*. Washington, DC.: U.S. Government Printing Office.

Gage, J. 2005. Quoted in "Defense Workers to Sue Pentagon," *Press Release*, American Federation of Government Employees, Washington: DC. February 10.

Gore, A. 1993. The Report of the National Performance Review: Executive Summary, *Creating a Government That Works Better and Costs Less*, Washington, DC: US Printing Office.

Greenhouse, S. 2005. "Unions Support Plan to Cut A.F.L.-C.I.O. Contributions." *The New York Times*.

Hays, S. W. and Reeves, T. Z. 1984. *Personnel Management in the Public Sector*, rev. ed. Dubuque, IA: William C. Brown Publishers.

Hyde, A. C. 1994. "Overcoming the Barriers: The Case of Customs and the NTEU." *PA Times* 17: August 11: 6.

Joyce, F. 2005. "Fate of the Union." *AlterNet* February 22. www.alternet.org/story/21312/.

Kelley, C. M. 2005. Quoted in "NTEU, Other Homeland Security Unions, File Federal Lawsuit to Stop DHS From Implementing Unlawful Personnel Regulations." *News Release*, National Treasury Employees Union, Washington, DC: 1–2. dhs.nteu.org/PressRelease.

Kennedy, J. F. January 1962. Executive Order 10988, *The Federal Register* 27:17, Washington, DC: US Government Printing Office.

Loy, J. 2003. Quoted in "TSA's Loy Determines Collective Bargaining Conflicts with National Security Needs." Transportation Security Administration, *Press Release* January 9, Washington, DC. www.tsa.gov/public/display.

Masters, M. F. and Atkin, R. S. 1995. "Bargaining, Financial, and Political Bases of Federal Sector Unions: Implications for Reinventing Government." *Review of Public Personnel Administration* 15: Winter: 5–23.

McCabe, D. M. March 21–25, 1982. "Problems in Labor-Management Relations Under Title VII of the Civil Service Reform Act." Paper presented to the *National Conference of the American Society for Public Administration*, Honolulu, HI.

Nigro, F. A. 1969. *Management-Employee Relations in the Public Service*, Chicago, IL: Public Personnel Association.

Nissen, B. 2002. *Unions in a Globalized Environment*. Armonk, NY: M. E. Sharpe, Inc.

Nixon, R. M. 1972. *Public Papers of the President: 1971*. Washington, DC: U.S. Government Printing Office.

Parker, M. and Slaughter, J. 1994. "From 'QWL' to Reengineering: Management Takes Off the Gloves." *Labor Notes* March: 8–11.

Rosenbloom, D. H. and Kravchuk, R. 2002. *Public Administration: Understanding Management, Politics, and Law in the Public Sector*, 5th ed. New York, NY: McGraw-Hill.

Roth, M. 2005. Quoted in "Homeland Security Unions Plan to Sue DHS," American Federation of Government Employees. *News Release*, January 26. www.afge.org.

Spero, S. D. and Capozzola, J. M. 1973. *The Urban Community and Its Unionized Bureaucracies*. New York, NY: Dunellen Publishing.

Stanley, D. T. 1972. *Managing Local Government Under Union Pressure*. Washington, DC.: The Brookings Institution.

Sweeney, J. 2005. Quoted in "Defense Workers Raise Voices and Signs to Protest New Personnel Changes." American Federation of Government Employees, *News Release*. February 8, Washington, DC: www.afge.org/Index.

Tobias, R. M. 1994. "Labor-Management Partnerships: The Union Perspective." *PA Times* 17: August 1: 6.

U.S. Department of Homeland Security and Office of Personnel Management. 2005. "Final Human Resource Regulations Fact Sheet."

U.S. Transportation Security Administration. 2003. "TSA's Loy Determines Collective Bargaining Conflicts with National Security Needs." January 9 Washington, DC. www.tsa.gov/public/display.

Chapter 9

Public Employees' Liability for "Constitutional Torts"

David H. Rosenbloom and Margo Bailey

Every person who, under color of any statute, ordinance, regulation, custom, or usage, of any State or Territory or the District of Columbia, subjects, or causes to be subjected, any citizen of the United States or other person within the jurisdiction thereof to the deprivation of any rights, privileges, or immunities secured by the Constitution and laws, shall be liable to the party injured in an action at law, suit in equity, or other proper proceeding for redress. For the purposes of this section, any Act of Congress applicable exclusively to the District of Columbia shall be considered to be a statute of the District of Columbia.

Civil Rights Act of 1871, as amended and
codified in 42 U.S. Code, Section 1983 (1982).

INTRODUCTION

Ever since the establishment of the Republic, public employment in the United States has been considered a "public trust." The concept that public employees have special obligations to the political community has prompted a variety of restrictions on their constitutional rights. For instance, the Constitution prohibits federal employees from being electors in the electoral college and from accepting gifts, offices, emoluments, or titles from foreign governments without the consent of Congress. The document also requires them to swear or affirm their support for it. As early as 1801, President Jefferson sought to restrict the First Amendment rights of federal employees to engage in electioneering because he deemed such activities ". . . inconsistent with the spirit of the Constitution and [their] duties to it" (Rosenbloom, 1971, pp. 39–40). Over the years, public employees have faced limitations not only on their political and economic activities, but also on their residency, privacy, speech and association, and general liberties (Rosenbloom, 1971; Rosenbloom and Carroll, 1990, 1995). Beginning in the 1970s, they also became potentially liable for "constitutional torts," which has had the effect of requiring public administration to comport more fully with constitutional law and values. The development of this additional legal obligation, its scope, and its consequences for public personnel management in the United States are the subjects of this chapter.

Constitutional torts are acts committed by public officials or employees, within the frameworks of their jobs that violate individuals' constitutional rights in ways that can be appropriately remedied by civil suits for money damages. For instance, the violation of an individual's Fourth Amendment right to privacy through an unconstitutional search is such a tort. So is a public employee's unconstitutional act of racial discrimination. Civil liability for money damages for constitutional torts can now be potentially attached to most federal, state, and local government employees. In general, they are vulnerable to both compensatory and punitive or exemplary damages. Under Eleventh Amendment interpretation, state governments and agencies cannot be sued in federal court for money damages for their constitutional torts (though other remedies for their unconstitutional acts are available). By extension, state employees cannot be sued as surrogates for state governments in such cases (*Will v. Michigan Department of State Police*, 1989). However, state employees can be sued in their *personal* capacities for constitutional torts committed while exercising official authority (*Hafer v. Melo*, 1991). Similarly, federal employees, but not agencies, can be sued for money damages in constitutional tort suits (*FDIC v. Meyer*, 1994). Local governments do not have Eleventh Amendment immunity. They are treated as "persons" in this area of the law, can be sued for compensatory, but not punitive or exemplary damages for constitutional torts caused directly by their policies (*Pembaur v. City of Cincinnati*, 1986; *City of Newport v. Fact Concerts*, 1981). Even public employees who never deal directly with members of the public may face liabilities for violations of their subordinates' constitutional rights.

This chapter focuses on public employees' *personal* liability for constitutional torts, which makes "constitutional competence" a matter of basic job competence by requiring public personnel to know the constitutional law that governs their official actions (Rosenbloom, Carroll, and Carroll, 2000, chapter 2). For human resource managers, avoidance of personal liability for constitutional torts necessitates: (1) understanding how the Constitution pertains to public employment and (2) building constitutionally required protections and procedures into administrative systems for recruitment, selection, employee development, promotion, adverse actions, reductions in force, equal opportunity, labor relations, background investigations, drug testing, and assisting employees with substance abuse and other problems that may jeopardize privacy rights.

PUBLIC OFFICIALS' ABSOLUTE IMMUNITY: THE TRADITIONAL APPROACH

Until the 1970s, under federal judicial interpretations, public employees at all levels of government generally held absolute immunity from civil suits stemming from the exercise of their official functions. Under this approach, when public officers are acting within the outer perimeter of their authority they cannot be sued personally for violating individuals' constitutional rights. For example, in *Stump v. Sparkman* (1978), a state judge enjoying absolute immunity was shielded from a damage suit even though he authorized the sterilization of a "mildly retarded" female high school student under circumstances that failed to protect her constitutional right to due process of law. Moreover, the judge acted without specific legal authorization, but not beyond the ultimate scope of his office. The rationales for granting legislators, judges, executive branch officials, and rank-and-file employees absolute immunity are all somewhat different. But at their root is the belief, developed in common law interpretations, that the activities of governmental functionaries should not be controlled or impeded by individuals' actual or threatened lawsuits. As the Supreme Court stated the principle in *Spalding v. Vilas* (1896), the first case on official executive immunity to reach it:

> In exercising the functions of his office, the head of an Executive Department, keeping within the limits of his authority, should not be under an apprehension that the motives that control his official conduct may, at any time, become the subject of inquiry in a civil suit for damages. It would seriously cripple the proper and effective administration of public affairs as entrusted to the executive branch of the government, if he were subjected to any such restraint (*Spalding v. Vilas*, 1896, p. 498).

This approach drew some of its legal strength from the centuries old common law principle of "sovereign immunity." In English law, sovereign immunity rests on the premise that "the king can do no wrong." Precisely why sovereign immunity was incorporated into U.S. constitutional law has never been wholly clear (*U.S. v. Lee*, 1882). However, it precludes suing the federal and state governments in some types of cases unless they have given their permission to be sued through a tort claims act or other legal device.

GENERAL LEGAL TRENDS RELATED TO OFFICIAL LIABILITY

Whatever the strength of the legal rationales for public employees' absolute immunity, by the 1970s judicial support for precluding civil suits against public employees for money damages had clearly weakened. The changing attitude toward absolute immunity was related to two major legal trends. First, civil liability was expanding throughout the American legal system. As Peter Schuck (1988, p. 4) reflected toward the end of the 1980s, "On almost all fronts and in almost all jurisdictions, liability has dramatically expanded. It does not seem to matter what kind of party is being sued. Doctor or public official, landlord or social host, government agency or product manufacturer—all are more likely to be held liable today." Although the number of suits initiated per capita may be no larger at present than in colonial times and other periods in United States history (Galanter, 1988, p. 19), plaintiffs appeared more apt to win or receive satisfactory settlements because of changing judicial interpretations. Schuck (1982), a leading student of "suing government," summarized the underpinnings of the emerging tort law:

> Although the new judicial ideology of tort law is complex and multifaceted, four elements stand out: (1) a profound skepticism about the role of markets in allocating risk; (2) a shift in the dominant paradigm of causation [from determinant to probabilistic causal relationships]; (3) a tendency to broaden jury discretion; and (4) a preoccupation with achieving broad social goals instead of the narrower, more traditional purpose of corrective justice between the litigants (Schuck, 1988, p. 6).

The second trend affecting the liability of public administrators for constitutional torts was the expansion of individual constitutional rights. Headed by the Supreme Court under Chief Justice Earl Warren (1953–1969), the federal judiciary demonstrated a new propensity to afford individuals greater constitutional protections vis-à-vis public administrative action (Rosenbloom and O'Leary, 1997). Whole categories of persons who formerly had very few constitutional protections when interacting with public bureaucracies were granted greater substantive, privacy, procedural, and equal protection rights under the First, Fourth, Fifth, Eighth, and Fourteenth Amendments. For instance, public employees were afforded substantial procedural due process protections in dismissals, greater freedom of speech and association rights (including such activities as whistleblowing and joining labor unions), and much stronger claims to equal protection of the laws. Clients or customers receiving welfare or public housing gained clear procedural due process protections of these benefits for the first time. The courts reinterpreted the equal protection clause to overturn the "separate but equal" doctrine that had previously permitted public services, such as education, to be racially segregated. Prisons were also desegregated under the Fourteenth Amendment and drastically reformed, via the Eighth and Fourteenth Amendments, to reduce overcrowding and brutal conditions. Individuals confined to public mental health facilities were granted a constitutional right to treatment or habilitation. The constitutional rights of persons accused of crimes were expanded to include "Miranda warnings" (*Miranda v. Arizona*, 1966) and other safeguards. The privacy and due process rights of persons engaged in "street-level" encounters were also enhanced, though somewhat modestly (Lipsky, 1980; *Terry v. Ohio*, 1968; *Delaware v. Prouse*, 1979; *Kolender v. Lawson*, 1983).

For the most part, the trend toward greater constitutional rights for individuals in their encounters with public administration continued during the Burger (1969–1986) and Rehnquist courts (1986–present). For example, in the 1990s, property rights were strengthened against administrative zoning regulations that effectively deprived individuals of legitimate uses of their land (*Lucas v. South Car-olina Coastal Council*, 1992; *Dolan v. City of Tigard*, 1994). New procedural due process protections were applied to civil forfeitures of real property (*U.S. v. James Daniel Good Real Property*, 1994). **Contractors'** free speech rights, which are now comparable to those of public employees, were also strengthened (*Board of County Commissioners, Wabaunsee County v. Umbehr*, 1996; *O'Hare Truck Service Inc. v. City of Northlake*, 1996). Constitutional equal protection also became more salient to con-tracting out (*City of Richmond v. J. A. Croson Co.*, 1989; *Adarand Constructors, Inc. v. Pena*, 1995). Under the Rehnquist court, a major exception to the general expan-sion of constitutional rights has occurred with regard to the Fourth Amendment's protection against unreasonable searches and seizures. Today, one can be arrested for a non-jailable (that is, "fine only") offense, such as not wearing a seat belt, police may use any traffic offense—no matter how minor—as a pretext for stop-ping a motorist whom they suspect of criminal wrongdoing, and individuals can face criminal penalties for refusing to identify themselves to police officers (*Atwater v. City of Lago Vista*, 2001; *Whren v. United States*, 1996; *Hiibel v. Sixth Judi-cial District Court of Nevada, Humboldt County*, 2004).

Taken together, the expansion of liability and constitutional rights brought about a revolution in the relationship of the federal courts to public administration at all levels of government. Federal judges became deeply involved in the man-agement of prisons, jails, public mental health facilities, and public schools. The courts also became far more salient to such public administrative matters as bud-geting and personnel (Rosenbloom and O'Leary, 1997; Horowitz, 1983; *Missouri v. Jenkins*, 1990, 1995). The intervention of federal courts in state administrative sys-tems added a substantial "juridical" element to federalism (Carroll, 1982).

When individuals possessed few constitutional rights in their encounters with public administrators, constitutional torts would necessarily be limited in number. Certainly police brutality or violations of the Fifteenth Amendment's guarantee of the right to vote regardless of race might have been the basis of suits, but by and large it was difficult for public administrators to violate individuals' constitutional rights simply because the public held so few substantive, procedural, and equal protection guarantees in their interactions with government agencies. As the courts expanded the constitutional rights of public employees, clients/customers, prison-ers, public mental health patients, individuals engaged in street-level encounters, property owners, and contractors, the potential number and scope of constitutional violations became substantial. Consequently, it was desirable to develop an enforcement mechanism that would protect individuals against unconstitutional administrative action and enable them to vindicate their rights. Enter liability.

FROM ABSOLUTE TO QUALIFIED IMMUNITY: THE RISE OF LIABILITY

As late as 1959, a plurality on the Supreme Court continued to adhere to the prin-ciple that:

It has been thought important that officials of government should be free to exercise their duties unembarrassed by the fear of damage suits in respect of acts done in the course of those duties—suits which would consume time and energies which would otherwise be devoted to governmental service and the threat of which might appreciably inhibit the . . . administration of policies of government (*Barr v. Matteo*, 1959, p. 571).

However, once the public was gaining an array of constitutional protections in their dealings with administrators and liability law was becoming more expansive, the courts sought to establish a better balance between the governmental requirement of efficient and effective administration, on the one hand, and the need to deter violations of individuals' rights and compensate for them, on the other. So remarkable had the changes in liability and constitutional law been that by the 1970s the concept of "absolute" immunity for most public officials was clearly out of place.

During that decade, the Supreme Court used two legal vehicles to redefine the liability of public administrators. First, in *Bivens v. Six Unknown Named Federal Narcotics Agents* (1971), the Court held that federal officials could be liable, directly under the Constitution, for breaches of individuals' Fourth Amendment rights. The Court reasoned that the Fourth Amendment gives victims of unconstitutional federal searches and seizures a constitutional right to sue the officials involved for money damages. Subsequently, the Court ruled that similar rights to redress exist under the Fifth and Eighth Amendments (*Davis v. Passman*, 1979; *Carlson v. Green*, 1980). Under ordinary circumstances, individuals can bring suits against federal officials for violations of the First Amendment as well (Lee and Rosenbloom, 2005, chapter 2; see *Bush v. Lucas*, 1983, for an exception).

Second, the Supreme Court dramatically reinterpreted the standards for liability regarding state and local public administrators and officials. The Court resurrected the Civil Rights Act of 1871, which is now codified as 42 United States Code section 1983, and generally called "section 1983." The relevant portion of the act is quoted in the epigraph to this chapter. Although well conceived in the Reconstruction Era (1865–1877) as a means of providing federal judicial protection to former slaves, the act was rendered virtually moribund by a number of judicial interpretations and doctrines that drastically restricted its coverage (Rosenbloom and O'Leary, 1997, chapter 8; "Section 1983 and Federalism," 1977). In terms of liability, the courts refused to interpret literally the act's explicit application to "every person who." Instead, the judiciary reasoned that in writing "every person," Congress did not intended to override the long-standing absolute immunity at common law enjoyed by many state and local government officials, such as legislators and judges, from civil suits for damages. Consequently, even though such officials might be directly responsible for the violation of individuals' federally protected rights, they could not be sued for money damages under the act. It was through the redefinition of official immunity during the 1970s that the act became a major force in public administration and American law.

The Supreme Court departed from past interpretations in *Scheuer v. Rhodes* (1974) when it abandoned the concept of absolute immunity for officials exercising executive functions. Instead, it opted for a "qualified immunity" that afforded many public officials immunity from civil suits for money damages only if they acted in good faith and reasonably. A year later, in *Wood v. Strickland* (1975, p. 321–322), "reasonably" was interpreted to mean whether the official "knew or reasonably should have known that the action he took within his sphere of official responsibility would violate the constitutional rights" of the individuals affected.

Bivens, Scheuer, and *Wood* opened the door to many suits against public administrators by individuals seeking money damages for alleged violations of their constitutional rights. Under the standard for qualified immunity these cases developed, suits could allege that the administrators failed to act in good faith by displaying malice or a reckless disregard of individuals' rights. In practice, defending against such a charge proved burdensome for the public officials involved. The issue of "good faith" is considered a matter of fact that may be submitted to juries for determination. Consequently, suits could be drawn out and very expensive to defend. Under such conditions, the process itself could be punishment, and public officials were consequently under substantial pressure to settle out of court, without strict regard to the merits of the charges against them. In an age of crowded dockets, elaborate trials in liability suits against public officials also took a toll on the courts. The Supreme Court sought to reduce these pressures in *Harlow v. Fitzgerald* (1982), which made it easier for public officials to defend themselves against constitutional tort suits.

The *Harlow* decision "completely reformulated qualified immunity along principles not at all embodied in the common law" (*Anderson v. Creighton,* 1987, p. 645). The new standard for qualified immunity relies on a procedure called "summary judgment" as the means of determining whether a suit can proceed to a full trial. A district court judge's decision regarding summary judgment can be appealed. However, once a decision to grant summary judgment to the defendant public employee or official is final, the case ends. It cannot proceed to a full-fledged trial. *Harlow* established the following standard for determining whether summary judgment should be granted: "government officials performing discretionary functions, generally are shielded from liability for civil damages insofar as their conduct does not violate clearly established statutory or constitutional rights of which a reasonable person would have known" (1982, p. 818). The defendant's motives and good faith are irrelevant at this stage. The key questions are whether the facts of what happened are sufficiently clear to make it unnecessary to determine them through a trial, and if so, whether the alleged conduct violated clearly established constitutional rights of which the administrator should reasonably have known. The judge grants qualified immunity if he or she concludes: (1) that based on the facts, there was no violation of the Constitution; (2) if the Constitution was violated, the law at the time was not clearly established; or (3) even if the law was clearly established, an administrator could not reasonably have known that the conduct involved would violate a constitutional right.

The great advantage of the *Harlow* approach is that summary judgments are far quicker and much less burdensome than jury trials. The immunity is from suit, not just a defense against liability (*Mitchell v. Forsyth*, 1985). The *Harlow* construction applies to federal officials and employees directly under the Constitution and to state and local personnel under section 1983.

THE LOGIC OF LIABILITY: DETERRENCE AND JUDICIAL INFLUENCE ON PUBLIC ADMINISTRATION

When the courts do something as dramatic as overturning the effects of centuries of common law, one is impelled to consider their rationale and the effects of the change. The logic of rejecting absolute immunity in favor of qualified immunity (or liability) is clear. First, the liability under consideration here is personal liability, not the liability of agencies or government entities. Personal liability is viewed by the Supreme Court as an excellent enforcement mechanism. In the Court's words, ". . . the *Bivens* remedy [that is, official liability], in addition to compensating victims, serves a deterrent purpose" (*Carlson v. Green*, 1980, p. 21), and the general point has been to "create an incentive for officials who may harbor doubts about the lawfulness of their intended actions to err on the side of protecting citizens' constitutional rights" (*Owen v. City of Independence*, 1980, pp. 651–652).

The deterrent effect of liability is magnified greatly by the potential assessment of punitive or exemplary damages against public administrators. In *Smith v. Wade* (1983), the Supreme Court had an opportunity to permit the federal courts to apply a tough standard for subjecting public administrators to such damages. Historically, there have been two general standards for these damages. One is whether the individual found liable acted with malice in violating the other party's rights, that is, displayed "ill will, spite, or intent to injure" (*Smith v. Wade*, 1983, p. 37). The other standard is recklessness, or a "callous disregard of, or indifference to, the rights or safety of others" (*Smith v. Wade*, 1983, p. 37). The Supreme Court allowed the lower courts to use recklessness, which is the weaker of the two. It reasoned that "the conscientious officer who desires . . . [to] avoid lawsuits can and should look to the standard for actionability in the first instance," that is, whether the action violated clearly established rights of which a reasonable person would have known (*Smith v. Wade*, 1983, p. 50). In other words, a finding that compensatory damages are appropriate will often support the assessment of punitive or exemplary damages as well because conduct at issue will manifest at least an indifference to the rights of the injured party. Reliance on recklessness rather than malice makes it easier to use damages to punish public administrators financially and to deter similar unconstitutional behavior on the part of others. Although punitive damages may trigger due process concerns, they are largely open-ended and not technically required to be tightly related to the injury involved (*BMW of North America v. Gore*, 1996). Consequently, in cases where qualified immunity is not granted, plaintiffs may allege malice (as well as recklessness) in the hope of recovering greater damages.

A second aspect of the logic of liability is more complex. The way that the courts constructed public officials' qualified immunity enables them to exercise considerable direction over public administration. In effect, the Supreme Court has made knowledge of constitutional law a matter of job competence for public administrators. As it stated in *Harlow* (1982, p. 819), "a reasonably competent public official should know the law governing his conduct." But what is that law? In the words of former Supreme Court Justice Lewis Powell, "Constitutional law is what the courts say it is" (*Owen v. City of Independence*, 1980, p. 669). Consequently, public administrators must take direction from judges, who determine how the Constitution bears upon their jobs.

Moreover, despite the qualifier in *Harlow* that the rights involved must be "clearly established," the Supreme Court has not limited liability to instances in which a materially similar or identical administrative action was already ruled unconstitutional (*Hope v. Pelzer*, 2002). Rather, the concept of "clearly established" extends to constitutional values and principles that should be known by a reasonably competent public official. Even if the constitutionality of some particular act has never been litigated, a public administrator engaging in it may be liable if the state of the law gives him or her "fair warning" that it violates the Constitution (*Hope v. Pelzer*, 2002).

Overall, therefore, public administrators' liability promotes two judicial objectives. It is a strong tool for enforcing the constitutional rights that the judiciary has established for individuals in their interactions with public administrators. It also enables the courts to exercise greater direction over public administration. The latter judicial interest has also been manifested in the courts' willingness to entertain suits seeking very broad reforms of administrative institutions or processes, such as public mental health facilities, public schools, and public personnel systems (Rosenbloom and O'Leary, 1997; Chayes, 1976; Horowitz, 1977, 1983).

THE IMPACT OF LIABILITY

It is difficult to assess comprehensively the impact of the change from absolute to qualified immunity. There is a lack of systematic knowledge about this area of the law. It is clear that thousands of suits have been brought against public employees, but less is known about their resolution (Lee, 1987; Farley, 1989). The likelihood of a public administrator losing a constitutional tort suit and paying damages personally appears relatively slim.[1] Nevertheless, public managers have been very concerned with potential liability and the costs of legal defense, settlements, and judgments (Friel, 1998; Rivenbark, 1998).

Even if more were known about case resolutions, settlements, and damages, however, it would still be very difficult to assess the overall impact of liability upon public administrative practices. Part of the intent of liability is to change public administrators' behavior to assure that it complies with constitutional requirements. To the extent that qualified immunity is successful, public administrators will be less likely to violate constitutional rights and there will be fewer grounds for suing them. For example, police today routinely do recite "Miranda warnings," and social service and personnel agencies have built constitutional due process into their standard operating practices. It would be surprising to find many constitutional violations in these areas. Nevertheless, there are surely many instances in which individuals whose rights are violated by public administrators fail, for one reason or another, to bring cases. Consequently, only limited inferences can be drawn from the number of cases filed, the absence of more filings, and the outcomes of cases. But clearly liability law is not a dead letter and the best defense is to know and respect individuals' constitutional rights (Lee, 2004; Lee and Rosenbloom, 2005).

EXCEPTIONS TO THE GENERAL PATTERN OF PUBLIC OFFICIALS' LIABILITY

There are some exceptions to the current standard for qualified immunity and to the availability of compensatory damages as a remedy for injuries. When public employees are engaged in adjudicatory or legislative functions they are likely to retain absolute immunity, as do judges and elected legislators (*Butz v. Economou*, 1978; *Bogan v. Scott-Harris*, 1998). It is important to remember that absolute immunity pertains to the function, not the official position description. For instance, an administrative law judge will have *qualified*, rather than *absolute* immunity when hiring or disciplining subordinate employees. Necessarily, the functional approach results in some ambiguity and even some public employees engaged in adjudicatory functions, such as public defenders and members of prison disciplinary committees, do not enjoy absolute immunity (*Tower v. Glover*, 1984; *Cleavinger v. Saxner*, 1985).

In *Bush v. Lucas* (1983), the Supreme Court held that liability suits were an inappropriate remedy for federal employees claiming to have been subject to illegal or unconstitutional personnel actions in retaliation for their exercise of freedom of speech. The Court reasoned that federal personnel law provides for elaborate remedies, including hearings before the Merit Systems Protection Board, for such employees. Therefore, in the Court's view, because Congress explicitly created these remedies, it would be improper for the judiciary to fashion additional ones through constitutional interpretation. *Bush's* broad reasoning precludes constitutional tort suits in federal personnel administration in a wide range of matters. However, where there is no alternative remedy for the violation of constitutional rights such suits may be appropriate. For example, in *Collins v. Bender* (1999) the U.S. Court of Appeals for the Ninth Circuit held that a former Drug Enforcement Agent could bring a constitutional tort suit against fellow agents who violated his Fourth Amendment rights by seizing personal firearms from his house without a warrant while he was on administrative leave. The seizure was not a personnel action subject to an administrative remedy. The *Collins* holding suggests that more viable constitutional tort suits by federal personnel may emerge as an unintended consequence of the reduction of civil service and administrative appeals rights for employees in the Departments of Homeland Security and Defense. *Bush*, of course, does nothing to prevent non-federal government employees from using section 1983 as a means of seeking compensatory and punitive damages for personnel actions taken against them in violation of any of their constitutional rights.

THE CONSTITUTIONAL RIGHT TO DISOBEY

Public administrators' potential liability for constitutional torts has generated a concomitant nascent constitutional right to disobey unconstitutional directives. In *Harley v. Schuylkill County* (1979, p. 194), a federal district court explained that:

> The duty to refrain from acting in a manner which would deprive another of constitutional rights is a duty created and imposed by the constitution itself. It is logical to believe that the concurrent right is also one which is created and secured by the constitution. Therefore, we hold that the right to refuse to perform an unconstitutional act is a right "secured by the Constitution. . . ."

The Supreme Court has not had occasion to consider the constitutional right of public employees to disobey unconstitutional orders. However, the district court's conclusion appears to be supported by strong policy reasons as well as by constitutional imperative. As Robert Vaughn (1977, pp. 294–295), points out: "Congress and the courts have already adopted the concept of personal responsibility by providing penalties for the wrongful acts of public employees. The courts now have the opportunity to vindicate the concept of personal responsibility by accepting the right of public employees to disobey under appropriate circumstances." To prevail in asserting a constitutional right to disobey unconstitutional directives, the employee may have to show: (1) that the refusal to obey was based on a sincere belief that the action at issue was unconstitutional, and (2) that he or she is correct in his or her legal assessment.

In practice, of course, disobedience is likely to be a last resort. Public employees also have a constitutional right to seek to eliminate unconstitutional practices through whistleblowing (*Pickering v. Board of Education*, 1968; *Givhan v. Western Line Consolidated School District*, 1979). In modern personnel and management systems, employees will also have the opportunity to discuss their reasons for not wanting to carry out an order with a supervisor, and some resolution short of litigation is highly likely.

CONSEQUENCES FOR PUBLIC PERSONNEL ADMINISTRATION

Public employees' liabilities for constitutional torts have several important consequences for public personnel administration. First, although such liability conveys great benefits by helping to protect constitutional rights, it also adds to the cost of government. The potential to be sued for constitutional torts makes public employment less desirable. Public personnel management is now infused with constitutional law and potential liability. In the past three decades or so, the Supreme Court decided several cases involving public employees' challenges to personnel actions allegedly violating freedom of speech or association, Fourth Amendment privacy rights, procedural due process, and equal protection.[2] The government plainly could have avoided some of the suits it lost by paying greater attention to clear constitutional doctrines in the first place.[3]

However, in some cases the law may appear clear to a judge but not necessarily so to a personnel manager. For example, affirmative action became deeply ingrained in the 1980s and 1990s and is still widely practiced in public personnel systems even though judges relying on the Supreme Court's reasoning in *Adarand Constructors v. Pena* (1995) and *Gratz v. Bollinger* (2003), might well find many instances of it unconstitutional (see Naylor and Rosenbloom, 2004).[4] In other cases, the law itself may be so unclear that affords little or no useful guidance. *Waters v. Churchill* (1994), which involved public employees' freedom of speech, is probably the preeminent example of just how fuzzy constitutional law can be (Rosenbloom, 1994). The key standard in Justice Sandra Day O'Connor's plurality opinion is that "only procedure outside the range of what a reasonable manager would use may be condemned as unreasonable" (*Waters v. Churchill*, 1994, p. 678). To which, Justice Antonin Scalia responded that "it remains entirely unclear what the employer's judgment *must* be based on" (*Waters v. Churchill*, 1994, p. 693).[5] Although such a lack of clarity would seem to relieve public personnelists of liability under the *Harlow* standard, they nevertheless need to follow the case law as it develops in lower court decisions, which may provide "fair warning" that a contemplated action is unconstitutional (*Hope v. Pelzer*, 2002).

Many public personnel systems protect their employees in liability suits by providing them with legal representation, legal insurance, and/or indemnification. These approaches go a long way toward eliminating the risk of being harmed financially in a lawsuit arising out of one's performance in public office. Nevertheless, sufficient insurance can be costly, the availability of legal representation may depend upon the specific circumstances involved, and indemnification may be incomplete or unavailable for punitive or exemplary damages. Moreover, any significant lawsuit will engulf one's time, attention, and energy. Consequently, liability remains an aspect of the public service that may be viewed as a drawback by prospective and current public employees.

Ironically, outsourcing public personnel functions may not reduce this problem. With the exception of the Thirteenth Amendment's ban on slavery and involuntary servitude, the Constitution does not ordinarily apply to interactions between private parties. However, the Constitution may control the behavior of private organizations and individuals when they take on public functions or become so deeply entwined with government that they are indistinct from it (that is, when they engage in "state action").[6] For instance, private physicians on part-time contracts to provide health care to prisoners and privately employed prison guards can be held liable for violating the Eighth Amendment's ban on cruel and unusual punishment (*West v. Atkins*, 1988; *Richardson v. McKnight*, 1997). Moreover, they have no immunity—either absolute or qualified—in such suits (*Richardson v. McKnight*, 1997).[7] Unfortunately for those making human resource management decisions, the law regarding state action is notoriously unclear (*Lebron v. National Railroad Passenger Corporation*, 1995; *Brentwood Academy v. Tennessee Secondary School Athletic Association*, 2001). There is a great deal of uncertainty regarding the specific characteristics of personnel functions or public-private partnerships that might make the Constitution apply to outsourcing arrangements. Perhaps the leading candidate for triggering state action doctrine is background investigations, which can involve Fourth Amendment privacy concerns.

Second, public personnel systems will have to take greater responsibility for teaching public servants to be constitutionally competent (Rosenbloom, Carroll, and Carroll, 2000). The public administrator's best defense against liability for constitutional torts is reasonable knowledge of the constitutional rights of those individuals upon whom his or her official actions bear. Universities can teach broad constitutional principles, values, and reasoning in their Master of Public Administration programs, but they are not well-suited for teaching the detailed constitutional law that controls specific jobs, such as that of a social worker, police officer, or prison guard. Constance Horner, former Director of the U.S. Office of Personnel Management (OPM), recognized the important role that personnel agencies can play in constitutional education by calling for "constitutional literacy" among higher-level federal employees (Horner, 1988). In 2004, OPM director, Kay Coles James, followed suit by highlighting the importance of the oath that federal employees take to support the Constitution (Barr, 2004). Local governments, in particular, should systematically follow constitutional law cases and integrate new rulings into their training and operational manuals. In *City of Canton v. Harris* (1989, p. 390), the Supreme Court held that a local government may be held liable for violations of constitutional rights caused by its failure to take "reasonable steps to train its employees."

Third, education and training in personnel and human resources management for the public sector should specifically and comprehensively cover the constitutional rights of public employees and applicants. Public servants have extensive constitutional rights to freedom of speech, association, privacy, due process, equal protection, and liberty (Rosenbloom, 1971; Rosenbloom and Carroll, 1995; Rosenbloom and O'Leary, 1997). Therefore, virtually any public administrator who engages in hiring, promoting, disciplining, or evaluating subordinates may potentially violate an individual employee's constitutional rights. Traditional personnel policies and those of the new public management and reinventing government movements, which heavily emphasize cost-effectiveness, should be tempered by substantial attention to public employees' constitutional rights. Personnelists who are poorly trained in the constitutional aspects of public employment will not be well positioned to develop policies that secure the due process, equal protection, privacy, and other constitutional rights of public employees.

Finally, contemporary liability doctrine has major implications for strategic human resources management (SHRM) within governmental entities. SHRM integrates human-resources planning into an organization's strategic management processes. Public employees liability for constitutional torts strongly suggests that government SHRM models are incomplete if they do not articulate clearly person-nelists' responsibilities for helping their organizations to guard against breaches of constitutional rights. Under SHRM, human resource organizations are expected to balance the roles of strategic partner, employee champion, change agent, and administrative expert (Ulrich, 1997). These roles give human resource professionals the opportunities to plan for and react to management decisions. As a strategic partner, human resource professionals have gained a "seat at the table." This allows them to work directly with executives to develop recruitment, compensa-tion, performance management, and other resource practices to achieve strategic goals. In their roles as employee champions, human resource professionals help managers understand and carry out their responsibilities for increasing employee commitment. The change-agent role requires human resource professionals to help both managers and employees cope with changes occurring within their organiza-tions. It is within the role of administrative expert that human resource profession-als will find their traditional responsibilities for establishing, implementing, and enforcing personnel rules. Encompassed within this role is basic legal compliance.

The general framework of strategic partner, employee champion, change agent, and administrative expert may limit the effectiveness of government human resources offices because it may not result in a comprehensive strategy for adhering to constitutional tenets and obligations. There may be a tendency to iso-late the analysis of constitutional compliance to staff attorneys or others with spe-cific responsibility for legal matters. This would be a mistake for two reasons. First, it ignores the responsibilities of those carrying out other strategic human-resource roles to ensure constitutional compliance. For example, strategic partners must be able to explain the constitutional consequences of outsourcing human-resource activities to the organization's executives. Employee champions must work closely with managers to help them understand their responsibility to pro-tect employees' freedom of speech, religious freedom, and privacy rights—even when administrative convenience or expedience alone might dictate some other course. In addition, employee champions can help employees fulfill their obliga-tion to protect the constitutional rights of the individuals to whom they provide goods and services. During reengineering activities, change agents should help management and employees to establish new practice that uphold constitutional protections, as well as to promote increased efficiency and effectiveness. Periodic "constitutional audits" are a useful approach for reviewing practices and official guidelines to ensure that they are current with the ever-changing constitutional law of public administration. To be most effective in the personnel context, human resource managers should participate on audit teams, along with legal experts, employee representatives, and program managers.

Second, the current SHRM framework does not promote constitutional compe-tence for government executives, managers, and employees. The *Harlow* decision requires public employees to make decisions that reflect reasonable knowledge of clearly established constitutional rights. Clearly, legal compliance is paramount not only because it is a basic requirement for democratic-constitutional government, but, more mundanely, because failure to protect constitutional rights adds substantially to the financial costs of government. An excellent example of how high the cost can be is the $535 million the federal government paid to settle sex discrimination cases against the Voice of America and the U.S. Information Agency[8]. This cost can be reduced substantially if government human resource professionals incorporate a role for constitutional compliance into their SHRM activities. In their SHRM roles as strategic partner, employee champion, change agent, and administrative expert human resource professionals gain access to the entire organization. Therefore, they are well positioned to educate managers and employees about the most effective methods to protect constitutional rights as they carry out their responsibilities.

Training human resource professionals to assess constitutional compliance across their different SHRM roles will help governments reduce the costs of public employees' liability. They will be more knowledgeable about how current case law impacts human resource activities and able to apply their knowledge when carrying out their responsibilities. This will help organizations establish practices that minimize the potential for litigation related to violations of constitutional rights. They can teach managers and employees how to reduce their liability for constitutional torts, perhaps with the added benefit of making public employment more desirable because managers and employees are given the opportunities to increase their constitutional competence.

NOTES

1. Yong Lee (1987) identified approximately 1,700 cases in the odd years from 1977 to 1983. This figure pertains only to reported cases. The number of unreported federal district court decisions in official liability cases is unknown, but presumably substantial. From 1993 to 1998, 7,000 federal employees sought legal representation by the Department of Justice, but only 14 were ultimately found personally liable in court (Friel, 1998, p. 1). Lee (1987, p. 169) lists the mean awards as follows: 1977, $48,552; 1979, $14,711; 1981, $63,031; 1983, $92,411. See also Yong Lee (2004) and Yong Lee and David H. Rosenbloom (2005).

2. Successful First Amendment challenges include the following: *Chicago Teachers Union v. Hudson*, 1986 (non-union employees in bargaining unit cannot be coerced to pay for a union's non-representational activities, including political activities, and a procedure for resolving amounts in dispute is required); *Rankin v. McPherson*, 1987 (remark by probationary employee in constable's office expressing hope that the next assassination attempt on President Ronald Reagan is successful is constitutionally protected and cannot be the basis for dismissal); *Rutan v. Republican Party of Illinois*, 1990 (partisan affiliation or support is an unconstitutional basis for personnel actions involving ordinary public employees' promotion, training, assignment, and similar actions, as well as hiring and firing); *Waters v. Churchill*, 1994 (speech-related dismissals require reasonable belief that employee made alleged remarks); and *U.S. v. National Treasury Employees Union*, 1995 (provision banning federal employee acceptance of pay for non-job related published and other expression violates free speech/press). Fourth Amendment decisions include the following: *O'Connor v. Ortega*, 1987 (administrative searches and seizures in public workplace must be reasonable in inception and scope if employee meets threshold test of having a reasonable expectation of privacy under the circum-

stances involved); and *National Treasury Employees Union v. Von Raab*, 1989 (suspicionless drug testing of some categories of customs employees is constitutional). Procedural due process was violated by dismissal from civil service job without prior notice and opportunity to respond (*Cleveland Board of Education v. Loudermill*, 1985). Equal Protection Clause prohibits dismissal of non-minority in violation of seniority rights to further equal employment opportunity/affirmative action (*Wygant v. Jackson*, 1986).

3. *Cleveland Board of Education v. Loudermill*, 1985, is perhaps the clearest example of an instance in which a minimal, almost costless procedure could have obviated a suit. *Wygant v. Jackson*, 1986, occurred because a school board agreed to race-based dismissals that would almost certainly result in litigation and, in high probability, loss as well. The statutory ban in *U.S. v. National Treasury Employees Union*, 1995, was exceptionally broad and the administrative rules pursuant to it were so complex as to appear irrational and arbitrary.

4. In *Adarand* (1995) the Supreme Court held that all racial classifications are constitutionally suspect and subject to strict judicial scrutiny. To be constitutional they must serve a compelling governmental interest in a narrowly tailored fashion. See also *Grutter v. Bollinger* (2003) and *Gratz v. Bollinger* (2003).

5. The question was whether a public employee could be disciplined for what her supervisor thought she said, or only for what she actually said. There was no majority opinion on the Supreme Court, but the guiding principles appear to be that: (1) the employer must reasonably investigate what the employee may have said, and (2) the employer must really believe the employee said it before imposing discipline.

6. "State action" means governmental action, regardless of whether at the federal, state, or local governmental levels.

7. Private organizations that become state actors by working for federal agencies are not subject to constitutional tort suits for money damages (*Correctional Services Corporation v. Malesko*, 2001). At the state and local levels, private organizations that are state actors can be sued under section 1983.

8. For 22 years, the federal government denied charges that Voice of America and the U.S. Information Agency discriminated against women when they applied for positions as broadcasters, broadcast technicians, writers, editors, and production specialists. Consequently, 1,100 women were awarded $508 million in the settlement of their class action suit. In separate cases, 46 women won an additional $22.7 million. Attorney fees were not included in these costs.

REFERENCES

Adarand Constructors, Inc. v. Pena. 1995. 515 U.S. 200.

Anderson v. Creighton. 1987. 483 U.S. 635.

Atwater v. City of Lago Vista. 2001. 532 U.S. 318.

Barr, S. 2004. "Federal Diary: OPM's Constitutional Confab." *Washington Post* November 12: B2.

Barr v. Matteo. 1959. 360 U.S. 564.

Bivens v. Six Unknown Named Federal Narcotics Agents. 1971. 403 U.S. 388.

BMW of North America v. Gore. 1996. 517 U.S. 559.

Board of County Commissioners, Wabaunsee County v. Umbehr. 1996. 518 U.S. 668.

Bogan v. Scott-Harris. 1998. 523 U.S. 44.

Brentwood Academy v. Tennessee Secondary School Athletic Association. 2001. 531 U.S. 288.

Bush v. Lucas. 1983. 462 U.S. 367.

Butz v. Economou. 1978. 438 U.S. 478.

Carlson v. Green. 1980. 446 U.S. 14.

Carroll, J. D. 1982. "The New Juridical Federalism and the Alienation of Public Policy and Administration." *American Review of Public Administration* 16: Spring: 89–105.

Chayes, A. 1976. "The Role of the Judge in Public Law Litigation." *Harvard Law Review* 89: 1281–1316.

Chicago Teachers Union v. Hudson. 1986. 475 U.S. 292.

City of Canton v. Harris. 1989. 489 U.S. 378.

City of Newport v. Fact Concerts. 1981. 453 U.S. 247.

City of Richmond v. J. A. Croson Co. 1989. 488 U.S. 469.

Cleavinger v. Saxner. 1985. 474 U.S. 193.

Cleveland Board of Education v. Loudermill. 1985. 470 U.S. 532.

Collins v. Bender. 1999. 195 F.3d 1076.

Correctional Services Corporation v. Malesko. 2001. 534 U.S. 61.

Davis v. Passman. 1979. 422 U.S. 228.

Delaware v. Prouse. 1979. 440 U.S. 648.

Dolan v. City of Tigard. 1994. 512 U.S. 374.

Farley, J. J. 1989. "The Representation and Defense of the Federal Employee by the Department of Justice." U.S. Department of Justice, Spring (mimeograph).

FDIC v. Meyer. 1994. 510 U.S. 471.

Friel, B. 1998. "Managers Rarely Found Liable in Lawsuits." *Government Executive (The Daily Fed)* May 19: 1.

Galanter, M. 1988. "Beyond the Litigation Panic." In Walter Olson, ed., *New Directions in Liability Law.* New York, NY: Academy of Political Science, pp. 18–30.

Givhan v. Western Line Consolidated School District. 1979. 349 U.S. 410.

Gratz v. Bollinger. 2003. U.S. Supreme Court, No. 02–516.

Grutter v. Bollinger. 2003. U.S. Supreme Court, No. 02–241.

Harley v. Schuylkill County. 1979. 476 F. Supp. 191.

Harlow v. Fitzgerald. 1982. 457 U.S. 800.

Hafer v. Melo. 1991. 502 U.S. 21.

Hiibel v. Sixth Judicial District Court of Nevada, Humboldt County. 2004. U.S. Supreme Court, No. 03–5554.

Hope v. Pelzer. 2002. 536 U.S. 730.

Horner, C. 1988. "Remarks on FEI's [Federal Executive Institute's] 20th Anniversary Dinner." Charlottesville, Va., Oct. 14, p. 14.

Horowitz, D. 1977. *The Courts and Social Policy.* Washington, DC: Brookings Institution.

Horowitz, D. 1983. "Decreeing Organizational Change: Judicial Supervision of Public Institutions." *Duke Law Journal* 88:3: 1265–1307.

Kolender v. Lawson. 1983. 461 U.S. 352.

Lebron v. National Railroad Passenger Corporation. 1995. 513 U.S. 374.

Lee, Y. 1987. "Civil Liability of State and Local Governments: Myths and Reality." *Public Administration Review* 47: March/April: 160–170.

———. 2004. "The Judicial Theory of a Reasonable Public Servant," *Public Administration Review* 64: July/August: 425–437.

Lee, Y. S. and Rosenbloom, D. H. 2005. *A Reasonable Public Servant.* Armonk, NY: M. E. Sharpe.

Lipsky, M. 1980. *Street-Level Bureaucracy.* New York, NY: Russell Sage.

Lucas v. South Carolina Coastal Council. 1992. 505 U.S. 1003.

Miranda v. Arizona. 1966. 384 U.S. 436.

Missouri v. Jenkins. 1995. 494 U.S. 33; 1990. 515 U.S. 70.

Mitchell v. Forsyth. 1985. 472 U.S. 511.

National Treasury Employees Union v. Von Raab. 1989. 489 U.S. 656.

Naylor, L. A. and Rosenbloom, D. H. 2004. "*Adarand, Grutter*, and *Gratz*: Does Affirmative Action in Federal Employment Matter?" *Review of Public Personnel Administration* 24: June: 150–174.

O'Connor v. Ortega. 1987. 480 U.S. 709.

O'Hare Truck Service, Inc. v. City of Northlake. 1996. 518 U.S. 712.

Owen v. City of Independence. 1980. 445 U.S. 622.

Pembaur v. City of Cincinnati. 1986. 475 U.S. 469.

Pickering v. Board of Education. 1968. 391 U.S. 563.

Rankin v. McPherson. 1987. 483 U.S. 378.

Richardson v. McKnight. 1997. 21 U.S. 399.

Rivenbark, L. 1998. "Protection Needed Against Lawsuits." *Federal Times* July 20: 3.

Rosenbloom, D. H. 1971. *Federal Service and the Constitution*. Ithaca, NY: Cornell University Press.

———. 1994. "Fuzzy Law from the High Court." *Public Administration Review* 54: November/December: 503–506.

——— and Carroll, J. D. 1990. *Toward Constitutional Competence: A Casebook for Public Administrators*. Englewood Cliffs, NJ: Prentice Hall.

——— and Carroll, J. D. 1995. "Public Personnel Administration and Law," in J. Rabin, T. Vocino, W.B. Hildreth, and G. Miller, eds. *Handbook of Public Personnel Administration*. New York, NY: Marcel Dekker, pp. 71–113.

——— Carroll, J., and Carroll, J. 2000. *Constitutional Competence for Public Managers: Cases and Commentary*. Itasca, IL.: F. E. Peacock Publishers.

——— and O'Leary, R. 1997. *Public Administration and Law*. New York. NY: Marcel Dekker.

Rutan v. Republican Party of Illinois. 1990. 497 U.S. 62.

Scheuer v. Rhodes. 1974. 416 U.S. 232.

Schuck, P. 1982. *Suing Government: Citizen Remedies for Official Wrongs*. New Haven, CT: Yale University Press.

Schuck, P. 1988. "The New Judicial Ideology of Tort Law." In Walter Olson, ed., *New Directions in Liability Law*. New York, NY: Academy of Political Science, pp. 4–14.

"Section 1983 and Federalism." 1977. *Harvard Law Review* 90: 1133–1361.

Smith v. Wade. 1983. 461 U.S. 31.

Spalding v. Vilas. 1896. 161 U.S. 483.

Stump v. Sparkman. 1978. 435 U.S. 349.

Terry v. Ohio. 1968. 392 U.S. I.

Tower v. Glover. 1984. 467 U.S. 914.

Ulrich, D. 1997. *Human Resource Champions: The Next Agenda for Adding Value and Delivering Results*. Boston, MA: Harvard Business School Press.

United States v. James Daniel Good Real Property. 1994. 510 U.S. 471.

United States v. Lee. 1882. 106 U.S. 196.

United States v. National Treasury Employees Union. 1995. 513 U.S. 454.

Vaughn, R. 1977. "Public Employees and the Right to Disobey." *Hastings Law Journal* 29: 261–295.

Waters v. Churchill. 1994. 511 U.S. 661.

West v. Atkins. 1988. 487 U.S. 42.

Whren v. United States. 1996. 517 U.S. 806.

Will v. Michigan Department of State Police. 1989. 491 U.S. 59.

Wood v. Strickland. 1975. 420 U.S. 308.

Wygant v. Jackson. 1986. 478 U.S. 267.

Chapter **10**

Hiring in the Federal Government: Political and Technological Sources of Reform*

Carolyn Ban

Hiring is one of the most critical personnel functions in any organization. And all organizations—public, private, and nonprofit—have adapted their hiring procedures to reflect the changing needs of the organization, the changing workforce, and new technology. But change in the public sector has been more difficult because of the political nature of the issues involved and because of the political process necessary for reform. This chapter will review the very real changes in hiring, focusing on both the political and technological sources of a period of reform that is still very much ongoing.

THE POLITICIZATION OF HIRING

Many people tend to see personnel management as essentially a technical field, but, at least in the public sector, it is squarely in the middle of many of the key political debates of our time. One of those debates concerns the appropriate role and size of government. As a result, the size of the federal workforce has been politicized for at least the past twenty-five years. Ronald Reagan's first act as President, in 1980, was to sign a retroactive hiring freeze (later found to be illegal), and Clinton's reinvention of government focused as much on shrinking the size of the federal workforce as on improving the management of government. In fact, "[f]rom January 1993 to January 2000, the Federal Government civilian

*My thanks to Ligaya Fernandez, Harry Redd, Laura Shugrue, and Paul van Rijn for their helpful comments.

workforce was reduced by 384,000 employees" (U.S. OPM, 2000a). But, especially in the Clinton administration, this desire to take credit for reducing the size of government was not linked to a political vision of a smaller role for government, so there was no parallel reduction in the number or scope of federal programs. The result was, in effect, a shell game, in which federal ranks shrank while the number of employees working for the federal government as contractors continued to swell (Light, 1999).

George W. Bush's Presidential Management Agenda (PMA) has continued to stress contracting out (termed "competitive sourcing") but has also identified strategic management of human capital as a key priority. The PMA noted that reductions in the size of the federal workforce were made in ways that were not "aligned with agency missions." One result has been an increase in "the average age of the federal workforce . . . to 46 years, compared to 42 in 1990" (U.S. OMB, 2002, p. 11). The PMA also identified as serious challenges weak human resources planning that was not responding adequately to expected high retirement rates, outdated compensation systems, and flawed processes for recruiting new employees (U.S. OMB, 2002, p. 11–12).

CONFLICTS OF VALUES AND INTERESTS

Attempts to reform the hiring process are complex as well because they reflect debates about core values of public service and public management. On the one hand, the civil service was based, from its founding, on the concept that employees should be selected on the basis of merit, rather than on party affiliation, inside contacts, or nepotism. On the other hand, both scholars and political activists have argued over what we mean by merit and how best to assess who is most meritorious.

The civil service system is also expected to reflect values of openness and equity and to be representative of the country's diverse population. In the early years of the civil service, that meant geographic representation, and state of residence was explicitly taken into consideration in hiring. More recently, the focus has been on demographic characteristics, such as gender and race or ethnic origin. Further, since the Civil War, the system has been designed explicitly to reward military service, and veterans still receive preference in hiring, but that value can be seen as conflicting with the goals of merit and equity.

The challenge is not only balancing sometimes-conflicting social goals but also the need to meet management goals, especially speed and efficiency. From the standpoint of managers, the ideal system would be cost-efficient to operate, would allow the public sector to identify and hire good candidates quickly, and would give managers flexibility to hire the people they identify and to offer them pay and benefits competitive with the market, thus providing incentives to managers to recruit aggressively for the best employees. But meeting these management goals while upholding the social goals discussed is a real challenge.

THE POLITICS OF REFORM: THE KEY POLITICAL ACTORS

Each of the values described earlier is reflected in the interests of the many actors who have been directly or indirectly involved in the ongoing cycles of reform of the hiring process. They include career managers, political appointees, and rank-and-file employees, as well as interest groups representing specific groups, including veterans, women, African Americans, and Hispanics. Change may take place via administrative reform, but major reforms require legislative approval, and proposals are revised and shaped during the legislative process. The courts, too, have, over the past twenty years, played a central role in reshaping hiring in the federal government. Reforms, thus, have taken place through the give and take of the political process as well as through the judicial process. The net result is a system that has moved from simplicity to complexity, from centralization to extreme decentralization, and, in the process, is still struggling to reconcile conflicting values.

TWENTY-FIVE YEARS OF REFORM: WHAT HAVE WE LEARNED?

In order to understand how the current system has evolved, it is useful to review briefly the major reforms of the past twenty-five years. They include a major legislative reform (the Civil Service Reform Act of 1978), an ongoing judicial reform (the *Luevano* consent decree), and a more recent series of administrative and legislative reforms (the National Performance Review under Clinton, the Bush administration's Presidential Management Agenda, and legislation giving individual agencies the authority to develop their own HR systems).

If we take as our baseline the system in place prior to passage of the Civil Service Reform Act of 1978, central to that system was a standardized examination called the PACE exam that was administered centrally by the Civil Service Commission and was used to select new employees for entry-level positions in more than 100 classes of jobs (Ban and Ingraham, 1988). That system was based on a core value, the merit system, but defined merit in a narrow way, as a score on a single test. PACE was an expensive system to operate, because the number of applicants was far greater than the number of positions available. The large number of applicants meant that, although a 70 was, in theory, a passing score, people who scored lower than the high 90s were rarely selected for jobs. This raised some troubling questions. One was the issue of test validity. This system was seen as relying strictly on merit, but merit came to be defined exclusively as high scores on the test. While the test was carefully validated using psychometric methods, even those who developed it did not argue that a person who received a 98 would necessarily be a more successful and productive employee than one who received a 97, or even a 95. Tests cannot tell us whether the job applicant is motivated, whether he or she gets along well with others, and, in the case of a general test like PACE, how quickly he or she can master the skills needed for a specific job.

PACE was an open system, in the sense that it was a clear and well-known route into government, and it was an apolitical system, in that only those who scored highly on the test could be considered for positions. But it had adverse impact (that is, the pass rate was lower for African Americans and Hispanics).

LEGISLATIVE REFORM: THE CSRA

President Carter's Civil Service Reform Act (CSRA) had the goal of modernizing the federal personnel system, making it more efficient and thus improving management and productivity of the civil service as a whole. While the teams planning the reform critiqued the slowness and inflexibility of the federal system for hiring, the bill itself included only modest reforms in this area. They focused on decentralizing the hiring process for those positions not covered by the PACE exam, giving agencies more control over the process with the assumption that in-house hiring processes would be faster and more responsive to managers' needs.

Why, given the lofty goals, were the reforms so narrowly drawn? One explanation lies in the political process and in the strength of some of the political actors mentioned earlier. For example, early drafts of the reform proposals included limiting veterans' preference, but the veterans groups were so well organized that it quickly became obvious that Congress would not support any change in this area (Ingraham, 1984).

Even this modest reform did not last long. Reagan's first appointee as director of the Office of Personnel Management (the successor agency to the CSC), Don Devine, moved to withdraw delegations of hiring authority in a number of cases. As a result, the net effect of the CSRA was minimal (Ban and Marzotto, 1984).

JUDICIAL REFORM: THE LUEVANO CONSENT DECREE

Far more radical reform resulted from the political process as played out in the courts. Late in President Carter's term, a group of Hispanic organizations brought a lawsuit against the federal government, charging that the PACE examination had adverse impact on minority groups,[1] and demanding that the federal government abandon its use. One of the last acts of the Carter administration was to sign what is called the *Luevano* consent degree (named for one of the parties of the suit) agreeing to do just that (*Luevano et al. v. Alan Campbell*, 1981; Ban and Ingraham, 1988). Many of the most important changes in the federal system flow from that consent degree and from the continued need to comply with it.

Abandoning the PACE examination forced a complete overhaul of the process for hiring entry-level professional and administrative employees, and the continued involvement of the courts in overseeing the implementation of the consent decree continues to shape the hiring process, sometimes with unintended consequences, as we will see next.

ADMINISTRATIVE REFORM: THE NPR

The National Performance Review (later renamed the National Partnership for Reinventing Government), headed by Vice President Gore, was a dramatic attempt to improve the quality of management throughout the federal government. The NPR report on Human Resources (National Performance Review, 1993) espoused sweeping reform of the federal personnel system centered on three key themes: deregulation, decentralization, and delegation. But, once again, the political process limited the opportunity for fundamental reform. Many of the reform proposals would have required legislation, but the Democrats lost control of Congress in 1994, dooming the chances for passing any civil service reform legislation.

Still, the NPR is a case study of the impact that can be made via administrative reform, without going through Congress. First, the NPR eliminated the Federal Personnel Manual, the 10,000-page guideline to personnelists on how to implement Title 5 (the law governing the civil service system) and the Code of Federal Regulations (the official regulations implementing that law).

A second focus of the NPR recommendations was decentralization. As a result, OPM abandoned its traditional role of gatekeeper of the civil service system. Authority for almost all examining was delegated to the agencies (with OPM oversight), and OPM stopped conducting exams centrally and maintaining central registers. Instead, it now offers consulting services to agencies on development of tests and other examination methods, as well as conducting examining for agencies, but on a cost-reimbursable basis.

Third, the NPR called for delegating more authority for managing the human resource function to line managers themselves. Giving managers more authority in hiring, classifying, and assessing the performance of their employees was seen as an integral part of breaking through the traditional culture of centralized control that characterized the civil service system (Ban, 1995).

The Clinton administration used the planned deregulation of the civil service system to justify dramatic cuts in the size of the human resources workforce, arguing that a simpler system would reduce staff needs (OPM, 1998a). "From 1992 to 1996, the number of people employed in personnel occupations declined by 18 percent" (Ban, 1998). While this argument was probably specious (especially absent legislative reform), the reduction in HR staff levels forced managers to take a more active role in the process and forced HR offices to find more efficient ways to carry out their work.

CURRENT CHALLENGES

The Bush administration has been a period of rapid change in the field of human resources, with some real progress in the areas of recruiting and hiring but also some enduring challenges. First, the trend of moving agencies out of the traditional civil service system and letting them develop their own systems accelerated rapidly. Second, legislation passed introducing important new flexibilities government-wide.

THE DEMISE OF THE TRADITIONAL CIVIL SERVICE SYSTEM

Absent government-wide reform, many agencies have, over the past two decades, sought their own routes around the system. Initially, some agencies used the demonstration provision in CSRA to try out new approaches.[2] They were, however, frustrated by the limitations in the demonstration provisions, such as the number of employees who could be included, and by the failure of OPM and Congress to make the systems that were found to be successful through demonstrations available to other agencies.

As a result, a number of agencies used a legislative approach, going to Congress to ask for authority to opt out of Title 5 and to set up their own personnel systems. This approach is not new. As a 1998 OPM report pointed out:

> In the Federal Government, the trend toward flexibility has manifested itself in a number of ways, including the attempt by a number of agencies to move away from the specific requirements of Title 5. Full or partial exemption from Title 5 is of course nothing new. Agencies such as the Tennessee Valley Authority and the Federal Reserve Board have been outside Title 5 for decades. But the movement in that direction has gained momentum, to the extent that nearly half of Federal civilian employees are now outside some aspect of Title 5 coverage (the U.S. Postal Service, with over 800,000 employees, constitutes the majority of the Title 5-exempt work force) (U.S. OPM, 1998b, p. 1).

Under the Bush administration, this approach has been used far more dramatically. The new Department of Homeland Security was created with the authority to develop its own HR system, and the Defense Department also received authority to create the National Security Personnel System. (Chapter 2 discusses this important change in detail.) With this dramatic development, the days of a single, standard civil service system have passed, and there are now proposals to make this official, and to give to all agencies the flexibilities that now cover a clear majority of the federal workforce.

What are the likely impacts on recruiting and hiring? Central to the new reformed HR systems is the concept of broad-banding, first tested well over twenty years ago in a Navy demonstration program (Ban, 1992). Under broad-banded systems, agencies move away from the traditional classification systems, which pigeon-hole employees into narrow categories and pay grades, to systems that group jobs into broad job classes and that have much wider pay bands. These systems, if well implemented, will give agencies more flexibility in designing entry-level positions with clear potential for growth and may also give managers greater flexibility in setting entry-level pay and in promoting rising stars quickly. These are changes that should make federal employment more attractive to top performers who seek challenging positions where they can learn new skills and have a good chance of promotion.

The approach of pulling agencies out of Title 5 on an individual basis does have its critics. Some fear "Balkanization," and it is true that having a large number of different systems might make it more difficult for individual employees to move easily across government. More flexible classification and pay systems may, indeed, result in those agencies with more resources setting salaries at a higher level and raiding the employees of less advantages agencies. Others argue that seeing the federal workforce as a single employer is unrealistic, as agencies have different missions and cultures, and HR systems should be designed to meet their specific needs (Ban 1995; Marzotto, 1988).

GOVERNMENT-WIDE LEGISLATIVE REFORM

While legislation is often the result of a slow and deliberative process, sometimes a crisis presents an opportunity for far more rapid change. The disaster of September 11, 2001 presented such an opportunity. Congress responded to the crisis by creating the Department of Homeland Security. And congressional leaders, especially George Voinovich, who had been working for some time on legislative proposals to modernize the civil service system governmentwide, took advantage of this opportunity to include in the Homeland Security Act of 2002 not only the new human resources system for the newly-created department discussed earlier but also new flexibilities for the entire civil service system.[3]

In the area of recruitment and hiring, the law included two very important changes: permitting agencies to use "category ranking" instead of the "Rule of Three," and using direct hiring for shortage categories. The traditional civil service system relied for many years on the "Rule of Three." Under the Rule of Three, managers are given a list of the top three scorers on a test and must make their appointment from that rather narrow group (U.S. MSPB, 1995). The Rule of Three reflected traditional values—in the name of reducing patronage or cronyism, it limited the choices of managers. Current reforms are based, in contrast, on recognizing that managers are professionals and on trusting them with greater discretion to manage their organizations.

Managers were also frustrated by their inability to compete effectively in recruiting, not only because the Rule of Three made it hard to hire very qualified people whom they had actively recruited but also because the system did not permit them to go out to a campus, and, for example, interview and make an offer (that is, use the "direct hire" approach). Rather, they had to tell applicants to submit a formal application to the HR office, and it might take months before a candidate could be selected and an offer made, by which time the best people were likely to have grown tired of waiting and accepted other positions. This created particularly serious problems in fields where there were shortages in the labor market, creating intense competition with private-sector employers.

The U.S. Department of Agriculture (USDA) took the lead in experimenting with a new approach, in a demonstration project, begun in 1990. Among its key initiatives were authorizing direct hiring for shortage categories and implementing an alternative candidate assessment method using categorical groupings instead of numeric scores. Specifically, in a category rating system, rather than ranking people by test scores, those evaluating job candidates put those who meet qualifications into two categories: quality and eligible. Managers can then select from the entire pool of those ranked qualified, rather than from only the three top scorers on a test. If the quality group has only one or two candidates, those in the eligible list may also be referred to the hiring official. While this demonstration obviously suspended the Rule of Three, it did not suspend veterans' preference; in fact, it gave veterans in the quality group absolute preference. Nonveterans could be selected only if all veterans were disqualified or if the agency approved a request to pass over the individual (U.S. OPM, 1992).

The reforms passed in the DHS bill in 2002 in essence made the flexibilities tested in the Department of Agriculture demonstration program available to all agencies. Yet agencies have been surprisingly slow to adopt them. The findings of a study conducted by the General Accounting Office (GAO) in 2004 are instructive. The GAO reported that "a majority (13 of 22) [of Chief Human Capital Officers] . . . said that their agencies were using category rating to 'little or no extent'" (U.S. GAO, 2004b, p. 4). The barriers most often mentioned were "lack of agency policies and procedures" and "lack of OPM guidance," so we may see an increase in use as agencies become more familiar with the legislation and how it is being interpreted by both OPM and their agencies (U.S. GAO, 2004a). As J. Christopher Mihm reported to Congress, the limited use of category rating was "somewhat unexpected" since many human resources directors had reported earlier that numerical ranking and the Rule of Three were "key obstacles in the hiring process" (U.S. GAO, 2004b, p. 3).

Steve Nelson, of the U.S. Merit Systems Protection Board, identifies another factor that may be limiting implementation:

> Line managers are generally the drivers of change, and many have not yet seen a compelling business case presented by their human resource (HR) partners for category rating. The HR community is often too busy implementing automation and dealing with day-to-day needs to undertake what may be viewed as just another initiative. Automating an improved process like category rating is far preferable to paving the cow-path of the Rule of Three (Nelson, 2004a, p. 2–3).

The 2002 law also permitted agencies to use "direct hire authority," bypassing the slow competitive process, in situations where there is a severe shortage or critical hiring needs, but, here, too, implementation has been limited. OPM's regulations allow OPM to decide whether there is a severe shortage of applicants in an occupation, either government-wide or in a specific agency or geographic location. Agencies may also request that OPM approve use of direct hire because they believe they are facing a severe shortage or critical hiring need (U.S. GAO, 2004a). Few agencies report that they are using direct hire authority. The barriers reported were similar to those for category ranking but also included "lack of [agency] expertise needed for implementation" (U.S. GAO, 2004b, pp. 8, 10). Since it issued its interim regulations in June 2003, "OPM had [by mid–2004] approved three governmentwide direct-hire authorities and seven agency-specific direct-hire authorities" (U.S. GAO, 2004a, p. 37). The net result was that, as of December 31, 2003, "fewer than 50 individuals had been hired under the new direct-hire authority" (U.S. GAO, 2004a, pp. 38–39).

CURRENT HIRING TRENDS AND CONTINUED MANAGEMENT CHALLENGES

The legislative changes discussed here may eventually be very significant, but many of the current challenges cannot be addressed through this or future legislation. Rather, they require management commitment, adequate resources, and creative use of technology. The greatest challenge is the fact that the federal government will have to increase dramatically its hiring.

For most of the past twenty years, the federal government was downsizing. The challenge was how to reduce the size of the workforce, and agencies often filled vacancies by hiring people who were already inside the federal system (NAPA, 1999). Now agencies are facing a number of challenges, ranging from increased retirements to new or expanded missions that require much more extensive hiring (U.S. GAO, 2001; U.S. MSPB, 2004a). According to the most recent data, "more than 50 percent of all federal employees are within five years of possible retirement and 70 percent of all senior managers will be eligible to retire by 2009" (Partnership, 2005, p. 5). In fact, actual retirements in 2003 exceeded projections by over 10 percent (Partnership, 2005). At the same time, the federal government will be experiencing an increasing demand for employees, particularly in the area of homeland security. The government is projected to need over 37,000 new employees in "security, enforcement and compliance assistance" (Partnership, 2005, p. 6). Even commentators who feel that the human capital crisis has been overstated, because actual retirement rates have not increased as predicted, agree that there may be higher turnover in selected occupations (Friel, 2003).

At the same time, projections are that, because of slow population growth and increased demand for technological skills, there will be an increased labor shortage, particularly in high-tech fields. Agency HR staffs and line managers are now learning how to recruit effectively in this labor market, albeit with limited resources and competing against other employers who are using very sophisticated recruitment techniques.

The first challenge for effective recruiting is deciding what kinds of people the organization will need in the future. This requires real planning and analysis. As Comptroller General David Walker explained:

> High-performing organizations establish a clear set of organizational intents—mission, vision, core values, goals and objectives, and strategies—and then integrate their human capital strategies to support these strategic and programmatic goals. However, under downsizing, budgetary, and other pressures, agencies have not consistently taken a strategic and results-oriented approach to human capital planning (U.S. GAO, 2001, p. 4).

As Walker points out, the Government Performance and Results Act (GPRA) is one vehicle for strategic planning that encompasses human capital needs. Nonetheless, a 2004 study found that "over a quarter of the organizations [studied] reported that they do not base recruitment decisions on any workforce analysis (U.S. MSPB, 2004a, p. 9).

Hiring in larger numbers also requires agencies to change from passive to active recruiting. For many years, if an agency had a vacancy, it would post that vacancy, physically—on bulletin boards—or, increasingly, on websites. The vacancy announcement was written in bureaucratic jargon, often very wordy and technical and difficult for an outsider to understand. The HR staff then sat back and waited for applicants to come to them. In only a few agencies were program staff actively engaged in going out and recruiting strong candidates and encouraging them to apply, and those were the agencies where managers expressed the most frustration with the system because the system then made it difficult to actually hire the people they had recruited (Ban, 1995).

Now agencies are rapidly developing staff capacity for external recruiting, both on a person-to-person basis and electronically. Agencies are now gearing up to go out on the road, recruiting at college campuses, job fairs, and professional meetings. Some are building long-term relationships with college career offices. And a number of the most successful are using senior managers to represent the agency. The best recruiters can convey the excitement and challenge of the job, as well as its technical requirements and opportunities for growth and advancement (NAPA, 2001; U.S. MSPB, 2004a). Involving the line managers in recruitment will be even more important as agencies increasingly use direct hire authority to make offers on the spot. Not all agencies, however, are providing the training that recruiters need to be fully effective (U.S. MSPB, 2004a).

This recruiting is taking place in an environment that is highly decentralized, with agencies posting their own jobs and applicants applying directly to the agency, rather than to OPM. This could increase the effort required by applicants, but, of course, the process of posting jobs has also changed. Now virtually all federal agencies have followed the lead of other employers and rely on their own websites to post their vacancies. The Office of Personnel Management requires all agencies to post all positions open to outside applicants on their website, USAJOBS, part of their Recruitment One-Stop Initiative, "which, as the name implies, would provide a one-stop website for federal job seekers by implementing a single application point that includes vacancy information, job application submission, application status tracking, employment eligibility screening, and applicant database mining" (U.S. GAO, 2004a, p. 20).

This is exactly the kind of integrated system that is needed. But getting there is still a challenge. As GAO reports, agencies, and the private contractors who work with them, have resisted a proposal that they shut down their own job search and resume-builder websites (U.S. GAO, 2004a). So applicants sometimes have to fill out the same information on multiple websites in order to apply to several agencies. Further, agencies are still working to upgrade their job announcements, which, in the past "were lengthy and difficult to read on-line, contained jargon and acronyms, and appeared to be written for people already employed by the government" (U.S. GAO, 2004a, p. 20. See also U.S. MSPB, 2003b).

Whether recruitment is in person or electronic, federal agencies continue to face a number of challenges. One is the negative image of the federal workforce as an employer. A summary of recent research states that "College graduates and public policy graduate students tend to view entry-level Government jobs as less challenging, rewarding, and developmental than private and nonprofit sector jobs. They tend to believe the private sector offers better compensation, more challenging work, and better developmental opportunities, while the nonprofit sector offers more rewarding work" (U.S. MSPB, 2004a, p. 18). Surveys and focus groups conducted for the Partnership for Public Service found an interesting distinction: Three-quarters of those sampled agreed that "there are great jobs for *regular people* in the federal government," but only half agreed that "there are great jobs for *people like me* in the federal government" (Partnership, 2004a, p. 8). The report attributes that difference to the perception of government as too bureaucratic and routine and as "a place that stifles creativity and entrepreneurial thinking" (Partnership, 2004a, p. 1).

This problem is compounded by the public perception that salaries in the government are not competitive. In fact, for many occupations, federal salaries and total compensation are very competitive, but this word is not getting out. In some cases, agencies are using the greater financial flexibilities that are now available, including paying off student loans for new employees,[4] paying moving costs, and paying what are, in effect, signing bonuses for new employees with specific needed skills, but agencies have limited budgets for using these recruitment tools.

Some agencies are addressing negative perceptions directly through campaigns to "brand" the agency—"to create a positive, familiar image of the agency in the minds of applicants so that they associate the agency's reputation with a positive place to work...[through] creat[ing] an integrated package of marketing materials...including displays, brochures, posters, print media, and recruitment websites" (U.S. MSPB, 2004a, pp. 11–12). "Branding" needs to communicate the organization's vision and convey compellingly the advantages of working there "in such a way to attract the type of employee desired" (NAPA, p. 2001, p. 8).

WHAT IS A "GOOD" TESTING METHOD?

Once applicants have been recruited, there needs to be a "good" method of evaluating their fitness for the position and of making a final selection. The problem is in differing definitions of "good." Personnel specialists define a good evaluation system as one that helps to identify the very best candidates for the position, supporting the core value in the U.S. government of the "merit system," which posits that employees are selected based on their merit for the job, not on political or family connections or on other extraneous non-job-related qualities. But there are differing definitions of "merit" and debates about what is the best method of ranking candidates (Riccucci, 1991). Indeed, recent discussions have focused less on the concept of merit and more on the values of fairness and equity (Woodard, 2005).

Traditionally, as we have seen, civil service systems relied heavily on written tests, and there developed a highly elaborated method of establishing the validity of these tests, i.e., their ability to accurately predict future performance on the job.

But agencies have moved away from formal tests, both because of the problem of adverse impact of these tests on minority applicants (leading to the *Luevano* consent decree, discussed earlier) and because, in the trade-off between speed of hiring and accuracy or test validity, most managers cared more about speed. Their fear has been that a slower process might, in theory, identify the very best prospects, but in doing so, would actually make it harder to hire those people, because they are the very applicants who are likely to find other jobs rather than waiting around for months.

In fact, the pressure for speed is so great that "OPM is urging agencies to implement a new 45-day hiring model, which measures the time-to-hire period from the date the vacancy announcement closes to the date a job offer is extended." Agencies will be evaluated on their progress towards speeding up hiring as part of their grades on the President's Management Agenda (U.S. GAO, 2004a, p. 14).

Nonetheless, the *Luevano* consent decree required that the Office of Personnel Management develop a battery of six examinations, each validated for a group of related occupations, and known collectively as the Administrative Careers with America (ACWA) examinations. OPM clearly intended ACWA to be a "major vehicle for college graduates and other candidates with equivalent experience to obtain federal employment" (U.S. GAO, 1994, p. 2). Although OPM spent a great deal of time and effort validating the six ACWA examinations, ACWA as a system was largely a failure. Managers found it too slow and were dissatisfied with the quality of applicants (U.S. GAO, 2004a). As a result, they proceeded to use every route possible to avoid hiring via ACWA. OPM then replaced the tests with a new version of ACWA, relying on a biodata approach—a lengthy questionnaire about the applicant's background and experience. But this was not a significant improvement, from the point of view of hiring officials. In fact, a number of reports have called for terminating both the use of ACWA and the consent decree itself (U.S. MSPB, 2000; NAPA, 2001; Partnership, 2004b).

A heavily-used route around ACWA for entry-level professional positions is the Outstanding Scholar program, also created in response to the *Luevano* consent decree, which allows agencies to hire applicants noncompetitively, based on their undergraduate grade point average. If the applicant has an undergraduate GPA of 3.5 or higher or is in the top 10 percent of his/her graduating class, he or she can be hired immediately without taking a test. Use of the Outstanding Scholar program has been heavy, since it meets managers' desire for speed and flexibility in hiring. But the program is controversial, first, because it has not been particularly effective in meeting the original goal of increasing minority representation. NAPA reports that, "of all the hiring methods, . . . outstanding scholar appointments produced the lowest percentage of minorities hired into the professional and administrative positions" (NAPA, 1999, p. 15). In fact, it is most often used to hire white women, who are not covered under the *Luevano* decree. Further, for some positions, more people were hired using the Outstanding Scholar program than via competitive appointments (U.S. MSPB, 2001b, pp. 1–4)

There is a lively debate concerning the validity of the Outstanding Scholars program's approach as a selection method. The U.S. Merit Systems Protection Board has questioned whether GPA or class standing are effective predictors of on-the-job performance, particularly since neither the quality of the institution nor the program of study is considered, and has argued that this process "has little more than speed of hiring to recommend it" (U.S. MSPB, 2000, p. 17; see also U.S. GAO, 2004a).

Agencies have also avoided use of ACWA through relying on internal promotions rather than hiring externally. Research has documented, however, that the people who moved into professional positions through internal promotion "do not advance as far as employees hired by other methods" (Partnership, 2004a), which may be an indicator of the quality of hires.

In general, developing valid selection tools is more difficult in a decentralized environment. The federal government has delegated examining authority for virtually all positions directly to the agencies. Decentralization has great advantages, but also considerable costs. One advantage is that, for most positions, agency HR staff and managers, who understand the work of the agency and its specific needs, are reviewing applications. That knowledge should increase the odds that the applicants' fit for the specific job is being assessed correctly. And decentralized hiring can, in many cases, be faster than a more centralized process. There are, however, significant costs in recruiting and reviewing applications. Particularly for smaller organizations, developing and validating a formal test is difficult or impossible, and, according to a GAO report, OPM officials say "that many agencies do not have the technical expertise, funding, or time to develop valid assessment tools" (U.S. GAO, 2004a). OPM does have those skills, but assistance from OPM is now available only on a cost-reimbursable basis, further disadvantaging smaller agencies.

The net effect of both *Luevano* and decentralization is that cognitive ability tests have virtually been abandoned as part of the federal hiring process, in spite of the fact that years of research have found them to be the most valid selection method (Schmidt and Hunter, 1998). Instead, agency HR staff score candidates numerically and rank them based on their self-reported training and experience. This approach is being used for over half of competitive new hires (Partnership, 2004b). Evaluating training and experience is relatively cheap, can be quite fast, and isn't likely to trigger court challenges. But one report concludes that it is "one of the least effective predictors of job performance" (Partnership, 2004b, p. 4). Agencies are also relying heavily on interviews, especially to make the final decision among finalists, but often use unstructured interviews, which are far less valid and reliable than more structured interviewing (U.S. MSPB, 2003a). A number of agencies have developed and validated their own selection methods for specific ACWA occupations as alternatives to ACWA, and studies document that there are a number of assessment approaches that are more valid, including not just written tests but also structured interviews, work samples, situational judgment tests, and others (Partnership, 2004b).

IS TECHNOLOGY THE ANSWER?

There is no doubt that technology has changed the way HR offices operate, including the processes of recruiting, testing, and selection. Some of the proponents of e-government see it as the panacea that will not only increase efficiencies but also improve the openness of government and the ability of citizens to connect to their government.[5] In the area of recruiting, it is clear that moving job postings to the web has opened up recruiting and reduced the costs to applicants of locating information about vacancies (although it may increase costs to agencies by encouraging larger number of applications). Technology is also seen as central to the goal of speeding up hiring, saving time while keeping costs low at every step of the process (U.S. MSPB, 2004b). As a GAO report describes it:

> Automation can facilitate almost every step of the federal hiring process. For example, an automated hiring system could electronically determine if an applicant met the basic qualifications and electronically provide timely notification to the applicant of the status of his or her application. Automation could also streamline the process by electronically rating and ranking applicants, or placing them in quality categories, eliminating the need to form panels to assess the applicants (U.S. GAO, 2004a, p. 23).

These systems may improve efficiency, but they may not use the full potential of technology. As the Merit Systems Protection Board found, when they reviewed systems in use, agencies are using the technology to assess applicants' training and experience (U.S. MSPB, 2004b). But the use of technology offers more—a way to return to more valid methods of assessing candidates, including written tests that can be tailored to a specific position and scored instantaneously. As the MSPB points out, technology allows agencies to combine and sequence assessment methods, for example, "to follow an initial rating of training and experience with other rigorous assessments, such as a structured interview or a work sample test. . . . However, relatively few agencies have used automated hiring systems to reengineer their hiring process" (U.S. MSPB, 2004b, p. 25).

It is important for agencies to recognize both the benefits of technology and its limitations. Implementing new systems requires significant start-up and training costs, and so gains in speed or efficiency may not show up immediately (U.S. MSPB, 2004b). Further, relying on these systems for making final selection decisions may not result in the best hires. They may be effective means for initial screening of applicants, but they "are better suited to make broad distinctions among applicants...than to making fine distinctions (e.g., selecting among highly qualified applicants)" (U.S. MSPB, 2004b, p. 46).

COMBINING ON-THE-JOB TRAINING WITH RECRUITMENT AND SELECTION: EXPANDED USE OF INTERNSHIP PROGRAMS

One of the reasons for the limitations of existing assessment methods, including those that are technology-based, is that successful hires need not only good technical skills but also strong motivation and the ability to communicate effectively and to work well with others, especially in the team-based work environment typical of many federal organizations. Structured interviews may assess some of these qualities, but neither reviews of training and experience nor formal written tests alone are generally effective in doing so. As a result, some agencies are trying a different approach—using internships as a way of recruiting and trying out potential job candidates.

Internships are not new. Government agencies have used a variety of internships and temporary employment programs for students for years. The current growth in interest reflects both the availability of new programs as well as the pressure to find better ways to recruit and hire. Discussions about these programs are complicated by the fact that the same term, "internship," is often used for two very different kinds of programs. The RAND Corporation study of intern programs in the Defense Department makes a very useful distinction between internships that are pre-employment programs (designed to provide part-time or temporary employment to students) and structured post-employment programs, which they term"early career professional development" programs (Gates and Paul, 2004, p. xiv).

The Presidential Management Internship program is one of the longest-running and best known of the post-employment programs, but it may have suffered from this terminological confusion, which may be one of the factors in its being renamed the Presidential Management Fellows program. It has been expanded under the Bush administration, both in number of appointments and in the fields covered but remains a relatively small prestigious program managed centrally by the Office of Personnel Management and offering formal training and job rotations leading to a permanent position. New employees recruited via the PMI (now PMF) are generally given high marks by their supervisors, and they are more likely to move into management than those hired through other routes, but there is some fear that the program may be losing its identity as a "vehicle to hire and train the Government's future managers" (U.S. MSPB, 2001a, p. ix).

A new internship program, the Federal Career Intern Program (FCIP), was introduced by executive order in 2000 (U.S. OPM, 2000b). It, too, is a post-education program, but, unlike the Presidential Management Fellows program, it is decentralized. Each agency can decide whether to create an internship program that will provide a vehicle for recruiting new employees, typically at the GS–5, 7, or 9 level, for a two-year program that will provide interns with formal training and developmental opportunities. At the end of the two years, interns can, at the discretion of the agency, be converted to the competitive career service (i.e., to permanent jobs). A number of agencies have set up their own internship programs under FCIP, but its utility is somewhat limited for positions covered by the *Luevano* consent decree[6] (Gates and Paul, 2004).

Agencies are also making increased use of pre-employment internships under a variety of authorities. Observing how interns respond to the challenges and pressures of the workplace over several months is certainly a more valid predictor of on-the-job performance than a written test or interview. Some agencies, such as the General Accounting Office (GAO) have made a conscious decision to rely heavily on interns as a source of new hires, since both the employer and employee have had a chance to try each other out.

Two of the main authorities for such programs are the Student Temporary Employment Program (STEP) and the Student Career Employment Program (SCEP).

They differ in that SCEP is a more structured program, which requires a clear relationship between the work being done and the student's area of study and career goals and which includes a formal development plan. In contrast, STEP is a more flexible program that allows hiring students to do any job. SCEP has a great advantage, in that students hired in a SCEP internship can be noncompetitively placed in a permanent position in any federal agency (not just in the agency where they held their internship) if they have completed 640 hours of work under SCEP and graduated from their academic program (Gates and Paul, 2004; Partnership, 2002).

These internship programs (both pre-employment and early-career post-employment) can play a useful role by giving agencies a chance to try out prospective employees before making a final commitment to them. Currently they provide a relatively small stream of new hires, and it is too early to say whether they will grow into programs large enough to address the majority of the predicted needs for new employees. If they do so, they raise questions about the extent to which they reflect the core value of merit, since they are technically noncompetitive methods of recruitment.

Of course, the probationary period is technically the final stage of the selection process, providing a similar chance to try out new employees on the job prior to making a final appointment, but it is not clear that managers fully understand the purpose and appropriate use of the probationary period.

CONCLUSIONS: PROGRESS BUT CONTINUED CHALLENGES

As we have seen, the processes of recruiting and hiring in the federal government are undergoing rapid change. The accumulated effects of years of piecemeal changes, including the decentralization of the process, recent more sweeping reforms in agency personnel systems, and legislation permitting agencies to move to category ranking and use of direct hire can, over the next several years, lead to systems for recruiting and hiring that are much more effective, but only if two remaining challenges are met: one is managerial and the other is judicial.

First, senior management needs to take the "human capital crisis" seriously. This means real attention, from the very top down, to the human capital needs of the agency, including careful planning of future staffing needs, thinking through up-front the human resource implications of new programs or reorganizations, and providing adequate staff and training (to both HR staff and line managers) to develop high-quality programs for recruiting and valid methods for selection. At the same time, OPM and agencies need to provide the regulatory and technical support to help operating HR offices to implement categorical ranking and to encourage its use. Further, as agencies finally begin to implement broad-banded pay systems, they need to "marry up the broader pay-band categories with matching competency levels for [hiring] qualifications" (Nelson, 2004b, p. 213).

Second, the *Luevano* consent decree has outlived its utility. The assessment methods that it has required are often either unworkable or lack validity. Worse, they often fail to help the very populations that the consent degree was designed to protect. Only the court can lift the decree, but agencies need to work with OPM and the administration to make this case, because, absent this change, agency managers will continue to find ways around the decree, increasing the costs and decreasing the effectiveness of hiring for positions that are vital to agency success (U.S. MSPB, 2000; Nelson, 2004b).

Finally, the current wave of reforms needs to be assessed based on its ability to meet the goals of efficiency and speed but also on the extent to which it upholds the value of merit. As changes are implemented we need to continue to ask the critical question: To what extent are these systems ensuring open access to the civil service and selection of employees who bring to the federal government both the technical skills and commitment to public service that will provide the leadership for the future?

NOTES

1. Technically, an examination or selection method is said to have adverse impact on a specific group if the pass rate for the group is less than 80 percent of the pass rate for whites. In the case of the PACE exam, "in 1978, about 42 percent of whites taking the test passed at 70 percent or higher, compared to only about 5 percent for blacks and 13 percent for Hispanics" (Ban and Ingraham, 1988, p. 709).
2. A provision of the Civil Service Reform Act allows agencies to suspend current civil service law (with a few exceptions) to test out new personnel systems. For more information, see Ban, 1992.
3. Title XIII of the Homeland Security Act of 2002 is referred to as the Chief Human Capital Officers Act of 2002. Pub. L. No. 107–296 (November 25, 2002).
4. The Student Loan Repayment Program permits agencies to repay student loans up to $10,000 a year, with a lifetime limit of $60,000 (U.S. MSPB, 2004b).
5. There is a rapidly growing literature on e-government. For a good overview, see Pavlichev and Garson, 2004. For a look at how one can measure the actual impact of e-government, see Stowers, 2004.
6. Under the *Luevano* consent decree, agencies would need to use the ACWA examination to fill covered positions, even when they are for excepted service appointments, such as under an internship program. The Merit Systems Protection Board has found that "this has led some agencies to stop publicly announcing these vacancies and has caused others to hire for those occupations above the GS–5/7 level to avoid the requirement to use the ACWA assessment tools" (U.S. MSPB, 2004a, p. 20).

REFERENCES

Ban, C. 1992. "Research and Demonstrations under CSRA: Is Innovation Possible?" In P. W. Ingraham and D. H. Rosenbloom, eds. *The Promise and Paradox of Civil Service Reform.* Pittsburgh: University of Pittsburgh Press, 217–235.

Ban, C. 1995. *How Do Public Managers Manage? Bureaucratic Constraints, Organization Culture, and the Potential for Reform.* San Francisco, CA: Jossey-Bass.

Ban, C. 1998. "Reinventing the Federal Civil Service: Drivers of Change," *Public Administration Quarterly* 22:1: 21–34.

Ban, C. and Ingraham, P. 1988. "Recruiting Quality Federal Employees: Life After PACE." *Public Administration Review* 48:3: 708–718.

Ban, C. and Marzotto, T. 1984. "Delegations of Examining: Objectives and Implementation." In P. W. Ingraham and C. Ban, eds. *Legislating Bureaucratic Change: The Civil Service Reform Act of 1978*. Albany, NY: State University of New York Press, 148–160.

Friel, B. 2003. "Data Shows 'Human Capital Crisis' May Be Overstated." *Govexec.com Daily Briefing* May 2. www.govexec.com/story_page.cfm?articleid=25526&printerfriendly Vers=1&.

Gates, S. and Paul, C. 2004. *Intern Programs as a Human Resources Management Tool for the Department of Defense*. Santa Monica, CA: RAND National Defense Research Institute.

Ingraham, P. W. 1984. "The Civil Service Reform Act of 1978: Its Design and Legislative History." In P. W. Ingraham and C. Ban, eds. *Legislating Bureaucratic Change: The Civil Service Reform Act of 1978*. Albany, NY: SUNY Albany Press, 13–28.

Light, P. 1999. *The True Size of Government*. Washington, DC: The Brookings Institution.

Luevano et al. v. Alan Campbell. 1981. Consent Decree, as amended. U.S. District Court for the District of Columbia (No. 79–0271).

Marzotto, T. 1988. "The Fragmentation of the Federal Workforce." Paper presented at the Annual Conference of the American Political Science Association.

National Academy of Public Administration (NAPA). 1999. *Entry-Level Hiring and Development for the 21st Century: Professional and Administrative Positions* (HRM Series V). Washington, DC: NAPA.

National Academy of Public Administration (NAPA). 2001. *The Quest for Talent: Recruitment Strategies for Federal Agencies*. Washington, DC: NAPA.

National Performance Review. 1993. Reinventing Human Resources Management. Washington, DC: U.S. Government Printing Office.

Nelson, S. 2004a. "The Challenge of Category Rating: Why Aren't You Using It?" *Issues of Merit* 10:1 January: 2–3.

Nelson, S. 2004b."The State of the Federal Civil Service Today: Aching for Reform." *Review of Public Personnel Administration* 24:3: 202–215.

Partnership for Public Service. 2002. *Tapping America's Potential: Expanding Student Employment and Internship Opportunities in the Federal Government*. Washington, DC: Partnership for Public Service.

Partnership for Public Service. 2004a. *A New Call to Service for an Age of Savvy Altruism: Public Attitudes About Government and Government Workers*. Washington, DC: Partnership for Public Service.

Partnership for Public Service. 2004b. *Asking the Wrong Questions: A Look at How the Federal Government Assesses and Selects its Workforce*. Washington, DC: Partnership for Public Service.

Partnership for Public Service and National Academy of Public Service. 2005. *Where the Jobs Are: The Continuing Growth of Federal Job Opportunities*. Washington, DC: Partnership for Public Service and NAPA.

Pavlichev, A. and Garson, G. D. 2004. *Digital Government: Principles and Best Practices*. Hershey, PA: Idea Group Publishing.

Riccucci, N. 1991. "Merit, Equity, and Test Validity: A New Look at an Old Problem." *Administration and Society* 21:1: 74–93.

Schmidt, F. and Hunter, J. 1998. "The Validity and Utility of Selection Methods in Personnel Psychology: Practical and Theoretical Implications of 85 Years of Research Findings." *Psychological Bulletin*. 124:2: 262–274.

Stowers, G. 2004. *Measuring the Performance of E-Government*. Washington, DC: IBM Center for the Business of Government.

U.S. General Accounting Office. 1994. *Federal Hiring: Testing for Entry-Level Administrative Positions Falls Short of Expectations*. GAO/GGD-94-103.

U.S. General Accounting Office. 2001. *Human Capital: Meeting the Governmentwide High-Risk Challenge*. Statement of David M. Walker, Comptroller General of the United States. Testimony before the Subcommittee on Oversight of Government Management, Restructuring, and the District of Columbia. Committee on Governmental Affairs. U.S. Senate. February 1. GAO-01-357T.

U.S. General Accounting Office. 2004a. *Human Capital: Additional Collaboration Between OPM and Agencies is Key to Improved Federal Hiring*. GAO-04-797, June.

U.S. General Accounting Office. 2004b. *Human Capital: Increasing Agencies' Use of New Hiring Flexibilities*. (Statement of J. Christopher Mihm.) GAO-04-959T, July.

U.S. Merit Systems Protection Board. 1995. *The Rule of Three in Federal Hiring: Boon or Bane?* Washington, DC: USMSPB.

U.S. Merit Systems Protection Board. 2000. *Restoring Merit to Federal Hiring: Why Two Special Hiring Programs Should be Ended*. Washington, DC: USMSPB.

U.S. Merit Systems Protection Board. 2001a. *Growing Leaders: The Presidential Management Internship Program*. Washington, DC: USMSPB.

U.S. Merit Systems Protection Board, 2001b. "Outstanding Scholar Hiring Inconsistent with OPM Guidance" *Issues of Merit* November: 1–4.

U.S. Merit Systems Protection Board. 2003a. *The Federal Selection Interview: Unrealized Potential*. Washington, DC: USMSPB.

U.S. Merit Systems Protection Board, 2003b. *Help Wanted: A Review of Federal Vacancy Announcements*. Washington, DC: USMSPB.

U.S. Merit Systems Protection Board. 2004a. *Managing Federal Recruitment: Issues, Insights, and Illustrations*. Washington, DC: USMSPB.

U.S. Merit Systems Protection Board. 2004b. *Identifying Talent through Technology: Automated Hiring Systems in Federal Agencies*. Washington, DC: USMSPB.

U.S. Office of Management and Budget. 2002. *The President's Management Agenda, Fiscal Year 2002* www.whitehouse.gov/omb/budget/fy2002/mgmt.pdf.

U.S. Office of Personnel Management. 1992. *U.S. Department of Agriculture Personnel Management Demonstration Project: First Annual Evaluation Report*. OS92-7. Washington, DC: USOPM.

U.S. Office of Personnel Management. 1998a. *Deregulation and Delegation of Human Resources Management Authority in the Federal Government*. Washington, DC: Office of Merit Systems Oversight and Effectiveness, USOPM. July. MSE-98-3.

U.S. Office of Personnel Management. 1998b. *HRM Policies and Practices in Title 5-Exempt Organizations*. Washington, DC: Office of Merit Systems Oversight and Effectiveness, USOPM. August. MSE-98-4.

U.S. Office of Personnel Management, 2000a. *Federal Human Resources Management for the 21st Century: Strategic Plan, FY 2000-FY 2005*. September 30.

U.S. Office of Personnel Management. 2000b. *OPM's Interim Rules on Federal Career Intern Program to Help Agencies Build Future Work Force*. OPM News Release. December 14.

Woodard, Colleen. 2005. "Merit by Any Other Name—Reframing the Civil Service First Principle." *Public Administration Review* 65:1: 109–116.

Chapter *11*

Strategic Human Resources Management

Dennis M. Daley

Strategic human resources management practices enhance employee productivity and the ability of agencies to achieve their mission. Integrating the use of human resource/personnel practices into the strategic planning process enables an organization to better achieve its goals and objectives. Productivity gains from the diffusion of technological innovations are now incorporated into both public- and private-sector organizations. Future productivity gains must focus on how people use these technologies.

The performance of organizations is the focus of intensive research efforts. How well an organization performs its mission and accomplishes its goals of program service delivery is of paramount concern. Human capital is a major component in this performance. Human capital, in a resource-based view of organizations, focuses on those factors that are actually within our power to effect. Improving human capital offers the most promise for improving organizational effectiveness.

Modern, knowledge-based organizations are ideal settings for the application of strategic human resources management practices. Inasmuch as their competitive advantage is attributable to techniques, which focus on people, these should prove to be directly linked to measures of organizational success. Civil service systems are designed to integrate the multiple values pursued by the public sector. While these rules can inhibit the adoption of progressive personnel practices, they are not necessarily rigid barriers to change. The public sector has been the venue of many experiments and innovations in recent years.

Combining human resource practices, all with a focus on the achievement of organizational goals and objectives, can have a substantial effect on the ultimate success of the organization. Resource-based theory posits that competitive advantage and the implementation of plans are highly dependent upon an organization's basic inputs, including its human capital (Wernerfelt, 1984; Barney, 1986, 1991, 2001; Peteraf, 1993; Boxall, 1991; Hitt, Bierman, Shimizu, and Kochhar, 2001). Human capital is seen as one of the factors offering organizations a competitive advantage. The human resource management systems, in as much as they are focused on developing and sustaining human capital, are seen as a significant instrument in this process (Lado and Wilson, 1994; Snell, Youndt, and Wright, 1996). Research on strategic human resource management offers empirical support for this thesis (Fitz-enz, 1990; Delery and Doty, 1996; Ulrich, 1997). In essence, the results of organizational strategic planning are, in implementation, linked to specific human resource practices (or perhaps more correctly, we judge our human resource practices in terms of how well they help us achieve our strategic plan).

STRATEGIC PLANNING

Strategic planning is rational analysis (Nutt and Backoff, 1992; Klingner, 1993; Perry, 1993; Berry, 1994; Mintzberg, 1994; Ledvinka, 1995; Bryson, 1996). It takes *what is* and develops ideas of *what should be* along with plans for *how to get there.* With a realistic organizational strategy focused on what the future should look like, strategic planning provides the "road map" for fulfilling that future.

While installing the strategic planning process appears relatively simple, in reality it requires that a learning organization exist. An organizational culture supportive of change must already be in place if strategic planning is to be anything other than a paper exercise. An organization must perceive that change may be desirable (i.e., recognize that the status quo is not the best of all possible worlds), be able to reflect and analyze that change (instead of following whatever is the current fad), have individuals who will champion the change, and, ultimately, the ability to institutionalize that change throughout the entire organization. Without this learning environment, strategic planning is for naught.

The problem of strategic planning is in implementation. Visions without implementation are merely delusions and hallucinations. As Theodore H. Poister and Gregory Streib (2005) indicate in their survey of municipalities only 44 percent claim to be engaged in strategic planning and, when implementation efforts are focused on, only 22 percent can still make the claim. While this represents a small proportion of municipalities, it also clearly indicates that strategic planning is indeed doable.

Through environmental scanning, strategic planning helps size up what the existing organization's capabilities are and defines the real world it exists in. The planning process explores alternatives—both in terms of the vision involved and the courses of action necessary to accomplish them. Finally, strategic planning helps an organization settle on one choice of direction and mesh it with the appropriate objectives and action plans. Strategic planning should also incorporate the human resources necessary for accomplishing its goals (Mesch, Perry, and Wise, 1995; Perry and Mesch, 1997; Tompkins, 2002). The foremost advantage derived from strategic planning is that it helps improve organizational performance.

Strategic planning focuses on the future—what should be. By focusing on the truly important, strategic planning takes attention away from the day-to-day fire-fighting and crisis management that so fruitlessly dissipate individual efforts. Its future-oriented techniques can warn an organization of dangers when there is yet time to prepare for them. Hence, it can be the basis for instilling habits fostering continuous improvement (Keen, 1994).

Strategic planning also helps to concentrate individual efforts into a team effort. It can assist in developing total quality management and objective-based performance appraisal systems. Accountability for results can be assigned. The strategic planning process itself can serve as a team-building exercise. Finally, the process itself transforms perceptions away from separate and distinct projects and towards the organization (and its goals) as a whole.

While vision is the chief responsibility of management, it is important that the vision be the organization's vision. A vision must be communicated and shared if it is to be an effective guide for performance. Leaders or management teams that "hammer out" a vision statement at some organizational retreat and then "broadcast" it to the organization are not providing a vision. Such catchy slogans are only a commercial message. A vision is also more than a "cult of personality" where the leader's personal vision, or merely his or her ego, is trumpeted loudly.

Visions are shared and voluntarily become guiding principles for each individual. While they will originate in some individual's personal vision, they are transformed as they are subscribed to or adopted by others. Often they are modified and transformed by this process of conversion. A vision statement displayed on the wall is only a physical reminder. Only when the vision is within an individual is there a real vision (Senge, 1990).

In addition to leadership support, those engaged in strategic planning need be aware of other potential problems. As occurs with all management techniques, individuals will need extensive training and refresher training (to answer unforeseen questions that arise in response to implementation). Conflict, confusion, and chaos will prevail initially and for some time thereafter. Only as individuals learn how to do it and see its value will the benefits of strategic planning be realized (Merjanian, 1997).

The value of strategic planning is highly dependent upon people in the agencies who assemble and provide the data realizing that it also helps them do their jobs better. Excessive requests for information and data unconnected to an organization's mission undermine the strategic planning process. While such information is useful in a command and control environment, strategic planning is essential for the more complex, knowledge-based organization's coaching and coordination. However, in such complex organizations the nonlinear nature of management is recognized. Strategic planning serves to define boundaries (Kiel, 1994). Planning is successful because it is useful (Merjanian, 1997).

The employment of needs assessment instruments for strategic planning and incentive systems for rewarding the successful implementation of plans are the alpha and omega of productivity.

Needs assessment brings into focus the general problems along with the directions the organization needs to go in seeking their solutions. Yet, it is up to individuals to actually accomplish these tasks. Focusing techniques concentrate on improving our understanding of an organization's goals and the means for achieving them. Goalsetting, brainstorming-scenario planning, and Ishikawa or cause-and-effect charts are but three methods used in focusing on problems and solutions.

Participatory goalsetting is quite simple; surprisingly it works extraordinarily well. Individuals work better with a goal in mind. Even when the reward for achievement is only intrinsic, goalsetting can be used to increase productivity. Goalsetting even in the looser form of work agendas helps focus efforts (Kotter, 1982; Barry, Cramton, and Carroll, 1997).

Participation allows the employees to clear up misconceptions and obtain a far better understanding of what is desired. It can also foster the sense of goal ownership that transforms motivation into commitment (Locke, Shaw, Saari, and Latham, 1981; Locke and Latham, 1984).

Brainstorming and related techniques, such as cognitive mapping and scenario planning, begin the goalsetting process. The human mind is designed to act quickly. It can readily draw conclusions based on little information. While an advantage to our ancestors and to us in emergencies, this facility can preclude the consideration of more complex, worthwhile options. Brainstorming exists to overcome this limitation. Since its purpose is to generate ideas, judgment is suspended at this stage in the process.

The ideas generated by the brainstorming process can be structured or grouped using techniques such as cognitive mapping of cause-and-effect charts. Cognitive mapping is a simple device wherein the various ideas are rearranged and grouped (easily done with the use of post-it notes) into similar topics. Complementary topic groups can be physically positioned near one another. More complex than cognitive mapping for structuring the ideas is the use of cause-and-effect charts. Devised by Kaoru Ishikawa (1976) as a TQM technique, the cause-and-effect chart (also referred to as fishbone diagrams) provides the skeleton around which individuals can structure their brainstorming. Participation, inasmuch as it creates this sense of shared ownership in decisions, enhances the commitment to succeed (Miller and Monge, 1986; Wagner and Gooding, 1987a, 1987b).

In a knowledge-based organization this, in itself, helps to coordinate the actions of the entire workforce. In essence, coordination by organization has been supplemented (or replaced) by the equally powerful coordination by idea (Fayol, 1916; Gulick, 1937). Goals should, in general, share a number of attributes: specificity, difficulty, feedback, participation, and competition (Sims and Lorenzi, 1992, 118–129).

If they are to direct effort, goals need to be specific as to "what is to be done." This, first and foremost, requires that they be clearly measurable. Individuals must be able to "keep score." They must be able to judge for themselves that the goal is doable, and how well they are doing. Measurable goals reduce vagueness in assessing success.

By attaching a degree of difficulty to a goal, it is invested with value. Goals that are simple and easy to accomplish do not succeed. Only if there is a challenge in its accomplishment, do humans invest a goal with the psychological attention that motivation calls for. This also means that goals should avoid being too difficult, i.e., deemed to be impossible to achieve. Organizations in creating goals (and individual objectives) have all too often "stretched" them beyond reality. The plans look nice, but they fail.

Goals require performance feedback. Employees need to know how well they are doing in order to continue or take corrective actions. This is especially important when goals are long term and big picture in nature. Intermediate and component assessments provide the small victories that encourage continuation.

STRATEGIC HUMAN RESOURCES PRACTICES

In the modern, knowledge-based organization, strategic planning should quite clearly include strategic human resources planning. In an empirical study noting the impact of strategic human resource management on organizational performance, John E. Delery and D. Harold Doty (1996), "replicated" in a public sector study by Dennis M. Daley and Michael L. Vasu (2005), identify seven general employment practices:

1. Internal career ladders
2. Formal training systems
3. Results-oriented performance appraisal
4. Employment security
5. Employee voice/participation
6. Broadly defined jobs
7. Performance-based compensation

Using the more narrowly focused outcome assessments of Return on Average assets (ROA) and Return on Equity (ROE) (measures with individual-level data drawn across organizations in the banking industry), Delery and Doty (1996) found strategic human resource management contributions of $R2 = .13$ (adj $R2 = .11$) for ROA, and $R2 = .09$ (adj $R2 = .07$) for ROE. In Delery and Doty (1996) relationships (standardized regression coefficients) with the outcome assessments were found between results-oriented appraisal (.14 ROA; .14 ROE), profit sharing (.31 ROA; .28 ROE), and employment security (.16 ROA).

However, the findings in this study are somewhat larger than those found by Hitt, Bierman, Shimizu, and Kochhar (2001) in their human capital findings in law firms ($R2 = .036$). The complex and somewhat less compatible goals entailed in public-sector organizations apparently do not limit the effectiveness or enhance the difficulty of strategic human resource management applications.

In a study of North Carolina County Social Services, Daley and Vasu (forthcoming) found that employment security assisted both in helping people stay off of welfare (increasing the odds five-fold) and in collecting child support (increasing the odds by a factor of six). These represent potentially substantial gains. However, these results may actually reflect an ability to withstand the pressure for the short term, a McJobs approach that welfare reform has often engendered. Training nearly tripled the odds for assisting people in going to work. However, training was also seen as having a negative effect on welfare decline (reducing the odds by four-fifths) and obtaining child support (decreasing the odds by a quarter). Perhaps this reflects not on training per se but on the nature of the training itself. Inappropriate training that takes professionals away from the doing their jobs is not going to make a positive contribution. Similar explanations may also underlie the failure of other practices (e.g., see Riccucci and Lurie, 2001, with regard to performance appraisal systems).

These human resource/personnel practices form the basis upon which the concept of strategic human resource management is constructed. These are clearly not the only such practices nor the only way in which they can be delineated. It can readily be argued that these personnel practices are rather "ordinary." Indeed they are.

Strategic human resource management is focused, for the most part, not on developing entirely new human resource practices, but on using the good practices already existing with an emphasis on how they assist in achieving organizational goals. Many of these practices are indeed to be found, more or less, in use among everyday organizations. However, the extent to which they are used strategically in achieving the organization's mission and goals may be open to question. Research has established linkages between HRM and various measures of organizational effectiveness (Arthur, 1992, 1994; Delaney and Huselid, 1996; Gerhart and Milkovich, 1990; Huselid, 1993, 1995; Terpstra and Rozell, 1993). Many studies link HRM to intermediate concepts such as efficacy, job satisfaction, organizational commitment, and trust. Hence, the strategic role of these personnel practices is cast as that of a necessary but not sufficient condition.

Much of this research has concentrated on private-sector organizations rather than on the provision of public social services (Selden, Jacobson, Ammar, and Wright, 2000). The general hypothesis is that each practice does indeed matter and individually (and collectively) contributes to organizational success. One should clearly see a linkage between the perceptions of personnel practices and goal achievement. Hence, the overall argument is one that strategic human resource management is eminently doable.

STRATEGIC HUMAN RESOURCES PRACTICES

INTERNAL CAREER LADDER

Strategically, the internal career ladder offers employees advancement opportunities within the organization for accomplishing the organization's mission and goals. Career ladders also focus attention on workforce and succession planning (Anderson, 2004; Johnson and Brown, 2004; Pynes, 2004). While succession planning highlights and identifies individuals who may succeed to key leadership positions, workforce planning is concerned with identifying key competencies that the organization will need and assuring that necessary training and development is provided.

A career system is necessary to focus individual attention on the strategic issues facing an organization over the long term. A long-term perspective induces organizational commitment and loyalty. It enables individuals and organizations to invest in training and productivity improvements knowing that they will reap the benefits from that enhanced knowledge and technique.

Internal selection is also easier. The employee has already been attracted. The questions on whether an individual will fit in and adapt to an organization's culture are now moot. The problems of orientation and socialization (which are fraught with disappointment and turnover) have been overcome. The not inconsequential costs of recruitment (which are often an unfortunate, limiting factor among governments) are dramatically reduced.

However, internal selection exposes an organization to the dangers of "inbreeding." While it promotes a more harmonious, homogeneous workforce, it also can blind the organization to what is going on in the world at large. Outside selection stirs up an organization. All the problems mentioned here that are avoided by internal selection are also lost opportunities.

FORMAL TRAINING SYSTEMS

The modern organization is indeed its people and the knowledge they possess. It can no longer be taken for granted that employees will arrive at work with all the requisite skills (Anderson, 2004; Pynes, 2004; Rothwell and Poduch, 2004). Too much of what goes on in today's organization requires specific adaptation. The most knowledgeable and skilled worker still requires training so as to fit into the organization and become a valuable contributor to the team (Quinn, Anderson, and Finkelstein, 1996). Strategically, training enables an organization to provide its employees with the precise skills that most effectively assist in achieving its mission.

Unfortunately, training and development are the most neglected aspects of government. Well into the 1950s and 1960s, governments denied the value of training and development. Individuals were hired for specific jobs and were assumed to already possess all the skills that would be needed. While the importance of training and development is now recognized, it remains a neglected area. New employees—like the buildings and equipment of government—are allowed to depreciate through an under-investment in maintenance (Quinn, Anderson, and Finkelstein, 1996).

RESULTS-ORIENTED PERFORMANCE APPRAISAL

Performance appraisal is used in making decisions pertaining to promotion, demotion, retention, transfer, and pay. It is also employed, as a developmental guide for training needs assessment and employee feedback. Performance appraisal also aids with a number of more general organizational functions as a means for validating selection and hiring procedures, promoting employee-supervisor understanding, and supporting an organization's culture. Modern performance-appraisal systems combine an objective appraisal instrument with supervisory and employee training. Performance-appraisal system failure is most often due to a failure to link the instruments to these purposes (Daley, 2000, 2001, 2003, 2005; Grote, 1996).

The objective performance-appraisal system links individual (and team) effort to the organization's goals. The "objectives" that are used to measure individual performance are derived from the strategic goals of the organization and its component units. Hence, both reward and development are focused on achieving the organizational mission.

Two formats dominate the arena of objective appraisal techniques: behaviorally-anchored rating scales (BARS) and management by objectives (MBO). BARS appraisals work best with large groups and subgroups of individuals whose job descriptions can be standardized; MBO, on the other hand, is more suited to cases that can be tailored to each individual job. MBO is best when it is focused on the results to be expected from job performance; BARS handles behavioral processes where outputs are more identifiable and assurable than outcomes.

EMPLOYMENT SECURITY

The knowledge-based environment also heightens the importance attached to employee rights along with the instrumental grievance and discipline system. Employees are human beings and work better when their humanity is recognized and respected. The employer-employee relationship is not that of master and servant (although much of the legal system is based on that design). Foreshadowed by the work of Mary Parker Follett and commencing with the Hawthorne studies in the late 1920s, motivational research has clearly pointed this out. With the transformation of the organization into an entity based on the skills of its employees rather than the efficiency of its machinery, this lesson becomes even more important.

Employee rights and the mechanism for enforcing them (i.e., the grievance process) serve as a safeguard for assuring that employees are accorded the basic dignity that every human being is entitled to. Like similar safety devices, we hope that we never will really need to use them. While most organizations would prefer to do without such legal and formal systems, reality requires them. If there were no past abuses, there would be no need for laws prohibiting such practices.

By providing, due-process rights focused on cause and protecting employees from abusive, arbitrary, and capricious behaviors, the organization assures that attention is placed on doing the job itself. This helps limit some of the "organizational politics" wherein an employee must build supportive alliances and networks devoted solely to self-protection.

Employee Voice/Participation

In *Exit, Voice, and Loyalty* Albert O. Hirschman (1970) proposes a typology of responses to dissatisfaction. A theory of individual self-interest that not only operates in terms of the economic market but with respect to socio-political values is primarily an attempt to explain an organization's survival. Although Hirschman's theory focuses on decisions regarding the acceptance/rejection of an organization's products or services, it can also be interpreted with regard to similar decisions by an organization's own personnel vis-a-vis the organization itself.

Exit is a conceptual representation of the market or economic system. The individual consumer chooses to buy or not buy; i.e., to stay or exit. By exiting a product line or service, individuals register their market judgment. Similarly, an employee can express dissatisfaction with the organization by leaving it. For such a market system to work, basic economic assumptions need to be met. The consumer or employee must have viable alternatives from which to choose (as well as the knowledge of the situation). Even so, Hirschman notes that the exit option, as such, is not made lightly. Hence, he suggests that prior to such a step being taken a consumer or employee is likely to make other attempts to rectify the perceived problems or dissatisfactions.

It is this effort to change the situation that gives rise to voice. *Voice* is seen to represent a political dimension, which can encompass a gamut of behaviors ranging from grumbling through participative management to full-scale democracy. It represents a viable, non-market means for assuring organizational survival. While voice focuses internally on the advocacy of reform, *loyalty* represents the employee's willingness to stand up for the organization. In this instance advocacy is in response to outside criticism and is an expression of confidence in the organization.

In a series of articles, Farrell and Rusbult (Farrell, 1983; Farrell and Rusbult 1981; Rusbult, 1980, 1983; Rusbult and Farrell, 1983; Rusbult, Farrell, Rogers, and Mainous, 1988) explicitly extend Hirshman's concept to personnel matters. As a result of a multidimensional scaling of job dissatisfaction, Farrell (1983) was able to demonstrate support for a modified version of Hirschman's typology. To the categories of exit, voice, and loyalty Farrell added one for neglect. *Neglect* indicates a condition in which employees give up but stay to draw a paycheck. Neglect may involve absenteeism and obstructionism or merely a passive "I don't care" attitude.

Broadly Defined Jobs

The "triumph of technique over purpose" is also evident here. The rigidity invested in the use of pay scales (and the commitant job analyses upon which they are based) denies organizations the flexibility to adjust to and meet change. Individuals cannot readily be reassigned duties. This is especially a problem if those duties are from jobs officially designated as having lower grades. Even if pay remains constant, a lower grade assignment might be seen psychologically as a career setback. Reward for exceptional performance is thwarted by the formal attachment of pay ceilings or maximum salaries to specific job grades. *Broadbanding* has been introduced as a means to cut through the Gordian knot of classification. Whether "broad grades" or "career bands" are used, management obtains greater flexibility. The employee is seen to benefit from both more challenging and meaningful work assignments and the possibility of pay increases (Risher and Schay, 1994; Risher, 1999).

Broad grades are simply a re-calibration of the existing pay scales. Under broad grades, a system of, for example, fifty pay grades is collapsed into one of ten or twelve grades. Career bands are more innovative and dynamic. While career bands also reduce the number of pay grades from, for example, fifty to ten or twelve, they do not impose any internal step structure onto this new system. Managers are given the flexibility to freely assign (and reassign) duties and salaries (limited only by overall budget figures). Individuals need not begin at the minimum, starting salary nor serve their time prior to receiving increases. Managers are often permitted to hire at any salary between the minimum and midpoint range; offers above the midpoint would be permitted but require approval. Ideally, salary determination within broadbanding is calculated from a midpoint base. The market or competitive salary sets the base, which should be the median or average salary.

PERFORMANCE-BASED COMPENSATION

Strategic pay requires that all decisions relative to compensation and benefits are designed to attract, retain, or motivate employees. As such, the entire organization's reward structure is designed to fully serve its mission or purpose. In reality, most organizations limit incentive pay to only a portion of the compensation package. All employees who perform satisfactorily are guaranteed a set base pay and benefits package. Even so, this guarantee serves to calm fears with regard to financial security and, hence, is a valuable tool in helping to attract and retain individuals.

Extrinsic incentives primarily use monetary rewards as their motivating factor. Career development and training opportunities that can lead to promotion or interesting, fulfilling assignments (which also provide intrinsic motivation through their recognition of merit) are another source of extrinsic motivation in the sense that in addition to higher compensation levels they pay individuals in terms of power and responsibility.

Pay-for-performance is an application of *expectancy theory*. Employee motivation is deemed to be extrinsic and follow the outlines of B. F. Skinner's (1904–1993) operant conditioning models. Expectancy theory posits that employees will be motivated to the extent to which their calculation of the desirability of rewards, the effort required to perform a task, and the probability of successful performance (and of the organization paying-off) are viewed favorably. Pay-for-performance schemes concentrate on providing or determining the right balance between extrinsic reward (pay) and required effort (performance).

A wide array of extrinsic pay-for-performance schemes exists. The modern pay-for-performance scheme builds upon a base-pay system. The salary or wage put "at risk" is to encourage or motivate the worker without jeopardizing his or her basic financial security. One can address overall individual performance or specific instances; focus can be on group performance at the organizational or team level. Individual systems based on merit pay step increases; annuities, bonuses, and suggestion awards as well as skill- or competency-based approaches abound. In addition, group or organizational rewards are the focus of gain or goal-sharing programs. Performance-appraisal systems are the trigger instrument for operationalizing pay-for-performance. The individual performance rating is used to determine which employees are eligible for individual and group awards as well as the amount of reward an individual is entitled to. Management by objectives systems may also serve as the measurement instrument for a pay-for-performance system (appraisal-by-objectives formally incorporates MBO into the performance-appraisal process).

REFERENCES

Anderson, M. W. 2004. "The Metrics of Workforce Planning." *Public Personnel Management* 33:4 : Winter: 363–378.

Arthur, J. B. 1992. "The Link Between Business Strategy and Industrial Relations Systems in American Steel Minimills." *Industrial and Labor Relations Review* 45: 488–506.

Arthur, J. B. 1994. "Effects of Human Resource Systems on Manufacturing Performance." *Academy of Management Journal* 37: 670–687.

Barney, J. B. 1986. "Strategic Factor Markets: Expectations, Lock, and Business Strategy." *Management Science* 32: 1231–1241.

Barney, J. B. 1991. "Firm Resource and Sustained Competitive Advantage." *Journal of Management* 17: 99–120.

Barney, J. B. 2001. "Is the Resource-Based 'View' a Useful Perspective for Strategic Management Research? Yes." *Academy of Management Review* 26:1: January: 41–56.

Barry, D., Cramton, C. D., and Carroll, S. J. 1997. "Navigating the Garbage Can: How Work Agendas Help Managers Cope With Job Realities." *Academy of Management Executive* 11:2: May: 26–42.

Berry, F. S. 1994. "Innovation in Public Management: The Adoption of Strategic Planning." *Public Administration Review* 54:4: July/August: 322–330.

Boxall, P. 1991. "The Strategic HRM Debate and the Resource-Based View of the Firm." *Human Resource Management Journal* 63: 59–75.

Bryson, J. M. 1996. *Strategic Planning for Public and Nonprofit Organizations*. San Francisco, CA: Jossey Bass.

Daley, D. M. 2000. "Performance Appraisal Techniques and Applications: Guides for Consultants." In Robert Golembiewski, ed., *Handbook of Organizational Consultation*. New York, NY: Marcel Dekker, pp. 243–253.

Daley, D. M. 2001. "Developmental Performance Appraisal: Feedback, Interview, and Disciplinary Techniques." In K. Tom Liou, ed., *Handbook of Public Management Practice and Reform*. New York, NY: Marcel Dekker, pp. 243–259.

Daley, D. M. 2003. "The Trials and Tribulations of Performance Appraisal: Problems and Prospects on Entering the Twenty-First Century." In Steven W. Hays and Richard C. Kearney, eds., *Public Personnel Administration: Problems and Prospects*. Upper Saddle River, NJ: Prentice Hall, pp. 154–166.

Daley, D. M. 2005. "Designing Effective Performance Appraisal Systems." In Steve Condrey, ed., *Handbook of Practical Human Resource Management*, 2nd ed. San Francisco, CA: Jossey-Bass, pp. 499–527.

Daley, D. M. and Vasu, M. L. 2005. "Supervisory Perceptions of the Impact of Public Sector Personnel Practices on the Achievement of Multiple Goals: Putting the Strategic into Human Resource Management." *American Review of Public Administration*. 35:2: 157–167.

Delaney, J. T. and Huselid, M. A. 1996. "The Impact of Human Resource Management Practices on Perceptions of Organizational Performance." *Academy of Management Journal* 39:4: August: 949–969.

Delery, J. E. and Doty, D. H. 1996. "Modes of Theorizing in Strategic Human Resource Management: Tests of Universalistic, Contingency, and Configurational Performance Predictions." *Academy of Management Journal* 39:4: August: 802–835.

Farrell, D. 1983. "Exit, Voice, Loyalty, and Neglect as Responses to Job Dissatisfaction: A Multidimensional Scaling Study." *Academy of Management Journal* 26: 596–606.

Farrell, D. and Rusbult, C. E. 1981. "Exchange Variables as Predictors of Job Satisfaction, Job Commitment, and Turnover: The Impact of Rewards, Costs, Alternatives, and Investments." *Organizational Behavior and Human Performance* 27: 78–95.

Fayol, H. 1949 [1916]. *General and Industrial Management*. London: Pitman.

Fitz-enz, J. 1990. *Human Value Management: The Value-Adding Human Resource Management Strategy for the 1990s*. San Francisco, CA: Jossey-Bass.

Gerhart, B. and Milkovich, G. T. 1990. "Organizational Differences in Managerial Compensation and Financial Performance." *Academy of Management Journal* 33: 663–691.

Grote, D. 1996. *The Complete Guide to Performance Appraisal*. New York, NY: AMACOM.

Gulick, L. 1937. "Notes on the Theory of Organization." In L. Gulick and L. Lyndall, eds. *Papers on the Science of Administration*. New York, NY: Institute of Public Administration.

Hirschman, A. 1970. *Exit, Voice, and Loyalty: Responses to Decline in Firms, Organizations, and States*. Cambridge, MA: Harvard Press.

Hitt, M. A., Bierman, L., Shimizu, K., and Kochhar, R. 2001. "Direct and Moderating Effects of Human Capital on Strategy and Performance in Professional Service Firms: A Resource-Based Perspective." *Academy of Management Journal* 44:1: February: 13–28.

Huselid, M. A. 1993. "Estimates of the Impact of Human Resource Management Practices on Turnover and Productivity." Paper presented at the annual meeting of the Academy of Management.

Huselid, M. A. 1995. "The Impact of Human Resource Management Practices on Turnover, Productivity, and Corporate Financial Performance." *Academy of Management Journal* 38: 635–672.

Ishikawa, K. 1976. *Guide to Quality Control*. Asian Productivity Organization.

Johnson, G. L. and Brown, J. 2004. "Workforce Planning Not A Common Practice: IPMA HR Study Finds." *Public Personnel Management* 33:4: Winter: 379–388.

Keen, C. D. 1994. "Tips for Effective Strategic Planning." *HR Magazine* August: 84–87.

Kiel, L. D. 1994. *Managing Chaos and Complexity in Government*. San Francisco, CA: Jossey Bass.

Klingner, D. 1993. "Developing a Strategic Human Resources Management Capability in Public Agencies." *Public Personnel Management* 22:4: Winter: 565–578.

Kotter, J. P. 1982. *The General Managers*. New York, NY: Free Press.

Lado, A. A. and Wilson, M. C. 1994. "Human Resource Systems and Sustained Competitive Advantage: A Competency-Based Perspective." *Academy of Management Review* 19:4: October: 699–727.

Ledvinka, J. 1995. "Human Resources Planning." In Jack Rabin, Thomas Vocino, W. Bartley Hildreth, and Gerald Miller, eds., *Handbook of Public Personnel Administration*. New York, NY: Marcel Dekker, pp. 217–240.

Locke, E. A., Shaw, K. N., Saari, L. M., and Latham, G. P. 1981. "Goal Setting and Task Performance." *Psychological Bulletin* 90: 125–152.

Locke, E. A. and Latham, G. P. 1984. *Goal Setting: A Motivational Technique That Works*. Englewood Cliffs, NJ: Prentice Hall.

Merjanian, A. 1997. "Striving to Make Performance Measurement Work: Texas Implements Systems Approach to Planning, Budgeting." *PA Times* 20:6: June: 1, 19–20.

Mesch, D. J., Perry, J. L., and Wise, L. R. 1995. "Bureaucratic and Strategic Human Resource Management: An Empirical Comparison in the Federal Government." *Journal of Public Administration Theory and Research* 5: 385–402.

Miller, K. I. and Monge, P. R. 1986. "Participation, Satisfaction, and Productivity: A Meta-Analytic Review." *Academy of Management Journal* 29:4: 727–753.

Mintzberg, H. 1994. *The Rise and Fall of Strategic Planning*. New York, NY: Free Press.

Nutt, P. C. and Backoff, R. W. 1992. *Strategic Management of Public and Third Sector Organizations*. San Francisco, CA: Jossey-Bass.

Perry, J. L. 1993. "Stategic Human Resource Management." *Review of Public Personnel Administration* 13:4: Fall: 59–71.

Perry, J. L. and Mesch, D. L. 1997. "Strategic Human Resources Management." In Carolyn Ban and Norma Riccucci, eds., *Public Personnel Management: Current Concerns, Future Challenges*. New York, NY: Longman, pp. 21–34.

Peteraf, M. A. 1993. "The Cornerstones of Competitive Advantage: A Resource-Based View." *Strategic Management Journal* 14: 179–191.

Poister, T. H. and Streib, G. 2005. "Elements of Strategic Planning and Management in Municipal Government: Status After Two Decades." *Public Administration Review* 65:1: January/February: 45–56.

Pynes, J. 2004. "The Implementation of Workforce and Succession Planning in the Public Sector." *Public Personnel Management* 33:4: Winter: 389–404.

Quinn, J. B., Anderson, P., and Finkelstein, S. 1996. "Leveraging Intellect." *Academy of Management Executive* 10:3: August: 7–27.

Riccucci, N. M. and Lurie, I. 2001. "Employee Performance Evaluation in Social Welfare Offices." *Review of Public Personnel Administration* 21:1: Spring: 27–37.

Risher, H. and Schay, B. W. 1994. "Grade Banding: The Model for Future Salary Programs?" *Public Personnel Management* 23:2: Summer: 187–199.

Risher, H. 1999. "Are Public Employees Ready for a 'New Pay' Program?" *Public Personnel Management* 28:3: Fall: 323–343.

Rothwell, W. and Poduch, S. 2004. "Introductory Technical Not Managerial. Succession Planning." *Public Personnel Management* 33:4: Winter: 405–419.

Rusbult, C. E. 1980. "Commitment and Satisfaction in Romantic Associations: A Test of the Investment Model." *Journal of Experimental Social Psychology* 16: 172–186.

Rusbult, C. E. 1983. "A Longitudinal Test of the Investment Model: The Development and Deterioration of Satisfaction and Commitment in Heterosexual Involvements." *Journal of Personality and Social Psychology* 45: 101–117

Rusbult, C. E. and Farrell, D. 1983. "A Longitudinal Test of the Investment Model: The Impact on Job Satisfaction, Job Commitment, and Turnover of Variations in Reward, Costs, Alternatives, and Investments." *Journal of Applied Psychology* 68: 429–438

Rusbult, C. E., Farrell, D., Rogers, G., and Mainous III, A. G. 1988. "Impact of Exchange Variables on Exit, Voice, Loyalty, and Neglect: An Integrative Model of Responses to Declining Job Satisfaction." *Academy of Management Journal* 31:3: September: 559–627.

Selden, S. C., Jacobson, W., Ammar, S. H., and Wright, R. 2000. "A New Approach to Assessing Performance of State Human Resource Management Systems: A Multi-Level Fuzzy Rule-Based System." *Review of Public Personnel Administration* 20:3: Summer: 58–74.

Senge, P. 1990. *The Fifth Discipline: Mastering the Five Practices of the Learning Organization.* New York, NY: Doubleday Currency.

Sims, H. P., Jr. and Lorenzi, P. 1992. *The New Leadership Paradigm: Social Learning and Cognition in Organizations.* Newbury Park, CA: Sage.

Snell, S. A., Youndt, M. A., and Wright, P. M. 1996. "Establishing a Framework for Research in Strategic Human Resource Management: Merging Resource Theory and Organizational Learning." In G. Ferris, ed., *Research in Personnel and Human Resources Management,* 14, pp. 61–90.

Terpstra, D. E. and Rozell, E. J. 1993. "The Relationship of Staffing Practices to Organizational Level Measures of Performance." *Personnel Psychology* 46: 27–48.

Tompkins, J. 2002 "Strategic Human Resources Management in Government: Unresolved Issues." *Public Personnel Management* 31:1: Spring: 95–110.

Ulrich, D. 1997. "Measuring Human Resources: An Overview of Practice and a Prescription for Results." *Human Resource Management* 36: 303–320.

Wagner, J. A. III and Gooding, R. Z. 1987a. "Effects of Societal Trends on Participation Research." *Administrative Sciences Quarterly* 32: 241–262.

Wagner, J. A. III and Gooding, R. Z. 1987b. "Shared Influence and Organizational Behavior: A Meta-Analysis of Situational Variables Expected to Moderate Participation-Outcome Relationships." *Academy of Management Journal* 30:3: 424–541.

Wernerfelt, B. 1984. "A Resource-Based View of the Firm." *Strategic Management Journal* 5: 171–180.

Chapter *12*

Employee Performance Appraisal in the Public Sector: Uses and Limitations

J. Edward Kellough

It is the task of management to help ensure that effective organizational performance is achieved. Toward that end, managers bring together material resources and personnel, coordinate and direct their utilization, and set policies and procedures to enhance productive activity. Of course, this focus on performance rests on the presumption that superior and inferior performance will be recognized when they occur. Management's ability to move an organization toward optimal productivity will certainly be obstructed if satisfactory and unsatisfactory levels of performance cannot be identified. But for that to take place, an adequate means of measuring performance is necessary. In some instances it may be possible to identify organizational goals and assess organizational productivity or performance comprehensively, or if that is not an option, the productivity of specific organizational sub-units might be scrutinized. More often, however, attention is focused on the productivity or performance of individual employees, and an assumption is made that greater individual productivity will lead to greater organizational performance. Obviously, there is no perfect relationship between the effectiveness of individual employees and organizational productivity. A host of factors, including changes in organizational environments and technology, may intervene to mediate that relationship. But employees can make a difference and it is true that one "key to improving productivity and quality services in the public sector is accurately measuring and controlling the performance of each worker" (Nigro and Nigro, 2000, p. 134). This chapter examines the concept of individual-level performance appraisal in the public sector. The central concern is on questions of (1) what precisely is appraised, (2) how should appraisals be conducted, and (3) how may the results of performance appraisals be utilized. Difficulties encountered in each of these areas of concern are addressed as the discussion proceeds.

IDENTIFYING PERFORMANCE CRITERIA AND STANDARDS

If we are interested in measuring the job performance of individual workers, our criteria for assessment should ideally be based on actual work outcomes or results. That is, we should focus on what it is that the workers produce and how well it is produced. An understanding or knowledge of job content, developed through systematic job analysis, is essential for identifying and specifying such criteria. Job analysis provides insight into the various tasks essential for the job, and work outcomes can be defined in terms of those tasks. Results-oriented measures could include such outcomes as the number of projects completed, number of forms processed, or the number of clients served. These types of measures by themselves, however, are obviously of limited utility. Allowance would have to be made for variation in the quality of the service or product delivered and differences in the level of difficulty of specific tasks. As a result, selection of criteria for performance evaluation is only half of the problem. The other half is determining appropriate standards of performance for each specified task. Such standards should reflect reasonable expectations of what is actually possible in terms of accomplishments. Those kinds of expectations come only from an understanding of the nature and context of the jobs under analysis and the documentation of previous levels of output or the utilization of time and motion studies (Carroll and Schneider 1982, pp. 131–134; Murphy and Cleveland, 1995, pp. 154–156).

Clearly, the development of performance appraisal systems based on results-oriented criteria and well-conceived performance standards may not be easily accomplished. In some instances, meaningful work outcomes at the level of individual employees are difficult to identify. What, for example, should be specified as measurable work outcomes for a county road maintenance crew worker whose specific tasks vary from day to day and are, at least in part, a function of weather and a variety of other factors that may not be easily predictable? Work products of numerous other types of employees in the public sector may also be difficult to ascertain. Consider, for example, a clerk in a local tax commissioner's office or a receptionist in a state agency whose specific duties will vary with fluctuations in public demand for the services of their respective units. Similarly, consider individuals who often work in teams such as a budget analyst or program auditor. What work outcomes are appropriately specified for their jobs when the fact is that much of what they do is dependent upon the work of others? Certain products or services may be identified for which the individual employee may be held accountable in each of these instances, but those outcomes may not capture the full extent of the responsibilities of the individual, and in addition, reasonable performance standards may prove to be illusive, especially when the nature of particular tasks vary in unpredictable ways. In such circumstances, appraisal may be skewed toward the assessment of work outcomes that are most easily measured even if they are not necessarily the most meaningful. Performance appraisal based on the quality and quantity of work outcomes produced by an individual are best developed when the individual's tasks are routine and focused almost exclusively on the production of tangible work products. Performance criteria and standards for individual employees whose tasks are diffuse, whose work depends on the actions of numerous other individuals, and whose effort is directed toward the production of less-than-tangible services or products may not always be readily identifiable.

For these reasons, performance appraisal is often based on other types of criteria that may not represent actual work product or outcomes but are nonetheless judged to be prerequisites for successful performance. Certain employee behaviors deemed to be essential for effective performance are used as such criteria. For example, the timely completion of required paper work or reports; efforts to assist co-workers; respectful, courteous, timely, and tactful interaction with agency clients; and the ready acceptance of direction and feedback from supervisors are all examples of behavioral criteria that could form the basis for the performance appraisal of individual workers. The advantage of behaviorally-based performance assessment systems is that for many jobs specific criteria—presumably effective job behaviors—are more easily identified than are work products or results for which the individual can be reasonably held accountable. It is also likely that similar behaviors may be relevant to a number of jobs so that separate criteria will not need to be developed for every distinct job, and employee behaviors should be relatively easy to observe and evaluate. A focus on behavior is not the same thing, however, as a focus on work product or actual employee accomplishments, and that is the major disadvantage of behavior-based criteria. An employee may complete a report on time, but that obviously is not a productive activity if the report contains errors or is otherwise of poor quality. In other words, the presence of desired behaviors by themselves may not be sufficient if the connection between those behaviors and organizational goals is tenuous (Riccucci and Lurie, 2001). Nevertheless, behavior-based approaches to performance appraisal are common. In the early 1990s, for example, the state of Georgia spent many months and an enormous amount of resources developing a new employee performance management system known as *GeorgiaGain* that rests largely (although not entirely) on behavioral criteria for individual performance (Kellough and Nigro, 2002).

Another approach to developing criteria for employee performance is to specify particular traits or personal characteristics presumed to be associated with effective performance. Employees may be evaluated in such systems on the basis of traits such as "dependability," "cooperativeness," "honesty," "diligence," or "initiative." Such evaluation systems are easily developed. It is not difficult to identify a set of presumably positive traits that are desirable as characteristics of employees. Trait-based approaches have been widely used in the past, and they can be used across a wide range of jobs, but their use is now typically discouraged because the linkage between apparent possession of particular traits and actual performance on the job may be quite weak, and the determination of the extent to which an individual employee exhibits an individual trait is highly subjective (Carroll and Schneider, 1982, p. 37; Tompkins, 1995, pp. 252–253). In addition, trait scales typically do not provide the kinds of specific information necessary to structure effective employee training and development efforts (Latham and Wexley, 1994, p. 38). Actual job behaviors and work outcomes (if they are specified) are typically much easier to observe, and will better identify training and developmental needs.

CONDUCTING THE APPRAISAL

While there are a variety of specific approaches including narrative essays written by supervisors and ranking or comparison methods (Cardy and Dobbins, 1994, pp. 64–67), performance appraisal is most often accomplished, regardless of whether the criteria are job outcomes, behaviors, or traits, through the use of a rating scale upon which the person conducting the evaluation indicates the observed level of performance, generally by simply placing a check mark in an appropriate box. For each performance criterion specified, for example, four or five performance levels may be identified. It is not uncommon to find performance levels defined as "unsatisfactory," "minimally satisfactory," "satisfactory," "highly satisfactory," "outstanding," or some variation of that scheme. The performance levels specified are assumed to reflect relevant standards for performance, but obviously, the actual definition or meaning of those standards will be determined by the judgment of the raters involved and that judgment may well vary from one person to another. In other words, "satisfactory" performance on a particular criterion or job dimension may rest in the eye of the beholder. To the degree that this is the case, an employee's appraisal can be as much a function of the rater's attitude and perception as it is actual performance.

To reduce this problem, it is necessary that performance levels be accompanied by at least brief narrative definitions. Trait- and behavior-based rating scales, for example, often utilize performance levels tied to behavioral anchors. Behaviorally-anchored rating scales (BARS) do not rely simply on ambiguous performance levels defined as "satisfactory" or "unsatisfactory" and various other gradients thereof. Instead, each level of performance is defined in terms of clearly articulated behaviors that are intended to be easily observable and are relevant to the particular job being performed. This procedure narrows somewhat the range of interpretative discretion exercised by the rater and thus helps to ensure consistency or uniformity in the application of the rating scale, although some discretion will necessarily remain in the hands of the evaluator. In instances where job outcomes or results are utilized as performance criteria, specific standards representing different levels of quality or quantity of work product should be specified. As noted earlier, these standards are unique to the tasks associated with each job and are developed through an analysis of the nature of the job and experience with the kinds of levels of productivity that are possible. But even in instances where meaningful individual-level work outcomes and performance standards tied to those outcomes can be defined, some judgment exercised by the rater will still be necessary.

In many, or perhaps most, organizations, individual performance ratings are conducted on an annual basis, although other schedules are certainly possible.

Regardless of the schedule, however, the results must be reported back to the employee. This communication can be accomplished simply by distribution of a copy of the rating sheet. It is far more desirable to take advantage of the opportunity that this stage of the process provides for counseling and direction from the employee's supervisor designed to provide the employee with information. Information not only about how well he or she performed, but also about what might be changed or altered so that performance can be improved (Carroll and Schneider, 1982, pp. 177–181; Daley, 1992, Klein and Snell, 1994). These appraisal interviews or briefing sessions may, in fact, be the most crucial aspect of the appraisal process. It is here that the supervisor may be able to explain the basis for judgments made in the evaluation and offer suggestions for employee improvement. In some systems, grounded on the concept of management by objectives (MBO) the supervisor and employee will set goals to be achieved during the upcoming performance cycle (Carroll and Schneider, 1982, p. 143). The individual goals are based on previously articulated organizational objectives, and it is assumed that directing employee efforts toward specific job-related goals tied to those objectives is one way of effectively promoting organizational productivity. Additionally, a substantial body of literature suggests that employee participation in the establishment of realistic yet challenging goals will enhance employee commitment to the organization and motivation to perform (Locke, 1983; Locke and Latham, 1984; Murphy and Cleveland, 1995, pp. 215–224; Roberts and Reed, 1996; Roberts, 2003; Reinke, 2003). Ultimately, however, the effectiveness of the goal-setting exercise and the appraisal interview itself will hinge on the skill, ability, and commitment of the supervisor involved.

It should be clear, then, that there may be a number of obstacles to effective performance appraisal. The process can never be entirely objective. Judgment must be exercised in the selection of criteria for appraisal, the definition of performance standards, and in the application of those standards to individual employees. A substantial commitment from the organization is necessary for performance criteria and standards to be adequately defined and for raters (usually supervisors) to be adequately trained in the proper application of the system. It is also important that sufficient time be allowed for effective counseling of employees during the performance briefing or interview, although that may be difficult to accomplish when supervisors are confronted with numerous other pressing demands on their time. In short, substantial organizational resources must be devoted to the performance appraisal process if it is to be made effective.

Because rater judgment is such a critical aspect of the appraisal process, some concern must be focused on the possibility of bias or error in the exercise of that judgment. Bias would occur, of course, when performance ratings are altered to conform to the rater's personal views of individual employees unrelated to work productivity. Bias can also obviously be the product of prejudice based on factors such as race, ethnicity, gender, age, or disability. Clearly, such considerations have no place in the appraisal process and evaluations made on such bases are legally proscribed. But in addition to bias, error can occur as a result of less invidious, but still unacceptable processes. A supervisor, for example, may have friends or "favorite" employees who are rated more generously than others. Several common errors are identified in the literature (e.g., see Cardy and Dobbins, 1994, pp. 27–33; Carroll and Schneider, 1982, pp. 39–41; Latham and Wexley, 1994, pp. 100–104). A discussion of some of the most important types of errors follows.

THE HALO EFFECT

Evaluators will often rate an employee, who performs well on one dimension of a job, high on all other aspects of the job. In this situation, it is as if the employee can do no wrong—hence the label "halo effect," but the process can also operate in the opposite direction. For example, poor performance in one area of work may lead the rater to judge the employee harshly in other areas. In general, the problem occurs whenever a rating in one dimension or aspect of a job (whether good or bad) is generalized to other dimensions.

THE FIRST-IMPRESSION ERROR

Raters, especially supervisors, may base subsequent performance appraisals on the impressions they formed of an individual employee when that person first came on the job. In other words, initial impressions, whether favorable or unfavorable, influence subsequent evaluations of performance. Information that is not consistent with the first impression formed is suppressed or discounted. For example, if during the first month on a job an employee had difficulty and performed poorly, the impression such behavior leaves with a manager may lead that manager to give the employee low performance ratings during later evaluations even though the employee's performance improved.

THE SIMILAR-TO-ME EFFECT

Performance evaluators may tend to judge employees more favorably whom they perceive as exhibiting behaviors or values similar to their own. In other words, "the more closely the employee resembles the rater in terms of attitudes or background, the stronger the tendency of the rater to judge that person favorably" (Latham and Wexley, 1994, p. 103).

COMPARISON OR CONTRAST EFFECTS

It may frequently be the case that employees are evaluated relative to each other rather than relative to actual job performance standards. An employee who is quite good, for example, may be rated as average simply because he or she is compared to others who are exceptional performers. Alternatively, an employee who is only average in performance, may be rated highly because by comparison, he or she looks good next to his or her mediocre colleagues. In either situation, an error occurs because performance is not judged relative to the actual requirements and standards set for the job but the reliance on employee contrasts or comparisons as a basis for performance appraisal is driven in part by the view of many managers that the appraisal process should produce a distribution of ratings that resemble a normal or bell-shaped curve (Latham and Wexley, 1994, p. 101; Lane, 1994).

The Central Tendency Error

This error is one of the most common in performance appraisal. It occurs when the rater judges all employees as "average" or "slightly above average." This problem may have the effect of limiting the usefulness of performance appraisal for some purposes, but the fact is the dynamics of the appraisal process often lead managers or supervisors into this difficulty. Typically there is no particular incentive in the process for a rater to judge a subordinate extraordinarily high. If such judgments are made in a few cases, the supervisor risks alienating the bulk of his employees who may feel resentment that some are favored at their expense. If higher ratings are given to numerous employees, upper management will undoubtedly question the rater's judgment and demand documentation to support that judgment. Alternatively, if employees are rated below satisfactory, the supervisor will risk the hostility of affected employees and will again need substantial documentation to support the judgment when it is challenged. In this situation, one can see readily that the path of least resistance for raters is to judge most employees as satisfactory or slightly above satisfactory unless truly extraordinary circumstances occur. As a result, there may be little variation in ratings among large numbers of employees, and actual scores will not reflect fine gradations in the quality of performance.

Reducing Bias and Error

While bias and error may never be completely eliminated from the appraisal process, it can be reduced if raters are adequately trained in the application of the appraisal system, are sensitized to the kinds of problems that can occur, and when clearly defined behavioral or results-oriented performance standards are established (Latham and Wexley, 1994, pp. 104–107). Additionally, error may be minimized when appraisal information is collected from a variety of sources. That is, supervisory appraisals may be supplemented with information from self-appraisals as well as with ratings by an employee's subordinates, peers, or customers (Campbell and Lee, 1988; deLeon and Ewen, 1997; Edwards and Ewen, 1996; Latham and Wexley, 1994, pp. 79–98; Murphy and Cleveland, 1995, pp. 133–142). Because these multi-rater approaches involve the collection of data from a number of points of view relative to the employee being evaluated, they are often referred to as *360-degree evaluations* (Bracken, et al., 1997; Tornow and London, 1998). Ratings by subordinates, peers, customers, and self-appraisals can provide useful supplements to the judgment of a supervisor who may not always be sufficiently familiar with an employee's work or who may not observe an employee often enough to render an informed judgment (Murphy and Cleveland, 1995, pp. 123–124). Of course, the expansion of the appraisal process to include other evaluators in addition to a supervisor can make the process more cumbersome, time consuming, and expensive.

LINKING PAY TO PERFORMANCE APPRAISAL RESULTS: A CRITICAL ASSESSMENT

Performance appraisals are conducted because it is believed that their results will be helpful in the process of improving individual employee performance and, ultimately, organizational performance. As noted earlier, the appraisal interview, if conducted effectively, provides an opportunity for the supervisor to guide employee behavior in productive ways. When an appraisal uncovers areas of performance that need improvement, that can be pointed out to employees and instructions as to how to improve can be provided (Roberts and Reed, 1996). In addition, in every organization some employees will be promoted while others will not, some will face adverse actions, some will be provided training opportunities that others will be denied, and some will receive larger pay increases than others. Ideally, we would have some rational basis to guide these decisions so that the process of distributing organizational rewards and sanctions actually promotes productive activity. Individual-based performance appraisal is the tool we rely upon to provide that foundation (Murphy and Cleveland, 1995, pp. 88–95). Obviously, however, the decisions made on that basis are only as good as the appraisal process itself.

The use of performance-appraisal ratings to determine annual employee pay increases is an interesting and important case in point. During the 1980s and 1990s, pay-for-performance systems enjoyed an enormous popularity in the public sector (Ingraham, 1993; Kellough and Lu, 1993; Kellough and Selden, 1997; Kellough and Nigro, 2002). In one approach, often known as *merit pay*, annual pay increases are tied to the outcomes of individual-level performance appraisals. An alternative approach is to use the outcomes of the individual-level appraisal process to award financial bonuses rather than increases in base pay. Merit pay systems are by far the most common pay-for-performance schemes. The federal government experimented with merit pay from 1981 to 1993, and numerous state and local government jurisdictions continue to rely on such systems. At a basic level, the concept of pay for performance has an appealing logic: one must simply determine which employees are superior performers and reward them with increased pay. Presumably, such a policy would prevent resentment or alienation of the best employees that could result when their superior contributions are not recognized, and they receive the same pay as their less-productive colleagues. At the same time, poorer performers are offered an incentive to improve their levels of productivity. Because of their apparent logic, pay-for-performance systems have a number of proponents including management consultants who sell the concept as a way of dealing with problems of organizational productivity (e.g., Risher, 2004).

The argument for merit pay rests closely on the principles associated with a set of ideas about worker motivation, known as *equity theory* (Adams, 1965; Mowday, 1983; Rainey, 1997). According to that perspective, individual employees will adjust their behaviors at work depending on their perception of how equitably they are being treated. In other words, employees' perceptions of equity at work will affect their levels of motivation. A superior performer who receives the same compensation as a much less-productive co-worker would perceive inequity, for example, and would over time adjust his/her output downward until the perceived inequity is no longer present. Such an employee could easily question why the extra effort necessary to achieve higher levels of productivity should be sustained if it is not recognized and rewarded (Schay, 1988). In fact, equity theory would suggest that the best way to ensure that top performers will continue to be productive is to find ways to acknowledge their higher levels of productivity— such as with pay differentials.

Additional theoretical support for pay-for-performance systems may be found in *expectancy theory* (Vroom, 1964; Porter and Lawler, 1968). This theory specifically addresses the psychological or cognitive processes associated with the development of motivation rather than questions of what incentives or motives are most effective. According to this view, individuals will be motivated to behave in productive ways depending upon their perceptions of the extent to which such behavior is possible, and if it is accomplished, will lead to valued rewards. More specifically, expectancy theory suggests that an individual will be most highly motivated to perform when he or she expects that (1) their effort will lead to higher levels of performance (the effort-performance expectation), (2) higher performance will lead to specified outcomes (the performance-outcome expectancy), and (3) the outcomes are desirable or valuable. Since higher pay would appear to be valuable to most, if not all, employees, proponents of pay for performance suggest that all that management must do to enhance employee motivation to perform is to offer financial incentives (either as bonuses or increases to base pay), encourage employees to believe that they can perform, and demonstrate that performance will be recognized and rewarded. It sounds like a simple idea, but in practice it does not appear to work as advertised.

In the early 1990s, after more than a decade of experimentation with pay for performance in government, examinations of the empirical literature could find little evidence that employee motivation or productivity was actually enhanced by such systems (Kellough and Lu, 1993; Milkovich and Wigdor, 1991). Difficulties with the concept of pay for performance arise in a number of ways. Consider, for example, the notion from expectancy theory that employees must believe that their levels of effort will lead to effective performance if they are motivated to perform. In many circumstances it will be difficult for management to promote that view among workers. Employees typically do not labor in isolation. Organizations are systems in which workers' efforts must be coordinated, and it is often the case that there are interdependencies among employees. A given individual's level of performance will, therefore, frequently depend upon the productivity of others in the organization. Other employees may make decisions or perform a variety of operations that will influence a specified individual's task difficulty and probability of success. Individuals in such situations will recognize this dilemma and will perceive that when this occurs, their own level of effort may make little difference in their ability to perform.

It is also essential, again from the view of expectancy theory, that employees perceive that performance is explicitly linked to pay, if pay-for-performance systems are to motivate workers. The issue referred to here is the performance-outcome expectancy. The difficulty at this point obviously lies largely in the performance appraisal process. As demonstrated earlier, individual-based performance appraisal is never entirely objective. Ultimately, the appraisal process rests on rater judgment. Employees recognize this characteristic of the process, and as a result, there is a tendency for employees to often question the accuracy of appraisal outcomes, especially when their performance is not rated as highly as they think it should be rated (Hamner, 1983). Efforts to base pay on the outcomes of performance appraisal have the effect of raising the stakes and increasing employee sensitivity to appraisal outcomes, and it should be stressed that employee perceptions of accuracy can have little to do with whether the appraisal outcome is in fact accurate. Ego involvement and a desire to rationalize unfavorable ratings may be more than sufficient to lead employees to question rater judgment, especially when pay is affected. Because employee perceptions are important determinants of employee motivation, i.e., expectancy theory requires that employees perceive that good performance is recognized in order for the performance-outcome expectancy and subsequent motivation to be high, perceptions that the appraisal process is less than fair will undermine the motivational potential of pay for performance.

Clearly, the dynamics of performance appraisal can exacerbate this difficulty. It should be recalled that it is often the case that raters, especially supervisors, are reluctant to draw sharp distinctions between employees. Low ratings and high ratings each require justification. The rater must be prepared to defend the judgments rendered, and such effort will divert time and energy away form what may be seen as tasks more instrumentally associated with the organization's mission. As a result, variation in appraisal outcomes is constrained and the perceived legitimacy of the process can be further undermined. Efforts to link pay to the outcomes of such a process would appear to invite employee alienation.

An additional difficulty is associated with the levels of pay increases or bonuses offered under pay-for-performance systems. The assumption that higher pay (as opposed to lower pay) is valued by public employees, which is also a necessary part of the foundation of pay for performance, seems reasonable on its face, but the motivational potential of pay increases or bonuses is surely linked to the size of those increases or bonuses, and for two reasons, this points to an additional difficulty, especially in the public sector. The first point is that there is a tendency, noted earlier, for there to be relatively little variation in the outcomes of performance appraisal processes. In addition, research has shown that when performance ratings are intended for use in making administrative decisions, including pay decisions, raters tend to be even more lenient than usual (Murphy and Cleveland, 1995, p. 96). As a result, the money available for distribution to employees under a pay-for-performance system is typically spread among a wide group so that, especially in the case of increases to base pay, most employees usually receive awards that are not much different than they would have received under an across-the-board distribution. Very few are denied increases and few receive substantial increases. In some organizations, outstanding ratings are actually rotated among employees in order to counter this problem, but, of course, that further undermines the perceived legitimacy of the system. The second point is that the difficulties caused by the frequently small, average pay increases under pay-for-performance systems in the public sector are often made worse because of an unwillingness on the part of many jurisdictions to adequately fund such systems. As a result, the amount of money available to reward performance may be relatively small. Typically, it is the case that payroll totals under pay for performance are not allowed to exceed what would have been available under a traditional pay system. While that approach may be understandable from a budgetary perspective, the effect is that larger pay increases for some employees must be offset by smaller pay increases for other workers—a fact that operates to further constrain variation in pay outcomes and limit the motivational potential of the system.

It should be acknowledged also, that even if pay-for performance mechanisms could succeed in increasing employee motivation, improvements in employee and organizational productivity may not follow. In other words, there are additional considerations beyond a failure to boost motivation that may lead to little observed impact of pay for performance on individual productivity. One factor, of course, is that such approaches to pay administration can lead to dysfunctional activities among employees. Effort might be directed toward tasks that are most easily measured, regardless of their relevance to organizational outcomes, and competition among employees for performance-based incentives can undermine teamwork and cooperation often necessary for organizational success. It is also the case, however, that even if motivation is increased as a result of pay for performance, motivation alone may not be sufficient to boost productivity. Employees must also have an understanding of what is expected, the opportunity to perform, and the ability to perform. Shortcomings in any of these areas can undermine individual productivity regardless of the level of employee motivation.

CONCLUSION

Performance appraisal is intended to be a tool through which management may direct individual behavior within organizations into productive channels. Appraisal outcomes are used also as the basis for a number of administrative decisions regarding training, promotions, adverse actions, and even pay. While the appeal of individual-based performance appraisal may be great from a managerial perspective, we have seen that there are a number of difficulties with the concept. The use of performance appraisal as a basis for allocating pay incentives is particularly troubling, and given the record in that area of activity, such action should be approached with caution. With respect to the appraisal process itself, at a minimum, an organization must be willing to commit substantial managerial time and other resources to the activity if there is to be any hope of its effective implementation. In fact, some observers, especially proponents of Total Quality Management, have argued that the problems with individual-based performance appraisal are so great that we would be better off to abandon the idea and focus on measuring the productivity of meaningful work units or larger organizational subdivisions or systems (Bowman, 1994; Deming, 1986; Juran, 1964). Such an approach may have the effect of allowing us to avoid the problem that individual performance is often a function, at least in part, of factors beyond the individual's control (Fox and Shirkey, 1997), but other performance-measurement problems associated with identifying appropriate performance criteria and standards will remain at such levels. In the end, we should approach individual-based performance appraisal guardedly. It may at times be a useful managerial tool, but our view must be tempered by a knowledge of the limitations inherent in the process.

REFERENCES

Adams, J. S. 1965. "Inequity in Social Exchange." In L. Berkowitz, ed., *Advances in Experimental and Social Psychology*. Orlando, FL: Academic Press.

Bowman, J. S. 1994. "At Last, An Alternative to Performance Appraisal: Total Quality Management." *Public Administration Review* 54:2: March/April: 129–136.

Bracken, D. W. et al. 1997. *Should 360-Degree Feedback Be Used Only for Developmental Purposes?* Greensboro, NC: Center for Creative Leadership.

Campbell, D. J. and Lee, C. 1988. "Self Appraisal in Performance Evaluation." *Academy of Management Review* 13: 187–196.

Cardy, R. L. and Dobbins, G. H. 1994. *Performance Appraisal: Alternative Perspectives*. Cincinnati, OH: South-Western Publishing Company.

Carroll, S. J. and Schneider, C. E. 1982. *Performance and Review Systems: The Identification, Measurement, and Development of Performance in Organizations*. Dallas, TX: Scott, Foresman, and Company.

Daley, D. M. 1992. *Performance Appraisal in the Public Sector*. Westport, CT: Quorum Books.

deLeon, L. and Ewen, A. J. 1997. "Multi-Source Performance Appraisals." *Review of Public Personnel Administration* 17:1: Winter: 22–36.

Deming, W. E. 1986. *Out of the Crisis*. Cambridge, MA: MIT Press.

Edwards, M. R. and Ewen, A. J. 1996. *360° Feedback: The Powerful New Model for Employee Assessment & Performance Improvement*. New York, NY: American Management Association.

Fox, C. J. and Shirkey, K. A. 1997. "Employee Performance Appraisal: The Keystone Made of Clay." In Carolyn Ban and Norma M. Riccucci, eds., *Public Personnel Management: Current Concerns, Future Challenges*, 2nd ed. New York, NY: Longman, pp. 205–220.

Hamner, W. C. 1983. "How to Ruin Motivation with Pay." In Richard M. Steers and Lyman W. Porter, eds., *Motivation and Work Behavior*. New York, NY: McGraw-Hill, pp. 264–275.

Ingraham, P. W. 1993. "Of Pigs in Pokes and Policy Diffusion: Another Look at Pay for Performance." *Public Administration Review* 23:3: July/August: 348–356.

Juran, J. M. 1964. *Managerial Breakthrough*. New York, NY: McGraw Hill.

Kellough, J. E. and Lu, H. 1993. "The Paradox of Merit Pay in the Public Sector." *Review of Public Personnel Administration* 13:2: Spring: 45–64.

Kellough, J. E. and Nigro, L. G. 2002. "Pay for Performance in Georgia: Employee Perspectives on *GeorgiaGain* After Five Years." *Review of Public Personnel Administration* 22:2: Summer: 59–61.

Kellough, J. E. and Selden, S. C. 1997. "Pay for Performance in State Government: Perceptions of State Agency Personnel Managers." *Review of Public Personnel Administration* 17:1: Winter: 5–21.

Klein, H. J. and Snell, S. A. 1994. "The Impact of Interview Process and Context on Performance Appraisal Interview Effectiveness." *Journal of Management Issues* 6: 160–175.

Lane, L. M. 1994. "Public Sector Performance Management: Old Failures and New Opportunities." *Review of Public Personnel Administration* 14:3: Summer: 26–44.

Latham, G. P. and Wexley, K. N. 1994. *Increasing Productivity Through Performance Appraisal*, 2nd ed. Reading, MA: Addison-Wesley Publishing Company.

Locke, E. A. 1983. "The Ubiquity of the Technique of Goal Setting in Theories of and Approaches to Employee Motivation." In Richard M. Steers and Lyman W. Porter, eds., *Motivation and Work Behavior*. New York, NY: McGraw-Hill, pp. 81–90.

Locke, E. A. and Latham, G. P. 1984. *Goal Setting: A Motivational Technique that Works*. Englewood Cliffs, NJ: Prentice-Hall.

Milkovich, G. T. and Wigdor, A. K., eds. 1991. *Pay for Performance: Evaluating Performance Appraisal and Merit Pay*. Washington DC: National Academy Press.

Mowday, R. T. 1983. "Equity Theory Predictions of Behavior in Organizations." In Richard M. Steers and Lyman W. porter, eds., *Motivation and Work Behavior*. New York: McGraw-Hill, pp. 91–113.

Murphy, K. R. and Cleveland, J. 1995. *Understanding Performance Appraisal: Social, Organizational, and Goal-Based Perspectives*. Thousand Oaks, CA: Sage Publications.

Nigro, L. G. and Nigro, F. A. 2000. *The New Public Personnel Administration*, 5th ed. Itasca, IL: F. E. Peacock Publishers.

Porter, L. W. and Lawler III, E. E. 1968. *Managerial Attitudes and Performance*. Homwood, IL: Dorsey Press.

Rainey, H. G. 1997. *Understanding and Managing Public Organizations*, 2nd ed. San Francisco, CA: Jossey-Bass.

Reinke, S. J. 2003. "Does the Form Really Matter?: Leadership, Trust, and Acceptance of the Performance Appraisal Process." *Review of Public Personnel Administration*. 23:1: Spring: 23–37.

Riccucci, N. M. and Lurie, I. 2001. "Employee Performance Evaluation in Social Welfare Offices." *Review of Public Personnel Administration* 21:1: Spring: 27–37.

Risher, H. 2004. *Pay for Performance: A Guide for Federal Managers*. Washington DC: IBM Center for the Business of Government.

Roberts, G. E. 2003. "Employee Performance Appraisal System Participation: A Technique that Works." *Public Personnel Management* 32:1: Spring: 89–99.

Roberts, G. E. and Reed, T. 1996. "Performance Appraisal Participation, Goal Setting, and Feedback." *Review of Public Personnel Administration*. 16:4: Fall: 29–60.

Schay, B. W. 1988. "Effects of Performance-Contingent Pay on Employee Attitudes." *Public Personnel Management* 17: 237–250.

Tompkins, J. 1995. *Human Resource Management in Government: Hitting the Ground Running*. New York, NY: HarperCollins.

Tornow, W. W. and London, M. 1998. *Maximizing the Value of 360-Degree Feedback: A Process for Successful Individual and Organizational Development*. San Francisco, CA: Jossey-Bass Publishers.

Vroom, V. 1964. *Work and Motivation*. New York, NY: Wiley.

Chapter *13*

Ethics Management and Training

Evan M. Berman and Jonathan P. West

*E*thics is defined as the standards by which actions are determined to be right or wrong (Kazman and Bonczek, 1998). Interest in ethics has grown in recent decades, fueled by political corruption cases in cities like Miami and Providence, and debacles at Enron, WorldCom, and elsewhere (Menzel with Carson, 1999; Petrick and Quinn, 1997; Weaver, Trevino, and Cochran, 1999a, 1999b). As these examples suggest, the challenge is to get individuals in organizations to adopt a common, shared set of standards that is consistent with organizations doing the "right" thing and avoiding wrong actions that cause harm to them and others.

Institutionalizing ethics in public organizations requires collaborative leadership. Human resource managers are in a strategically advantageous position to work with others in creating and maintaining an ethical organization. These individuals can help increase ethical awareness, cultivate ethical reasoning, encourage ethical action, and exercise ethical leadership. Human resource managers' responsibilities in the areas of hiring, orientation, compensation, training, performance appraisal, and adverse actions provide leverage points for introducing the ethics factor into decisions. Ethical implications for HRM are also evident in diversity initiatives; union-management relations; human resource information systems; health, safety, and accessibility issues; and privatization (West, 2003). Together with others on the management team, human resource managers can assist in shaping and implementing HR systems and processes that reinforce an ethical workplace.

There are many different sources of ethical behavior in organizations. One source is *professional conduct*, from which norms develop regarding standards for professional knowledge and skills, having a constructive, professional attitude about working with others, and promoting excellence. A second source is *serving the public interest*, from which norms are derived about respecting democratic processes and the roles of citizens and elected officials in those processes, making

190

decisions that best promote the public interest, and promoting fairness and justice, including due process. A third source is *personal honesty and integrity*, from which norms arise about telling the truth, following through on what has been promised, taking responsibility for one's mistakes, and serving as a model of ethical leadership. A fourth source stems from *knowing and respecting the law*, such as avoiding discrimination, conflicts of interest, taking bribes, and other prohibited activities. Each of these examples is a widely recognized source of ethics.

It is often noted that ethical behavior and legal behavior are not necessarily equivalent. Generally, ethical norms concern a broader class of conduct. What is illegal is usually unethical, though the converse is not always true. For example, leaving work a few minutes early each day is not illegal but it is unethical because it violates norms of personal integrity and fails to serve the public interest. Also, while there is an ethical obligation to avoid the appearance of conflict of interest or discrimination, the legal standard often is narrower; namely, to avoid committing specific acts, that often are carefully circumscribed and defined by law. Because ethics concerns a broader class of actions than just legal ones, legal woes often can be avoided by attention and commitment to ethics. Attention to ethics often gives a margin of error, of safety, in avoiding unintentional legal missteps.

But two of the greatest challenges today are getting organizations to (a) articulate and (b) manage a set of common, specific values and standards. It is not so much that organizational leaders are unaware of the importance of ethics in organizations. They hear and read the news, just like everyone else. Indeed, often their organizations have identified many of the broad values stated here. But leaders, especially those in HR, need to inform members of their organizations about the specific forms of conduct that are either prohibited or especially welcomed. For example, what exactly does promoting the public interest mean in the context of doing a background check on a prospective employee? Specifically, how much time and money should the organization spend? Or, in the interest of promoting professionalism and excellence, exactly how much training should be given to employees and in which areas? These are very important practical questions that require specific, detailed answers; broad values alone do not provide operational clarity and, as such, they do not suffice.

Another problem is consistency and follow-through. Organizations and their leaders cannot realistically expect good results if they do not devise and manage those activities through which standards of specific conduct are set. Managers and employees need to be informed of these expectations and also to be expected to put them into practice. Performance in these areas needs to be monitored and measured, and individuals should receive feedback and experience consequences of their behaviors in a systematic way. That is, there needs to be management of these expectations. Some time ago, we called this *ethics management*, and this term is now frequently used (Berman, et al., 1994). While most organizations could do a better job of managing ethics, many institutions are laying the groundwork, and quite a few have even made substantial gains in this area.

This chapter begins, first, by identifying and briefly discussing six principal elements of a systematic strategy of ethics management. Second, the current state of the art of ethics training in U.S. cities, an important human resource management activity, is reported in greater detail. Third, the purpose of ethics training, the breadth and depth of topics covered, pedagogical approaches to instruction, and the correlates of training are considered. Finally, we show a statistical model that depicts the impact of ethics training and the factors affecting its use.

ETHICS MANAGEMENT

The need to manage an organization's values is no different from that of other resources, such as technology or money, but it does take on its own form. The main ingredients are leadership, assessment, articulation, training, feedback, and consequences.

Leadership is the cornerstone of the moral foundation of organizations. This is a historic truth. Leaders set the tone, and through their actions and conduct they model this behavior for everyone else. As noted by an interviewee in one of our studies: "There is truth to the old saying 'a fish stinks from the head down.' If there is mediocrity at the top, it permeates the organization" (Berman and West, 2003). The same holds true for moral corruption. It is certainly no coincidence that leaders of morally corrupt organizations often are prosecuted for specific, illegal acts that they committed. Conversely, when we asked several years ago about sources of ethical leadership in organizations, the most frequent response by senior managers was "exemplary moral leadership" (West et al., 1993). There is no doubt that leaders set the tone of the organization. If ethics is to be taken seriously, it must start at the top. This is reflected in their specific actions ("don't do as I say, do as I do"), as well as in their commitment to ensuring ethical standards throughout the organization, by their own commitment to the activities discussed later.

Of course, no amount of ethics management can avoid any and all forms of ethical wrongdoing. To expect this is to be truly naïve. Additionally, personnel selection processes in HRM are uncertain at best. When it comes to ethics, we know very little about the ethical philosophies and practices of those whom we hire. However, undertaking ethics management reduces the risk and amount of ethical wrongdoing. This system will sometimes catch unethical action at an early stage before even more damage is done while in other instances the system will entirely preempt it. Ethics management also provides a shield for organizations, enabling them to better distance themselves from the unethical acts of individuals. It is better to have to acknowledge having had one or two bad apples in the barrel, than to appear as though the barrel is half full of them.

If the purpose of ethics management is to increase ethical conduct, then managers need to know the current state of ethics in their organizations (Berman, 2003; Bonczek, 1998). They need to know what is working well, and what is not. They need to know what is important, but not yet on the radar screen of employees and managers. This proactive approach is called *assessment*, and there are several ways in which this is done. Leaders can rely on their own sense of what is lacking, informed by broader discussions in society and reinforced through conversations with others in the organization. This allows them to gauge the sense of ethics in both general and specific terms. For example, leaders may find that matters of personal integrity and professionalism receive little emphasis in personnel appraisals, or that ethics is a minor factor in promotion decisions—both crucial HR functions. They may also discover a surprising lapse in knowledge concerning major provisions of law, or a rash of ethics violations. Some organizations also conduct employee surveys that may include such items as: "My department has a defined standard of integrity, and I know what it is" or "My supervisor encourages me to act in an ethical manner." Responses to such statements can be quite illuminating.

After assessing the ethical climate and conduct, the next step is to clearly *articulate* what is expected. This is often contained in codes of ethics or standards of conduct that are found in many jurisdictions and offices (ICMA, 1998). These documents usually contain general statements, such as "we are committed to honesty and integrity in all of our actions" or "we are committed to providing the highest level of customer service." Numerous examples of these standards and codes can be readily found on the Internet. However, as stated earlier, managers will need to operationalize these generalities in order to provide guidance for specific situations that their employees encounter. Employees are rightly skeptical of ethics plaques that are not buttressed with specifics. As Payne (1996, p. 313) notes, "Ethical knowledge is not only 'knowing that' a particular conduct is wrong but also 'knowing how' to cope with one's responsibility in regard to such conduct."

For example, in an HR department, specific ethics standards would relate to procedures for protecting the confidentiality of employee information, proactively assisting employees to ensure that their benefits selection is in their best interest, ensuring that recruitment and selection are done in ways that promote organizational interests, informing managers of sources of possible litigation and procedures to avoid, and requiring that managers instruct their employees about provisions in the code of ethics and standards of conduct. Such specific measures go beyond generalizations such as "serving as role models for maintaining the highest standards of ethical conduct" or "being ethically responsible for promoting and fostering fairness and justice for all employees and their organizations," which are found in the Society for Human Resource Management's "Code of Ethical and Professional Standards in Human Resource Management." In order to be effective, the principles actually must be applied.

Ethics management can never entirely foresee the myriad ways in which ethics principles need to be applied. People are challenged on a daily basis to make ethical decisions. Some of these are new and lack precedents. For example, what about the manager who wants to go to a conference in Las Vegas but stays an extra day at public expense to enjoy the sights? What about the employee who spends half an hour every day surfing the Internet pursuing his or her own personal interests? While job applications should identify the most important candidate qualifications, *ethics training* helps to both ensure a broad sensitivity to matters of ethics and provide employees with a process for identifying and dealing with thorny ethical dilemmas. Most ethics training includes processes of identifying warning signs and cultivating moral reasoning skills. When in doubt about ethical matters, it is often helpful to raise the issue and discuss it with others.

Organizations vary greatly in the extent and depth of their ethics training. There is substantial room for improvement. Beyond training, another aspect of ethics management is the monitoring of performance and provision of feedback. Today, monitoring is seldom a systematic activity, and often episodic, based on whether lapses in ethics judgment have become apparent. However, one systematic approach involves the use of an ethics "scorecard" with various measures for assessing ethical conduct in different areas. This is clearly a cutting edge concept that is yet to be mainstreamed. Rather, supervisors are more likely to "monitor" by becoming informed when something has gone wrong, such as when a client, employee, or staff person in another department brings to their attention some questionable behavior or conduct.

This, then, affords the opportunity for supervisors to provide feedback and consequences. *Feedback* is important because it is the starting point of human learning and change. People need to know that what has been done is wrong. While some unethical acts are intentionally committed, it is usually more common that unethical behavior is either conducted unknowingly or by people who simply make bad judgments in difficult situations. Perhaps these individuals were unaware of standards or of the options available to them in dealing with a particular situation and feedback can provide a genuine learning opportunity for avoiding such problems in the future. Feedback can be provided in meetings between employees and their supervisors. Such sessions can provide a summary of the facts of what has occurred, the nature of the unethical conduct, the standards that apply, and a statement of more desirable actions and decisions. For example, one of our managers shared this experience:

> We had an incident whereby a manager hung some of her colleagues out to dry by blaming them for a problem and thereby deflecting her responsibility for a mistake. In counseling with her, I used the GFOA Code of Ethics to explain why her conduct violated a provision of the professional code. She recognized the problem, and there has been no recurrence of unethical behavior (Berman & West, 2003, p. 36).

Consequences are the next step of ethics management. Reinforcement matters. All organizations send strong signals about ethics, and consequences are a powerful message. For example, when unethical conduct is known to constitute a disqualification for salary raises and promotion, a signal is sent that ethics matter. When individuals are punished (negative consequences) for unethical acts, a similarly strong signal is communicated. When leaders praise individual and organizational acts of ethical leadership and exemplary conduct, the importance of ethics is reinforced. Consistency of consequences, whether positive or negative, shapes both managers' and employees' perceptions about what is expected, what they need to do, and what to avoid. By contrast, when organizations are inconsistent or unclear regarding consequences employees may conclude that ethical conduct is not very important, especially compared to other things that receive greater emphasis.

Ethics management, then, is a systematic approach to managing the values and actions of the organization's members. It consists of leadership, assessment, articulation, training, feedback, and consequences. Beyond consequences, the cycle is closed through a renewed leadership assessment of the current situation regarding ethics, and so on. Ethics management can shape conduct and thereby reduce the amount of failure, in the process helping organizations to deal with unethical situations that may develop. Yet, while the desirability and vision for it is clear, the practice of ethics management is still variable and underdeveloped. This is because the notion of ethics management is new and because many leaders fail to make ethics an important priority. Others may agree that ethics management is important, but view it as a matter of personal responsibility and therefore not an appropriate organizational concern. Ironically, failing to make ethics management a priority increases the risk of a serious ethics failure, thereby making it an urgent priority when failure does occur. Ethics management initiatives are likely to increase in the future as ethical conduct continues to be a salient societal issue. The remainder of this chapter focuses on a crucial component of ethics management: ethics training.

ETHICS TRAINING

Ethics training has become a centerpiece of corporate and government compliance and values-oriented initiatives (Berman, West, and Cava, 1994; Bruce, 1996; Wells and Schminke, 2001; West et al., 1998). It sharpens participants' awareness and competence in dealing with a myriad of issues that often arise in the work life of employees and managers. Ethics training is part of an integrated view of ethics management. Of course, it can also be viewed and studied as a form of workforce training; focusing on skills and abilities in matters of ethics and ethical decision-making. The following is adapted from our article "Ethics Training in U.S. Cities" (West and Berman, 2004), which explores the nature of this relatively new form of training and its use in local governments.[1] It should be noted that our survey focused on the use of ethics training in cities generally, and was not limited to human resource managers or their departments.

Managers who decide to undertake ethics training have various tools at their disposal. For example, in 1998, ICMA published "Ethics in Action" which provides a participant's and leader's handbook. This publication contains situational exercises, ice breakers, presentation slides, ethics definitions, and applications. Topics include corruption, conflict of interest, disclosure, and fairness of treatment, for example, as well as strategies for decision-making. There is also an additional collection of professional articles on ethics, and a CD-ROM with interviews and further exercises. Many other professional organizations have also developed materials for their members that deal with situations they are likely to face. Generally, it would appear that a broad range of training materials are available. It should also be noted that there are a vast number of organizations and consultants that offer to provide ethics training.[2]

We find that 64.1 percent of jurisdictions offer training that meet our definition of "activities that increase participants' knowledge of the standards of conduct within an organization (and) deals with what is right and wrong, giving both guidelines and specific examples for identifying and addressing issues of ethical concern." Only about 36.8 percent of respondents call this training "ethics training." Use does not vary significantly by region or form of government; however, large cities are more likely to offer ethics training. Among those that offer training, about one-third (37.3 percent) provide it as mandatory training for all employees, and 43.5 percent offer it as voluntary. Most of the remainder includes that which is offered only to managers, to new staff, or to violators. Thus, there exists considerable variation in the use of ethics training.

The purposes of ethics training are now widely accepted to include a "high" road and a "low" road (Paine, 1994). The low road (which is also sometimes referred to as "defensive") focuses on legal compliance and helps organizations avoid the embarrassment associated with allegations of legal wrongdoing. The high road (which is sometimes called "aspirational") includes efforts to develop employees' capacity to identify, articulate, and resolve ethics issues. Such training often includes additional efforts to increase openness, communication, and accountability. Many authors view this as a desired state to promote ethical conduct, and others additionally view this as a way to increase organizational productivity.

Our findings support the view that ethics training supports both purposes. Regarding the "low road," reducing the frequency of unethical conduct is widely mentioned by 82.5 percent of respondents, as is heightening familiarity with key legal requirements (77.3 percent), avoiding litigation (75.2 percent), and reducing the legal liability of the jurisdiction (74.6 percent). Among cities that use training, 84.8 percent mention at least one of these defensive purposes. But ethics training also serves aspirational purposes, or at least has aims beyond narrow, legal concerns. Two-thirds of respondents' state that a purpose of ethics training is to encourage critical thinking about ethics and three-fourths mention that a purpose is to offer practical guidance. Also, 43.3 percent use ethics training as a means of transforming the organizational culture, and 82.5 percent view it as a means of reinforcing the organizational culture. Eight in ten respondents mention at least one of these purposes. Also, 77.0 percent use training to communicate and discuss ethical standards and expectations, which can be used for either reinforcing or transforming organizational culture.

The topics of ethics training reflect these purposes. Some topics emphasize general awareness of ethical principles and decision-making, whereas other topics provide specific applications of ethics in specific areas of administration or ethical situation. By and large, respondents state that many topics are covered "in-depth" or "adequately," such as being a good role model (82.1 percent), making decisions that are fair and just (84.8 percent), due process (80.7 percent), respect for individual rights (80.4 percent), and how to decide whether something is unethical (73.2 percent). Additionally, 82.7 percent also state that they deal with ethics issues in specific areas, such as law enforcement, in adequate or in-depth ways, as do 79.1 percent of respondents with regard to explaining what "conflict of interest" is in operational terms, and "personal honesty" (65.1 percent). Somewhat less frequently addressed are potentially perplexing problems for busy public managers, such as: detecting warning signs of unethical behavior (63.4 percent), dealing with inadvertent mistakes (53.2 percent), and balancing legal and ethical considerations (67.9 percent). Ethics audits, however, are only rarely covered in ways that are in-depth or adequate (11.7 percent). Many authors find this a significant omission (Van Wart, 1998; White and Lam, 2000).

However, the median duration of voluntary ethics training for employees is only about four hours per year, and about three hours for training that is mandatory. Although this is a very modest amount of training (about two half-mornings a year), it frequently occurs in conjunction with other forms of ethics management activities, which also help clarify what is expected of employees. For example, among those that provide ethics training, 58.3 percent state that they also monitor adherence to a Code of Ethics, 51.3 percent also use ethics as a criterion in hiring and promotion, 52.5 percent regularly communicate with employees on matters of ethics, and 57.5 percent require financial disclosure. Also, among those that require training, 82.8 percent also state that "exemplary moral leadership" by senior managers is used as a strategy for ensuring an ethical climate. Further analysis suggests that ethics training often is one of several activities in an overall ethics strategy.

With so little time devoted to ethics training, a reasonable question would be: What is the depth of coverage? Jurisdictions that offer two or more hours of mandatory training agree more frequently that these topics are covered thoroughly, than jurisdictions that provide less than two hours. For example, whereas 44.8 percent of respondents with two or more hours of mandatory training agree that "warning signs of unethical behavior are covered thoroughly or in-depth," only 15.0 percent of those who offer less than two hours of mandatory training agree. Likewise, the percentages regarding "dealing with inadvertent ethical missteps" are 25.0 percent and 5.0 percent; explaining what "conflict of interest" means in operational terms, 41.4 percent versus 17.9 percent; and examples of professional conduct, 42.9 percent versus 22.5 percent. In short, respondents report that more training allows for a more thorough (deeper) coverage of the topics. It is important to note that training is not the only source of information on these topics in organizations (inter-departmental memos, presentations by senior managers, on-the-job discussion, and hiring/promotion decisions), and in this sense the purpose of ethics training is to clarify and strengthen ethics expectations and procedures established by managers and their organizations.

Because in-service training involves adult learners, adapting training to adult learning styles is important. Several learning considerations and instructional methods need to be considered in designing an effective program. Best practices for ethics training have been summarized by Larry Ponemon (1996), who identifies a dozen features crucial to success: live instruction, use of a professional trainer, a powerful message from the manager, small class sizes, at least four hours of training, a decision-based focus, significant group interaction, realistic case materials, comprehensive involvement of employees, separate course for compliance areas, follow-up communications, and new employee programs. Although the authors may differ in their assessment of essential features, the literature reflects a clear preference for reality-based, varied, active learning adapted to the needs of adult trainees, thus allowing sufficient time for digesting information, encouraging trainee participation, using experiential teaching techniques to supplement traditional lecture methods, and emphasizing competency-based learning applicable to workplace decisions (Van Wart, Cayer, and Cook, 1993; Knowles, 1973; LeClair and Ferrell, 2000).

Ethics training in cities often is reality-based and practical, and includes hypothetical scenarios (82.5 percent), case materials (80.9 percent), role plays or short exercises (67.89 percent), and has a decision-based focus (57.5 percent). These methods are consistent with most descriptions of best training practices (see Ponemon, 1996) and with knowledge concerning adult learning styles. The schedule for training often involves different points in time (84.1 percent) and training is delivered with optimal class sizes (81.7 percent with 30 or fewer trainees). The training is tailored to the needs of the jurisdiction (79.6 percent) and delivered in ways that minimize time away from the job (81.6 percent). Professional trainers or outside consultants are used in most cities (64.3 percent) and the lecture format is the primary means of delivery (61.4 percent). Post-training materials for later reference are provided (81.4 percent) and in-class evaluation of training is conducted (72.3 percent). These results clearly reflect that ethics training has become, in many ways, "professionalized." Most training is offered in the form of live instruction with very limited use of Web-based or other forms of electronic instruction (9.6 percent).

Correlates and Impact

Why do some cities provide broad coverage and use numerous methods of ethics training while others do not? To examine this question, some factors mentioned in the previous framework are considered. Having adequate resources for training is associated with use of more ethics training, even controlling for the size of the jurisdiction. Training is also associated with respondents' perceptions that their jurisdiction frequently develops new, innovative programs. However, perceptions of the amount of litigation or employee grievances are not associated with the use of ethics training. Such perceptions may be related to other, non-ethics factors as well. Ethics training is also (weakly) associated with using ethics as a criterion in hiring and promotion. It stands to reason that employees need to be informed and trained in that for which they are held accountable.

These associations are stronger for more targeted ethics training efforts. Consistent with the model of adult learning, a six-item index variable was made of training content, which emphasizes warning signs of unethical behavior, the importance of getting facts, dealing with inadvertent ethical missteps, addressing ethical complaints, consequences of ethical violations, and ethical issues in specific areas (such as law enforcement). This broad measure is more strongly associated with using ethics as a criterion in hiring and promotion. It is also associated with monitoring adherence to the Code of Ethics.

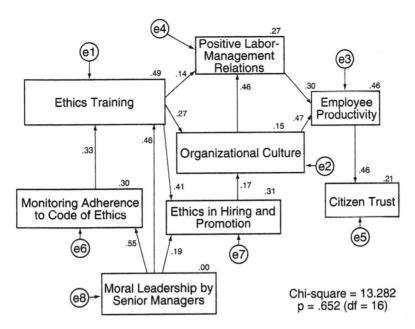

FIGURE 13.1 Structural Equation of Model of Ethics Training, Leadership, and Outcomes

To examine the impact of training, an index variable of revitalized "organizational culture" was developed, measured as a construct of the following items: "in our city, people are strongly supported to put forth their best effort," "our organizational culture encourages creativity and new ideas," "our organization encourages open and constructive dialogue," "our organization rewards passionate commitments to accomplishment," and "in our city, people are encouraged to take on rather than avoid new challenges." In the sample, 51.8 percent agree or strongly agree with these statements. Ethics training is significantly associated with improvements in the organizational culture. Among jurisdictions offering training, 67.2 percent report having a revitalized organizational culture, compared to only 29.0 percent of those that do not do ethics training. Similarly, among jurisdictions that have applications-oriented ethics training discussed earlier, 79.6 percent report having a revitalized organizational culture compared to only 25.0 percent of those that do not do such training.

These associations do invite questions of causality: for example, does ethics training cause improvements in the organizational culture, or is a revitalized organizational culture more likely to use ethics training? Moreover, is the impact direct or indirect, caused by other intervening variables? Such questions of causation and immediacy are explored in Figure 13.1, a Simultaneous Equations Model (SEM) of the impact of ethics training, and factors affecting its use.[3] A variety of conclusions can be drawn from this model. First, the model uses the applications-oriented measure of ethics training; a general measure of ethics training often is not associated with the following paths that are significant for the measure of targeted ethics training efforts. Thus, this corroborates the earlier emphases on targeted measures of training. Second, the model shows that although the relationship of ethics training to citizen trust and employee productivity is complex, training is significantly associated with improvements in the organizational culture and positive labor-management relations. However, the relationship between ethics training and the outcomes is indirect; no direct relationship is significant, and it is therefore not shown.

Third, it can be calculated that the effect of ethics training on perceptions of employee productivity is about the same as the effect of moral leadership by senior managers on employee productivity, though both effects are less than the direct effects of organizational culture and having positive labor-management relations.[4] Fourth, Figure 13.1 also shows that, interestingly, the moral leadership of senior managers does not directly affect perceptions of employee productivity and citizen trust (those paths are not shown, because they are insignificant). The use of ethics training is affected by moral leadership of senior managers, monitoring of employees' adherence to the code of ethics (if an organization has one), and using ethics as a criterion in hiring and promotion. In summary, Figure 13.1 clearly shows the complex, but real relationship of ethics training in connection with other ethics activities, leadership, and important organizational outcomes.

CONCLUSIONS

Ethics is defined as the standards by which actions are determined to be right or wrong and ethics management as those activities through which organizations define and implement such standards, and thereby affect the conduct of employees and managers. As a concept, ethics management is about a decade old, but it is just now catching on. The main ingredients of ethics management are: leadership, assessment, articulation, training, feedback, and ensuring consequences.

Ethics training is thus one of several strategies through which leaders manage their organization's ethics. Based on our study, about 64 percent of cities offer some form of ethics training, although only 36 percent call it "ethics training." This training covers a broad range of topics that include both legal aspects as well as broader concerns that help employees to recognize instances of questionable ethics and to adopt appropriate responses to such situations. We also found that training is associated with fostering organizational cultures of openness, accountability, and performance that, in turn, are associated with increased employee productivity. This study further reveals considerable variation in the extent of ethics training, and in the depth with which different topics are covered. The results also suggest that the perceived effectiveness of training is greatest when it is applied to specific problems and when managers monitor ethics implementation.

While ethics training has been substantially "professionalized" in the last decade, progress is still needed. The depth of training is modest at best, about a half day or so a year. Although ethics training is not the only source of ethics-related information and priorities in organizations, it is important from the perspective of reinforcing management priorities. Why is more not being done? The usual reasons still exist in some organizations, such as managers considering ethics to be a private or confidential matter for individuals to resolve, or perceiving that addressing ethics can be construed as an affront suggesting that co-workers are deficient in some way. In others instances, the need for ethics management and training has not yet surfaced on the radar screens of managers and leaders. Paradoxically, the lack of adequate attention to ethics increases the risk of ethics failure and, hence, ensures that ethics will require greater attention in the future.

NOTES

1. Data were collected as part of a 2002 questionnaire mailed to city managers and chief administrative officers (CAOs) in all 544 cities with populations over 50,000. Two hundred (200) usable responses were received after three rounds of mailing, for a response rate of 36.8 percent. Survey respondents report having extensive government experience, 20 years, of which 11 of those years are spent with their current jurisdiction. Respondents hold a variety of very senior positions, so we refer to the response groups as "senior managers." We also conducted in-depth telephone interviews among a sample of respondents.

2. Other valuable ethics training resources that can complement instructional activities include ASPA (1998); Berman, et al. (1998); Cooper (2001); Brattebo & Malone (2002); Gueras & Garofalo (2002); Kazman & Bonczek (1998); LGI (1995–1998); NCSL (2003); Pasquerella, et al. (1996); and http://www.aspanet.org/ethicscommunity/compendium.

3. Although path analysis can also be used to estimate this recursive model, the approach used here includes additional tests for the appropriateness (specification) of the overall model. Figure 13.1 satisfies the usual goodness-of-fit standards (chi-square = 13.28, p > .05). See West and Berman (2004) for a complete discussion of other fit measures. Although this is not statistically the most parsimonious model, it does show the theoretically relevant linkages.

4. The respective effects on employee productivity are .208 (ethics training), .191 (moral leadership), .608 (organizational culture), and .304 (labor-management relations). These are the beta coefficients. Indirect effects are calculated as the product of coefficients. For example, the indirect effect of organizational culture on productivity through labor-management relations is .46*.30 = .138. The direct effect is .47, hence, the total effect is .608. Other indirect effects are calculated in the same manner.

REFERENCES

American Society for Public Administration. 1998. *Applying Standards and Ethics in the 21st Century*. Washington, DC: ASPA.

Berman, E. 2003. "Implementing Ethics." In: Jack Rabin, et al., eds. *Encyclopedia of Public Administration and Public Policy*. New York, NY: Marcel Dekker, pp. 461–464

Berman, E. and West, J. 2003. "Solutions to the Problem of Managerial Mediocrity: Moving Up to Excellence Part 2." *Public Performance & Management Review*, 27:2: December: 28–50.

Berman, E., West, J., and Bonczek, S., eds. 1998. *The Ethics Edge*. Washington, DC: ICMA.

Berman, E., West, J., and Cava, A. 1994. "Ethics Management in Municipal Government and Large Firms: Exploring Similarities and Differences." *Administration & Society* 26:2: 185–203.

Bonczek, S. 1998. Creating an Ethical Work Environment. In E. Berman, J. West, and S. Bonczek, eds. *The Ethics Edge*. Washington, DC: International City/County Management Association, pp. 77–79.

Brattebo, D. and Malone, E., eds. 2002. *The Lanahan Cases in Leadership Ethics & Decision Making*. Baltimore, MD: Lanahan.

Bruce, W. M. 1996. "Codes of Ethics and Codes of Conduct: Perceived Contribution to the Practice of Ethics in Local Government." *Public Integrity Annual* 17: 23–29.

Cooper, T. 2001. *Handbook of Administrative Ethics*. New York, NY: Marcel Dekker.

Gueras, D. and Garofalo, C. 2002. *Practical Ethics in Public Administration*. Vienna, VA: Management Concepts.

International City Management Association. 1998. Code of Ethics with Guidelines, as adopted by ICMA Executive Board.

Kazman, J. and Bonczek, S. 1998. *Ethics in Action*. Washington, DC: International City/County Management Association.

Knowles, M. 1973. *The Adult Learner: A Neglected Species*. Houston, TX: Gulf Publishing.

LeClair, D. T. and Ferrell, L., 2000. "Innovation in Experiential Business Ethics Training." *Journal of Business Ethics* 23: 313–322.

Local Government Institute. 1995–1998. *Honesty and Fairness in the Public Service*. Tacoma, WA: LGI.

Menzel, D. with Carson, K. 1999. "A Review and Assessment of Empirical Research on Public Administration Ethics: Implications for Scholars and Managers." *Public Integrity* 1:3: 239–264.

National Conference of State Legislatures. 2003. *The State of State Legislative Ethics*. Denver, CO: NCSL.

Pasquerella, A., Killilea, X., and Vocino, M., eds. 1996. *Ethical Dilemmas in Public Administration*. Westport, CT: Praeger.

Paine, L. 1994. "Managing for Organizational Integrity." *Harvard Business Review* 106–117.

Payne, S. L. 1996. "Ethical Skill Development as an Imperative for Emancipatory Practice." *Systems Practice* 9:4: 307–316.

Petrick, J. A. and Quinn, J. F. 1997. *Management Ethics: Integrity at Work*. Thousand Oaks, CA: Sage.

Ponemon, L. 1996. "Key Features of an Effective Ethics Training Program." *Management Accounting* October: 66–67.

Van Wart, M. 1998. *Changing Public Sector Values*. New York, NY: Garland Publishing, Inc.

Van Wart, M., Cayer, N. J., and Cook, 1993. *Handbook of Training and Development*. San Francisco, CA: Jossey-Bass.

Weaver, G. R., Trevino, L., and Cochran, P. 1999a. "Corporate Ethics Programs as Control Systems: Influences of Executive Commitment and Environmental Factors." *Academy of Management Journal* 42: 41–57.

Weaver, G. R., Trevino, L., and Cochran, P. 1999b. "Corporate Ethics Practices in the Mid–1990s: An Empirical Study of Fortune 1000." *Journal of Business Ethics* 18: 283–294.

Wells, D. and Schminke, M. 2001. "Ethical Development and Human Resources Training: An Integrative Framework." *Human Resources Management Review* 11: 135–158.

West, J. P. 2003. "Ethics and Human Resource Management." In S. Hays and R. Kearney, eds., *Public Personnel Management: Problems and Prospects*. Upper Saddle River, NJ: Prentice Hall, pp. 301–316.

West, J. P. and Berman, E. 2004. "Ethics Training Efforts in U.S. Cities: Content and Impact." *Public Integrity* 6:3: 189–206.

West, J. P., Berman, E., and Cava, A. 1993. "Ethics in the Muncipal Workplace." *The Municipal Yearbook 1993*. Washington, DC: International City/County Management Association, pp. 3–16.

West, J. P., Berman, E., Bonczek, S., and Kellar, E. 1998. "Frontiers of Ethics Training." *Public Management* 80:6: 4–9.

White, L. and Lam, L. 2000. A Proposed Infrastructural Model for the Establishment of Organizational Ethical Systems. *Journal of Business Ethics* 28: 35–42.

www.aspanet.org/ethicscommunity/compendium.

Chapter *14*

Privatization and Its Implications for Human Resources Management

Sergio Fernandez, Hal G. Rainey, and Carol E. Lowman

Privatization of public services has been one of the most significant developments in public administration over the last several decades. Around the world, trillions of dollars worth of activities have been privatized or considered for it. In the United States and some other countries, much of this privatizing has taken the form of contracting out, and such arrangements have spread widely and rapidly. These developments have important implications for human resources management in government, and this chapter discusses many of the most important ones. After some background on the privatization trend, the discussion turns to general implications for public management. Then, the chapter addresses one of the main issues for human resources management, the skills and knowledge needed to manage contracting out and similar arrangements, and we enumerate many of these by identifying skill requirements for a well-developed contracting process. We discuss specific issues that privatization raises for human resources management, including organizational design issues and the professionalization of the procurement workforce (the experts on contracting and procurement) through education and certification requirements. Next, the chapter covers one of the most important challenges: managing relations with employees and unions in privatization situations. This section discusses employee and union opposition to contracting out, its impact on employees' job security and wages, and how human resources managers and other officials need to address these issues to deal with such opposition and to treat employees fairly. Finally, the chapter reports on developments in a recent trend towards privatization or "outsourcing" of human resources management functions themselves. All these topics represent challenges for everyone involved in human resources management in government, and reflect the imperatives to increase our capacity to respond to such challenges.

THE PRIVATIZATION TREND

Privatization as a service delivery method dates at least as far back as the sixteenth century during the reign of Elizabeth I (Kent, 1998), and in the United States predates the foundation of the Republic. The adoption of privatization in its different forms increased considerably during the last two decades, however (Donahue, 1989; Savas, 1987, 2000; Sclar, 2000; Greene, 2002; Salamon, 2002). Privatization has been a central component of the new public management reforms, the National Performance Review, numerous efforts to reform or reinvent state and local government in the United States, and more recently, of the Bush Administration's President's Management Agenda (see Ingraham, 1997; Kettl, 2002; Peters; 1996). In the United States, governments have owned few commercial or industrial enterprises, so privatization in this country has commonly taken the form of contracting out. Contracted services in the U.S. have spanned the wide spectrum of governmental functions, from development and production of atomic weapons to the delivery of social services at the state and local level. By most indications, the use of contracting out as a service delivery approach continues to spread in the United States, indicating that privatization has become firmly entrenched in our system of governance (Kettl, 1988; Donahue, 1989; Kelman, 2002; Martin, 1999).

Governments have joined this privatization movement in pursuit of cost savings, better quality of service and better performance, and for access to new alternatives and skills. They were pushed in this direction by economic problems in many nations in the 1970s and 1980s, and by strong claims about the benefits of privatization from some academics and theorists. These theoretical rationales came from advocates of privatization representing perspectives such as neoclassical economics theory, liberal political philosophy, and public choice theory. Economists of the public choice school, such as Downs (1967) and Niskanen (1971), contend that bureaucrats, lacking a competitive market for their outputs and thus protected from competition, have more incentive to maximize their own budgets than to maximize efficiency or to be responsive to citizens. Privatization, then, becomes a way to break the monopolistic power of public bureaus and to force government to offer citizens more choices about government services. Relatedly, some economic theorists assert that in the absence of competition and profit incentives, public agencies are unlikely to produce public goods or services at minimal cost (Pack, 1987, p. 527). According to Averch (1990), the quantity of output of a good or service produced by a budget maximizing public bureaucracy is "technically and allocatively inefficient," so that the public bureau will produce a level of output greater than the socially efficient level and for a higher than minimal cost (p. 60). Government can overcome this obstacle by allowing profit-maximizing businesses to bid competitively for the production of public goods and services. Similarly, Pack (1987) contends that, "competitive bidding by profit-maximizing firms for a well specified output guarantees that the product will be produced at the lowest cost" (p. 527).

From the perspective of liberal political philosophy, the coercive power of the state poses a grave danger to the personal freedom of the citizenry. Privatization therefore has value as a way of countering the power of the encroaching state that increasingly takes more of people's earnings, and makes decisions about the use of this money in an unresponsive manner (Savas, 2000, p. 10). Interestingly, recent empirical evidence is beginning to indicate that privatization has entered a less ideological phase in which its adoption has gained wide acceptance, independently of ideology (Brudney, et al., 2005; Auger, 1999; Kelman, 2002).

While one can debate these assumptions and assertions at length (e.g., Moe, 1987), they gained wide acceptance during the 1970s and 1980s, as economic woes and other developments fueled a trend in many nations towards regarding government as too big and too inefficient (Moe, 1987). Political leaders, such as Ronald Reagan and Margaret Thatcher, championed privatization as a solution for these problems. Savas (1987) published one of the most significant books about this movement, in which he concluded from a review of empirical research that the private sector, under contracts and other privatization procedures, delivered public services more efficiently and as effectively as government.

The burgeoning privatization movement, however, elicited a response from authors and experts who challenged the view of privatization as a panacea for government's ills. By the end of the 1980s, a new stream of literature was enumerating the many problems posed by privatization, addressing the challenge of how best to manage it and to avoid its shortcomings (e.g., Sclar, 2000; Cooper, 2002; Donahue, 1989; Kettl, 1993; Moe, 1987, 1996; Rehfuss, 1989). These authors tended to portray the strong claims for privatization as naïve in their assumptions that contracting out would automatically bring benefits, and to point out that "successful privatization requires effective management by government officials" (Gill and Rainey, 1998, p. 1). Donahue (1989), for example, argued that for privatization to be successful, the government must be capable of specifying clearly the product or service it desires, and must ensure the presence of effective competition if any gains in efficiency are to be realized. Government must also establish well-designed contract administration and monitoring systems to ensure accountability (p. 218). Concerning these requirements, Rainey (2003, p. 371) comments that "the chief irony of privatization is that proponents tout it as a cure for bad government, but it takes excellent government to make it work" (see also Moe, 1996).

This latter current in the literature on privatization has focused on a number of different contingencies on which the success of privatization hinges. These include effective design of the contracting process (Wallin, 1997; Avery, 2000), improved contract management practices (Rehfuss, 1989; Kettl, 1993; Prager, 1994; Crawford and Krahn, 1998; Dicke and Ott, 1999), frameworks for deciding which functions to contract out (Ferris and Graddy, 1986; Donahue, 1989; Rehfuss, 1989; Moe, 1987), and methodological advice on how to make fair and accurate comparisons of public with private service delivery (Barnekov and Raffel, 1990; Prager and Desai, 1996; Sclar, 2000; Fernandez and Fabricant, 2000).

Part of this countertrend arose because the aggressive claims of privatization proponents have not been clearly supported by the available evidence. On the question of whether contracting out to private providers results in greater efficiency and higher quality of service, the results of empirical research are mixed. Savas (2000), for instance, reviews many studies comparing public with private service delivery in solid waste management, street sweeping, street paving, traffic-signal maintenance, bus transportation, administrative services, custodial work, tree maintenance, lawn maintenance, and corrections. He concludes that contractors selected through competitive bidding performed more efficiently than public agencies and performed work of equal quality (Savas, 2000, p. 153). Similarly, Siegel's (1999) review of research about twenty local government service areas concludes that contracting improves efficiency and effectiveness and leads to cost savings in a number of service areas (p. 374) (see also Dilger, Moffett, and Struyk, 1997).

On the other hand, many individual studies and examples have indicated problems with privatization. For example, Kamerman and Kahn's (1989) analysis of privatized child care programs in North Carolina found that gains in efficiency were attained only through a reduction in the level of service provided, particularly by creaming off the easier and less costly cases. The news media have reported numerous horror stories about the corrupt or abusive behaviors of non-profit or for-profit private organizations that provide services under contracts with government. Donahue (1989, p. 62) notes that one of Savas' own studies found that open competition among private garbage collection services made the service more costly than either government provision or government contracting out of the service. Larger studies have also found evidence that privatization falls short of its proponents' optimistic claims. Hodge (1999) reports a meta-analysis of numerous empirical studies comparing public with private service delivery in different nations. He concludes that overall, contracting out produces cost savings, but that the savings actually concentrate in a few service areas such as garbage collection, cleaning, and maintenance (p. 467). Savings through privatization in other service areas were either much lower or nonexistent. In addition, no general difference could be ascertained between cost savings through contracting with the private sector and through contracting with other public sector organizations (p. 464). Sclar (2000) asserts, "although there are clear situations in which contracting works well, there are at least as many, if not more, in which the existence of direct public service is a rational economic strategy" (p. 68). Even Greene (2002, pp. 49–50), who concludes that the evidence of efficiency is favorable toward privatizing municipal services, admonishes that cost-savings may often be less than reported, and that greater efficiency is generally a result of competition rather than private service delivery.

In summary, research on privatization has produced a controversy over its value. Most parties to the controversy, however, would almost certainly agree on several points. Privatization has been a strong movement and will continue to represent a major alternative for government decision-makers. Privatization offers advantages and disadvantages, and even those skeptical of it see that it can provide useful strategic options for government, including such advantages as flexibility and the ability to attain skills and services not readily available in government. On the other hand, even those devoutly supportive of privatization tend to agree that the procedures and conditions for effective privatization have a significant bearing on its success, and hence the sound management of it becomes imperative. Sound management of any enterprise requires sound management of the human resources involved.

PRIVITIZATION AND HOW IT IS REDEFINING THE ROLE OF THE PUBLIC MANAGER

To be successful, contracting for services must be managed well, and doing so requires special managerial knowledge, skills, and abilities. In fact, some experts have argued that the growth in contracting for services is forcing a redefinition of the role of the public manager, in ways that have many implications for human resource management. As Moe explains (1996), "the assignment of public functions to third parties, while it may decrease the need for direct government employment, does not eliminate, or even substantially reduce, the requirements of government management, it simply changes the character of this management. Privatization, contrary to conventional wisdom, often results not in less but in new and more sophisticated demands being placed on public management, demands at present little recognized or appreciated by either privatization advocates or the public sector management community itself" (pp. 135–136; see also Milward, et al., 1993).

Specifically, what demands does privatization place on public managers? First, privatization requires that public managers have the ability to write contract specifications and to design effective contract documents, or that they acquire staff to do so, and have sufficient knowledge to deal effectively with that staff. Public managers must possess a good understanding of the technical aspects of the service or function that is being contracted out and at least some familiarity with procurement practices and contract law. They also must have the ability to plan the transition to external service delivery, anticipate problems or contingencies that might affect the contractual relationship before it begins, and address these contingencies in the contract document.

Second, public managers must be prepared to take effective steps to ensure accountability and performance when hiring external providers to deliver services. Contracting out does not eliminate concerns about accountability and performance. In fact, issues of accountability and performance become even more pressing and difficult to manage when contracting for services. Relying on external providers to deliver services tends to strain the lines of authority and accountability (National Academy of Public Administration, 1989; Kettl, 1993). As Kettl (1993) puts it, the trend leans toward more sharing of power with nongovernmental actors. In some cases, he points out, contractors actually have been making important policy decisions, and increasingly taking over important governmental functions. Other observers express related concerns that government and its leaders and managers may have a reduced ability to defend values such as social equity and opportunity for the disadvantaged. According to the prevailing view in the literature, ensuring accountability and performance seems to involve a combination of competitive bidding, rigorous monitoring of contractor performance, and the crafting of an effective package of contract incentives and sanctions to curb opportunistic behavior.

A third new demand is that public managers engaged in contracting for services must be knowledgeable of private markets for contracted services and must have the ability to influence, and sometimes even to shape, private markets. As Warner and Hebdon (2001) argue, governments do not passively respond to market conditions but are active participants in shaping markets. Public managers should be familiar with service providers that are available to them, including the capacity and performance record of these providers. This knowledge helps to prevent awarding a contract to a provider that is ill equipped to deliver a service; it also allows local governments to seek alternate providers quickly if an existing contract goes awry or new services are needed on an emergency basis. Local governments also can takes steps to stimulate markets by advertising bids widely, by encouraging firms to bid on contracts, and by offering grants or small purchases and contracts to smaller providers to help build their capacity. Knowledge of private markets also gives public managers an indication of when they may need to contract "back in" by reverting to in-house service delivery.

Finally, public contract managers must be able not only to monitor and control the behavior of contractors, they must also be able to manage interorganizational relationships based on trust and mutual consent between partners (Cooper, 2002). This requires even greater levels of certain skills and abilities that all managers need, including persuasion, negotiation, and coordination within and across organizational boundaries; good problem-solving skills; and the ability to build trust and a shared culture between contracting parties.

THE CONTRACTING PROCESS AND HUMAN RESOURCES NEEDS

No one has ever prepared a conclusive list of the human resources needs related to privatization, because the skills, people, training, and other needs should be flexibly defined and will vary in different settings. One way of developing suggestions about such needs, however, involves examining a well-developed contracting process for indications. A well-developed process, such as the ones used in many federal agencies, includes three phases: the pre-award phase, during which the organization specifies its needs; a second phase involving evaluation of bids or proposals; and the post-award contract administration phase. Public employees and managers need knowledge and skills pertinent to each of the three phases.

The pre-award specification phase requires personnel with substantive knowledge of the program or function to be contracted out, as well as the analytical, communication, and writing skills necessary to draft clear contractual requirements and statements of work. Knowledge of the market, including such matters as the extent of competition between potential providers, also plays a crucial role during this phase. Moreover, public managers must have skills in promoting effective communication and cooperation between the people in the procurement department (who are specialists in contracting and procurement procedures) and the people in the "user" departments (the operating units that want to contract out a function, and thus want to use the contractor and its services). These linkages, essential to ensuring that the contractor understands and meets the needs of the organization, require skillful management of integration devices, such as cross-functional teams that come together to identify the organization's needs and draft technical requirements.

The evaluation phase of the contracting process demands personnel with the knowledge and skills to compare bids or proposals. This includes substantive knowledge of the program or function being contracted out, financial skills such as cost-benefit analysis and marginal analysis, and some knowledge of microeconomic principles including such topics as transaction cost economics.

Many authors have pointed to inadequate skills and training in contract administration as a serious problem in privatization processes (Moe, 1994; Kettl, 1988; Handler, 1996; Prager, 1994; Wallin, 1997). To ensure that government gets what it pays for, contract administrators need training in the areas of quality assurance, project management, inspection, statistical sampling, accounting, auditing, and record-keeping. Ideally, contract administrators should have skills in negotiation, persuasion, and conflict resolution, and sound knowledge of the law that applies to the contracting process.

For the phases of the contracting process just described, human resources managers and governmental personnel systems face decisions about how to design and deliver appropriate training. They also need to blend this training with other ways of acquiring needed skills, such as through hiring appropriate people or through still more contracting with providers who can meet those needs. In many instances, public organizations have contracted with consultants to draft technical specifications, with attorneys to provide legal advice related to procurement, and with large accounting or management firms to monitor other contracts. This creates an intricate web of external suppliers that can strain the lines of accountability and weaken the authority of public managers.

Also, as described later, privatization and contracting out can increase the need for knowledge and skills for which human resources managers in government already have responsibility. Contracting out may require a reduction-in-force (RIF) and may involve "Rights of First Refusal," "Veterans Preference," and governmental early retirement programs. These matters require knowledge of governmental laws, rules, and procedures about how to carry them out.

THE PROFESSIONALIZAITON OF THE PROCUREMENT WORKFORCE

The skills and knowledge requirements for privatization are evolving, in part because governmental authorities such as legislative bodies are becoming involved in identifying them. At the federal level, Congress has taken action to enhance the professionalization of personnel involved in procurement and contracting out, in ways that increase their discretion and that make the required skills more open-ended. In the Federal Acquisition Reform Act (FARA) and the Federal Acquisition Streamlining Act (FASA), Congress decreased and streamlined the elaborate regulations that previous legislation had imposed on federal procurement and contracting out. FARA and FASA increase contracting officers' discretion by allowing them to "exercise business judgment" and by allowing such changes as the use of oral proposals in place of written proposals in some instances.

In conjunction with this trend of providing for more professional discretion and skill in the procurement workforce, Congress has moved to professionalize these employees through increased requirements for education, training, and certification. The Defense Acquisition Workforce Improvement Act, for example, requires that procurement/acquisition personnel have a college degree or 24 hours of college credit in business topics. The Act also establishes certification requirements, and requires that certified personnel complete 80 hours of continuing education every two years. Additional legislation has strengthened such requirements and extended them to the entire federal procurement workforce. These developments reflect recognition in the legislative branch that more emphasis on privatization and contracting out will require corresponding increases in knowledge and skill on the part of government employees. Experts have sometimes cited limited expertise in contracting out as a problem for privatization in some state and local agencies (Chi, 1994), so this trend of seeking to enhance the professional preparation and certification of the personnel involved will disseminate to other levels of government.

ORGANIZATION DESIGN ISSUES: SEPARATING GOVERNMENT AND CONTRACT PERSONNEL

In addition to the need for acquisition of skills and personnel, increasing privatization raises still more challenges for government managers and personnel systems. Some of these involve issues of organizational design. One important example of this arises when government managers need to avoid mixing together government and contractor personnel. Government frequently contracts for services such as health, refuse collection, landscaping, and janitorial services, where the government does not simply buy a product, but contracts for the knowledge and work of the contractors' personnel. At the federal level, the Federal Acquisition Regulation (FAR) forbids "personal services" contracts (with some exceptions) where the contractor's personnel appear to be, in effect, government employees (FAR 37.101). The FAR forbids such contracts because government normally hires employees through Civil Service rules, and personal service contracts can bypass the Civil Service system. To prevent this, FAR requires that government managers avoid direct or even indirect supervision of the contractor's employees (FAR 37.104(d)(6)). In some situations, government managers have to prevent these problems by physically separating the two types of employees, using various procedures (such as identification badges) to clearly identify the difference, and making sure that official documents such as organization charts emphasize the difference. Government managers may have to set up organizational designs that make sure that tasks and directions are relayed to contractor employees through the contractor's supervisory chain, and not the government's, and specify the differences in duties and responsibilities in formal organizational documents. It is important to emphasize that such arrangements provide one example of the many issues and requirements that government managers may have to take into account. Actually, in many contracting-out situations, governmental and contractor employees unavoidably must work closely together with a lot of communication and interdependence. This can blur the lines of accountability between public and contractor employees, and pose challenges for government managers that cannot readily be resolved through simply separating the two types of employees or relaying instructions through the contactor's chain of command.

PUBLIC EMPLOYEE AND PUBLIC UNION OPPOSITION TO PRIVATIZATION

The possibilities of reductions in force and of contractors' employees taking over governmental functions show why privatization gives public employees reasons to worry about their jobs, and why public employee unions display tremendous concern about privatization. A study by the National Commission for Employment Policy concluded that, "by far the most contentious issue associated with contracting out is its impact on public sector workers" (1988, p. 11). Typically fervid in their opposition to privatization, public employees and public unions pose a formidable barrier to contracting out of services at all levels of government. This section discusses employee opposition to privatization; the various forms this opposition can take; empirical findings on the actual impact of privatization on public employment levels, wages, and benefits; and suggestions for public managers on how to cope with this important contingency when designing and implementing a privatization initiative.

The available literature and evidence indicates that union opposition can present a real obstacle to the adoption of privatization. Ferris and Graddy (1986) found that the extent of public employee unionization had a significant negative effect on the likelihood that a city will contract out for a service. Boyne (1998) reviewed numerous privatization studies and found a general negative relationship between the percentage of the population employed by the public sector and contracting out, although the link between unionization and contracting out appeared to be more tenuous. He concluded that the balance of the evidence points toward a negative relationship between public employee strength and the incidence of privatization (see also Becker, Silverstein, and Chaykin, 1995). In addition, a large survey of sanitation collection services in U.S. cities with populations over 10,000 revealed that unionized cities were less likely to consider contracting out than non-unionized cities. The survey also found that opposition to contracting out was significantly higher in unionized cities than in non-unionized cities, and that cities that considered contracting out but never did so reported significantly higher levels of opposition from both city employees and residents than cities that ultimately contracted out for sanitation collection services (Chandler and Feuille, 1991). A recent study from Georgia found that an individual's employment in the public sector correlated negatively with support for privatization, suggesting that opposition to privatization might transcend organized union efforts to include rank and file employee opposition. Other research, however, has found that labor and union opposition has little or no effect on the decision to privatize (Warner and Hebdon, 2001; Brudney, et al., 2005).

Public employee opposition to contracting out stems in large part from fears of job displacement and loss or reduction in wages and benefits. Opponents of privatization have also asserted that privatization does disproportionate harm to minorities employed in the public sector. In a county in Florida, the mere prospect of privatization sparked sufficient resistance among employees to bring the initiative to a halt (Becker, et al., 1995). The primary concern among most public employees not only focused on the loss of job security, but the loss or reduction in benefits also posed a significant barrier to privatization. Specifically, employees expressed outrage over the considerably lower retirement benefits and lower family health care coverage that the contractors offered (Becker, et al., 1995). Interestingly, the issue of wages never became a stumbling block, since the contractors offered salaries competitive with those of the county.

Public employees and public unions have employed various methods to influence or obstruct privatization initiatives. In many instances, public unions have mounted legal challenges to municipalities or agencies attempting to contract out a service. These legal challenges have contended that the decision was not taken to improve efficiency or effectiveness; that political favoritism drove the decision; and that the agency or unit of government failed to bargain in good faith with unionized employees. In addition, the legal challenges contended that the agency or unit of government acted in an unlawful, unilateral manner that caused it to violate its duty to bargain (Elam, 1997). Though public unions' success in the courts has varied in this regard (Naff, 1991), the mere threat of a lawsuit may convince decision-makers to reconsider their decision to contract out. Moreover, the ability of public employees to obstruct privatization reaches beyond the courtroom. For instance, public employee unions have mounted both local and national public relations campaigns against privatization in order to garner political support and public sympathy for their cause. Particularly at the local level, political opposition from public unions can pose a significant barrier to privatization. Local elected officials may be disinclined to antagonize public unions by proposing privatization, since they depend on union members to deliver important services to constituents (NCEP, 1988). Moreover, public employees tend to vote more frequently than the average citizen, and their collective voting power can influence the results of local elections significantly.

IMPACT OF PRIVATIZATION ON PUBLIC SECTOR JOB SECURITY, WAGES, AND BENEFITS

While the available empirical evidence on the impact of privatization on public-sector job security, wages, and benefits should allay some of the fears held by public employees and their unions, it seems to confirm others. Do many public employees become displaced when contracts are awarded to private or nonprofit firms? Although the evidence is not conclusive, it tends to refute the claim that contracting out results in lay-offs of significant numbers of public employees. Based on a review of Department of Defense (DOD), General Accounting Office (GAO), and Office of Management and Budget (OMB) studies of military and civilian agency contracts, the National Commission for Employment Policy (1988) concluded that federal employee job displacement from contracting out was very low. Only about one in twenty federal workers became unemployed as a result of contracting out with the private sector. Moreover, the Commission also conducted its own multiple-case study of seventeen city and county governments and found that few workers were laid off because of contracting out. In all but two of the seventeen cases, workers who were terminated were given opportunities for other jobs within government. Most of the cities established a "no lay-off" policy as a condition to awarding contracts. The findings from the multiple case study, however, did reveal that former public employees subsequently hired by contractors tended to work for them for less than two years.

Donahue (1989) recently examined trends in the size of the public workforce and in the incidence of government outsourcing and concluded that the effect of privatization on the size of the public workforce has been quite small. As he explains, "a greater readiness to rely on private delivery almost surely has had a smaller influence on the size of the public workforce than have shifts in the size and composition of government's mission, productivity growth, and simple austerity. Far from cutting to the heart of public employment, privatization seems to have been (at least so far) nibbling around its edges" (p. 275); Greene (2002) reached a similar conclusion. Light (1999) has argued that there is circumstantial evidence of a link between the decline in the size of the federal workforce and the surge in the size of the shadow workforce, but he admits that further research is needed to determine if government employees are truly being replaced by contract workers (p. 25). Given the significance of this issue, further research is needed, particularly panel studies and other longitudinal studies to assess the long-term impact of privatization on public employees.

The same multiple-case study by the National Commission for Employment Policy (1988) found, as did Becker et al. (1995), that private contractors generally offered higher wages than cities and counties. However, other studies have shown that wages paid by private contractors were generally lower than those paid by cities and counties, sometimes by as much as half (NCEP, 1988). Many advocates of privatization contend that public-sector employees are significantly overcompensated. As Sclar (2000) notes, however, when one controls for education, skill level, and job tenure, the evidence indicates that public-sector employees actually make 4 to 5 percent less than their private counterparts. "Hence, as the nature of public-service work subjected to privatization becomes more skill- and education-intensive, the utility of private-sector wage differentials as a source of savings diminishes rapidly" (Sclar, 2000, p. 61). On the impact of privatization on employee benefits, the limited empirical evidence seems to confirm the concerns expressed by public employees and public unions about considerably lower benefits packages offered by private contractors (NCEP, 1988; Becker, Silverstein, and Chaykin, 1995).

Concerning whether privatization does disproportionate harm to minorities employed in the public sector, the evidence is also mixed. Savas (2000) and the NCEP (1988) concluded that contracting out is not disproportionately harmful to minorities. Yet, when fiscal stress prompted the city of St. Louis to close down its public hospitals and enter into an agreement with a private provider, the city lost almost half of its African-American workforce (Stein, 1994). In 1979, the city's hospital division employed 3,344 workers, 74 percent of whom were African-American. By 1990, however, with both public hospitals closed, the same division employed only 178 workers, of whom only 39 percent were African-American.

REDUCING BARRIERS TO PUBLIC EMPLOYEE OPPOSITION TO PRIVATIZATION

Even though the evidence on the impacts of privatization is mixed, public managers must treat public employee and public union opposition to privatization as a critical contingency when implementing privatization. The literature on the topic provides valuable advice on how to cope with public employees' and public unions' resistance. First, public managers can take steps to minimize the number of employees who lose their government jobs as a result of privatization (NCEP, 1988; Eggers and O'Leary, 1994). Municipalities or agencies can contract out only for new or expanding services, or can establish a "no lay-off" policy when contracting out for existing services. Employees can also be transferred to other departments or given hiring preference for new job openings in the municipality or agency. Reductions in workforce through attrition, by means such as early retirement incentives, can also help persuade employees to leave voluntarily. Finally, in some instances such as the "competitive sourcing" initiatives of the Bush administration, public employees have been granted the right to bid for those services being contracted out.

For those public employees who become displaced, measures can be taken to assist them in securing alternate employment in the private sector or elsewhere (NECP, 1988; Eggers and O'Leary, 1994; Jackson, 1997). Resources can be directed toward employee assistance programs and services such as retraining, job placement, counseling, and reimbursement for lost pension and other benefits that can facilitate the transition to new jobs. Municipalities or agencies can also give preference to bidders who offer to hire displaced employees as part of their bid or proposal. Finally, contractors can be compelled to offer displaced public employees the right of first refusal to new jobs created as a result of privatization. In the federal government, many contracts for the purchase of commercial or industrial products and services fall under the authority of Office of Management and Budget Circular No. A–76 (Revised). The circular requires that under certain circumstances federal agencies must perform a cost comparison between providing goods and services in-house and through contract. When the results of the cost comparison suggest that private provision of goods and services is preferable to governmental provision, the circular mandates that resulting contracts contain the "Right of First Refusal of Employment" clause.

Under the Rights of First Refusal of Employment clause, the contractor who wins the cost comparison against the government must offer public employees affected by privatization the right of first refusal of any jobs on the contract for which they are qualified. While this clause offers some protection for government employees, it by no means guarantees another job, since under certain conditions contractors face no requirement to offer the right of first refusal. Note that these conditions and the reference to this provision as a "right" make this right of first refusal a good example of how important it is for human resources managers to know about such conditions and specifications in the laws and rules, and to ensure careful compliance with them, and to foster this knowledge and practice in other officials.

Another possible strategy for reducing barriers to privatization involves creating incentives to make privatization more acceptable to public employees (NECP, 1988; Eggers and O'Leary, 1994). Municipalities or agencies can tie pay levels to productivity improvements and efficiency gains to encourage support for privatization. Government organizations can create employee stock ownership plans (ESOPs) to offer public employees an ownership interest in new private enterprises that are created in privatization initiatives. A related strategy involves encouraging groups of employees to buy out government service delivery operations and run them as employee-owned businesses. Governments can encourage such arrangements by transferring capital assets to the employee-owned business, granting the new business continued access to public facilities, providing financial and legal start-up assistance, and guaranteeing the initial contract award to the employee-owned enterprise.

Undertaking a significant privatization initiative represents a major organizational change for a public agency. Over the years, experts who have explored the issue of reducing resistance to change have frequently cited widespread employee participation as an effective approach for reducing such resistance (Rainey, 2003; Armenakis, Harris, and Field, 2001; Burke, 2002; Kotter, 1995; Judson, 1991; Kemp, et al, 1993; Thompson and Sanders, 1997). The authors of a study of large-scale privatization in the city of Charlotte go so far as to claim that "employee participation at all levels is key to ensuring the success of the privatization initiative" (Jurkiewicz and Bradley, 2002, p. 380). The literature indicates that involvement by organizational members helps to reduce barriers to change by creating psychological ownership, promoting the dissemination of critical information, and encouraging employee feedback so that the innovation can be fine-tuned during implementation. Public employee and union resistance to privatization might be reduced, therefore, by allowing employees to participate in the decision-making about whether or not to privatize, in the design of the program, and in its implementation. It is important to note, however, that participation is not a magic bullet for overcoming resistance to change (Bruhn, Zajac, and Al-Kazemi, 2001; Bryson and Anderson, 2000; Shareef, 1994; Piderit, 2000). Managers must commit sufficient time, effort, and financial resources to the participation process and recognize and value employee contributions; failure to effectively manage participation can be counter-productive in terms of wasted time, morale, and resources (Bruhn, Zajac, and Al-Kazemi, 2001).

Of course, one of the major reasons that government officials have to deal effectively with employee opposition to privatization arises from the possibility that public employee unions can mount a legal challenge to the decision to contract out. As described earlier, unions have brought legal challenges claiming various improprieties in the contracting process. If the court finds that the government entity or the contractor acted improperly in making and implementing the decision, the court might award monetary damages for breach of contract by the contractor or award back pay to displaced public employees. Elam (1997) offers suggestions for overcoming the legal barriers to privatization that tend to address the points on which the legal challenges have been brought. First, state clearly the purpose for contracting out. Second, compile fact-based evidence with which to demonstrate that privatization will promote greater effectiveness or efficiency in service delivery. Third, draft clear specifications and performance requirements, and employ competitive bidding (or other objective merit-based methods for selecting a contractor), to guard against claims of improper behavior or politically motivated contract awards. Fourth, seek legal counsel if considering refusal to bargain or negotiate. Finally, if contracting meets the criteria of mandatory negotiation, prepare to engage in extensive bargaining. This entails early acknowledgement of the duty to bargain; allowance of ample time for bargaining; notification to unions of the possibility of contracting (thereby initiating the formal bargaining process) no later than the day the agency announces its invitation for bids/solicitation for proposals; avoidance of unnecessary and burdensome time constraints; use of mediation when agreement cannot be reached; and the allowance of some concessions so as to maintain an atmosphere of good faith during the negotiations.

RUNNING A RIF: MANAGING REDUCTIONS IN FORCE

The suggestions for avoiding legal action show that while human resources managers and other officials in government need to consider many of the strategies and procedures described in previous sections, they must do so within a lattice of governmental statutes, laws, and rules that regulate the privatization process and related human resources practices. Knowledge and skill in these matters becomes another important resource that human resources managers need to provide or foster. Managing RIFs provides another good illustration of this point.

As noted earlier, there is not much evidence that privatization displaces a great number of public employees, but it still does raise the possibility that a government entity will have to carry out a RIF. Substantial literature offers advice on managing the sensitive issues involved in "downsizing" or reducing employment in organizations of all types, through steps such as those described earlier in the discussion of dealing with employee resistance to privatization, such as finding new jobs for displaced employees. Governmental human resources managers, however, have to consider how to apply this advice within the context of governmental personnel systems.

Concerning the management of a RIF, for example, at the federal level the United States Office of Personnel Management (OPM) regulates the RIF process in accordance with Title 5 of the United States Code. The law designates a complicated process that agencies must follow in carrying out a RIF. It requires, for example, that when there are more than fifty government employees involved, the agency must get the approval of Congress before beginning the process. The law also requires that agencies base decisions about which employees must leave or be moved to lower positions on factors such as the employee's type of appointment, status as a military veteran (veteran's preference), length of service, and performance ratings. Agencies thus have to do careful analysis and planning of who the RIF will affect and how. These days, the RIF plans are usually done with computer software, for which the human resources personnel provide a database on the agency workforce. The computer then identifies the employees that the RIF will affect, and in what way. Obviously, an understanding of this computerized process and of details involved, such as the nature of veteran's preference criteria, becomes important knowledge for human resources management personnel.[1]

Once they have determined the impacts of the RIF, human resources personnel have to send RIF notices to all the employees affected, specifying the implications for them at least sixty days before the RIF takes effects. For example, an employee might be notified that he will be reduced by one grade, or that he will be reassigned to another organization. Sometimes labor agreements provide for longer notice periods and alter other details of how the RIF can be conducted, so human resources personnel have to be aware of the pertinent labor agreements and their legal requirements.

Since the RIF might involve voluntary separations or early retirements, human resources personnel at the federal level need familiarity with two incentive programs that Congress has created, the Voluntary Separation Incentive Pay (VSIP) and Voluntary Early Retirement Authority (VERA).[2] Personnel who are separated under the RIF may receive benefits under one of these programs, including pay for accrued leave time and lump sum amounts that take into consideration the employee's length of service, age, and other factors. All these procedures and calculations need to be handled accurately and properly.

Indeed, all the steps and procedures described here must be managed accurately and properly, because after the RIF is complete, all affected employees have various rights to grieve or appeal under either local labor agreements or under the auspices of the Merit System Protection Board. Thus, the running of a RIF serves to illustrate the various forms of expertise that privatization may require of governmental managers and personnel.

OUTSOURCING THE HUMAN RESOURCES FUNCTION

While expertise on the part of governmental personnel remains essential, one of the important recent developments in the area of human resources management has been the practice of outsourcing all or part of the human resources function. Private firms, which have customarily performed the human resources function internally, are now increasingly turning to external providers to perform human resources activities in an effort to reduce costs and gain access to specialized knowledge and skills (Greer, Youngblood, and Gray, 1999; Sunno and Laabs, 1994; Csosko, 1995, as cited in Klaas, et al, 1999). Growing evidence also points to a significant incidence of this sort of outsourcing of the human resources function in the public sector. An International City Management Association (1989) survey of larger cities and counties conducted in 1988 found that approximately 8 percent of the respondents contracted out for personnel services. About ten years later, a similar survey of the 100 largest cities in America found that approximately 24 percent of the respondents reported contracting out for employment and training activities (Dilger, et al., 1997, p. 22). Finally, a study of 22 federal agencies by the National Academy of Public Administration (NAPA, 1996; see also U. S. General Accounting Office, 1998) found that more than half outsource one or more human resources functions, most often with franchise programs (i.e., federal agency administrative offices, which operate on a self-sustaining reimbursable basis by offering services to other public agencies). This and other evidence has prompted one author to characterize the outsourcing of the human resources function as "a trend that is more than transitory" (Siegel, 1999, p. 226; see also Lawther, 2003).

Public agencies have at their disposal various types of alternative service providers with which to contract for one or more human resources functions. These include private firms specializing in human resources services; central human resources offices from neighboring agencies or units of government; intergovernmental consortia that market their services to personnel departments in other agencies; and public employee-owned enterprises such as Employee Stock Ownership Plans (ESOPs). The alternatives also include federal franchise programs like the U.S. Department of Treasury's Center for Applied Financial Management and the Office of Personnel Management's Personnel Resources and Development Center, which were set up to provide human resources services to other public agencies.

According to Siegel (2000), except for outsourcing of training and development functions, governments tend to outsource human resources functions peripheral to core human resources management (i.e., drug-testing, health and benefits administration, or information systems operations), while private firms are more likely to outsource most human resources functions (p. 228). Other studies have identified training (Shafritz, et al., 2001) and employee assistance programs (Lawther, 2003) as areas that have experienced significant growth in outsourcing. A NAPA (1997) study identified human resources functions that are not inherently governmental, and for which competitive bidding is possible, as potential candidates for outsourcing. These functions include administrative and technical functions, employee development, staffing and classification, affirmative employment and diversity programs, employee and labor relations functions, human resources development, career transition services, employee assistance programs, organizational development services, management consulting functions, payroll processing, benefits administration, and health and safety services (pp. 29–35).

Why would a public agency consider outsourcing all or part of its human resources function? Outsourcing such functions offers public agencies several potential advantages over in-house provision. By contracting with larger firms that specialize in particular functions or services, a public agency may be able to take advantage of economies of scale to reduce the cost of service provision. Outsourcing can free up existing human resources staff, allowing them to focus on core competencies and play a more strategic role within the agency. Outsourcing may also enable an agency to procure services of higher quality from leading human resources providers. Finally, contracting out with external providers can enable an agency to procure specialized knowledge and skills not immediately available from within the agency. Dilger et al.'s (1997) survey of America's largest cities found that among the 16 cities contracting out for one or more human resources functions, 9 reported being satisfied to some extent with the services received and 7 were neither satisfied nor dissatisfied (p. 23). Beyond this study, however, little empirical evidence is available from the public sector on whether these potential advantages from outsourcing actually materialize in practice.

Outsourcing the human resources function is no panacea or "magic bullet" (NAPA, 1997; Siegel, 2000), for it requires effective management on the part of public managers and raises the sorts of challenges described earlier in this chapter. For example, contracting out requires that a public agency retain sufficient in-house knowledge and resources to effectively monitor the performance of human resources contractors, and to ensure that the contract be designed with performance measures and incentives that encourage the contractor to behave in the best interest of the agency. Government officials also have to face the problem that contracting out the human resources function may result in loss of control over vital organizational functions such as recruitment, staffing, and training. In summary, successful outsourcing of human resources functions requires the sorts of knowledge and skills that this chapter has prescribed for the management of privatization in general.

NOTES

1. Veteran's preference can reduce managers' flexibility in retaining workforce members during a RIF (Cayer, 1995, p. 291). OPM regulations, based on the Veterans' Preference Act of 1944, require that veterans receive additional "points" for time served in the

military during specific timeframes, for disabilities of more than 30 percent, and for service during a campaign or expedition when a campaign medal was authorized. Veterans are often male and veteran's preference can therefore influence the number of males and females retained during a RIF. It can thus have an impact on the equal opportunity posture of an agency undergoing a RIF.
2. Under the VSIP, the Government pays an employee a lump sum to leave civil service, up to a maximum award of $25,000, based on average pay, years of service, age, and similar variables. Employees who choose the VERA incentive have the option of retiring before they have reached the age or length of service normally required for full retirement, although with a 2 percent penalty for every year short of the retirement age.

REFERENCES

Armenakis, A. A., Harris, S. G., and Field, H. S., 2001. "Paradigms in Organizational Change: Change Agent and Change Target Perspectives." In R. T. Golembiewski, ed., *Handbook of Organizational Behavior*. New York, NY: Marcel Dekker, Inc.

Auger, D. A. 1999. "Privatization, Contracting, and the States: Lessons from State Government Experience." *Public Productivity and Management Review* 22, 435–454.

Averch, H. 1990. *Private Markets and Public Intervention: A Primer for Policy Designers*. Pittsburgh, PA: University of Pittsburgh Press.

Avery, G. 2000. "Outsourcing Public Health Laboratory Services: A Blueprint for Determining Whether to Privatize and How." *Public Administration Review* 60: 330–337.

Barnekov, T. K. and Raffel, J. A. 1990. "Public Management and Privatization." *Public Productivity and Management Review* 14: 35–52.

Becker, F. W., Silverstein, G., and Chaykin, L. 1995. "Public Employee Job Security and Benefits: A Barrier to Privatization of Mental Health Services." *Public Productivity and Management Review* 19: 25–33.

Boyne, G. A. 1998. "The Determinants of Variations in Local Service Contracting: Garbage In, Garbage Out?" *Urban Affairs Review* 34, 149–162.

Brudney, J. L., Fernandez, S., Ryu, J. E., and Wright, D. S. 2005. "Exploring and Explaining Contracting Out: Patterns Among the American States." *Journal of Public Administration Research and Theory*. 15.

Bruhn, J. G., Zajac, G., and Al-Kazemi, A. A. 2001. "Ethical Perspectives on Employee Participation in Planned Organizational Change: A Survey of Two State Public Welfare Agencies." *Public Performance and Management Review* 25, 208–228.

Bryson, J. M. and Anderson, S. R. 2000. "Applying Large-Group Interaction Methods in the Planning and Implementation of Major Change Efforts." *Public Administration Review* 60, 143–162.

Burke, W. W. 2002. *Organization Change: Theory and Practice*. Thousand Oaks, CA: Sage.

Cayer, N. J. 1995. "Merit System Reform in the States." In Hays, S. and Kearney, R., eds. *Public Personnel Administration: Problems and Prospects*, 3rd ed. Englewood Cliffs, NJ: Prentice-Hall, pp. 291–305.

Chandler, T. and Feuille, P. 1991. "Municipal Unions and Privatization." *Public Administration Review* 51: 15–22.

Chi, K. 1994. *Privatization in State Government: Trends and Issues*. Lexington, KY: The Council of State Governments.

Cooper, P. J. 2002. *Governing by Contract*. Washington, DC: CQ Press.

Csoko, L. S. 1995. *Rethinking Human Resources: A Research Report*. The Conference Board, Report No: 1124–95-RR.

Crawford, J. W. and Krahn, S. L. 1998. "The Demanding Customer and the Hollow State." *Public Productivity and Management Review* 22: 107–118.

Dicke, L. A. and Ott, J. S. 1999. "Public Agency Accountability in Human Services Contracting." *Public Productivity and Management Review* 22: 502–516.

Dilger, R. J., Moffett, R. R., and Struyk, L. 1997. "Privatization of Municipal Services in America's Largest Cities." *Public Administration Review* 57: 21–26.

Donahue, J. D. 1989. *The Privatization Decision: Public Ends, Private Means*. New York, NY: Basic Books.

Downs, A. 1967. *Inside Bureaucracy*. New York, NY: Little, Brown.

Eggers, W. D. and O'Leary, J. 1994. "Overcoming Public Employee Opposition to Privatization." *Business Forum* 19: 16–20.

Elam, L. B. 1997. "Reinventing Government Privatization Style: Avoiding the Pitfalls of Replacing Civil Servants with Contract Providers." *Public Personnel Management* 26: 15–29.

Federal Acquisition Regulation, Subpart 37.101, "Definitions."

Federal Acquisition Regulation, Subpart 37.104, "Personal Service Contracts."

Fernandez, S. and Fabricant, R. 2000. "Methodological Pitfalls in Privatization Research: Two Cases from Florida's Child Support Enforcement Program." *Public Performance and Management Review* 24: 133–144.

Ferris, J. and Graddy, E. 1986. "Contracting Out: For What? With Whom?" *Public Administration Review* 46: 332–344.

Gill, J. M. and Rainey, H. G. 1998. "Public Management, Privatization Theory and Privatization in Georgia State Government." Paper presented at the Annual Meeting of the American Political Science Association, Sept. 3–6, 1998.

Greene, J. D. 2002. *Cities and Privatization: Prospects for the New Century*. Upper Saddle River, NJ: Prentice Hall.

Greer, C. R., Youngblood, S. A., and Gray, D. A. 1999. "Human Resource Management Outsourcing: The Make or Buy Decision." *Academy of Management Executive* 13: 85–97.

Handler, J. 1996. *Down From Bureaucracy: The Ambiguity of Privatization and Empowerment*. Princeton, NJ: Princeton University Press.

Hodge, G. A. 1999. "Competitive Tendering and Contracting Out." *Public Productivity and Management Review* 22: 455–469.

Ingraham, P. W. 1997. "Play It Again, Sam; It's Still Not Right: Searching for the Right Notes in Administrative Reform." *Public Administration Review* 57: 325–331.

International City Management Association. 1989. *Service Delivery in the 90s: Alternative Approaches for Local Government*. Washington, DC.

Jackson, C. Y. 1997. "Strategies for Managing Tensions Between Public Employment and Private Service Delivery." *Public Productivity and Management Review* 21: 119–136.

Judson, A. S. 1991. *Changing Behavior in Organizations: Minimizing Resistance to Change*. Cambridge, MA: Blackwell Business.

Jurkiewicz, C. L. and Bradley, D. B. 2002. "Making Privatization Work: Utilizing a Scorecard Model of Human Resource Strategy." *Public Organization Review* 2: 365–385.

Kamerman, S. B. and Kahn, A. J., eds. 1989. *Privatization and the Welfare State*. Princeton, NJ: Princeton University Press.

Kelman, S. J. 2002. "Contracting." In L. M. Salamon, ed. *The Tools of Government: A Guide to the New Governance*. New York, NY: Oxford University Press.

Kemp, E. J., Funk, E. J., and Eadie, D. C. 1993. "Change in Chewable Bites: Applying Strategic Management at EEOC." *Public Administration Review* 53: 129–134.

Kent, J. 1998. "Elizabeth I and the Limits of Privatization." *Public Administration Review* 21: 59–64.

Kettl, D. 1988. *Government by Proxy.* Washington, DC: Congressional Quarterly.

Kettl, D. 2002. *The Transformation of Governance.* Baltimore, MD: Johns Hopkins University Press.

Kettl, D. F. 1993. *Sharing Power: Public Governance and Private Markets.* Washington, D. C.: Brookings Institution.

Klaas, B. S., McClendon, J., and Gainey, T. W. 1999. "HR Outsourcing and its Impact: The Role of Transaction Costs." *Personnel Psychology,* 52: 113–136.

Kotter, J. P. 1995. "Leading Change: Why Transformation Efforts Fail." *Harvard Business Review* March/April, 59–67.

Lawther, W. C. 2003. "Privatizing Personnel: Outsourcing Public Sector Functions." In Hays, S. W. and Kearney, R. C., eds. *Public Personnel Administration: Problems and Prospects.* Upper Saddle River, NJ: Prentice Hall.

Light, P. C. 1999. *The True Size of Government.* Washington, DC: Brookings Institution Press.

Martin, L. L. 1999. *Contracting for Service Delivery: Local Government Choices.* Washington, DC: International City/County Management Association.

Milward, H. B., Provan, K. G., and Else, B. A. 1993. "What Does the 'Hollow State' Look Like?" In Bozeman, B., ed. *Public Management: State of the Art.* San Francisco, CA: Jossey-Bass.

Moe, R. C. 1987. "Exploring the Limits of Privatization." *Public Administration Review* 47: 453–460.

Moe, R. C. 1994. "The 'Reinventing Government' Exercise: Misinterpreting the Problem, Misjudging the Consequences." *Public Administration Review* 54: 111–120.

Moe, R. C. 1996. "Managing Privatization: A New Challenge to Public Administration." In B. G. Peters and B. A. Rockman, eds., *Agenda for Excellence 2: The Administrative State.* Chatham, NJ: Chatham House, pp. 135–148.

Naff, K. C. 1991. "Labor-management Relations and Privatization: A Federal Perspective." *Public Administration Review* 51: 23–30.

National Academy of Public Administration. 1989. *Privatization: The Challenge to Public Management.* Washington, DC.

National Academy of Public Administration. 1996. *Alternative Administrative Service Delivery: Improving the Efficiency and Effectiveness of Human Resources Services.* Implementing Real Change in Human Resources Management, Phase II: Practical Applications. Washington, DC.

National Academy for Public Administration. 1997. *Alternative Service Delivery: A Viable Strategy for Federal Government Human Resources Management.* Implementing Real Change in Human Resources Management, Phase III: Practical Tools. Washington, DC.

National Commission for Employment Policy. 1988. *Privatization and Public Employees: The Impact of City and County Contracting Out on Government Workers.* A study prepared by Dudek and Company for the National Commission for Employment Policy.

Niskanen, W. A. 1971. *Bureaucracy and Representative Government.* Hawthorne, NY: Aldine de Gruyter.

Pack, J. R. 1987. "Privatization of Public Sector Services in Theory and Practice." *Journal of Policy Analysis and Management* 6: 523–540.

Peters, B. G. 1996. *The Future of Governing.* Lawrence, KS: University of Kansas Press.

Piderit, S. K. 2000. "Rethinking Resistance and Recognizing Ambivalence: A Multidimensional View of Attitudes Toward an Organizational Change." *Academy of Management Review* 25: 783–794.

Prager, J. 1994. "Contracting Out Government Services: Lessons from the Private Sector." *Public Administration Review* 54: 176–184.

Prager, J. and Desai, S. 1996. "Privatizing Local Government Operations: Lessons from Federal Contracting Out Methodology. *Public Productivity and Management Review* 20: 185–203.

Rainey, H. G. 2003. *Understanding and Managing Public Organizations*, 3rd ed. San Francisco, CA: Jossey-Bass.

Rehfuss, J. A. 1989. *Contracting Out in Government*. San Francisco, CA: Jossey-Bass Publishers.

Salamon, L. M. (Ed.) 2002. *The Tools of Government: A Guide to the New Governance*. New York, NY: Oxford University Press.

Savas, E. S. 1987. *Privatization: The Key to Better Government*. Chatham, NJ: Chatham House.

Savas, E. S. 2000. *Privatization and Public-Private Partnerships*. New York, NY: Chatham House.

Sclar, E. D. 2000. *You Don't Always Get What You Pay For: The Economics of Privatization*. Ithaca, NY: Cornell University Press.

Shafritz, J. M., Rosenbloom, D. H., Riccucci, N. M., Naff, K. C., and Hyde, A. C. 2001. *Personnel Management in Government: Politics and Process*, 5th ed. New York, NY: Marcel Dekker.

Shareef, R. 1994. "Subsystem Congruence: A Strategic Change Model for Public Organizations." *Administration and Society* 25: 489–517.

Siegel, G. B. 1999. "Where Are We on Local Government Service Contracting?" *Public Productivity and Management Review* 22: 365–388.

Siegel, G. B. 2000. "Outsourcing Personnel Functions." *Public Personnel Management* 29: 225–235.

Stein, L. 1994. "Privatization, Work-force Cutbacks, and African-American Municipal Employment." *American Review of Public Administration* 24: 181–191.

Sunno, B. P. and Laabs, J. J. 1994. "Winning Strategies for Outsourcing Contracts." *Personnel Journal* 73: 69–76.

Thompson, J. R. and Sanders, R. P. 1997. "Strategies for Reinventing Federal Agencies." *Public Productivity and Management Review* 21: 137–155.

U.S. Code, Title 5, Sections 3501-3503.

U.S. General Accounting Office. 1998. *Management Reform: Agencies' Initial Efforts to Restructure Personnel Operations*. GAO/GGD–98–93. Washington, DC.

Wallin, B. A. 1997. "The Need for a Privatization Process: Lessons from Development and Implementation." *Public Administration Review* 57: 11–20.

Warner, M. and Hebdon, R. 2001. "Local Government Restructuring: Privatization and Its Alternatives." *Journal of Policy Analysis and Management* 20: 315–336.

Chapter 15

Human Resources Management Challenges for Nonprofit Organizations

Joan E. Pynes

Charitable 501 (c) (3) nonprofits are private organizations that serve a public purpose. Because of their nondistribution constraint, they cannot pay dividends on profits to members or other individuals. If for some reason they must dissolve and no longer operate, their remaining assets must be distributed to a nonprofit organization. For those reasons, it is believed that they possess a greater moral authority than for-profit organizations. Nonprofits often perform public tasks that have been delegated to them by the state or perform tasks for which there is a demand that neither government nor for-profit organizations provide. They provide a myriad of services such as helping the disadvantaged, providing medical services, supporting museums and cultural activities, preserving the environment, and funding medical research. Many nonprofits are the recipients of government contracts and grants. Government has some influence on nonprofits through the conditions it may place on agencies that receive public funds, but it can quickly disassociate itself from programs when things go wrong.

Public and nonprofit organizations are similar in many respects. They define themselves according to their missions or the services they offer and they are responsible to multiple stakeholders. Nonprofits are primarily responsible to supporters, sponsors, clients, interest groups, and government sources that provide funding and impose regulations, while public agencies are primarily responsible to their respective legislative and judicial branches, to taxpayers, interest groups, cognate agencies, political appointees, clients, the media, and other levels of government.

There are, however, some interesting differences between public and nonprofit organizations in regard to issues that may influence human resources management practices. This chapter will discuss some important differences in HRM for nonprofits; the rights of nonprofits given their status as voluntary associations, permission to discriminate on the basis of religion, the rights and responsibilities of nonprofit organizations in the management of volunteers, and collective bargaining and labor relations.

THE VOLUNTARY AND LOCAL NATURE OF NONPROFIT ORGANIZATIONS

Nonprofits are often referred to as voluntary organizations because they receive much of their financial support from private contributions and depend on volunteers to contribute their time and energies to serve charitable purposes. Because of their voluntary nature, which is reinforced by the First Amendment's protection of the freedom of association, nonprofits were often considered exempt from the application of nondiscrimination laws. The behavior and activities of voluntary associations were considered to fall within the sphere of private activity (Rosenblum, 1998, p. 161).

This changed in 1984, when the United States Supreme Court ruled in *Roberts v. United States Jaycees* that local chapters of the Jaycees could admit women. The local St. Paul and Minneapolis chapters of the Jaycees sued their national organization. The national Jaycees had threatened to revoke the local charters because the local chapters had voted to admit women, a violation of the national organization's bylaws. The national Jaycees claimed that requiring them to admit women as regular members violated its organization's constitutionally protected freedom of association. By ruling in favor of the local chapters, the United States Supreme Court expanded the scope of a "public accommodation" to include voluntary associations like the Jaycees and limited their freedom of association when in conflict with the state's compelling interest to eradicate discrimination (*Roberts v. United States Jaycees*, 1984).

Examples of public accommodations include, but are not limited to, hotels, restaurants, shops, hospitals, theaters, libraries, camps, swimming pools, meeting places, amusement and recreation parks, colleges, and universities. Three specific exemptions to public accommodations in most nondiscrimination laws are organizations that are "distinctly private," a religious institution or "an educational facility operated and maintained by a bona fide religious or sectarian institution," or the right of a natural parent, or the *in loco parentis* exception (in the place of a parent; acting as a parent with respect to the care and supervision of a child).

An organization's "expressive rights of association" refer to the right to associate for the purpose of engaging in those activities protected by the First Amendment: the right to speech, assembly, petition for the redress of grievances, and the exercise of religion. Any government intervention to regulate an organization's internal operations, such as membership or personnel policies, must be balanced against the organization's expressive rights of association. Nondiscrimination laws that force organizations to accept members whom they may not desire violate an organization's freedom of expressive association if the organization can demonstrate that these new members would affect in a significant way the group's ability to carry out its mission and express its private viewpoints (*Board of Directors of Rotary International v. Rotary Club*, 1987; *Hurley v. Irish-American Gay Group of Boston*, 1995; *New York State Club Association v. City of New York*, 1988).

Another important characteristic of nonprofit organizations is their local orientation. Most social service agencies, schools, libraries, hospitals, museums, theaters, advocacy groups, foundations, clubs, and other common types of nonprofit organizations focus primarily on local constituencies and local issues. Even nonprofits linked with national organizations such as the American Red Cross are coordinated and run through local chapters with substantial local discretion. They raise and spend most of their money and employ most of their staff and volunteers through the local chapters (Oster, 1992; Young, 1989, p. 103).

Because of their local orientation, nonprofit managers must walk a thin line when defining and defending their membership and personnel policies. The complex environment that nonprofit administrators must operate in became exacerbated when the U. S. Supreme Court in a 5–4 decision held that the application of New Jersey's public accommodation law to the Boy Scouts violated its First Amendment right of expressive association (*Boy Scouts of America v. Dale*, 2000). The Boy Scouts argued successfully that, as a private organization, it has the right to determine criteria for membership. The Supreme Court heard this case on appeal from the Boy Scouts of America in response to the New Jersey Supreme Court's decision against its position.

The New Jersey Supreme Court held that the Boy Scouts of America is a place of "public accommodation" that "emphasizes open membership" and therefore must follow New Jersey's anti-discrimination law. The court further held that the state's law did not infringe upon the group's freedom of expressive association (*Dale v. Boy Scouts of America and Monmouth Council Boy Scouts*, 1999). The court reasoned that the New Jersey legislature, when it enacted the anti-discrimination law, declared that discrimination is a matter of concern to the government, and that infringements on that right may be justified by regulations adopted to serve compelling state interests.

The New Jersey Supreme Court noted the BSA's historic partnership with various public entities and public-service organizations. Local BSA units are chartered by public schools, parent-teacher associations, firehouses, local civic associations, and the United States Army, Navy, Air Force, and National Guard. The BSA's "learning for life" program has been installed in many public school classrooms throughout the country. Many troops meet in public facilities. The BSA in turn provides essential services through its Scouts to the public and quasi-public organizations. This close relationship underscores the BSA's fundamental public character.

Nonprofit administrators must stay current with the changing and sometimes contradictory community norms and legal requirements across a diverse set of local communities and reconcile them with mandates from the national/parent organization. This is especially true for sexual orientation discrimination. When confronted with sexual orientation discrimination, nonprofit managers find themselves in a complex legal environment. No federal legislation has been passed defining a national standard; thus, nonprofit managers face a patchwork of state and local laws, executive orders, and judicial and commission decisions barring such discrimination. The organizations that have withdrawn their support from the Boy Scouts have clearly stated that they cannot fund or support organizations that have policies that conflict with their own anti-discrimination policies. Despite the U. S. Supreme Court's ruling supporting the Boy Scouts of America's exclusionary policy, the stand of the Boy Scouts' National Council to refuse local councils to determine local policy has jeopardized their funding and support from *their* local communities.

The New Jersey Supreme Court's analysis of the public nature of the Boy Scouts is shared by many. The Boy Scouts of America's decision to exclude homosexuals has become controversial. The State of Connecticut dropped the Boy Scouts from the list of charities that receive donations through a state employer payroll-deduction plan. The Boy Scouts sued the state, saying that the ban was unconstitutional. The Scouts lost in two federal court decision and the U.S. Supreme Court declined to hear the case letting the lower court rulings stand (*Boy Scouts of America v. Wyman*, 2003, 2004). The state is also considering whether to block the Scouts from using public campgrounds or buildings. Fifty-three local United Way offices have revoked their funding of the Boy Scouts until the BSA rescinds its policy of discrimination against gays and atheists. Many school districts across the country restricted access to their schools for meetings and events, prompting the passage of The Boy Scouts of America Equal Access Act, 20 U. S. C. § 7905 (2003). The Act prevents public schools and local educational agencies that receive federal funds from denying equal access and fair opportunity to meet, or from discriminating against groups officially affiliated with the Boy Scouts of America or any other youth group listed in Title 36 of the Untied States Code as a patriotic society for reasons based on the membership or leadership criteria or oath of allegiance to God and country.

While the Act no longer permits school districts to have the right to restrict access by the Boy Scouts to their facilities (without jeopardizing federal funds), private corporations such as Levi Strauss and Company, J. P. Morgan, American Airlines, Wells Fargo of Portland Oregon, Hewlett Packard, The Providence Journal, IBM, Textron, and CVS Pharmacy have withdrawn hundreds of thousands of dollars in support to the Boy Scouts.

The City of San Diego agreed to pay nearly $950,000 to settle a lawsuit with the American Civil Liberties Union over land it leases to the Boy Scouts for a nominal charge and will ask a federal judge to void the lease. The ACLU contends the Scouts should be evicted from the parks because the organization discriminates on the grounds of sexual orientation and religion. The Boy Scouts refuse to let atheists and agnostics be members or leaders of the Boy Scouts believing that one must believe in God to maintain a high standard of morality and ethics. Decisions dating back to 1992 have held that the Boy Scouts are not a public accommodation or business establishment and fall within the private club exception (*Welsh v. Boy Scouts of America*, 1992, 1993; *Seabourn v. Coronadao Area Council*, 1995; *Randall v. Orange County Council, Boy Scouts of America*, 1998).

On November 15, 2004, the Defense Department agreed to end the direct sponsorship of Boy Scout Troops in response to a religious discrimination lawsuit brought by the ACLU. The ACLU of Illinois charged that the Boy Scouts of America required troops and pack leaders, and in this case government employees, to compel youth to swear an oath of duty to God. The ACLU charged that the Boy Scouts' policy violates the religious liberty of youth who wish to participate but do not wish to swear a religious oath and that direct government sponsorship of such a program is religious discrimination. The settlement does not prohibit off-duty public employees from sponsoring Boy Scout troops on their own time and the Boy Scouts will still have access to any military facilities that are currently made available to other nongovernmental organizations.

What does this mean? The U. S. Supreme Court upheld the right of voluntary associations to discriminate in regard to their employees and volunteers. The most appropriate policy however, is for national nonprofit organizations to permit local chapters, sensitive to their community norms, to formulate their own nondiscriminatory policies. Other nonprofits such as the Girl Scouts of America have deferred to the norms of each local community and let each troop decide how to handle this potentially divisive issue. The issue of local values is becoming more pronounced in the nonprofit sector. Just a few years ago, local United Ways were concerned over the increasing centralization of the United Way of America governance structure, precipitating the early resignation of the president.

LAWS THAT ADDRESS RELIGIOUS DISCRIMINATION

TITLE VII OF THE CIVIL RIGHTS ACT OF 1964

Most of us are aware that Title VII of the Civil Rights Act of 1964 forbids any employer to fail to hire, to discharge, to classify employees, or to discriminate with respect to compensation, terms, conditions, or privileges of employment in any way that would deprive any individual of employment opportunity due to race, color, religion, sex, or national origin. However, there are exemptions to Title VII that specifically state employers may discriminate on the basis of sex, religion, or national origin if the characteristic can be justified as a "bona fide occupational qualification (BFOQ) reasonably necessary to the normal operation of the particular enterprise" (Title VII Sec. 703e).

Nonprofit organizations that provide secular services but that are affiliated with and governed by religious institutions are exempt from the law under Section 702 of the Civil Rights Act of 1964, which states: "This title shall not apply to an employer with respect to the employment of aliens outside any State, or to a religious corporation, association, educational institution, or society with respect to the employment of individuals of a particular religion to perform work connected with the carrying on by such corporation, association, educational institution, or society of its activities (as amended by P.L.92–261, eff. March 24, 1972).

Section 702 of Title VII permits religious societies to grant hiring preferences in favor of members of their religion. It states: "this title shall not apply to an employer with respect to the employment of aliens outside any State or to *a religious corporation, association, educational institution, or society with respect to the employment of individuals of a particular religion to perform work connected with the carrying on by such corporation, association, educational institution, or society of its activities* (as amended by P. L. 92–261, eff. March 24, 1972).

Section 703(e)(1), (2) provides exemptions for educational institutions to hire employees of a particular religion if the institution is owned, controlled, or managed by a particular religious society. The exemption is broad and is not restricted to the religious activities of the institution.

In *Mormon Church v. Amos* (1987) the Supreme Court upheld the right of the Mormon Church to terminate a building engineer who had worked at its nonprofit gymnasium for 16 years, because he failed to maintain his qualification for church membership. The Court claimed that the decision to terminate was based on religion by the religious organization and thus exempted from the Title VII prohibition against religious discrimination. The Section 703(e)(2) exemption is broad and is not limited to the religious activities of the institution.

Although the language of Title VII allows religious or faith-based organizations to discriminate on religious grounds only, courts have interpreted the religious exemptions to Title VII more broadly and have allowed religious organizations and affiliated nonprofits to discriminate against applicants or employees not only on the basis of religion or religious beliefs but in regard to gender, and conduct that is inconsistent with the tenets and teachings of the religious institution.

The courts have also read a "ministerial exception" into Title VII under the Free Exercise Clause that allows religious organizations to discriminate on gender, race, and age. For example, a female officer took the Salvation Army to court after she was discharged for complaining that she received less compensation than did male officers of equal rank (*McClure v. Salvation Army*, 1972). The U. S. Court of Appeals for the Fifth Circuit ruled that the Salvation Army was a religious organization and that Congress did not intend for Title VII to regulate the employment relationship between a church and its minister. The employment of ministers was not subject to gender discrimination suits under the Civil Rights Act, even though the statute itself contained no such exemption.

In a recent case concerning the Salvation Army, for four years, Wendy and her husband Gary Spearin served as officers in the Salvation Army. Officers are sent through a two-year training program preparing them to manage a Salvation Army center anywhere in the United States. Married couples are graded individually and graduate separately as individual officers. Allowances are paid to both single men and single women; however, once a woman becomes married she loses her individual pay and becomes listed as a spouse for income tax purposes. Salaries are given to the husband only. The Spearins received a joint salary that was paid bi-weekly to Mr. Spearin. As a result, Wendy Spearin has no official tax records of her employment and upon reaching retirement, she will not be eligible to receive the Social Security benefits that she would have accrued had she received a salary in her own name. Nor does she have any reported income for tax or credit purposes. Mrs. Spearin filed a sex discrimination claim with the EEOC, charging that the Salvation Army's pay policy violates Title VII of the 1964 Civil Rights Act. The Salvation Army responded that Mrs. Spearin was an ordained minister at the charity, which is a religious organization. Therefore, it is exempt from Title VII in regard to how it compensates its ministers. In addition, Salvation Army officers typically view their work as voluntary service for which they receive an allowance (Williams, 2000, p. 26). The Salvation Army says its behavior is consistent with the law, because Mrs. Spearin was an ordained minister at the charity. Mrs. Spearin claims that the duties she performed were administrative and not spiritual, and that the decision to discriminate was a business decision, not a religious one.

Additionally, religious organizations have been permitted to refuse to hire or to dismiss employees on the basis of the applicant's or employee's marital status (e.g., seeking an annulment as in *Little v. Wuerl*, 1991), sexual behavior (e.g., adultery as in *Gosche v. Calvert High School*, 1998), sexual orientation (*Hall v. Baptist Memorial Healthcare Corp.*, 2000), or beliefs that are supportive of abortion rights (*Maguire v. Marquette University*, 1987), race (*Young v. Northern Illinois Conference of United Methodist Church*, 1994) and age (*Sanchez v. Catholic Foreign Society of America*, 1999). Courts have expanded the definition of clergy to include lay employees of religious institutions whose primary duties consist of teaching, spreading the faith, governance, supervision of a religious order, or supervision or participation in religious ritual and worship.

Pedreira v. Kentucky Baptist Homes for Children (2001) was a federal district court case that addressed the personnel policies of a religiously-affiliated nonprofit organization that provides government-funded social services. Americans United for the Separation of Church and State and the American Civil Liberties Union filed a lawsuit in the Federal District Court in Kentucky against the Kentucky Baptist Homes for Children (KBHC) alleging religious discrimination in violation of Title VII of the Civil Rights Act of 1964, and the Kentucky Civil Rights Act for terminating Alicia Pedreira who was identified as a lesbian, and on behalf of Karen Vance, who, as a lesbian, felt deprived of the opportunity to apply for work at KBHC because its policy against hiring homosexuals was well known. The U.S. District Judge ruled that KBHC was not guilty of religious discrimination when it fired Pedreira, nor because its hiring policy discouraged Vance from applying for work. The judge found that any discrimination practiced against Pedreira was due to her sexual orientation, not her religion, and rejected the argument that because her dismissal was motivated by KBHC's religious tenets, it constituted discrimination on the basis of religion. KBHC did not, the judge noted, establish any religious tests for its employees, nor are they required to attend religious services or be members or believers in any particular religion or religious group. The decision stated that Title IIV "does nor forbid an employer from having a religious motivation" for discharging somebody because of some other trait or conduct not covered under the law. "While KBHC seeks to employ only persons who adhere to a behavioral code consistent with KBHC's religious mission, the absence of religious requirements leaves their focus on behavior, not religion. KBHC imposes upon its employees a code of conduct which requires consistency with KBHC's religious beliefs, but not the beliefs themselves; the civil rights statute protects religious freedoms, not personal lifestyle choices" (*Pedreira v. Kentucky Baptist Homes for Children*, 2001, pp. 4–5).

CHARITABLE CHOICE AND THE PERSONAL RESPONSIBILITY AND WORK OPPORTUNITY RECONCILIATION ACT OF 1996 (PRWORA)

The Personal Responsibility and Work Opportunity Reconciliation Act of 1996 (PRWORA) was passed to "reform welfare as we know it." *Charitable choice* was passed as part of the Act. States could enter into funding relationships with any faith-based institution to provide social services using federal TANF (Temporary Assistance for Needy Families) dollars. *Charitable choice* permits religious organizations or faith-based organizations to receive federal funds for use in providing social services to their communities. As recipients of federal funds they still retain their autonomy as independent organizations, while remaining in control of their religious mission and their organizational structure and governance. Faith-based organizations have a right to display religious art, scripture, and icons, and retain their right to use religious criteria in hiring, firing, and disciplining employees. However, none of the funds received to provide services may be "expended for sectarian worship, instruction, or proselytization." Like their secular counterparts, faith-based service providers are subject to financial audits for the funds received under government grants and contracts. Under charitable choice, clients are given the right to choose among religious and nonreligious providers and cannot be refused services on the basis of their religion, religious beliefs, or religious practices. Charitable choice explicitly prohibits participating faith-based organizations from denying services to people on the basis of religion, a religious belief, or refusal to actively participate in a religious practice. Clients who feel they are discriminated against can bring civil suits against providers (De Vita, 1999).

Congress passed additional legislation involving charitable-choice provisions, including the Welfare-to-Work program (1997); the Community Services Block Grant program funded by the Health and Human Services Reauthorization Act (1998); and drug treatment programs funded by the Substance Abuse and Mental Health Services Administration (SAMHSA) (2000).

Public monies are allocated in a variety of ways. TANF funds are provided through block grants that are distributed in lump sums to states, who can choose to administer the funds at the state or local levels or at both levels. For CSBG programs, the states are required to pass through at least 90 percent of their federal block grant allotments to primarily community action agencies to provide services directly or subcontract them out. Substance Abuse Prevention and Treatment (SAPT) funds are block grants distributed to states, which have broad discretion on how they distribute the funds, as long as the funds are passed on to a public or nonprofit entity. Welfare-to-Work has two funding streams; 75 percent of WTW funds are distributed to states through formula grants to pass on to local work-force boards though sub-grants. The remaining 25 percent of WTW funds are des-ignated for competitive grants, which are distributed at the federal level by the Department of Labor directly to local applicants. Because federal funds are dis-bursed at multiple levels and to a variety of contractors it is difficult to track the pervasiveness of faith-based services (GAO, 2002; Montiel, Keyes-Williams, and Scott, 2002).

FAITH-BASED INITIATIVES

To further expand the use of religious organizations and religious affiliated non-profits in the delivery of public services, President George W. Bush signed five executive orders requiring executive branch agencies to identify and remove bar-riers that served as a deterrent to faith-based organizations in participating in executive agency programs. These executive orders are referred to as *faith-based initiatives.* He first signed Executive Orders 13198 and 13199 in January 2001, fol-lowed by Executive Orders 13279 and 13280 in December 2002, and Executive Order 13342 was signed in June 2004 requiring executive branch agencies to *eliminate regulatory, contracting, and other programmatic obstacles to the participation of faith-based and other community organizations in the provision of social services.* The executive orders established the White House Office of Faith-Based and Commu-nity Initiatives, as well as offices in the departments of Agriculture, Commerce, Education, Health and Human Services, Housing and Urban Development, Jus-tice, Labor, and Veterans Affairs, the Agency for International Development, and the Small Business Administration (White House, 2001). The initiatives have also been promoted in the Corporation for National and Community Service and other government offices overseeing programs ranging from home ownership and busi-ness development to energy conservation (Farris, Nathan, and Wright, 2004).

While the faith-based initiatives address a number of issues, in the context of human resources management the executive orders now allow federally-funded religious or faith-based organizations to consider religion in the selection of employees whether the jobs to be performed are sectarian or not. While faith-based service providers are permitted to require applicants to be a member of a particular denomination in hiring personnel, they are still prohibited from dis-criminating on the basis of race, gender, disability, or national origin.

While Catholic Charities, Lutheran Social Services, United Hebrew Charities, the Salvation Army, and other religious-affiliated nonprofits have received signifi-cant government grants and contracts dating back to the 1800s to provide services to the needy (De Vita, 1999), Chaves (2002) notes that what is significant about charitable choice and faith-based initiatives is the encouragement of government funding of congregations, whose primary purpose is to provide religions to their members, not social services to their clients (p. 288).

Why should the compensation practices of the Salvation Army and other sec-tarian nonprofits be of concern to public administrators? One needs to question if a greater influence of religious institutions in the provision of social/human/educational services will disadvantage women. As it now stands, women significantly contribute to their families' income, despite weekly earnings of only 80 percent of what men are paid (U. S. Department of Labor, Bureau of Labor Statistics, 2004). The nonprofit sector has always been a predominantly female workforce. In 1998, 71 percent of employees in the nonprofit sector were female (Weitzman, Jalandoni, Lampkin, and Pollak, 2002). One needs to question whether the increased participation of religious organizations in the provision of social or educational services will further depress the salaries of women working in the nonprofit sector (Steinberg and Jacobs, 1994), as well as attempt to restrict certain employer-provided benefits they are entitled to.

The California Supreme Court ruled earlier this year that Catholic Charities must offer birth control coverage to its employees. This ruling is consistent with 20 states that have concluded that private employee prescription plans without contraception benefits discriminated against women (Elias, 2004). In addition to concerns about salary and benefits, what might happen if the practices of some faith-based organizations diminish the role of women and their contributions to society or choose to neglect certain social problems like domestic violence, homelessness, and services to individuals with HIV and AIDS?

Another reason why public administrators should pay attention to the adoption of faith-based initiatives is the increase in litigation that often accompanies their introduction. The Wisconsin-based Freedom from Religion Foundation has brought a lawsuit claiming that faith-based initiatives favor religious groups over secular ones, violating the First Amendment, and a lawsuit has been filed in the U.S. District Court, Southern District of New York alleging that the Salvation Army has unlawfully discriminated on the basis of religion with respect to its professional employees working in child welfare services funded by New York State and New York City. The plaintiffs charge that the Army's New York division tried to force them to sign forms revealing the churches they had attended over the past ten years, naming their ministers, and agreeing to the Army's mission "to preach the Gospel of Jesus Christ." The employees felt forced to violate their professional obligations and codes of ethics. For example, the children assigned to receive foster care and other social services include sexually active teenagers who are at risk for HIV, sexually transmitted infections, and unintended pregnancy. However, the Salvation Army condemns nonmarital sexual relations, contraceptive use outside of marriage, homosexuality, and abortion (*Lown v. The Salvation Army, Inc.; Commission, New York City Administration for Children Services and Others,* 2004).

Nonprofit organizations have been at the forefront of many HRM issues such as developing fair employment policies, the hiring and promotion of women and minorities, and providing domestic partnership benefits to their employees. What might be the societal implications for services for disenfranchised groups if secular nonprofits lose out on public monies to provide services to faith-based organizations?

MANAGING VOLUNTEERS

There is a tradition of volunteerism in this country that began with religious-affiliated organizations and local government councils. Today a wide range of non-profit organizations provide a variety of volunteer opportunities ranging from serving as board members of nonprofit organizations to serving on local government boards and commissions. Volunteers are used to assist employees in meeting their agency's mission, and thus become an important part of strategic human resources management and planning. In 1998 about 5.7 million individuals or 62 percent of all volunteers worked in the independent sector. Volunteer employment contributed over $200 billion in unpaid human resources to the economy (Weitzman, Jalandoni, Lampkin, and Pollak, 2002, p. 19). The increase in volunteer activities has necessitated the increasing professionalism of volunteer administration. Organizations such as the National Volunteers Center, the National Information Center on Voluntarism, the National Center for Voluntary Action Center, and the Minnesota Office on Volunteer Services provide books, pamphlets, training materials, and videos targeting the recruitment and management of volunteers. These agencies also provide training related to the recruitment and use of volunteers.

Recruiting volunteers can be difficult as there has been an increase in competition among public and nonprofit agencies for volunteer talent. Contributing to the difficulty in recruiting volunteers is the nature of today's society. The United States ranks among the highest on a global scale in the percent of employees working fifty hours per week or more. Many workers are finding it difficult to balance job and family demands (Jacobs and Gerson, 1998) without adding volunteer work. Many Americans believe that the time pressures on working families are getting worse (National Partnership for Women and Families, 1998). The increased pressure on working adults with families has forced many nonprofits like the Girl Scouts to target new audiences for recruiting volunteers. One poster to recruit Girl Scout troop leaders shows a girl with green hair and fingernails, and another poster shows a girl sporting a tattoo of the Girl Scout trefoil on her back. The message "Sure we wear green. But a lot else has changed." The posters are designed to attract young single volunteers in their 20s and 30s, not the stay-at-home moms who anchored the volunteers corps since its inception (Wyatt, 2000). As a result of the many economic and demographic changes affecting communities, some Girl Scout Councils wanting to provide services in rural and urban communities and unable to recruit volunteers, have begun to pay "program specialists" (Davis, 2001, pp. 1B, 7B).

Other nonprofits are rethinking the assignments they give to volunteers in terms of time, location, and length of commitment. Many communities have established volunteer banks where volunteers can be assigned to projects that do not require a long-term commitment to the agency or require volunteers to work scheduled hours each week.

Ellis (2002) discusses the possibilities of using the agency's website to recruit volunteers. Visitors to an agency's website should be able to find information regarding volunteer opportunities, and be given the name, telephone number, or email address of a person to contact about volunteering. Other nonprofits are using online or Internet volunteering as a way to fit volunteering into their busy and sometimes unpredictable schedules. iMentor is a nonprofit that encourages volunteers to exchange emails with New York high-school students. Volunteers and students exchange email messages several times a week on topics such as career development and college applications. Best Buddies is a Miami nonprofit that matches online volunteers with people with mental retardation. Volunteers make a one-year commitment to exchange email messages at least once a week with their e-Buddies. The email exchanges encourage participants to develop computer skills and helps to ease some of the social isolation they might be experiencing (Wallace, 2001).

The research on why individuals volunteer indicates that both intrinsic and extrinsic rewards motivate them. Intrinsic rewards include satisfaction, a sense of accomplishment, and being challenged, which results from the work itself. Extrinsic rewards are benefits granted to the volunteers by the organization. Many individuals use volunteering as a means for career exploration, others to develop skills that may enhance their paid positions. Some people volunteer because it provides them with the opportunity to meet new people. Some volunteer as a way to contribute and give back to the community. Others volunteer because they value the goals of the agency, and still others volunteer because they desire personal growth or external recognition.

There is no one reason that individuals volunteer. Therefore, the volunteer experience should attempt to provide satisfying and interesting opportunities and some form of external recognition. Nonprofit agencies need to recognize the different needs of volunteers and be flexible in developing volunteer assignments and working hours.

Attention should be paid to the recruitment, selection, training, evaluation, and management of volunteers. While volunteers can be tremendous assets to any organization, they also present new human resources management challenges. Administrative responsibilities are increased as agencies must keep records and extend their liability insurance and worker's compensation policies to volunteers. Managing volunteer programs requires the development of personnel policies and procedures to assist with the integration of volunteers into the everyday operations of the agency. Paid staff, unions, and board members need to support the use of volunteers; oversight needs to be provided so that volunteers are properly utilized; and strategies need to be developed to motivate and retain volunteers.

One group of very important volunteers in nonprofit organizations is the governing board, often referred to as the board of directors or board of trustees. The governing board is responsible for developing policies relating to the nonprofit's management. It is the responsibility of the board of directors to make sure that the public purpose of the nonprofit organization is implemented. Some of the basic responsibilities of nonprofit boards include the following: determining agency mission and purposes, selecting the executive director and evaluating her/his performance, participating in strategic and long-range planning, establishing fiscal policy and oversight, monitoring the agency's programs and services, promoting the agency in the community, and participating in the development of personnel/human resource management policies and strategies. Governing boards should not be involved in the day-to-day activities of the nonprofit, but instead develop policies to guide the agency and provide oversight to ensure that it is fulfilling its public purpose. Because of the variety of knowledge and skills needed by nonprofit boards, agencies must make an effort to recruit board members who can assist the organization. The recruitment strategy includes seeking board members with diverse backgrounds and professional expertise. Nonprofit boards should be sensitive to the community and organizations they are serving. When possible, there should be a distribution of ages, gender, color, and representatives of the constituency being served by the organization. Expertise is needed in the following areas: personnel/HRM, finance, law, fundraising, and public relations.

Volunteers are critical to the success of most nonprofit organizations. Agencies should develop volunteer recruitment strategies to reach individuals whose interests and skills are likely to match the needs of the organization. To facilitate good staffing decisions, key staff should be involved in the development of the job descriptions for the volunteers they will supervise. This information will enable the agency to match the interest and skills of the volunteers with the positions in the organization. For example, a volunteer who wants to interact with other individuals would be unhappy working in isolation. Taking the time to match volunteer interests and skills with the needs of the agency in advance of their placement should help to minimize frequent turnover or absenteeism. The turnover rate and absenteeism of volunteers are some of the greatest challenges facing nonprofit administrators. Volunteers, like employees, should also receive training on how to perform their tasks and on the performance standards of the agency.

LABOR RELATIONS AND COLLECTIVE BARGAINING

Nonprofit labor relations and collective bargaining are governed by the same laws that govern for-profit private-sector labor-management relations. They fall under the provisions of the National Labor Code, which consolidated the National Labor Relations Act of 1935, the Labor-Management Relations Act of 1947, and the Labor-Management Reporting and Disclosure Act of 1959. The National Labor Relations Board (NLRB) is the administrative agency responsible for enforcing the provisions of the laws. Until the 1970s, the NLRB excluded nonprofit employees from coverage. In 1974, Congress amended the National Labor Relations Act to bring nonprofit health care institutions under the law's coverage (P. L. 93–360, 88 Stat.395). The health care amendments indicated that Congress had no objection to bringing nonprofit employers under federal labor law. In 1976, the National Labor Relations Board (NLRB) began to treat nonprofit and charitable institutions in the same way it treats businesses operated for profit. If a nonprofit employer has revenues that exceed certain amounts, then the NLRB can become involved in labor-management disputes. The NLRB has established a table of jurisdictional standards that provides the dollar amounts required for nonprofit organizations to come under its jurisdiction (NLRB, 1997). For example, symphony orchestras fall under the NLRB's jurisdiction if they have gross annual revenues of one million dollars or more. Employers who provide social services come under the NLRB standards if their gross annual revenues are at least $250,000; nursing homes, visiting nurse-associations, and related facilities come under the NLRB standards if their gross annual revenues are at least $100,000.

Unlike federal government employees and some state and local public employees, nonprofit employees are permitted to negotiate over wages. They can also negotiate over hours and working conditions. Also, unlike many public employees, nonprofit employees are permitted to strike. Earlier this year, in New York City home health care aides and child care employees went out on strike, seeking higher wages (Greenhouse, 2004; Kaufman, 2004). As of November 2004, the Chicago Symphony Orchestra, the Philadelphia Orchestra, and the Cleveland Symphony have expired contracts and are threatening to go on strike. Graduate assistants and adjunct faculty at many nonprofit universities have gone out on and/or threatened to go on strike (Arenson, 2004).

The uncertainty of many workplace changes has shaken the confidence of many employees that their jobs are secure and that their wages will remain competitive. Professional employees are the fastest growing group in the labor force, and unionization has been viewed as a mechanism to defend professional autonomy and improve working conditions. Unions have stepped up efforts to organize them. The old-line unions that historically represented blue-collar workers have realized that, if they are to remain viable, they must follow the job growth. The projected job growth is in the service sector, for both higher paid technical and professional positions as well as low-paid service workers such as custodians, nursing assistants, and child care workers.

The impact of competition and organizational restructuring has become an issue in nonprofit organizations. Contracts have called for employers to notify employees of impending layoffs and to offer voluntary leaves of absences to employees before reducing their hours. In other circumstances, unions have been called on to defend professional autonomy and improve working conditions. Unions have sought to expand the scope of bargaining to include such issues as agency-level policy-making, agency missions, standards of service, and professional judgment. Other negotiated topics have included coverage for malpractice and professional liability insurance, legal representation of workers, workload issues, the provision of in-service training, financial assistance for licensing examinations, and remuneration for enhanced education.

As more and more public services become privatized and former public employees enter nonprofit agencies, nonprofit managers can expect to see an increase in union activities. If nonprofit organizations wish to keep adversarial labor-management relations at bay, nonprofit administrators and boards of directors must work with their staffs to develop progressive and relevant human resources polices that respect employees. Employees must feel that their jobs are important and that they are contributing to the mission of the agency. Performance evaluations, promotions, and merit pay systems must be administered in an equitable and consistent manner. Career enrichment opportunities must be provided. Organizations that provide employees with the opportunity to participate in the decision-making process tend to have less labor strife (Peters and Masaoka, 2000).

FUTURE CHALLENGES

New cultural and social changes are affecting the workplace. There have been substantial increases in the number of female, minority, disabled, and older workers. Not only have the nonprofit workforces become more demographically diverse but the values of employees have also changed. They want challenging jobs, and they want to exercise discretion in those jobs. If nonprofit organizations are going to be able to attract qualified employees and volunteers, they need to be flexible and have progressive HRM policies and programs in place. To accommodate the changing workforce and to minimize conflict, organizations should promote a greater awareness of diversity issues and cultural differences. It is also important that they audit their human resources functions to ensure that they are free from bias. Recruitment selection, training and development, performance evaluation, and compensation and benefits should be administered in an equitable fashion.

At one time nonprofits could afford to be more complacent about HRM issues. Many nonprofits originated as a response to new societal needs, such as hospices for the terminally ill, rape crisis support organizations, domestic violence shelters, and daycare centers. They thus have missions that appeal to employees. Other nonprofits, such as museums, zoos, historical societies, and symphonies, are thought to be interesting places to work. However, interesting places to work can become less interesting, and employees' and volunteers' commitments to agency missions can erode if they are not treated with respect and allowed to grow professionally. Nonprofits must be innovative not only in how they treat and reward their employees and volunteers, but they also must be creative in how they recruit employees and volunteers. Nonprofits can employ individuals who possess the motivation to work in public service, but who also may want to work in smaller, less bureaucratic organizations. Preston (1990) found that the opportunity to perform a variety of work and enhance one's skill development has been instrumental in attracting women to nonprofit organizations. Many women choose to work in nonprofits despite the often lower pay they provide in order to take advantage of the opportunities they offer. In this competitive environment, nonprofits need to be concerned not only about their compensation and benefit packages, and professional development opportunities, but also their anti-discrimination policies. Many potential employees and volunteers may choose to seek opportunities in organizations that are inclusive.

REFERENCES

Arenson, K. W. 2004. "Pushing for Union, Columbia Grad Students are Set to Strike." *New York Times*. Retrieved 4/17/2004, from nytimes.com, www.nytimes.com/2004/04/17education/17columbia.html?ex=1083242121ei=1en=b0379abdad6c4029.

Board of Directors of Rotary International v. Rotary Club. 1987. 481 U.S. 537, 544, 107 S.Ct. 1940, 1945, 95 L. ED. 2d 474, 483–484.

The Boy Scouts of America Equal Access Act. 2003. 20 U. S. C. § 7905.

Boy Scouts of America v. Dale. 2000. No.99–699 U. S. Supreme Court, June 28, 2000. supct.law.cornell.edu/supct/html/99-699.zo.html.2000.

Boy Scouts of America v. Wyman. 2004. 03-956, March 8, 2004.

Boy Scouts of America v. Wyman. 2003. 335 F. 3d 80, 90 2d Cir.

Chaves, M., 2002. "Religious Congregations." In Lester M. Salamon, ed., *The State of Nonprofit America*. Washington, DC: Brookings Institution Press and Aspen Institution, pp. 275–298.

Civil Rights Act of 1964, Title VII, Secs. 70.

Dale v. Boy Scouts of America and Monmouth Council Boy Scouts. 1999. A-195/196-97, N.J. Sup. Ct. August 4, 1999. lawlibrary.rutgers.edu/courts/supreme/a-195-97.opn.html.

Davis, R. 2001, March 5. "To Keep a Pledge, Scouts Pay." *The St. Petersburg Times* 1B, 7B.

De Vita, C. J. 1999. "Nonprofits and Devolution: What Do We Know?" In E. T. Boris and C. E. Steuerle, eds., *Nonprofits and Government: Collaboration and Conflict*. Washington, DC: The Urban Institute Press, pp. 213–233.

Elias, P. 2004, March 2. "Calif. Justices: Catholic Charity Must Cover Birth Control." *The Washington Post*. Retrieved 3/2/04 from washingtonpost.com, washingtonpost.com/ac2/wp-dyn/A20797-2004Mar1?language=printer.

Ellis, S. J. 2002, May 1. "Your Web Site: Does It Welcome Prospective Volunteers?" *The Nonprofit Times* 16:9: 18.

Farris, A., Nathan, R. P., and Wright, D. J. 2004. *The Expanding Administrative Presidency: George W. Bush and the Faith-Based Initiative*. Albany, NY: The Roundtable on Religion and Social Welfare Policy.

Gosche v. Calvert High School. 1998. 997 F. Supp. 867 Dist. Ct., Northern Ohio.

Greenhouse, L. 2004, June 8. "Thousands of Home Aides Begin a Strike." *New York Times*. Retrieved June 8, 2004, from nytimes.com., www.nytimes.com/2004/06/08/nyregion/08strike.html?ex=1en+d56f1e33f714a7aa.

Hall v. Baptist Memorial Healthcare Corp. 2000. 215 F. 3d 618 6th Cir.

Hurley v. Irish-American Gay Group of Boston. 1995. U. S. No. 94–749.

Jacobs, J. A., and Gerson, K. 1998. "Who are the Overworked Americans?" *Review of Social Economy* 564: 442.

Kaufman, L. 2004, June 9. "Strike Today to Complicate Day Care for Poor." *New York Times*. Retrieved 6/9/2004, from nytimes.com, www.nytimes.com/2004/06/09nyregion/09strike.html?ex=1087792993ei=1&en=25c859634e4fdbb2.

Little v. Wuerl. 1991. 929 F. 2d 944, 3rd Cir.

Lown v. The Salvation Army, Inc.; Commission, New York City Administration for Children Services and Others. February 24, 2004.

McClure v. The Salvation Army. 1972. No. 71–2270, 460 F.2d 553; 1972 U. S. app. LEXIS 10672.

Maguire v. Marquette University. 1987. 814 F. 2d 1213, 7th Cir.

Montiel, L. M., Keyes-Williams, J., and Scott, J. D. 2002, September. *The Use of Public Funds for Delivery of Faith-Based Human Services.* Albany, NY: The Roundtable on Religion and Social Welfare Policy.

Mormon Church v. Amos. 1987. 483 US 327.

National Labor Relations Board. 1997. *A Guide to Basic Law and Procedures Under the National Labor Relations Act.* Washington, DC: U. S. Government Printing Office.

National Partnership for Women and Families. 1998. Family matters: A national survey of women and men. www.nationalpartnership.org/survey/survey8.htm.

New York State Club Association v. City of New York. 1988. 108 S. Ct. 2234.

Pedreira v. Kentucky Baptist Homes for Children. 2001. United Sates District Court of the Western District of Kentucky, July 23, 2001, 2001 U. S. District LEXIS 10283. LEXIS-NEXIS Y/document?_ansset=A-WA-A-DB-MsSEZE-UUW-EEDBEAVUZ-WZWZWUVAA-DB-U&08/07/2001.

Peters, J. B., and Masaoka, J. 2000. "A House Divided: How Nonprofits Experience Union Drives." *Nonprofit Management and Leadership* 10:3: 305–317.

Personal Responsibility and Work Opportunity Reconciliation Act of 1996 (PRWORA , Section 104 of P. L. 104–193).

Preston, A. E. 1990. "Women in the White Collar Nonprofit Sector: The Best Option or the Only Option?" *The Review of Economics and Statistics* 72: 560–568.

Oster, S. M. 1992. "Nonprofit Organizations as Franchise Operations." *Nonprofit Management & Leadership* 2: 223–258.

Randall v. Orange County Council, Boy Scouts of America. 1998. 952 P. 2d 261 Cal.

Roberts v. United States Jaycees. 1984. 468 U.S. 609, 104 S.Ct. 3244, 82 L.Ed. 2d 462.

Rosenblum, N. 1998. *Membership and Morals: The Personal Uses of Pluralism in America.* Princeton, NJ: Princeton University Press.

Sanchez v. Catholic Foreign Society of America. 1999. 82 F. Supp. 2d 1338.

Seabourn v. Coronado Area Council. 1995. 891 P.2d 385, Kan.

Steinberg, R. J. and Jacobs, J. A. 1994. "Pay Equity in Nonprofit Organizations: Making Women's Work Visible." In T. Odendahl and M. O'Neill, eds., *Women and Power in the Nonprofit Sector.* San Francisco, CA: Jossey-Bass, pp. 79–120.

U. S. General Accounting Office. 2002, September. *Charitable Choice: Federal Guidelines on Statutory Provisions Could Improve Consistency of Implementation,* GAO–02–887. Washington, DC: Author.

U. S. Department of Labor, Bureau of Labor Statistics. 2004, September. *Highlights of Women's Earnings in 2003.* Report 798. Washington, DC: Author.

Wallace, P. 2001. *The Psychology of the Internet.* Cambridge, MA Cambridge University Press.

Welsh v. Boy Scouts of America. 1993. 787 F. Supp. 1511 N. D. Ill.; 1992, 993 F. 2d 1267 7th Cir., cert.denied, 510 U. S. 1012.

Weitzman, M. S., Jalandoni, N. T., Lampkin, L. M., and Pollak, T. H. 2002. *The New Nonprofit Almanac and Desk Reference: The Essential Facts and Figures for Managers, Researchers, and Volunteers.* San Francisco, CA: Jossey-Bass.

White House. 2001. *Unlevel Playing Field: Barriers to Participation by Faith-based and Community Organizations in Federal Social Service Programs.* www.whitehouse.gov/news/releases/2001/08/unlevelfield.html.

Williams, G. 2000, January 27. "Rank and File: Former Salvation Army Officer Charges that Charity's Policy on Pay for Married Couples Violates Her Civil Rights." *Chronicle for Philanthropy:* XII, 7, 25–26.

Wyatt, K. 2000, October 22. "Girl Scouts' Recruiting Drive Tells Old Image to Take a Hike." The Associated Press. In *The Tampa Tribune,* p. 23.

Young v. Northern Illinois Conference of United Methodist Church. 1994. 21 F. 3d 1984.

Young, D. 1989. "Local Autonomy in a Franchise Age: Structural Change in National Voluntary Associations." *Nonprofit and Voluntary Sector Quarterly* 18:2: 101–117.

Index